On the radio of my natal home sat a statue of three squatting monkeys—See No Evil, Hear No Evil, Speak No Evil. In the original symbol, imported from India, four monkeys sat side by side. The fourth had its hands over its genitals. By lopping off that fourth monkey, Victorian society did not eliminate sex but only public acknowledgment of it. That severed monkey fell into the unconscious, where it acquired the mischievous and obsessive power of the forbidden.

The fourth monkey represents all that any person, or family, or institution, or society strives to repress. Because Western society has devoted itself to the materialistic, the technological and the pragmatic, its fourth monkey represents all that is intuitive, psychical, spiritual and mystical. Instead of forming a natural part of our lives, these are now experiences for which we must go in search. . . .

D1495214

By the same author:

Pandora

The Candy Factory

A Casual Affair

The Emperor's Virgin

Berlin Solstice

My Father's House

THE QUEST FOR THE FOURTH MONKEY

A THINKER'S GUIDE TO THE
PSYCHIC AND SPIRITUAL REVOLUTION

SYLVIA FRASER

KEY PORTER BOOKS

Key Porter Books Limited
70 The Esplanade
Toronto, Ontario
Canada M5E 1R2

ISBN 1-55013-594-5

Original version published in Canada by Doubleday Canada Limited
as *The Book of Strange*.

Distributed in the United States of America by National Book
Network, Inc.

Printed and bound in Canada

94 95 96 97 98 6 5 4 3 2 1

To my sister Irene

1931–1990

CONTENTS

Acknowledgements

I wish to express my appreciation to the readers of my manuscript-in-progress for their useful criticisms: the late Adele Wiseman, June Callwood, Jack McClelland, Lily Poritz Miller, Kelly Kelly, my agent Sterling Lord and my editors David Kilgour and Shaun Oakey. A special thanks to Professor Jim Prentice, Physics Department of the University of Toronto, for his comments on key sections of the manuscript; to John Pearce for his incisive editorial advice, and to Maggie Reeves for her expertise in production.

A ton of gratitude to Anna Porter for her generous support of this and all of my books, as well as to the rest of the warm and fuzzy Porter clan.

Introduction

"The Universe is stranger than we imagine."
— Albert Einstein

The 1950s were the apogee of guilt-free, Western materialism. Our side had won The War through superior technology, and now we civilians were entitled to our booty in the form of new cars and refrigerators.

For kids, this amazing chromium affluence was experienced in the trickle-down effect: toys of metal instead of cardboard! Real chocolate bars instead of popcorn dipped in brown wax! The sighting of a 1947 Studebaker—the first all-new, postwar car to make it to curbside—was greeted with as much awe as a flying saucer. Kids would toss down their bats and ropes to run a block on the strength of rumor. As we stood in an ever-more-jaded circle, one would brag: "I've seen four." "That's nothing, my brother's seen seven." Boredom set in at a legitimate dozen, but by then other giddy marvels had materialized on other streets and even in our own houses—electric irons, kettles, blenders, hair-dryers, coffee-makers, washer-dryers, crescendoing in four-tone cars and TV sets in Italian provincial cabinets.

Against this everyday world of wonders, the Sunday miracle of wine from water or the multiplying of loaves and fishes could scarcely compete. Though as a kid of ten I already possessed a collection of inscribed Bibles attesting to perfect Sunday School attendance, religion seemed to offer little beyond a place to go when stores and theaters and schools were barred and bolted. With skepticism politely placed, like a pair of galoshes, on the rug marked "Faith, Hope and Charity," I would sit in the gallery with the other kids comparing the ratio of feathered to flowered hats while a succession of preachers struggled to arouse their dozing flocks. Hell and brimstone no longer worked: the world had been through hell—War Is Hell—and we had survived. The more modern ministers appealed to pseudo-spiritual minds with pseudo-scientific questions: Is Noah's ark still parked on Mount Ararat? Was the star of Bethlehem a supernova? And then, expanding into a social vacuum: Should dancing and bingo be allowed in the church basement? Or, proving psychological relevance: Does a Christian kiss on a first date?

At high school, I was taught nineteenth-century knowledge in fifty-minute bites by conscientious teachers who didn't seem to know they were already a few decades out of date. Physics meant learning the principle of the lever and other inviolable laws of nature. Chemistry meant pouring a test tube of x into one of y and getting z—sometimes explosively. Botany meant classifying flowers by counting their petals and measuring their pistils versus their stamens. Zoology meant studying the cardiovascular system of humans by dissecting frogs. History meant listing the eleven reasons for the fall of the Roman Empire. Geography meant reciting six products of Trinidad or Cuba—each citrus fruit separately, if you could get away with it. No one was interested in why something was, only in how it worked. After several months of balancing equations of increasing complexity, I boldly asked my math teacher: "Sir, what is algebra for?" His reply was quintessential fifties: "Sit down. You've always been a troublemaker."

Even in English literature, where creative thought was pastured like a ruminating cow, we spent our time analyzing

Romantic poetry by scanning rhythm and counting metaphors. During my final year of high school, a sadistic English teacher stunned our class by instructing each of us to write a poem. This was unprecedented, unfair! Our job as students was to dissect poetry, not to create it. After our outrage died down, we set about our appointed task, offering up some forty blissfully tortured stanzas about clouds, about daffodils, about "bee-loud glades." Though we lived in an industrial city where we saw lambs on our plates far more often than in the fields, everyone in the class assumed poetry meant a lyric about nature in the style of Wordsworth or Bliss Carman. That was the sum of our experience—our reality—and it took a first-year college course for me to discover that poets had ever been inspired by anything else.

Although it's easy to mock the fifties' educational system, with its rigidly patrolled specialties, those of us who passed through its revolving door found ourselves equipped for a materialistic society that, in its basic assumptions, hasn't changed very much for very many people until very recently. Despite the best efforts of visionaries like Einstein, most of us still behave as if the Universe is a machine. Time is absolute and irreversible. Knowledge is acquired only by observation and experimentation. *Homo sapiens sapiens* evolved from the ape and is distinguished from his simian ancestors only by greater intelligence. Disease is caused by the invasion of germs or the wearing out of parts, and cure means killing off or cutting out. The concrete is more real than the abstract, words more real than thoughts, actions more real than feelings, and the unknown is simply that which hasn't yet been quantified.

I was in college before I was presented with a genuine choice about the kind of Universe I might believe in. That was where I discovered that great thinkers seemed to come in pairs: for every philosopher who taught that the ultimate reality of the Universe was matter, an equally compelling one taught that the ultimate reality of the Universe was psyche or spirit.

Today we honor the ancient Greeks for their mathematics, logic and reason while ignoring the fact that many of the greatest were also mystics.

In the sixth century B.C., Pythagoras discovered that by varying the length of a string he could alter its pitch in a precise and predictable way. Out of this has emerged the seven-note scale on which Western music, from Mozart to Motown, is based. Having proven that music could be described by numbers, Pythagoras wondered if shapes could also be so defined. Representing the digit 1 by a single point, he joined two points to produce a straight line; three to produce a triangle; four to produce a square; all points equidistant from a single point to produce a circle.

Through such ruminations, Pythagoras invented the geometry bearing his name; he also demonstrated that mathematical formulas can describe the physical Universe—the basis of the science of both Newton and Einstein. However, Pythagoras's appreciation of numbers went far beyond their use as a tool of calculation. To him, they stood above and prior to the sensory world, which was merely their physical manifestation. They were the ultimate reality of the Universe. "All things are numbers."

The competing materialistic school, founded a century later by Democritus, taught that everything that exists is composed of indivisible particles of matter, which ceaselessly collide in empty space, with those of coarser texture creating the physical world and with those of the finest texture creating the mental world. Democritus called these particles atoms, meaning that which can't be cut.

Between them, Pythagoras the mystic and Democritus the materialist defined the poles of early Greek thought. Discouraged by how slowly his materialistic theory was winning converts, Democritus complained: "I came to Athens, and no one knew me." However, if he were to make that same journey from Abdera today, he would find a sign dominating a main artery—Democritus Nuclear Research Laboratory—while thousands of computers spit out Pythagorean numbers without reverence, as if they were just digits.

The matter–spirit debate was crystallized for the Western world by the opposition between the fourth-century B.C. philosopher Plato and his student Aristotle.

Considered by many to be the wisest person who ever lived, Plato believed, like Pythagoras, that the material world was just the manifestation of a greater psychic Reality. In Plato's cosmology, this Reality contained the abstract Form or Idea of everything, mental and physical, that existed in the sensory world. This included the eternal pattern for Tree, out of which all trees on earth had been created, and the Idea of absolute Justice, which inspired the human concept of justice.

Although Plato's eternal Reality cannot be perceived directly by the senses, it can be grasped by intuition aided by reason. To him, it was the source of humanity's loftiest ideals—our concepts of beauty and truth and compassion which go beyond the bare needs of survival; our enduring conviction that life has meaning surpassing human understanding; our spiritual thirst for contact with something transcending ourselves.

Plato's basic idea—that psyche predates and transcends matter—underlies all religious systems. It was the premise on which the great civilizations of the East were founded. It was the starting point for the first Middle Eastern cities, established around 6000 B.C. as temple compounds.

Though Plato's mysticism defies the reach of logical language, he demonstrated his meaning in a famous allegory in which he likened everything in the material world to shadows cast by firelight on the walls of a cave. Since most humans are chained by ignorance with their backs to the cave's mouth, they mistake these flickering shadows for Reality. However, the wise person can struggle from the cave toward the sun—the metaphor Plato used to represent the highest Idea, containing all others, which he called the Good. That is the goal of existence—a spiritual journey that Plato, like Pythagoras, believed continued through many incarnations.

By contrast, Aristotle was a natural scientist who favored biology, observation and the study of causation over mathematics and mysticism. Laying the foundation for the science of Newton and Darwin, Aristotle stated that all that exists is matter, moving in space. Humans are nothing but rational animals, entirely subject to the laws of matter and hence without immortal souls. All human knowledge derives from sense experience; intuition and reason do not represent some rarefied way of understanding, as Plato claimed, but are just sophisticated byproducts of our ordinary five senses. Morality is a human collective agreement—a branch of politics. Values such as courage and justice do not exist apart from human exercise of them, and the overriding goal for every living thing in the Universe, whether human or flatworm, is to become the best it can become within this materialistic framework.

So brilliantly and yet divergently did Plato and Aristotle define human knowledge that nineteenth-century poet Samuel Coleridge was moved to remark: "Every man is born either a Platonist or an Aristotelean."

Even while Aristotle was classifying all the knowledge of Greece, its Golden Age was drawing to a close. Though the shift of power to Rome meant a pendulum swing from the mysticism of Plato to the natural science of Aristotle, it also meant a shift from philosophy to empire-building, from contemplation of beauty to accumulation of wealth, from sculpting to road-building, from ethical inquiry to law-making, from the values of the Acropolis to those of the Coliseum.

When the Roman Empire itself began to crumble, after a half-dozen centuries of triumph, mysticism experienced a revival in the form of Neoplatonism; this was matched with renewed enthusiasm for the ancient Greek Mystery cults, dedicated to gods and goddesses such as Dionysus and Demeter. Vying as one cult among the many was that of the Jewish teacher Jesus Christ. After Emperor Constantine converted to this faith in the fourth century, St. Augustine grafted the Christian idea of one God onto the Platonic Idea of the Good. In this way, he provided a rational foundation for what had been merely a religion based on faith.

Nine centuries later, St. Thomas Aquinas again employed Greek prestige to redefine Christianity for a new age—this time for the Renaissance, just over the horizon. What history would declare to be the proxy marriage of Plato to Jesus Christ was now completed by the baptism of Aristotle. Aristotle's laws of nature were interpreted by Aquinas as the laws of God. His flatworm striving for perfection was defined as the struggle of all things toward the the perfection of God. Most importantly, Aristotle's fixation on the natural world was glorified as humankind's worship of God through the study of His creation.

Just as European society was poised to unleash its pent-up fascination with life in the here and now, Aquinas had flung open the Church door, giving papal permission. However, Galileo's telescope soon revealed a cosmos at odds with creation as described by biblical scriptures. When the seventeenth-century's Sir Isaac Newton proved that planets moved around the sun according to predictable laws, the Universe began to look more like a giant clock than a morality play. Increasingly, it was the Church that had to scramble to justify its views and to shore up its dwindling powers.

The new outlook became known as the Enlightenment. Though based on the supremacy of matter, that capitalized name with its aura of revealed truth served notice that science itself was about to become an ideology, perpetrated by an elite as authoritative as the one in Rome. When Charles Darwin's theory of evolution seemed to prove that humans were nothing but rational apes, as indicated by Aristotle, the last claims on behalf of mysticism were confidently dismissed. Dubbing everything before Newton as belonging to an Age of Ignorance, the new materialists recast the old matter–spirit debate as science versus superstition.

For the next hundred years, that materialistic viewpoint was the legitimate one, while the spiritual view was designated "the other." Since science, as well as political history, is written by the winning side, the record of Western culture has been distorted to reflect this materialistic bias. While Darwin was elevated to stardom, the cofounder of evolution—Alfred Russel Wallace—was consigned to history's dustbin; Wallace's crime was to argue that natural selection and survival of the fittest could not alone explain human consciousness or culture, for which he postulated some designing, shaping spiritual force. Though Newton is known to every school kid, few have heard of Gottfried Leibniz, the seventeenth-century mathematician who shared with him invention of the calculus; yet Leibniz proposed a competing mystical cosmology, based on energy fields, which shows stunning parallels to the latest subatomic theory.

Even when celebrating its heroes, Western society has often toasted only half a brain. Ironically, materialists forged their clockwork Universe in the name of Sir Isaac Newton, a devout Christian, a practicing occultist and a fervent alchemist. Historians have trivialized alchemy as a get-rich scheme for converting lead into gold, yet deeper study has suggested it was intended to be a symbolic ritual for transmuting the dross of human experience into spiritual gold. According to Newton's obsessive mystical writings, the Universe is a vast riddle in which God planted clues for unifying all of nature under Him in the myths of Olympus and in alchemical formulas. It was this quest for spiritual truth that fired his interest in how the laws of matter worked.

In summing up Newton's dazzling career as a physicist, biographer J.W.N. Sullivan commented that Newton "was a genius of the first order at something he did not consider to be of the first importance." Having squeezed most of his scientific discoveries into what he described as "the two plague years," Newton gave himself over to what he really wanted to be: a magician.

As a philosophy undergraduate, I was aware that my professors seemed biased toward the Platonic model. However, as a child of wars recently won and the myth of progress, I chose materialism. In my suspicious mind, Plato with his transcendental moral values seemed too much like Christianity in Greek drag. I was tired of an all-perfect God who felt it His right to judge the second-to-second doings of His flock while brooking no questioning of His own ways; who believed an eternity of hell-fire to be suitable for those who did not bow before His throne; whose biographical highlights, such as His divine birth and resurrection, had been stolen from earlier religions; who valued chastity and obedience, above all in women; who wielded guilt like a cat-o'-nine-tails and then—the largest outrage—demanded unconditional love. That itchy Christian hairshirt, which I had inherited along with Original Sin and the other trappings of a worn out faith, was something I was delighted to junk. If the pew doesn't fit, burn it.

In my sophomore year, I became the first atheist in my dorm—or, as philosophy had taught me to succinctly phrase it, an agnostic acutely slanted toward atheism. A thrilling, dialectical introversion gripped me until nearly graduation, when practical career questions jarringly surfaced. Suddenly, my four years of philosophy seemed rather like a wrong-way Tower of Babel, dug ever-downward in search of a non-existent first premise. If this were a materialistic, one-shot Universe, as I had decided, then I'd better get on with living inside it.

In 1957, women without rare talent or beauty had a choice of three basic careers: secretary, nurse or teacher, with "glamor" jobs in social work and public relations just opening up. I decided to become a magazine journalist because, after four years of intellectual hair-splitting, I lusted to lead an extroverted and adventurous life. During the next eleven years, I researched my fantasies, both frivolous and serious, while being paid for the privilege. Specifically, I lived briefly with an Inuit family in an igloo, danced with Masai warriors in Kenya, chased a stockbroker on the lam in Panama, dined with an Indian prince at Maxim's in Paris, visited TV's Batman in his Hollywood batcave. Since my career traversed the psychedelic sixties, I also tracked that demographic bulge of postwar babyboomers who produced the sexual revolution, the psychedelic implosion, the Aquarian Age, the politics of protest, "Peace not War," Woodstock, under-thirty millionaires and, eventually, black power and the feminist movement.

More personally, I explored the human psyche as a member of a loosely linked group of questers dubbed the Human Potential Movement. This included research into Freudian analysis, encounter groups, primal therapy, massage therapy, bioenergetics and, several years later, Jungian analysis. My motivation, I thought, was curiosity—especially about that seventies' obsession, relationships.

Eventually, I began to write novels full of a dark sexual violence that mystified me. This task also grew obsessive. The crisis toward which I was moving revealed itself in December of 1983 when, for the first time in my adult life, I suddenly recalled my father's sexual abuse of me. This is the story I told in *My Father's House: A Memoir of Incest and of Healing.* It is not one I wish to repeat here, except to note that the piecemeal return of my memory was frequently marked by odd events of the sort labelled paranormal. Even after my past had been resurrected and then laid to rest, these weird phenomena continued: telepathy, disconcerting webs of coincidence, premonitions, dreams of prophecy—subtle yet powerful, enriching and unnerving. For example:

NOVEMBER 10, 1988

I am preparing for bed in my Toronto apartment when the telephone rings. As I pick up the receiver, I sense this call will be a significant one. The report of the death of a cousin from cancer makes it so.

Now lying in bed, I brood about my cousin's death and about death in general. From some intuitive well, I hear this message: "When someone who is genetically linked to you dies, the door is open for a little while."

What door? "The door between realities."

Since I assume this to be the "door" between life and death, I ask to see my mother who died the previous year, age eighty-six. Immediately, she appears in my mind's eye as a woman of about forty, in glowing health, wearing a mahogany dress – an odd detail since my mother disliked brown. After shyly lifting the folds of her skirt as she used to lift her apron, she rushes forward to embrace me.

Moved by this healing fantasy, I ask to see my former husband who died six months before my mother at age fifty-five. He, too, appears, looking youthful and joyful. As he approaches, I impulsively blurt: "Am I making all this up or can you give me some sign?"

My husband and I suddenly seem to be walking along the shore of Lake Erie, where his parents once owned a cottage. As the water laps the pebbles at our feet, he tells me: "Tomorrow you will see a pebble where you wouldn't expect to see a pebble and you will be very surprised. Don't expect it to be pretty. It will be quite ordinary, even unattractive." I know he is referring to the colorful pebbles we used to collect along this beach and warning me not to expect the same.

Next day as I board the bus from Toronto to Hamilton for my cousin's funeral, I remember the prophecy and wryly ask myself: "How far am I going to have to force events to make it come true?" Still tongue-in-cheek, I decide: "If I find a pebble in the center of a bus seat, that will be a pebble out of place. If I see one on the floor, that will not." I see no pebble on a seat or on the floor.

After my cousin's funeral, I join the cortège to the gravesite, where an Anglican sister delivers a few words of farewell. As I turn to walk away, a relative touches my arm. "Look! Isn't that charming—the children are putting pebbles on the coffin."

Startled, I watch as my deceased cousin's two grandchildren, ages seven and four, place pebbles from the frozen ground onto her shiny coffin, where they rest like ill-formed buttons.

This event did not fit the materialistic philosophy I had chosen; yet, given its complexity, power and purposefulness, I could not dismiss it as mere coincidence. Attempts to share it and similar experiences too often resulted in an indulgent, glazed-eye smile, or such a gullible outpouring of the improbable that *my* eyes would glaze over. Communication with the dead, prophecy and telepathy were topics I had discussed at adolescent pajama parties, then abandoned as a sign of maturity. However, I was unwilling to discard a compelling experience just because it was at odds with a preconception. Had I actually been given a sign by my dead husband? Alternatively, had I telepathically influenced the children to carry out my unconscious wishes? Had I hallucinated the future?

As a journalist I know it's often the detail that doesn't fit that points to a deeper, underlying truth. Attempts to force my life into the materialistic framework were growing increasingly futile, like trying to confine musical notes in a cage. I felt compelled to discover why unicorns were wandering through my life and where they could possibly be leading me.

I began to read books on biology, neurology, cosmology, physics. Though I had been aware of radical changes in those fields since 1905, when Albert Einstein redefined space and time, I was not prepared for how complete and wide-ranging these changes had become, or how consistent: the new world still-in-prototype seemed far closer to the one envisioned by Plato and Pythagoras and Leibniz and Wallace and the mystical half of Newton than the one conceived by Democritus and Aristotle and Darwin and the mechanical side of Newton. It also displayed striking parallels to the mystical Universe intuited thousands of years ago by Hindu and Buddhist seers. As confirmed by physicist J. Robert Oppenheimer: "The general notions about human understanding ... which are illustrated by discoveries in atomic physics are not in the nature of things wholly unfamiliar, wholly unheard of, or new. Even in our own culture they have a history, and in Buddhist and Hindu thought a more considerable and central place. What we shall find is an exemplification, and encouragement, and a refinement of old wisdom."

I now believe the sixties spawned two important social revolutions—spiritual as well as sexual. The sexual revolution ran full course, sweeping across barriers of age, race and religion to carry its liberating message mainstream. By contrast, the spiritual revolution was stillborn, discredited not only because of its youthful proponents' reliance on drugs but also because of their gut disdain for authority, causing them to scorn the movement's intellectual roots. While you can get a fast sexual fix you can't get a fast spiritual one. "What's your sign?" is no substitute for the *Dialogues* of Plato. "Do your own thing!" does not equate with a Tibetan monk's lifetime of meditation. "Don't trust anyone over thirty" means refuse to grow up. Magic mushrooms—though successfully eliminating the middleman—do not guarantee a direct line to God.

    Sixties' spiritual frustration sublimated itself in yuppie greed, neoconservatism and the hard drug trade. Yet the spiritual impulse did not die. A couple of decades later, the Aquarian Age has resurfaced as the New Age, with mainstream ambitions accompanying its slicked-down name. In popular culture, this expresses itself as a restless fascination with everything Eastern, mystical, native, mythological or paranormal—reincarnation, channeling, psychic healing, yoga, shamanism, trance-meditation, near-death experience. On the surface, conversations about *chakras* and crystals and spirit guides may sound every bit as credulous as the buzztalk of the sixties, and much of it probably is. However, this time its adherents are searching for, rather than rebelling against. This time acceptance no longer requires them to park their heads along with their hats at the door. This time much of the new movement's leadership comes bearing doctorates and even Nobel laureates.

The Quest for the Fourth Monkey is divided into two sections. In "The Self," I investigate the human psyche through events in my life that challenge orthodox science: experiences of telepathy, of multiple personality, of dreams that seemed more than dreams and death that seemed less than death. I also explore theories of psychic and holistic healing that are now emerging through a greater understanding of Eastern and shamanic medicines, as well as from radical new insights in biology and subatomic physics. Throughout, my emphasis is on bridging the mind-body split that currently undermines the effectiveness of Western healing.

In "The Universe," I investigate such topics as prophecy, reincarnation, possession and spiritualism within a framework of ancient thought, tribal wisdom and modern physics, once again spearheaded by my own compelling experiences.

Because each chapter is structured on the exploration of ideas, I've employed my biographical material anecdotally, without regard for chronological order; nonetheless, powering this book is a spiritual journey, shaped by the most significant events of my life. My model in relating both the personal and the impersonal is that of the travel guide who reports on exotic territory with more of a passion to share than to prove. As in travel, the juxtaposition of the naive and the sophisticated may sometimes seem jarring; however, it is my intention to reunite ways of seeing that have been falsely separated, to honor the intuitive as well as the intellectual, the anecdotal as well as the more objective.

Throughout, I have emphasized the psychic viewpoint over the materialistic viewpoint because that is the one that has been so grossly underrepresented in Western society for the past three hundred years. However, since both have persisted in the face of relentless persecution, both must be important to the human race. Indeed, the discovery that we humans house a split brain, within a single skull, suggests that these opposing ideas may appeal to the disparate halves of our brains: the left with its fondness for linear reasoning and concrete analysis, the right with its bias toward the metaphoric, abstract and holistic. Thus, the historical matter–psyche debate could be a partial projection of the constant shifting and balancing that take place within our own skulls. At present, most branches of science fiercely reflect this Aristotelean–Platonic split, with orthodoxy favoring the first while the thrust of change is increasingly toward the second. If the materialistic Universe can be described as a clock, then a deep suspicion is growing among many scientists that it may be a pocketwatch kept in the vest of an intelligence some call God.

Nothing in philosophy or science, old or new, proves such a contention. Yet the psychic paradigm provides a forum in which the existence of soul, or afterlife, or transcendental morality, or divine purpose, or meaningful design can be fruitfully debated without the harassment of a closed mind posing as a rational mind.

I once saw a television documentary about a satellite that was sent into space to detect cosmic objects in the infra-red spectrum of light. Since most infra-red rays are screened out by the earth's atmosphere, the human eye has not adapted to seeing in that spectrum. What the satellite revealed, in regions astronomers thought to be empty space, was a vast other universe: unknown galaxies, stars in the process of being born, clouds of infra-red dust thousands of light years wide. The implications were immense since physicists believe the amount of matter in the Universe to be crucial in determining its ultimate fate.

Similarly, the wondrous other world I belatedly set out to explore was one that always had existed in the dark, silent spaces of my life but that I had failed to see because I had chosen not to see it. The implications for me were also immense, since this newly discovered other world has animated my familiar world with greater meaning, purpose and mystery. However, I hope that the importance of this book lies not in what it says about my own journey but in the invitation it extends to every reader to search for the meaning of the fourth monkey in your own life.

The Self

Telepathy:

THE FAX OF NATURE

"And though it is most certain, that two lutes being both strung and tuned to an equal pitch, and then one played upon, the other will warble a faint audible harmony in answer to the same tune; yet many will not believe there is any such thing as sympathy of souls; and I am well pleased that every Reader do enjoy his own opinion."

—Sir Izaak Walton

APRIL 15, 1943

All morning I feel peculiar as if something inside me were about to hatch. When the noon bell rings, I stick my head in my desk instead of racing to the door with the other kids, afraid to go home, without knowing why.

I hear my grade two teacher's sturdy black oxfords approach. Her voice, as sensible as her shoes, inquires: "Don't you think you'd better go home for lunch? Your mother will be wondering where you are."

Under her solicitous eye, I force myself from my seat, then out the door, then up the street, dragging each foot along the gritty sidewalk, being especially careful not to step on any cracks, growing more and more fatigued, like a wind-up doll that is running down.

At the last corner I stop, too tired to turn, and too scared. I plunk down on a neighbor's muddy lawn, then ever so slowly crawl around the hedge. Parked in front of my house, six doors away, I see what I had already envisioned in my mind: a strange black car, out of place on such a modest street—very long, very shiny and without windows. Two white-uniformed men carry a stretcher, bearing something lumpy, swathed in a white sheet, while my mother—ringed by neighbors, sober and supportive—dabs her eyes with a handkerchief from her apron pocket.

My maternal grandmother, age sixty-nine, has died of a heart attack. Everyone else in the family is shocked by this sudden death. I am surprised by their surprise. The night before, suspended between waking and sleeping, I silently talked with my grandmother in her bedroom a staircase below, hearing the ululation of her dying and, in some strange way, participating in it. Death had become a cold and physical presence in the house. I sensed him in spaces deeper than wells, and knew for whom he had come.

Of all the mind's disputed superpowers, telepathy is the one most of us find easiest to accept, perhaps because of the many engaging games it seems to play at the edge of everyday consciousness: like the times we've sensed as soon as the phone started ringing that it would be bad news; or spontaneously called someone only to discover that person was about to call us; or mistaken a stranger on the street for a friend, only to have that friend appear on the next block.

Telepathy even appeals to some pragmatists as a shoe that almost fits: if only scientists were to stretch their theories a little more, while we ordinary people shoved our anecdotes a little harder, they might slip inside the materialistic tradition; then, telepathy could be used to explain away even more troublesome phenomena, like so-called fortune telling, which could be dismissed as siphoning information from other people's heads. However, orthodox science still rejects telepathy—defined as communication other than through the five senses—because it can't be proven in materialistic terms to exist. Worse, no one can explain how it could work, if it did work. Therefore, most scientists prefer to deny everyone's personal experience of it. They tell me that I, as a child, could not have witnessed my grandmother's death the way I thought I witnessed it. I could not have known, before I turned the corner, that a death car was parked at the curb of my house. I've misremembered the evidence, put it together wrongly, children are such unreliable observers.

Yet, five decades later, I have only to catch a whiff of gardenia to restore the whole event: the pulpy white corsage on my grandmother's death pillow, exuding the fragrance that would become the memory's fixative; the heaviness of her flesh like a soufflé that had fallen; the glow of her mahogany casket replacing our parlor piano, and—perpetually parked at our curb—that long black death car without windows. Given a choice between the vividness of my memory and scientific doubt, I'll take my own experience: I was there; science was not. Though that may sound arbitrary, among scientists themselves a belief is escalating that subjective evidence, with its emphasis on the detailed and the unique, has been foolishly downgraded in favor of conclusions exaggerating the commonality of experience. Metaphorically, this is like describing a bank of yellow and blue flowers in terms of its average color: green.

At the root of many scientists' difficulty in accepting "paranormal" experience is the narrowness with which they have defined "normal" experience. A post-Darwinian invention, psychology was established for the laboratory study of the human animal in its physical environment. Eager to prove the credentials of their fledgling discipline, pioneers were often guilty of mistaking the controllable activities of white rats in cages for those of people in a free environment. In the 1920s, John Watson, then North America's most influential psychologist, not only denied the existence of human consciousness but also managed to convince his peers and legions of parents that infants had no inborn instincts, no innate ideas, no inherited character traits or talents. By turning nurseries into laboratories of manipulation and regulation, Watson—who, incidentally, ended his career as an advertising executive—maintained that parents could produce any child-model they chose, as predictably as ordering a green Chevrolet or a black Buick. As he declared in *Behaviorism*: "Give me a dozen healthy infants, well-formed, and my own specified world to bring them up in and I'll guarantee to take any one at random and train him to become any type of specialist I might select—doctor, lawyer, artist, merchant chief and, yes, even beggar-man and thief, regardless of his talents, penchants, tendencies, abilities, vocation, and race of his ancestors."

Watson came to these conclusions by watching rats and cats and chimps run through mazes, push levers and ring bells, convincing him that all learning was trial and error, supported by reward and punishment. Meanwhile, psychologist Wolfgang Köhler of Berlin had demonstrated that, even if Watson's children could not learn through creative insight, his chickens could. For hundreds of trials, Köhler presented them with grain scattered over paper colored in two shades of gray; after he had repeatedly chased them from the lighter paper, they learned to peck the grain only on the darker paper. So far, this was typical of Watson's experiments: Köhler's chickens had learned through trial and error backed by punishment and reward. However, Köhler then replaced the lighter paper with sheets even darker than those on which the hens had been permitted to feed. Now, when presented with choice, most of the hens pecked the grain from the darker paper rather than from the paper to which they had been conditioned. Thus, they were not reacting mechanically, out of habit, as behaviorism predicted; instead, they had grasped the light-dark relationship and deduced that darker meant "yes." From these and other experiments, Köhler concluded that creative insight, not trial and error, was the lynchpin of learning. Watson's chimps and children had responded mechanistically only because their choices were so restricted they could not do otherwise.

As the Watson–Köhler controversy demonstrated, laboratory evidence is not always as authoritative as it appears. Nor is personal anecdote so sorry a source of information when the test-subject is the human animal. In assessing the story of my grandmother's death, the professionally trained mind often makes many hidden assumptions based on how science has done business over the past couple of hundred years. These include the conviction that the mental must prove itself in terms of the material; that the objective is superior to the subjective; that "how" is more relevant than "why"; that skepticism is more truthful than open-mindedness. Thus, they focus on the perceptual content of the story of my grandmother's death—that a child claimed to know, while still outside of sensory range, that a death car would be parked outside her house. However, this event is not, at heart, about the transfer of sensory information, but about love and grief. That was its dynamic context. To witness it otherwise is to perceive the photo of a child joyfully bicycling down a hill as being about spinning wheels and wind velocities. Science has been so phobic for so long about emotion as an enemy of truth that it blocks it out even when it is central to a story, rather like defining an orange only in terms of its rind, ignoring the pulp inside. The visual information of my grandmother's death—the black hearse at the curb—was transmitted to me because I loved my grandmother and I was losing her. Emotion was the motivator of the event—perhaps the part containing the most vital clues, as we will later consider.

Even scientists who accept telepathy usually see it as a regressive trait, more relevant to our species' evolutionary past than to our present. This view is based on the fact that the human brain is triune—actually three brains fitted together with the outer two encasing the third, like seashells. The brain stem, the deepest and oldest, is often called the reptilian brain because it resembles the entire brain of the reptile; in humans, it contains instinctive programs for basic survival, such as those governing killing and mating.

Encasing the brain stem is the mammalian brain, developed by a nocturnal, shrew-like ground-dweller who used it to interpret smells. When one evolutionary line took to the trees, its brain grew more complex—at first through the demands of daylight vision, then through the need for prolonged child nurturing.

Enfolding both these brains is the cerebrum, which exploded frontally after a tribe of primates left the trees for what proved to be a more hazardous and challenging life on the ground. Though this outer brain today serves as our chief executive officer, all three remain active in our daily lives, with functions roughly corresponding to instinct, emotion and reason. During a crisis the responses of the three may clash, with impulses of fear or sexual desire or love sometimes overwhelming reason.

Telepathy is hypothesized to be a function of the lower two brains: the reptilian one cued to survival and the mammalian one geared to family bonding. As evolution favored language over telepathy and individuality over tribal consciousness, our nervous system learned to block psychic messages from other tribal members so that each of us could concentrate on the task at hand, without the silent chatter of tribal gossip to distract us.

As expressed by British psychologist Sir Cyril Burt: "'Osses,' said the coachman to Tom Brown, 'as wears blinkers, so's they see only wot's in front of 'em: and that's the safest plan for 'umble folk like you and me.' Nature seems to have worked on much the same principle. Our sense organs and our brain operate as an intricate kind of filter which limits and directs the mind's clairvoyant powers, so that under normal conditions attention is concentrated on just those objects or situations that are of biological importance for the survival of the organism and its species. . . . As a rule, it would seem the mind rejects ideas coming from another mind as the body rejects grafts coming from another body."

Nonetheless, over the past twenty years, researchers in the increasingly specialized field of prenatal study have discovered that telepathy may still play a vital role in infant survival. According to this theory, hormonal changes during pregnancy create a mother-fetus psychic unit, allowing a woman to sense danger to her fetus in advance of medical evidence. In a dramatic example, cited by childbirth authority Carl Jones in his book *From Parent to Child: The Psychic Link*, anthropologist Robbie Davis-Floyd could not shake the feeling that her unborn son was strangling in his umbilical cord. Employing telepathy, she suggested to him that he use his hands to adjust the cord. When the child was born one week later, he was clutching his umbilical cord with both hands. In another example, Nancy Holroyd, a registered nurse, dreamed vividly of giving birth to a dark-haired, elfin-like child with Down's syndrome before producing such a child.

This mother-fetus bond is also said to be the source of powerful intuitions in which the mother suddenly "knows" the sex of her unborn child, and other physical features, such as hair and eye color. In a study of 1,048 prenatal dreams from sixty-seven mothers, Dr. Patricia Maybruck, a clinical psychologist in San Francisco, determined that perhaps 6 per cent represented communication between mother and fetus. In one such example, Peggy O'Neill of Richmond, Virginia, a pregnant health-care worker, dreamt she was shown a roomful of fourteen-month-old boys from which she was supposed to identify her own. This was a shock, since she had her heart set on a girl. However, as soon as she saw a certain blond, blue-eyed boy, she happily selected him. Then, three days after the birth of a son, who grew to look like the child in the dream, O'Neill, her husband and a friend simultaneously dreamed, during naps in separate rooms, that the child's name should be Jonathan.

This story illustrates another peculiarity of the mother-child forcefield: its reputed power to telepathically draw in other caregivers. In a 1960s study by British psychiatrist W.H. Trethowan, 11 per cent of the expectant fathers were found to suffer from couvade syndrome, a condition with symptoms such as weight gain and morning nausea, imitating pregnancy. Though the fathers-to-be were usually unconscious of the origin of their distress, Trethowan noted that the condition might be psychologically functional, since the wives of such men tended to remain symptom-free. Trethowan's observations have been confirmed by the experience of other health-care professionals, as well as by World War II medical reports, linking the abdominal cramps of soldiers in the field with their wives' labor pains, even when the births were off-schedule. Obstetricians have similarly found themselves hooked up to the prenatal hot-line. Stated Dr. Peter Hope of New Hampshire: "I have often awakened, noticed the time, then later received a call from a woman whose labor began at the time I was awakened."

Recent evidence indicating that newborns may be more aware than suspected strengthens the extrasensory thesis. In 1983, psychologist David B. Chamberlain used hypnosis to compare the birth memories of mothers and children who had never discussed the subject. One mother described the first sight of her baby: "I pick her up and smell her. I smell her head. I look at her toes and say, 'Oh God! She has deformed toes.'" Her daughter described the same scene: "She's holding me up, looking at me. She's smelling!" Correctly, the daughter added: "She asked the nurse why my toes were so funny. The nurse said that's just the way my toes are and that they weren't deformed." Dr. Chamberlain concluded that babies have "an intuitive basis for communication apart from language, a knowing deeper than words."

New York psychiatrist Jan Ehrenwald agreed. To him, the mother-child biological unit is the origin of telepathy in humans—the "cradle of ESP." However, as the child matures, Western culture's emphasis on individuality requires the child to establish a

barrier between its thoughts and its mother's. Experiences of telepathy then become taboo, since they carry the taint of infantilism.
Confirmed Ehrenwald: "The rejection and repudiation of the telepathic factor by the growing child's ego has become mandatory in
our culture."

The dramatic decline of psychic ability in very young
children as speech develops has been verified by a number of
researchers. In a five-year British study involving 1,000 subjects
and using simple guessing games, parapsychologist Ernesto
Spinelli found that children aged three to three and a half had
telepathic scores 17 per cent above chance; by four and a half to
five years, this had declined to 15 per cent above chance; by five to
seven years, to 4 per cent; from eight years onwards, to a level
expected by chance.

Some researchers believe telepathy accounts for the incredible speed with which the very young absorb the subtleties of
culture before this dropoff. This, they say, is reflected in games
featuring chanting, skipping, bouncing and other repetitive
rituals—all suggestive of, or conducive to, a trance state. As
language takes over, ego-consciousness prevails. Telepathy is tossed
into the toybox like a worn-out teddy bear, awaiting crisis to
resurrect it.

Among two groups of birth-bonded pairs, the expected
dropoff in psychic intensity does not always seem to occur:
between mothers of severely handicapped children, and between
identical twins. In the psychological literature, a subject known
only as the Cambridge boy had spastic diplegia and congenital
cataracts in both eyes, yet could "read" eye charts as long as his
mother was also looking at them; Bo, a retarded Georgia boy of
eleven, was similarly able to read and do mathematical calculations
as long as his mother was so engaged.

Of particular interest to researchers are identical twins born
from the same fertilized egg but raised in different environments
with no communication between them. In a 1980s study of sixteen
such pairs, psychologist Tom Bouchard of Minnesota reported
astonishing parallels in the lifestyles, choices and personalities of

most of them, even though many were meeting for the first time and some hadn't even known they possessed twins.

Adopted by families in different Ohio cities in 1939, James Lewis and James Springer had no contact from their separation at birth until their reunion at age thirty-nine. As children, both had owned dogs they named Toy. Both married and divorced women named Linda, then married women named Betty. James Lewis called his first son James Alan, while James Sprinter varied the spelling to James Allan. Both had worked as part-time deputy sheriffs, filling station attendants and at McDonald's. Both regularly vacationed at the same three-hundred-yard Florida beach, drank Miller's Lite beer, chainsmoked Salems and drove Chevrolets. Both enjoyed household chores and scattered love notes around their homes for their wives. Both built furniture in basement workshops and had constructed white benches around trees in their gardens. In school, both had loved math and hated spelling. Both used the same slang words. Both liked stock-car racing and disliked baseball.

Like the "Jim twins," Dorothy Lowe and Bridget Harrison were separated weeks after birth in 1945, and did not meet until they were thirty-four. Adopted into different British social classes, they lived lives that also showed amazing parallels, even though neither knew she had a twin. Both had cats named Tiger. Both had sons—one Richard Andrew and the other Andrew Richard. Both had daughters—one Catherine Louise and the other Karen Louise. (Bridget claimed she had wanted the name Catherine but changed to please a relative.) Both had studied the piano to the same grade, then stopped after the same exam. Both loved historical novels; one was an avid fan of Catherine Cookson, the other of Caroline Marchant—Catherine Cookson's alternate pen name. Both picked at their cuticles and crossed their limbs in the same way. Both wore the same perfume and collected cuddly toys. At their reunion, each gave the other a teddy bear. For their next birthday, both decided in advance to exchange the same present. Tempted by a completely different choice, Dorothy stuck to the agreement; tempted by the same item that Dorothy had spotted, Bridget bought it for Dorothy.

Even more suggestive: during 1960, but only during that year, both girls kept a diary—the same make and color. Though the entries were unalike, both filled in most of the same days while leaving the others blank.

Parallel choices and unlikely coincidences marked the lives of most of the other Bouchard twins, some far more than others. There were twins who showed up for their first meeting in similar hairstyles and identical dresses (one borrowed); twins who married on the same day; twins who shared a single ailment—one possessing a wasted leg muscle who had suffered no pain and the other possessing no injury who had suffered chronic leg pain; twins brought up in opposing cultures—one as an Israeli Jew and the other as a member of Hitler Youth—who first met in the Minnesota airport, age forty-six, wearing clipped mustaches, identical rectangular spectacles and shirts with epaulettes.

Since any two lives are a potentially rich source of coincidence, it is difficult to present Tom Bouchard's twin harmonics in a statistically relevant way. One reassuring aspect for those who distrust all psychic research is the extent to which Bouchard himself downgraded telepathy, since he was investigating the influence of heredity.

ANIMAL TELEPATHY

JULY 1945

My best-beloved cat, Smoky, is missing. This is not an entirely unpredictable event since, in the four years my family has owned him, he's gone AWOL every time we prepared to drive home from whatever cottage we rented for our summer vacation. Assuming that he is alerted by the ritual of packing the car, my sister and I have learned to lock him up in advance, with the result that Smoky has learned to disappear earlier. In the past, after hours of desperate search and encirclement, we've always recaptured him at the last minute—chasing frogs down on the beach or even huddled under the car. Now that last minute has come and gone. My sister and I revisit all Smoky's favorite

nooks while my mother tries to calm our father, growing loga-
rithmically more irritable at the thought of the Sunday traffic. Finally,
we must leave. Distraught, my sister and I beg cottagers up and down
the Lake Ontario community of Peacock Point to phone us the instant
when—we dare not say "if"—Smoky returns. It is a long and brutal
ride home.

No phone call from Peacock Point ever comes. Smoky never
returns there. However, two months after the trauma of our rupture the
raking of claws down the screen door of our Hamilton house, in a way
expressly forbidden, causes me to spin. A skinny gray cat hangs
suspended where a fat one used to. Smoky!

How he tracked us we will never know. He had travelled the
sixty-mile route to this particular rented cottage only once, snoozing in
the back seat. As a child, I was quick to proclaim a miracle. Out of
sentiment, I still do.

While extrasensory perception (ESP) may be a suspect
quality in humans, doting pet owners often freely assign it to their
dogs and cats and birds and gerbils. Pride of ownership notwith-
standing, sometimes the facts do suggest telepathic ability.

In a 1963 study, researchers J.B. Rhine and Sara Feather
investigated "psi trailing" in pets—incidents in which an animal,
separated from its owner, follows that person through unfamiliar
territory under conditions not allowing for sensory tracking. Their
criteria included positive identification of the animal, availability of
the animal for inspection, reliable source of information and
independent corroboration. Out of several dozen cases, Rhine and
Feather chose twenty-five that met their standards, involving
distances of thirty to three thousand miles.

Because my Smoky had once traveled the sixty-mile route
from our Hamilton home to our rented cottage at Peacock Point,
he would not have qualified under the strict Rhine-Feather
guidelines. However, four-year-old Chat Beau, who went missing
while his Louisiana family was moving three hundred miles to
Texas, did. Four weeks later, the white Persian turned up, in fragile

condition, at the Texarkana school attended by his family favorite, Butchie. Though the cat ran from other children, he sought out Butchie, who immediately exclaimed, "It's Chat Beau!" Not only did this cat have a uniquely scarred eye but he also bore a smear of tar the family had been unable to wash off in Lafayette. The family's collie, who had raised Chat Beau along with her pups, welcomed her with familiarity.

Sugar, a cream-colored Persian, was reluctantly left with a neighbor when a Californian principal moved his family to Oklahoma. After less than three weeks, Sugar took off; fourteen months later, a cat leapt onto the principal's wife's shoulder as she stood with her back to an open window, causing her to joke, "Sugar has come to see us!" To her astonishment, examination revealed Sugar's distinctive left-hipbone deformity. An exceptionally strong male who had proved himself in combat with dogs and coyotes, Sugar was judged vigorous enough for the 1,500-mile odyssey.

As amazing as the endurance of these pets was their ability to hone in on their human targets, using a talent that seemed telepathic. Since animals often use their sharpened five senses in ways that appear supernatural to humans, scientists are chary about assigning to them a sixth sense. For example, birds and even bees are thought to chart their migratory or nectar-foraging routes by the sun, the stars and/or the earth's magnetic fields; however, it is difficult to imagine how such navigational aids would help an animal tracking humans in a car over busy highways through foreign territory to an unknown destination.

The response of pets to human tragedy is another rich source of anecdotal lore: whimpering dogs that hide in closets simultaneous with a beloved owner's death, berserk horses that break out of stalls, bristling cats that climb trees and won't come down. Better documented than most is the story of Flak, the canine mascot of a World War II bomber crew stationed in Tunis, North Africa. Though Flak always met his masters' plane on its arrival from a mission, one day he refused to go out onto the flight line, preferring instead to cower by himself, howling mournfully. Did Flak sense that his crew had been shot down hours before in Italy?

A less typical story centers on young Rheal Guindon of Opatsika, Ontario, who found himself alone in the bush after his parents drowned in a fishing accident. As reported by CP news service in November 1956, with the temperature below zero, the exhausted and shivering youngster lay on the ground and prayed. Suddenly, in the darkness, he felt something warm and furry. Gratefully, he hugged it, without even knowing what kind of animal it was. Next morning, Rheal found three large beavers snuggled against him. Rejuvenated from his sleep, he was able to limp, on bleeding feet, to the town of Kapuskasing.

Even more contentious than a pet's psychic response to personal crisis is the potential role of telepathy in the interaction and learning of all animals. In 1952, a species of monkey, domiciled over several Japanese islands, was introduced to sweet potatoes. Eventually, a monkey on the island of Koshima was observed dunking its sweet potato in the ocean to wash off the sand. Soon all members of this troop were dunking their potatoes and, very soon after that, monkeys on every island had reportedly picked up this trick. In his controversial theory of the Hundredth Monkey, South African biologist Lyall Watson speculated that when enough members of a species have learned a useful habit it becomes easier for all members of that species to acquire the same habit—hypothetically, through telepathy. He called the number necessary for psychic transmission the critical mass.

As a second example of critical mass learning, Watson cited the abruptly acquired ability of English sheep to cross grids of rollers by lying down and sliding. After one flock had demonstrated this talent, sheep over the whole of England were suddenly rolling their way to greener grass and greater freedom. Similarly, widely scattered British bluetits seemed mysteriously and simultaneously to learn to peck through milk-bottle tops to drink the cream.

Traditional debate over animal learning pitted the innovators, who believed that the same discoveries were made many times in many places, against the diffusionists, who believed they occurred only once, then spread by imitation. Of course, both sides attacked

Watson's Hundredth Monkey theory, with the first claiming that if one monkey is clever enough to wash its sweet potato, then all monkeys are, and the second insisting that Watson's island monkeys were better swimmers than he knew. Such criticism has not stopped the grassroots popularity of Watson's theory, which continues to gain converts—perhaps soon to become a critical mass—who intuitively accept its validity.

Evidence for some kind of a group mind operating among insects is even more striking. For example, colonies of harvester ants build radiating roads to food sites half a mile away; when a road becomes blocked, police ants arrive in a phalanx to construct a detour. Experiments, using a stopwatch, have verified that these ants appear on site before an alarm could be relayed by any known sensory or chemical means.

Even more suggestive is the behavior of the flattid bug. To hide from predators, clouds of these tiny insects—in graduated shades of coral and green—arrange themselves on twigs to look like a single flower with a green tip. When disturbed, the colony instantly reassembles like a well-drilled flashcard section. How do individuals learn this trick of coordination? How do they manage to transmit their learning from generation to generation, so that the right number of precisely shaded insects—some half pink and half green—continue to reproduce?

Summed up Watson in his book *Supernature*: "Without telepathy it is difficult to see how an elaborate instinctive pattern can develop at all in invertebrate animals that are highly unlikely to acquire new habits by imitation or by tradition."

TELEPATHY IN THE LAB

1950–1953

As a teenager, desiring more control over my life, I engage in a series of what I call mind experiments.

On days when I have done no homework, and my sister has not been thoughtful enough to write the answers in my inherited textbook,

I attempt to prevent the teacher from calling upon me through my exercise of will. As the teacher travels up and down the rows, systematically extracting answers, I stare at my text, while repeating with the fiercest of conviction: "I am not here!" More often than not, the teacher—to the awe of my classmates—skips me, and only me, without seeming to notice any oversight.

By concentrating on a deck of cards, I also find I can sometimes pull out four aces in about six tries. Though I imagine this might equip me to psychically control the Crown & Anchor wheel at local carnivals, I find it does not. Yet, I discover that, on those occasions when I am about to win through the ordinary laws of chance, I suddenly feel a peculiar certitude even while the wheel is still spinning.

Eventually, boredom ends these experiments. Psyching out the teacher, I discover, takes as much concentration as doing the homework. Similarly, the satisfaction of knowing when I am going to win at Crown & Anchor hardly compensates for the quarters lost.

During experiments with psychic healing in the late nineteenth century, doctors devised a technique that became known as hypnosis. In this highly suggestible state, it was discovered, subjects experienced dramatically heightened extrasensory ability. Now, at last, researchers could study paranormal events at will and with controls.

Beginning in 1885, French neurologist Pierre Janet and his assistant Dr. Gibert demonstrated that they could hypnotize, at a distance, a woman they called Madame B. Described as a peasant of limited intelligence prone to sleepwalking, Madame B. did not like to be hypnotized because, she said, it "makes me look silly." Far from being flattered by this distinguished attention, she sometimes dowsed her hands in cold water to counteract the psychic pull.

On the evening of April 22, 1886, Gibert attempted to hypnotically lure the unknowing Madame B. to his Le Havre study two-thirds of a mile away. Classical scholar Dr. F.W.H. Myers, who coined the term *telepathy*, took the following notes: "At 9:22 . . .

observed Madame B. coming halfway out of the garden gate, and again retreating. Those who saw her more closely observed that she was plainly in the somnambulic state, and was wandering about and muttering. At 9:25 she came out (with eyes persistently closed, so far as could be seen) . . . and made for M. Gibert's house. . . . She avoided lamp-posts, vehicles, but crossed and recrossed the street repeatedly. . . . After eight or ten minutes she grew much more uncertain in gait, and paused as though she would fall . . . it was 9:35. At about 9:40 she grew bolder, and at 9:45 reached the street in front of M. Gibert's house. There she met him, but did not notice him, and walked into his house, where she rushed hurriedly from room to room on the ground-floor. M. Gibert had to take her hand before she recognized him. She then grew calm.

"M. Gibert said that from 8:55 to 9:20 he thought intently about her; from 9:20 to 9:35 he thought more feebly; at 9:35 he gave the experiment up, and began to play billiards; but in a few minutes began to will her again. It appeared that his visit to the billiard-room had coincided with her hesitation and stumbling in the street. But this coincidence may of course have been accidental."

Over the next several decades, hundreds of telepathy experiments were conducted by members of the Society for Psychic Research, founded in Britain in 1882 for study of the paranormal. Included in the SPR's ranks were Victorian society's most eminent scholars and scientists—physicists Sir Oliver Lodge, Sir William Crookes, J.J. Thompson and Lord Rayleigh; authors Lewis Carroll, Mark Twain, Alfred Lord Tennyson and John Ruskin; American psychologist William James; French philosopher Henri Bergson; French physiologist Charles Richet.

One indefatigable SPR experimenter was classical scholar Gilbert Murray, who drafted the Covenant of the League of Nations. While he waited behind closed doors, his colleagues would silently write down a subject that he, on rejoining them, would try to guess, with his words recorded verbatim. Of Murray's first 505 experiments, 60 per cent were judged positive, some astonishingly so. To the subject "Crimean soldiers receiving medals from Queen Victoria at Horse Guards," Murray replied: "Is it the

King giving V.C.s and things to people?" In response to "*Lusitania*," Murray replied: "I have got this violently. I have got an awful impression of naval disaster. I should think it was the torpedoing of the *Lusitania*."

As Murray stated in an address to the SPR, "Fraud, I think, is out of the question; however slippery the behavior of my subconscious, too many respectable people would have had to be its accomplices."

Despite the sterling reputation of Murray and other SPR investigators, later researchers rejected their evidence because their controls were not judged stringent enough. Modern study of telepathy is, therefore, said to have begun in the 1930s, when parapsychologist J.B. Rhine established a laboratory at Duke University in North Carolina. For forty years Rhine and his colleagues attempted to prove telepathy through the statistical analysis of card-guessing games. Selecting a card from a pack of twenty-five, bearing five different symbols, a tester would concentrate on it while a subject tried to guess the symbol by reading the tester's mind. Since chance would account for five successes in twenty-five, consistently higher scores would point to telepathy.

Rhine's initial results, involving thousands of trials, produced odds-against-chance ratios estimated at one million to one. This bombshell inspired both a rush of imitators and a bath of vituperative denouncing his procedures. Such polarization still defines the psychic field. Like the French experts who rejected communication by telephone because they were sure a ventriloquist must be hidden under the table, hardcore critics of telepathy regard positive results as *prima facie* evidence of fraud or carelessness. Yet despite the unscientific tone of churlishness running through the skeptical literature, the case for caution is a just one. After a series of apparently successful experiments, French philosopher Henri Bergson found one cheater had been reading words reflected in his eyes—backward letters 1/250 of an inch high!

With the imposition of ever-more stringent controls, parapsychologists often found themselves unable to replicate their early successes—an apparent victory for their critics. However, investigators soon began to suspect that the controls were toxic to the ability they were trying to measure. This was supported by a new analysis of old statistics, revealing that most subjects scored well at the beginning of a series, slumped in the middle, then improved near the end—a curve fluctuating with their enthusiasm.

The connection between emotional engagement and psychic success had earlier been stressed by SPR experimenter Gilbert Murray: "I do feel there is one almost universal quality in these guesses of mine which does suit telepathy and does not suit any other explanation. They always begin with a vague emotional quality or atmosphere . . . and it is notable that I never had any success in guessing mere cards or numbers, or any subject that was not in some way interesting or amusing."

Some parapsychologists also began to doubt Rhine's original hypothesis: that telepathy was a faculty possessed by everyone. Instead, they reasoned, it might be a gift, like musical talent, requiring selection and nurture. In 1945, psychologist Gertrude Schmeidler of New York divided subjects into sheep and goats according to whether they believed in extrasensory perception. During 1,300 tests spanning a decade, she found that sheep consistently scored above chance while goats consistently scored below, at odds of one million to one. Thirteen studies by other researchers verified Schmeidler's results, with personality tests indicating that extroversion, openness, confidence and an ability to recall one's dreams correlated with psychic talent. Schmeidler also found that new mothers scored exceptionally high, and that results were significantly better between identical twins and other emotionally bonded pairs than between strangers.

Eventually, some researchers came to believe that even the attitude of testers influenced scores. In one experiment, conducted by British psychiatrist Donald J. West and researcher G.W. Fisk, packs of randomly shuffled cards were sent to participants, who attempted to guess their order without opening them. One factor was found unexpectedly significant: packs shuffled by Fisk were correctly guessed at a much higher rate than those shuffled by West.

Such observations led to the labelling of testers who consistently collected negative scores as psi inhibitory. Here, at last, was a foolproof response to critics who rejected psychic evidence out-of-hand: to succeed you had to believe! Unfortunately, in adopting such a defence, parapsychology had turned full circle. Once again telepathy was a matter of faith instead of science.

FIELD RESEARCH

JULY 20, 1974

I am teaching at Banff Centre in the Rockies when my mother phones from Hamilton, Ontario, to tell me that my eighty-two-year-old father is dying. In preparation for returning home the next morning, I complete various tasks, feeling increasingly sluggish, like a clock that is running down. Eventually, I go to my room, where I fall into a heavy doze.

Fifteen minutes later I am jolted to attention by an unearthly and unidentifiable shriek. Instinctively, I look at my watch: exactly three o'clock. I think: "My father could be dying at this moment and I wouldn't even know it." A garbled quote from a John Donne sermon passes through my mind: "Do not ask for whom the bell tolls. It tolls for thee."

At five that evening I phone my mother. Her line is busy. It stays that way until nearly six. By the time she answers, I've already guessed her message: "Daddy passed away. It happened at five." She adds, as if providing important information, "I know it was exactly five because I looked at my watch."

After hanging up the phone, I grow puzzled: five o'clock. Had my father died even as I was trying to call home?

That night I am again jolted awake by a shriek, which I now recognize as a train whistle, weirdly amplified by the mountains. It is a sound I might have heard a dozen times a day but chose to notice only twice: now and at three that afternoon. With a queasy feeling I make the connection I previously blocked: my father died at five o'clock Eastern Time, meaning three o'clock Mountain Time—the instant both my mother and I looked at our watches.

The above event, like the anecdote involving my grandmother, sprang from a one-of-a-kind crisis: death. Though radiantly meaningful to me, no matter how sincerely I try to share it, the incident remains confined to the private theater of my head. Even to review it alters it emotionally without recapturing it. That is the truth proclaimed by the Greek philosopher Heraclitus: "No one can ever step into the same river twice." More than two millennia later, American philosopher William James translated that thought into psychological language: "No state of consciousness, once gone, can recur and be identical with what it was before."

Reflecting this belief, a new breed of parapsychologists has rejected J.B. Rhine's efforts to trap ESP in the laboratory through card-guessing games. In their view, telepathy is not routine, predictable, replicable, quantifiable or objective. Instead, it is creative, startling, spontaneous, singular, significant and subjective. To attempt to analyze it in materialistic terms is like trying to explain the horror of Edgar Allan Poe's "The Tell-Tale Heart" through reference to a medical textbook.

That I had two experiences of telepathy centered on death does not produce statistical odds for my producing another. Yet this lack of predictability in no way renders either event less real. Mental events cannot be quantified or isolated any more than Heraclitus's river can be dissected. As French philosopher Henri Bergson stated, "You cannot have a ton of love . . . or a yard of hate or a gallon of numinous awe; but love and hate and awe are just as real as a ton of flour or a yard of linen or a gallon of petrol, more real indeed, because they have immediate significance, they are not simply means to ends like making bread, a pillow case or haste."

In *The Science of the Paranormal*, parapsychologist Lawrence LeShan puckishly summed up the absurdity-in-principle of Rhine's attempts to trap psychic events in his laboratory by comparing them to a hypothetical laboratory study of falling in love: "Males and females were brought into the laboratory, and delicate scales measured their attraction and repulsion to each other. They were presented to each other under varying conditions, including with and without the ingestion of coffee, alcohol and barbiturates. . . .

Experimenters would continually try to devise a 'repeatable experiment' [in which subjects would] . . . always demonstrate the existence of the phenomena by always falling in love with each other." By contrast, LeShan himself has opted for the release of telepathy, like a frisky lab animal, from its statistical cage for free-range study. For this, he accepts personal testimony, prudently weighed, so as to learn how telepathy operates: when and where it is likely to occur, who is likely to experience it and what purpose it serves.

After reviewing a wealth of anecdotal evidence, LeShan concluded that the most striking incidents happened when a loved one was in danger and other forms of communication were blocked. Most often this took place between parent and child or deeply bonded mates. Typically, the event reflected the emotional history of the two persons, with the endangered one reaching out to someone who provided comfort in the past. However, it isn't information that is exchanged, as between two computers. Instead, two minds create a dynamic forcefield, vibrant with the meaning of their relationship. In such a union, distance is irrelevant. Whether the communicators are a few rooms apart, as with my grand-mother, or half a continent away, as with my father, the process, which appears to be instantaneous, remains unaffected. Most importantly, the experience is transformational, perhaps creating changes in the values of one or both persons. It is not about fact. It is about meaning.

JULY 1986

While I am staying in Los Angeles, a Siamese cat I love disappears under circumstances suggesting theft. After days of frantic search, I am forced, by earlier plans, to fly home to Toronto. As I sit in a friend's backyard, telling of my cat's disappearance, a milkweed parachute floats by. Though this friend is of the no-nonsense variety, she impulsively urges: "Make a wish!"

Plucking the silky tuft from the air, I wish for news about my cat; then I let the breeze spirit away the tuft, carrying my wish.

Next day my sister hands me a gift, purchased on impulse: it is a paperweight with a milkweed parachute imbedded in acrylic. Though my cat never returns, I take this gift as a sign of some benign principle at work in the Universe. It is a gift that will continue to float through my life, in strange and subtle ways, like a milkweed on the wind, with its presence growing in significance as I come to realize that my sister, too, has embarked on a short journey toward death.

My sister's timely gift was not random: it evoked in my consciousness a whole backyard of childhood experiences connecting us, like a spiderweb suddenly illuminated by sunlight. Yet the skeptic demands to know: How could any two people be in contact without telephone wires or radio waves connecting them? How is it possible for a message to travel between two brains with no known energy source or conductor?

With the whole weight of Newtonian physics on one side of the weighing scales, my bit of milkweed gossamer seems grossly incapable of balancing the other; yet, surprisingly, some very reputable scientists have put their authority down onto the pan with the milkweed fluff. In particular, they reject the skeptic's question about conductors and energy sources because they believe it to be grounded on a misassumption: that brain and mind are inseparable. According to their increasingly influential view, thought is not a product of the brain as sight is of the eye. To destroy the eye is to destroy the sight, but to destroy the brain is not necessarily to destroy the mind.

Though this brain-versus-mind debate goes back at least as far as Plato and Aristotle, its modern phase began in 1859. That was when Charles Darwin published his evolutionary theory stating that *Homo sapiens sapiens* had developed by trial and error from the single-celled organisms that once teemed in Earth's primordial oceans. At each progressive stage, life-forms had adapted to environmental conditions, with those genetic mutations most useful for survival prevailing. In this random fashion—combining natural selection with survival of the fittest—all present organisms had evolved. Therefore, humans were not the product of purpose or design but merely accidental descendants of shrews and primates, from whom they differed only in complexity.

In the cranky quarrel between Darwinians, who traced their lineage to apes, and Creationists, who traced theirs to Adam, the name Alfred Russel Wallace was all but lost. Yet, working independently, Wallace had simultaneously formulated the same theory as Darwin, and is so credited by history. However, Wallace did not believe that material causes alone could account for the origin of life, the origin of a new species, the creation of human consciousness or the beginnings of culture. As he wrote in an 1869 letter to Darwin: "Natural selection could only have endowed the savage with a brain a little superior to that of the ape, whereas he possessed one very little inferior to that of an average member of our learned society." To account for these gaps in evolution, Wallace postulated some driving, shaping, guiding, designing or willing force, which could come only from "the unseen universe of spirit." A dismayed Darwin replied: "I hope you have not murdered completely your own and my child."

Whereas Darwin easily won the nineteenth-century debate, modern opposition has crystallized around Wallace's arguments.

Far from being random in its thrust from amoeba to mammal to monkey to Michelangelo, evolution has strongly favored intelligence and greater organization. Similarly, "survival of the fittest" is not a purely mechanistic principle but a metaphysical one, embracing both individual and collective will: Why, and to what end, does any cell or group of cells struggle for existence against the raw forces of nature? Why does one member of a species risk its life—like a worker bee defending its queen, like a salmon swimming upriver to spawn, like a human going into battle—to protect and perpetuate its kind? Far from being the triumph of aggression, evolution is the story of species cooperation.

Most problematic: How did mechanical processes produce the human brain? Often cited as the most amazing structure in the Universe, this three-pound, convoluted gray mass is composed of some one hundred billion nerve cells, with one pinhead of cortex perhaps containing ten trillion connections. To create such a complex organ from natural selection, millions of separate parts would have to develop simultaneously and become genetically fixed even though each had no survival value in itself. In mechanistic terms, this is as if a heap of sand and pebbles being swept down the Tiber, were to collect on shore to randomly construct the Vatican.

Besides, recent fossil evidence indicates that the human brain took far less time to evolve than Darwin estimated. Instead of proceeding through small mutations, changes occurred explosively, discontinuously and in quantum leaps over the past 250,000 years *in advance of* the needs or the abilities of prehistoric races to use them. Therefore, the human brain was not created through gradual adaptation of the primate brain to a changing environment; first came improvements to the brain, then came our species' more skillful manipulation of the environment, leading to all the effects Darwin described.

Even biologists who accept that evolution may have started mechanistically believe that Darwin did not allow for a quantitative difference escalating into a qualitative one. Just as a forest fire, ignited by the abrasion of two sticks, can no longer be defined by the properties of those sticks, so the human brain exploded frontally with a dynamism that renders it unanalyzable in terms of its primate origins. Theoretically, this occurred when society began to affect the brain's development more than the natural environment did. Alone among all species, humans are culture-producing animals. Even isolated groups create art and religion, spurred not by survival but by their passion to understand the human predicament. It is this search for meaning, rather than intelligence, that distinguishes humans from primates: how else can one explain the great gap between a cry of warning and a Hamlet soliloquy? Said biologist Sir Julian Huxley: "The brain alone is not responsible for mind, even though it is a necessary organ for its manifestation. Indeed, an isolated brain is a piece of biological nonsense as meaningless as an isolated individual."

The cornerstone of culture is language, developed out of a desire not only for communication but for self-reflection.

During an intensive language program begun in 1966, a young female chimpanzee named Washoe was taught American Sign Language in a social setting where all the humans communicated only by signing. During the first year and a half, Washoe's ability to acquire signs outstripped that of a child, exposed to the same setting, indicating no want of intelligence on Washoe's part. Eventually, she learned a vocabulary of 130 signs, which she linked meaningfully in sentences of up to four words. However, it soon became apparent that Washoe did not use her "language" as a child would. While successful in signing for food or attention, she did not attempt to acquire other words, to inquire about her environment, to describe, argue or "talk" to others—all things a child naturally does. She gave no indication of any inner use of language, such as thinking or reflecting, and she did not pass on her skill to her offspring. Language remained a trick she had learned to get what she wanted in a particular setting, without her ever gaining any intuitive grasp of its greater meaning.

Other language-training programs have so far confirmed that, even when sharing a vocabulary and environment with humans, chimps do not enter the same social universe. As Sir John Eccles, winner of the 1963 Nobel prize for medicine, wrote: "The history of humanity establishes that there are human attributes—moral, intellectual, and aesthetic attributes—that cannot be explained *solely* in terms of the material composition and organization of the brain. . . . We reject materialism because, as we have seen, it doesn't *explain* our concepts but denies them."

A major difference between the human brain and that of other species is that ours is delivered at birth with a vast number of blank circuits. As learning takes place, our neural cells branch into dendrites, which connect to other neural cells by means of chemical links called synapses. This rich escalation of connections occurs simultaneously with the gradual but permanent lifetime loss of about one billion neurons; therefore, with every passing year, each of our brains becomes less of a physical "thing" and more of a biochemical-electrical network, reflecting our unique and hazardous journey from birth into the unknown. For this reason, many neurologists eschew physical models of the functioning mind, seeing it instead as a process separate from the brain, in the same way that a symphony exists apart from the orchestra that performs it. If someone were to machine-gun all the members of the orchestra during a performance, do they kill the symphony or just the orchestra members? And even though the audience will no longer hear the rest of the piece, what happens to the music that has already been played? Does it disappear as if it had never been, or does it exist in frequencies finer than those picked up by the human ear? In a materialistic world, such questions make no sense; in a psychic one, they are quintessential.

Though Greek physician Hippocrates lacked modern neurological knowledge, he intuited in the fifth century B.C. that the human mind was separate and superior to the human brain: "To consciousness the brain is messenger. . . . The brain is the interpreter of consciousness." More than two thousand years later, Montreal neurosurgeon Wilder Penfield concurred: "I, like other scientists, have struggled to prove that the brain accounts for the mind. But now, perhaps, the time has come when we may profitably consider the evidence as it stands." After decades of surgery, during which conscious patients conversed with him while he removed portions of their brains to control epileptic seizures, Penfield concluded that mind was not only distinct from brain but superior to it, in the same way that the intelligence programming a computer is superior to the computer.

Penfield's categorical conclusion: "One cannot assign the mind a position in space." Therefore, the fact that two brains are a thousand miles apart does not mean that two minds are, and the question of how thought travels physically from consciousness to consciousness becomes a specious one. Thoughts are not things but processes. Even inside the brain you can't meaningfully describe one thought as being an inch away from another, as if both were apples; the idea of a thought occupying space or zooming like a sports car on a freeway between two heads is equally absurd. Thus, telepathy— if it exists—operates independently of space so that "here" and "there" become irrelevant concepts. It is a property of consciousness, unbound by Newtonian science based on sensory experience. As British astrophysicist Sir Arthur Eddington summed up: "To those who have any intimate acquaintance with the laws of chemistry and physics, the suggestion that . . . [consciousness] could be ruled by laws of allied character is as preposterous as the suggestion that a nation could be ruled by laws like the laws of grammar."

The evolutionary debate between Darwin and Wallace has produced an ironic footnote, for it was during a period of strange lucidity brought on by malaria that Alfred Russel Wallace, then an unknown biologist on a field trip to what is now Indonesia, rapidly drafted a paper, which he mailed next day to Charles Darwin. When Darwin read Wallace's letter, he was astounded: here was a description of natural selection almost identical to his own still unpublished theory. As Darwin testified: "I never saw a more striking coincidence." Had Wallace, in a fever state conducive to telepathy, tuned into Darwin's thought processes? Had he, like a bus seatmate, read Darwin's thesis over his shoulder? Is that why he instinctively sent the manuscript to Darwin? If so, both men remained faithful to the source of their inspiration, for while Darwin grew ever more mechanistic in applying his theory, Wallace grew more spiritual and—some insisted—downright weird.

For a hundred years, the scientific community overwhelmingly favored Darwin. Now, the pendulum is swinging.

A GROUP MIND?

AUGUST 1965

As a journalist for the Toronto Star Weekly, *I have been assigned to write a story about Namu the killer whale, being tugged in a floating pen from the northern British Columbia cove where he was captured to his purchasers at the Seattle Aquarium. His caretakers for the voyage are two marine biologists, a disc jockey who owns the tugboat, and a Seattle reporter, dispatched to cover this story as light relief from America's Vietnam doldrums.*

After a day spent prowling the west coast of Georgia Strait, I am unable to find the whaling party. Discouraged, I check into a hotel in Campbell River on Vancouver Island, knowing that my story is at anchor in some anonymous cove, ready to sail away on the next tide.

About four A.M., *I jerk out of a deep sleep: I have dreamt that a whale is thrashing in the hotel lobby—a whale so gargantuan it has catapulted me out of bed. After throwing on my coat, I race downstairs to the lobby to confront the night clerk with an unlikely question: "Where's Namu?"*

To my surprise, he gives a bemused shrug, then points to a retreating back. "Ask him. He's the captain."

I streak across the lobby, fling myself in front of the departing stranger. "Wait!" Then I plead my case.

Once aboard the tugboat, I soon determine that the four men of the whaling party are not in a normal state of mind. After a week charting the tricky currents of Georgia Strait, they have fallen into some kind of trance, centered on the whale in the pen they are dragging. The Seattle reporter, a seasoned pro who has written about the Korean and Vietnam wars, confides with tears coursing down his cheeks that he has never covered such an important story. The disc jockey is being threatened by loss of job and wife because he refuses to return home. The marine biologists are equally dotty. Like Captain Ahab, all four men are obsessed with the whale: they have whale-bonded.

In southern France there are miles of caves with walls and domes magnificently painted with musk-oxen, reindeer, bison. Some scientists theorize that these paintings, estimated to be more than twenty thousand years old, were used in sacred rites in which hunters attempted to telepathically fuse their minds with those of their prey so as to track them.

Such rituals are still practiced by the pygmies of the Congo, who draw sand pictures of animals they wish to kill, and among some Inuit hunters, who use carvings. The Naskapi Indians of the eastern Arctic traditionally contact caribou and bear through what they call the Big Dream, in which a shaman telepathically seeks out a herd, then asks its spirit for permission to hunt its members. As an Iglulik once explained to Danish anthropologist Knud Rasmussen: "The greatest peril of life lies in the fact that human food consists entirely of souls. All the creatures that we have to kill and eat, all those that we have to strike down and destroy to make clothes for ourselves, have souls, souls that do not perish with the body and which must therefore be pacified lest they should revenge themselves on us for taking away their bodies."

Was it the lure of tribal rites, unconsciously remembered, that overwhelmed four modern whale hunters, separated from their urban lives by wind and water? Did isolation cause them to fuse their minds with that of their captured whale? Did this radiating group mind create a psychic forcefield strong enough to allow a female reporter—in mock reversal of hunting ritual—to track them?

As astonishing account of the apparent use of telepathy to communicate with porpoises was provided by Arthur Grimble, a former land commissioner in the Gilbert Islands of the South Pacific. While Kumba villagers prepared for feasting, their porpoise-caller retired to his hut, where he put himself into a trance. Hours later, with tables set and pots boiling, the ecstatic caller rushed down to the seashore, shrieking, "They come!" As Grimble stood at water's edge, he saw a flotilla of porpoises approaching at two- or three-yard intervals, as far as the eye could see. "So slowly they came, they seemed to be hung in a trance." While crooning encouragement, the villagers eased the porpoises over the sandbars. "It was as if their single wish was to get to the beach."

As members of an agrarian society, the Hopi Indians of Arizona use telepathic rituals to grow their crops. In their mystical world, even to think about a stalk of corn leaves a psychic trace on it. More important than soil preparation and planting are the long and intricate ceremonies preceding these activities. Because of the concentration involved, that's when the Hopis believe their hardest work is done.

According to anthropologist Tomas Roessner, the natives of eastern Peru enhance their natural telepathic ability with a hallu- cinogenic drink made from "the vine of the soul." This, they believe, allows them as a group to project their minds to other places. On one occasion, they decided, "Let's see cities!" After completing their psychic journey, they questioned their anthropologist guests, full of excitement: "What were those strange things (*aparatos*) which run so swiftly along streets?" They were describing cars, which they had never before seen.

Today, vestiges of tribal hunting rites appear in sporting rituals that emphasize male bonding. Often teams are named for admired animals—the Boston Bruins, the Hamilton Tigercats—while mascots, decked out in team colors, replace the small animals once sacrificed as bait. Coaches psych their players with pep talks emphasizing team spirit, and players repeat good-luck rituals or carry charms. On the field of combat, drum bands and cheerleaders exhort fans to provide the same positive atmosphere sought by the Hopis for rain making and corn growing, while a scoreboard records the symbolic "kills."

Though modern electronic communications have made telepathy redundant for the spread of information, human emotions and even emotion-drenched ideas may still be transmitted by telepathy. Perhaps telepathy is even our *chief* means of emotional transmission, so omnipresent in our lives that we seldom notice it. Perhaps it is telepathy that makes a hockey game or a rock concert or a political rally or live theater such an electrifying experience: instead of reacting individually to the same stimuli as traditionally explained, members of the audience become psychically fused into a vibrating whole that responds as one. Perhaps this explains the power of television: not only do spectators witness the same events but they do so at the same time, creating a pulsating group mind that is larger than the sum of its parts.

Perhaps it is the same emotional forcefield—once useful in securing cooperation for war and the hunt—that fuels all political, religious and nationalistic movements, countering the separateness and self-interest fostered by our intellects. Perhaps telepathy explains how populist movements like the sixties' sexual revolution and the stunning collapse of communism can sweep like wildfire through whole populations, leaving institutions in ruins, with the leadership and even the media scrambling to catch up. Perhaps telepathy also explains how people can behave in a riot or an orgy or a war in a bloodthirsty way that mocks their rational selves as well as their emotional history. Are they, perhaps, telling the truth when they claim to have been driven by emotions not their own?

Is it emotion, telepathically shared by our mammal brains, that distinguishes all close bonding, including that enigma known as romantic love? Could the world's great love poetry—not to mention the miles of greeting-card doggerel—be correct? Are lovers emotionally joined in a single, dynamic forcefield, accounting for their sense of oneness and immediacy, even during separation? Is that why they so often talk and act alike, even claiming to read each other's minds?

TOWARD A RADICAL NEW BIOLOGY

In 1953, the highly respected British biologist Sir Alister Hardy put forth a paper in which he suggested that animals might share the evolutionary information vital for their development through a group mind, which he described as "a sort of psychic blueprint between members of a species." Hardy also speculated that all species might be linked in a cosmic mind, capable of carrying evolutionary information through space and time.

It was this theory that biologist Rupert Sheldrake developed in *A New Science of Life*, under the label morphic resonance. According to Sheldrake, species develop and behave as they do because of pre-existing psychic blueprints, which he called morphogenetic fields. Every individual inherits the field specific to its own species along with the genetic contents of its DNA. This psychic field directs the development of the embryo, using DNA as building blocks. Though causative in the way an architectural blueprint is causative, a morphogenetic field also possesses the drive to complete itself and to continue to direct the behavior of an organism throughout its life. It does this by psychically absorbing the experience of all species members, circulating new information among them, and storing the accumulation for future generations. In this way, it functions as architect, builder, office manager, president and librarian all in one.

A morphogenetic field can't be perceived by humans except through its physical effects. Thus, the morphogenetic field of a tulip can be seen only through the production of a tulip. In this, it resembles an electromagnetic field, which can be detected only through its effect on iron filings. When you sweep away the iron filings, the electromagnetic field still exists, and the same is true for a morphogenetic field: if you burn a tulip to ashes, the form continues to exist, though it is no longer visible.

To demonstrate how a morphogenetic field affects learning, Sheldrake cited the experiments of psychologist William McDougall of Harvard University. In the 1920s, McDougall exposed thirty-two generations of white rats to a water tank with two escape gangways—one brightly illuminated but producing an electric shock, the other unlit and without shock. Since McDougall randomly changed the lighting on the gangways, learning occurred when a rat discovered illumination always meant shock. Though some first-generation rats required 330 immersions, the last learned nearly 90 per cent faster. Since McDougall was studying inherited learning, this was the effect he wanted. However, he noted "the disturbing fact" that control rats from genetically unrelated stock also upped their learning speeds. When McDougall's experiments were repeated by F.A.E. Crew of Edinburgh, the first-generation rats began with the average scores McDougall's rats had achieved after thirty generations, with some rats performing perfectly without a single shock.

According to Sheldrake, unrelated rats were able to learn a skill with increasing speed simply because other rats had previously done so. Literally, they picked the information out of the air.

More radical than Lyall Watson and his Hundredth Monkey, Sheldrake hypothesizes that what any *one* member of a species learns becomes telepathically accessible to the rest. He also believes that all information fields are interconnected hierarchically, with the field of "mammal" guiding and restricting that of "primate," which in turn guides and constrains "chimpanzee." The more similar any two species, the more readily they can exchange information. Sheldrake also speculates that solutions produced on one planet could become available throughout the Universe, and that inanimate forms may also have morphogenetic fields. As evidence of the latter he cites how chemists often have great trouble inducing new chemicals to crystallize the first time, but afterwards find the same chemicals crystallize under the same circumstances with increasing rapidity.

Though still unproven, Sheldrake's morphic theory would resolve one of the greatest mysteries in biology: how a fertilized egg evolves into a tiny replica of its parents. Since identical copies of DNA are passed to all cells, what tells one group to sprout a wing and others to transmogrify into a heart? In a set of experiments in the 1890s, biologist Hans Driesch discovered that even mutilating a system did not prevent its normal development. When he destroyed one of a sea-urchin's two embryonic cells, the remaining cell always gave rise to a small, complete sea-urchin. Similarly, the fusion of two embryos resulted in a single, giant sea-urchin. Despite extreme damage, some unknown organizing principle was able to redirect matter in an apparently intelligent way to fulfill an intention: the production of a healthy sea-urchin.

Sheldrake's theory is also versatile enough to account for other evolutionary enigmas: the magic leap by which a chimpanzee brain, in the slow process of becoming a better chimpanzee brain, suddenly explodes frontally to become a human one; the similarities in structure between dramatically different species, such as the circulatory system common to humans and frogs; the evidence of group planning, from generation to generation, in lowly species like the flattid bug, and of group learning in advanced species like the potato-washing monkeys of Koshima island; the complex solutions arrived at by simple organisms, such as the pivoting, butt-wagging dance by which a honeybee, with all the agility of a Fred Astaire, reports the longitude, latitude and flying distance of a rich cache of nectar.

Here, in Sheldrake's morphogenetic fields, is evolution's driving, shaping, guiding, willing force, as demanded by Alfred Russel Wallace. Here, too, is an echo of Plato's transcendental Forms. However, where the latter were eternal and existed above matter as unattainable Ideas, Sheldrake's evolve with matter, both shaping it and being shaped by it.

JULY 6, 1987

I awaken in a state of exhaustion. Though I try to get dressed, I am too dizzy. Uncharacteristically, I stay in bed till noon, with images of death suffusing my mind—fragments of dreams I can't quite grasp but compelling enough to cause me to cancel a lunch date. Later that afternoon, I impulsively visit the grave of my former husband, who died precisely six months previous. On my return, I find a message from my sister: our eighty-six-year-old mother died that afternoon after a bus trip to visit a niece.

The eight-hour funeral-parlor visitation, two days later, proves an ordeal. My mother was deservedly admired for her goodness and optimism, and the description on everyone's lips is "a saint." Two months before, I had told my mother that I was writing a memoir about my incestuous relationship with my father. Though she was supportive, I now believe the pending publication of my book hastened her death. As mourners file into the funeral parlor, I am struck by another horrendous thought: since I have no proof of the incest beyond my own recovered memories, how do I know it's true? What if my "recollections" are nothing but a self-deceiving fantasy?

The room distorts, blurs, begins to pulsate. Drawn to my mother's casket, I stare into her closed eyes, pleading for insight and guidance: "If I am wrong, how can I make things right?" Then I go into a private lounge to pull myself together.

When I return to the visitation room for the final half-hour, my sister tells me a man is waiting to speak with me. Though I've never met him, I recognize his name as someone who was professionally involved with my father. Leaning against the wall in a way that cuts me off from the rest of the room, he reminisces in an easy, jovial tone that belies his words: "Your mother was a gem. She really sparkled after your father died. He was such a greedy man. Everyone loved your mother but your father was relentless. He never let up. He made her life hell."

After the eight-hour wash of well-intentioned sentimentality, here is a conversation with graininess and complexity that confirms my own reality. In relief, I blurt: "I have the desire to tell you something."

"What?"

"My father sexually abused me."

"I know that. He and I talked about it several times."

"You what?"

"He and I talked about it."

"But I didn't know! I'd blocked it out."

"Well, you know now, don't you?"

My world rights itself: once again the ceiling is over my head where it belongs, and my feet find solid ground. "Yes."

When I leave the funeral parlor, it is with a profound sense of gratitude, convinced that I inhabit a benign and meaningful Universe in which human needs are recognized and, if possible, met, however mysteriously,

Though Sigmund Freud scorned telepathy as a neurotic and regressive capability left over from an earlier evolutionary stage, Carl Jung respected it as a valuable means of communication with our own unconscious, the unconscious of others and what he called the collective unconscious.

Just as Sheldrake hypothesized morphogenetic fields to account for biological evidence, so Jung hypothesized the collective unconscious to account for psychological evidence. In his clinical work, Jung was impressed by how often clients produced the same remarkable images, used in the same way. He was also struck by the stunning repetition of plots and symbols in the myths of societies widely scattered in time and space: the birth of a magical child; the incarnation, death and resurrection of a god; the destruction of the world by a flood. From this, he hypothesized a common psychic source—the collective unconscious, which he described as the spiritual heritage of humankind, born anew in the brain structure of every individual. Deposited by our ancestors from prehistoric times, this instinctive and intuitive wisdom is there to guide each of us, especially during periods of transition or crisis.

Psychologist William James expressed a similar belief in a group mind that transcended time and space: "There is a continuum of cosmic consciousness against which our individuality builds but accidental fences, and into which our several minds plunge as into a mother sea."

Access to this collective storehouse, whether during sleep or while awake, seems best achieved by powerful emotion, urgency, openness and the need for meaning. All these coalesced at my mother's lying-in. In my opinion, the very special circumstances— the mythic quality of a mother's death, my trance-like state and powerfully articulated need—allowed me to pluck information, like a milkweed tuft, from the air. In this transaction, two minds were in contact—that of the man who provided the confirmation I desired, and my own. Yet I cannot shake the feeling that a third was involved—the one I addressed, the spirit-mind of my dead mother, either as itself or as part of the cosmic consciousness.

William James has estimated that most people use only 5 per cent of their mental capacity and that Einstein employed a probable 15 or 20 per cent. Similarly, geneticists estimate that the human brain uses only 1 per cent of its DNA for its complicated coding, leaving 99 per cent unaccounted for. What is the function of that silent matter in our heads? Does it represent something we have lost, something unconscious, something we have yet to develop?

As Lyall Watson marveled in *Supernature*: "Nature seldom does things without good reasons and yet she has gone to some trouble over the past ten million years—a very short time by her usual standards—to equip us with an enormous cerebral cortex of seemingly unlimited capacity. . . . What was the hurry? . . . At the moment, we are like a small family of squatters who have taken over a vast palace but find no need to move beyond the comfortable, serviced apartment in one corner of the basement."

Scientists in many fields have been predicting that the next stage in human evolution will be psychical. American psychologist Carl Rogers stated: "I do not know how this world of the paranormal may change us. . . . Perhaps we are entering a transitional stage of evolution similar to that of the first sea creatures who laboriously dragged themselves out of the swamp bogs to begin the difficult and complex task of coping with the problems of living on land."

And just as our primate ancestors could not visualize a human, so we can't imagine the form into which we may evolve. As an unfinished species, we inhabit a zone somewhere between Aristotle's flatworm and the stars.

Psychic Power:

HEALING THE
HEADLESS HORSEMAN

"Miracles do not happen in contradiction to nature, but only in
contradiction to that which is known to us of nature."

—St. Augustine

MARCH 1977

I lie on a table, breathing deeply as instructed, while a masseuse "reads" my body for places where I store tension. The setting is typical of counterculture therapy in the seventies—a deliberately overheated basement with exposed pipes painted in psychedelic colors and aromatic with incense.

Without warning, the therapist zeroes in on my well-defined jaw, pressing hard on the taut musculature with her thumbs. "You hold it like a vise." When I stoically endure, she grows indignant on my behalf: "Doesn't that hurt? Let out the sound! Speak the words released by the pain."

My first response is a dutiful "ouch." However, as the torture intensifies under her unrelenting thumbs, adult embarrassment gives way to annoyance and then—unexpectedly—to a child's towering sense of injustice and grief. Startled, I hear myself protest: "It's not fair! It's not fair of you to make me cry and then not let me!"

I experience a flood of memories associated with a childhood incident in which my mother accuses me of using tears to get my own way when, in fact, I am clenching my jaw to hold them back since I know they will be discounted. I want to shriek: "Why would I cry when you never believe I feel anything?" It is a very old and deep hurt, hidden for decades behind the defensive anger of a permanently set jaw.

After months of therapeutic prodding, I learn to trace each emotion to the physical place where I typically harbor it. I also learn to experience my feelings more fully as I encounter them in life, often just by asking, "Where does this hurt / feel good?" Of a sudden, I become conscious of an answering tightness in my chest or a pleasurable tingling in my legs, allowing me to savor or discharge the emotion rather than to store it as tension that might transmogrify into disease.

In this way, my body becomes a vital river of subtle currents flowing through my life, rather than a hunk of matter I notice only when it is troubling me.

Before entering massage therapy, I was prepared to believe that relieving body tension would release emotions. However, what astonishes me is the power and precision of that process: not only are many feelings embedded in tissues as deeply as driven stakes but they are incident-specific: who would guess that my jaw possessed memory?

Previously, I prided myself on my high pain threshold, my stoic ability to blot out hot and cold, and my inherited good health. Now, I realize that my body was not so much complaint-free as deprived of a voice. Though it was struggling to call out to me, I did not understand because I was a physical illiterate.

Most cultures but our own have looked to the psyche for the prevention, cause, diagnosis and cure of disease. In tribal societies, a healthy person was one who dwelt in harmony with nature, the community, the gods and the self, while a sick one harbored unclean, harmful or sorrowing thoughts, had fallen under an evil spell, had broken a taboo or otherwise displeased the gods.

In Egypt, circa 2000 B.C., temples were hospitals where ailing persons slept to encourage incubation dreams, which might contain diagnostic advice from the gods. This ritual continued throughout Greece and Rome into the third century A.D. as part of the worship of Asclepius, god of healing. Frequently, sufferers donated sculptures of the body part they wished healed, resulting in the peculiar sight of temples bristling with penises. Even Hippocrates valued the diagnostic insights provided by incubation rites; however, he believed the dream information came from the body drawing attention to its needs, and not from the gods.

How do mind and body interact? Since the desire to move a finger results in muscle contraction, they obviously do; yet the process by which a thought turns into an action has never been isolated.

In A.D. 130, a physician named Galen from Asia Minor observed that the pulse of a female patient quickened each time he mentioned a certain male dancer. Diagnosing her condition as love-sickness, he concluded that temperament might be a cause of disease. This supported Hippocrates' belief that disease was the product of a person's total personality, leading him to comment, "I would rather know what sort of person has a disease than what sort of disease a person has."

Unfortunately for the development of Western medicine, French philosopher René Descartes persuaded his seventeenth-century peers that mind and body occupied different realms of reality and operated according to different rules: physical effects were produced by physical causes and mental effects by mental causes. Therefore, what looked like interaction was just parallel action. Though Descartes failed to explain satisfactorily how this coordination occurred, he did provide a diplomatic solution to a thorny political issue: Europe's centuries-old power struggle between religion and science. From now on, the Christian Church could rule over the invisible world of mind and spirit while science lay undisputed claim to the material one, then in a state of exuberant expansion.

Freed of all churchly and mystical constraints, science took off like the jet engine it would become. In disciplines like geology this "Cartesian split" scarcely mattered. However, in the field of healing, the ax severed the subject matter itself, leading to medicine as the study of headless cadavers and psychology as the study of torsoless heads.

When Freud, as a young neuropathologist, began his career by tracing physical symptoms, without organic cause, to their psychological origins, he seemed about to bridge this gap. However, as psychoanalysis developed under him and his disciples, it became a rarefied "insight" treatment in which the head used clever jargon to discount and control "primitive" body impulses, especially sexual ones. Since this reflected Victorian bias, Freudian therapy served well enough for several decades. However, after the 1960s sexual revolution, Freud's sense of sin no longer seemed so relevant or his interpretations so galvanizing. By the 1970s, word was spreading: psychoanalysis doesn't work. After years of authoritative couch talk, patients were emerging with their heads full of sophisticated insights but with their neuroses unrelieved and their feelings untouched.

The result was the Human Potential Movement, spearheaded by breakaway Freudians who believed healing had to be more than just a "head trip." They were followed by thousands of North Americans, in a hungry search for self-knowledge. Often middle-class and middle-aged, they were too old for the sexual revolution but not too old to feel its shockwaves through divorce and other life-changes unthinkable a generation before.

Most radical of the new therapies were those that appealed to the emotions through the body. Although these took off in several directions, all were rooted in the work of one man: the controversial—some say mad—Wilhelm Reich.

Born in Galicia in 1897, Reich's unique contribution to healing began when he became more interested in how patients on his analytic couch responded to questions with their bodies than in what they said. As Friedrich Nietzsche had declared before him: "One can lie with the mouth, but with the accompanying grimace one nevertheless tells the truth." Through his extraordinary powers of observation, Reich concluded that anxiety left its mark in muscular rigidity, which he called body armoring. Such armoring usually resulted from too harsh infantile treatment, causing the child to repress emotions by holding the breath, clenching the jaw, constricting the throat and otherwise tightening the musculature. Prolonged distress led to habitual shallow breathing, combined with a body frozen into characteristic postures, gestures and expressions. The result was an adult imprisoned in plates of armor—a mutant Ninja Turtle, trapped in infantile rage and deadened to real feeling.

Reich described this body armor as consisting of seven muscular rings: the ocular, encircling the eyes; the oral, involving the jaw and throat; the deep neck and upper back; the chest, encasing the heart; the diaphragm, stomach and solar plexus; the large abdominal muscles; and the pelvis. Working downward, he might request the patient to widen or roll the eyes; then he might press the jaw to liberate sobbing, which he described as a body softener. "Usually, there is severe rage held down by the motion of crying. If the patient let go in crying fully and freely, he would feel that he had to commit murder."

Typically, the voice of an armored person is thin and reedy. Reich might instruct his patient to tickle the back of the throat, causing a gag reflex, perhaps even vomiting—the healthful opposite to swallowing one's emotions. Throughout, he urged his patients to breathe deeply while he watched for places that seemed dead and uninvolved. Though the point of bodywork was the release of emotions through the release of physical tension, it might also activate vivid causal memories. "Every muscular rigidity contains the history and the meaning of its origin. It is thus not necessary to deduce from dreams or associations the way in which the muscular armor develops; rather, the armor itself is the form in which the infantile experience continues to exist as a harmful agent."

Softening this armor produced energy that could be felt in streaming—pleasurable currents of energy coursing through the body. When powerful enough, they became convulsive—what Reich described as the orgasm reflex, also occurring during sex. Since he believed sex to be the body's way of spontaneously ridding itself of tension, Reich declared orgasmic potency to be the goal of therapy, which meant releasing the inhibited pelvic ring. However, time and again as patients were on the verge of bursting through their defensive armor, they experienced a sudden dread of being overwhelmed by sensuous feelings after a lifetime without them. Reich called this "pleasure anxiety." He also noted that patients nearing orgasmic potency often developed a symbolic fear of falling—actually, fear of losing control of their pent-up emotions.

Reich thought his work a deeper development of Freud's: under the skin of civilized man, Freud had discovered a lustful beast, but under the protective armoring of that beast Reich had found a grieving child, crazed at being forced to give up loving, sensuous feelings. Freud was incensed. Far from wishing to release his clients from their defensive cages, he remained unalterably committed to building higher walls with narrower bars. As he enunciated in 1929 in *Civilization and Its Discontents*: "The intention that man should be 'happy' is not included in the 'scheme of Creation'. . . . Civilization is built on renunciation of instinctual gratifications. . . . Hence the restrictions on sexual life."

Branded a pervert, Reich was expelled from the International Psychoanalytic Society. He was also drummed out of Vienna and Berlin, where he had established sex hygiene clinics that gave advice on birth control, abortion, premarital sex and masturbation.

Relocated in Oslo, Reich turned to laboratory research to prove his theories were biologically sound. Using electrodes attached to the erogenous zones of human subjects, he discovered that foreplay and orgasm caused electrical currents to stream toward the skin, creating a rise in voltage: during sex the air *was* electric, as romanticized in popular fiction, with genital moisture serving as a conductor. He also found that unpleasant feelings caused bio-electrical currents to stream away from the skin, resulting in a sharp drop in voltage. His offbeat conclusion: emotion was energy in motion—*e-motion.*

Hounded out of Norway, Sweden and Denmark because of his radical sexual views, Reich re-established his practice in New York in 1939. Now working as a self-taught microbiologist, he noted the same streaming of energy within living cells that he had observed in humans on the macro level: during pleasure, cells expanded, but under stress they contracted.

Comparing the blood cells of healthy donors with those of cancer patients, Reich isolated differences in composition that he judged to be the result of long-term stress, meaning long-term constriction: deprived of emotional stimulation, the cells had run down like batteries, leaving the whole organism vulnerable to disease. Based on such observations, he developed a blood test for diagnosing cancer *before* the appearance of tumors, anticipating the Pap smear by more than a dozen years. However, this announcement reaped only professional scorn: while other microbiologists were still obsessed with finding a virus or some other toxin as the cause of cancer, Reich had hit upon immunological breakdown.

As a group, Reich observed his cancer patients to be inhibited in their expression of anger and abnormally resigned. They also exhibited the same muscular rigidity, shallow breathing and reedy voices as his neurotic patients. Just as he had earlier theorized a connection between emotion and body type, he now theorized one between personality and such diseases as asthma, allergies, arthritis and stroke. He also found the organ under attack to possess symbolic significance. For example, disease of a sexual organ might result from sexual abuse, and asthma from smothering by an overprotective parent.

Reich now embarked upon the most controversial phase of his unorthodox career. As the result of both his microscopic and clinical findings, he claimed to have isolated an unknown energy in free circulation—what he called orgone. Massless and weightless, it radiated from the sun, entering our bodies through the breath; there it caused each cell to pulsate, while extending beyond the skin of the whole organism in a bluish-white field.

Since Reich's experiments showed that orgone was reflected by metal and absorbed by organic substances like wool and wood, he constructed a metal-lined wood box, which he called an orgone accumulator; into this, he put cancerous mice for thirty minutes a day. While mice in his control group lived an average of only seven months, his orgone-treated mice lived nine and a half months, with vastly superior appearance and vigor.

In May 1941, Reich treated his first cancer patient, a woman with a breast tumor who had been given no more than two months to live. After three weeks of thirty-minute orgone treatments, her pain had subsided, enabling her to sleep without morphine; the hemoglobin content of her blood was higher and she was no longer bedridden. After ten weeks, her tumor had disappeared and her vigor had returned. However, Reich now found himself confronted with the same contrary principle he discovered while treating his neurotic patients. When the woman's personal life did not improve along with her health, she developed an intense fear of falling. Eventually, she did fracture a leg, leading to the reappearance of tumors and a rapid decline. Observed Reich: "As long as she was ill, the tumor and resulting suffering had absorbed all interest. . . . In a phase of particularly intense depression, the patient confessed that . . . she did not see how she could suffer this life."

Of the fifteen "hopeless" cancer patients Reich treated from 1941 to 1943, all reported their pain greatly alleviated, leading to elimination or reduction of morphine; all showed decrease or disappearance of their tumors. Three lived only as long as expected; six prolonged their lives by five to twelve months; six improved enough to return to work, and five of those were still alive in 1943, when Reich published his results.

According to his analysis, when an organism was threatened, the body's sympathetic system employed anxiety for flight or fight by accelerating heartbeat and breathing, and by constricting blood vessels; when danger had passed, the parasympathetic system was supposed to relax the organism for pleasure by reversing these processes. However, chronic childhood anxiety froze the organism in a state of permanent siege, cutting off pleasurable feelings and leading to depletion of the organism's vitality. By nurturing his patients' energy systems, Reich's orgone accumulators had reputedly enabled their cells to breathe and pulsate, reversing early damage.

Eager to share his discovery, Reich founded the Orgone Institute Research Laboratories for rental of his orgone boxes at minimal cost. His medical critics, once merely derisive, were now outraged. With the encouragement of the American Psychiatric Association, the U.S. Food and Drug Administration began an investigation of Reich, not only for cancer "quackery" but also on the old charges of perversion, stemming from his sex clinics in Europe. When Reich—with arrogance fed by a developing paranoia—failed to defend himself with appropriate diligence, his orgone boxes were destroyed under federal supervision, tons of his books and papers were burned, and he was sentenced to two years in prison.

On November 3, 1957, after serving seven and a half months, Reich died at age sixty, a broken man.

What can be said of the career of this Promethean man? Three decades after his death, Reich's innovative approach to cancer, emphasizing immunological breakdown, is now a highly credible one; his biological studies, connecting disease with personality, have attracted many adherents; he is regarded as a pioneer in holistic healing, which recognizes the vital connection of mind to body. In *Fury on Earth: a Biography of Wilhelm Reich*, Myron Sharaf states that twenty studies of varying quality have verified the existence of orgone, and that limited experiments in Canada and Europe, using accumulators to treat both cancerous mice and humans, have produced positive results.

In the therapeutic field, Reich's views on sex have gone mainstream. "Reichian" is now a respectable epithet, right along with Jungian and Freudian, and Reich's bodywork has spawned hundreds of imitators and innovators, most notably in the persons of Alexander Lowen and Arthur Janov.

A writer of critically acclaimed texts linking personality with body language, Lowen replaced Reich's hands-on body manipulations with exercises, such as the beating of pillows, geared to release repressed emotions. The goal of this technique, which he calls bioenergetics, is to heal the mind-body duality by treating the whole individual as a single unit.

Like Reich, Lowen believed psychological and physical symptoms to be interchangeable and even mutually exclusive: where one stressed person might produce an allergy, another might feel depressed. In mid-life, symptoms often switched so that the person who typically became depressed might suddenly acquire an allergy, while the hypochondriac might just as suddenly become depressed. Lowen believed such crossovers to be hopeful since they indicated that an individual's psyche was in a state of dynamic flux. As he stated in *Betrayal of the Body*: "My clinical experience is that schizophrenics rarely manifest the symptoms of common cold; when they do, I regard it as a sign of clinical improvement. It is also well documented that states of intense emotional excitement and upheaval may alleviate physical afflictions in normal individuals."

The inventor of primal therapy, Dr. Arthur Janov, diagnosed neurosis as a disease of feeling. Echoing Reich, he believed an adult might carry infantile emotion locked in the tightness of a jaw, in blocked sinuses, in layers of fat, in stunted growth. His solution: the adult must go back and dare to cry. This meant re-enacting those childhood scenes that caused emotional shutdown in the first place, thus draining one's secret "primal pool" of pain. Since the storage-bin for this pain seemed to be the gut, released tension often emerged through the mouth in what Janov called the primal scream. "Many describe it as a lightning bolt that seems to break apart all the unconscious control of the body. . . . Suffice it to say that when a feeling can convulse a human being, when it can produce earth-shaking screams, it testifies to the enormous pressure the neurotic must be under continually."

Again like Reich, Janov believed good mental health meant dismantling the defences rather than strengthening them, as Freud advocated. "I am continuously struck by how unaggressive and non-violent people are when their so-called civilized fronts are removed. . . . The angry man is the unloved man. Make anger real and it will disappear."

Despite the shaping hand of Wilhelm Reich on these and many other modern therapies, he is still officially described as a crackpot who thought he could cure cancer with an "orgasm" box.

MEDICINE: HEADLESS CADAVERS

FEBRUARY 1977

While watching a rerun of the movie Snow White, *I experience such severe abdominal pain that I am forced to leave the theater. For the next several hours, I roll around my bed in feverish discomfort, hallucinating scenes from my childhood. Subsequently, I am diagnosed as having fibroids of the uterus, requiring a hysterectomy. Though these growths are sufficiently advanced to have caused pain well before this, they did not do so. This seems odd, but I am now well enough versed on mind-body interaction to have an explanation.*

As I tell my doctor: "It was the movie Snow White *that caused the attack. I had the same reaction when I was a kid. The instant the queen turned into the wicked witch, I screamed so hysterically I had to* be removed from the theater. Now I understand why. The theme of Snow White is *mother-daughter jealousy*. This time when I saw the movie, I realized what I intuited as a kid: how much jealousy existed between my mother and myself. It was a terrible shock—I'd blocked that from my consciousness, as I'm sure she did. I guess that's why the initial attack was so fierce. I had no idea pain could be stored like fat!"

Though my doctor eyes me with the bemusement of one who has just heard that leeches cure acne, I am convinced what I'm saying is true. Unfortunately, what I don't yet understand is that fueling the mother-daughter jealousy is our much dirtier family secret: my incestuous relationship with my father. However, because I can see from persistent nightmares that my medical problem has a powerful psychological substructure, I try to tell two more doctors a streamlined version of my Snow White story. Neither is remotely interested and, in fairness, the medical system offers no model for incorporating that kind of information.

Since I have a strong constitution and no complicating medical history, my operation is considered routine. However, twenty-four hours out of the anesthetic, I am still too nauseated to eat or to sit up. When a nurse insists I take a shower, I am too dizzy to obey. Since her instruments say I should be fine, she assumes I'm being uncooperative.

Without machines to mislead them, my friends see instantly what the medical staff is missing: I am dying. Fortunately, I count among them writer and social activist June Callwood. Just as June is challenging the hospital system on my behalf, a lowly thermometer—humble amidst more sophisticated medical paraphernalia—at last registers a dangerous fever. Within hours, I am in emergency surgery for the removal of an abscess, virulently filling the cavity vacated by the fibroids.

In retrospect, I can only say that if a thumb pressed into an adult jaw can release deeply repressed childhood grief, what can be expected of a knife plunged into the womb of an incest victim harboring a forty-year secret? In my view, the fibroids were a 3-D photograph of that secret. When they were surgically removed before I was emotionally ready, a deadlier substitute filled the vacuum. As stated by Freud and Reich and Janov and Lowen, the psychological truth and the physical symptom are the same.

Since Western medicine evolved out of the dissection of cadavers, it was natural that the most prestigious cure would become cutting out or lopping off, with ever-more-awesome surgical precision. Simultaneously, the information explosion caused by high-tech inventions such as the x-ray machine led to narrower, ever-more-discrete specialties, creating a medical model of the human body like a side of beef, divided into steaks and cutlets of expertise and authority. Or, as a *New Yorker* cartoon once put it: a surgeon emerges from the operating room, wiping his brow and exclaiming, "Whew! One-hundredth of an inch to the left and I would have been outside of my specialty."

Though the split between physical and psychological disease may be convenient in theory, it is illusory in practice, as countless studies have shown. In 1955, Dr. Henry Beecher found 35 per cent of patients suffering severe pain from wounds and angina experienced relief when injected with salt water that they thought to be morphine. This became known as the placebo effect—Latin for "I will please," referring to the patient's desire to please the doctor as an authority figure by getting well. In a 1978 review of similar studies, psychiatrist Jerome David Frank concluded that "at least 50 per cent of the effect of any drug that influences patients' subjective states is due to the physician's expectations as transmitted to the patient—that is, at least 50 per cent is a placebo effect." Harvard doctor and biologist Andrew Weil was even more decisive in his 1983 study of modern medicine, *Health and Healing*: "The history of medicine is actually the history of the placebo response."

Though many medical doctors may suspect they are treating psychological problems as often as physical ones, most solemnly take their blood tests and dispense their pills according to the rules of their specialties. Not to do so would offend their patients, also trained to expect physical cures from physical doctors. A physician who suggested to his lawyer patient that his sinus trouble might be caused by unshed tears from childhood grief would be in danger of convincing the patient he himself was in need of psychiatric help.

Holistic treatment within the medical power structure is still a rarity, rather like finding a monk hand-copying manuscripts at a large publishing firm. However, U.S. surgeon Bernie Siegel is one of those anomalies. In his 1986 bestseller, *Love, Medicine and Miracles*, Siegel told of his conversion to emotion-based healing at a 1978 seminar conducted by tumor specialist Carl Simonton and his wife, psychologist Stephanie Matthews.

After relaxing their cancer patients with hypnotic rituals, the Simontons typically instruct them to vividly and repeatedly imagine their body's disease-destroying white cells to be sharks or rocketships eating or blasting their cancer cells, like exterminators in a video game. Such a method takes advantage of the body's inability to distinguish between a real experience and a powerfully imagined one: through intense visualization, the body apparently believes the cancer cells to be undergoing destruction and kicks in with its own immunologic resources. This is similar to the techniques once employed by East bloc coaches to psych their Olympic teams to gold medals: envisioning perfect physical moves that culminated in victory reputedly helped produce that reality.

In the Simonton/Matthews first group of 159 "terminal" patients, 19 per cent eliminated their cancer, 22 per cent went into remission, and the rest, on average, doubled their predicted survival time. Siegel was galvanized: "Here I was, an M.D., a 'Medical Deity,' and I didn't know what went on in the head at all! The literature on mind-body interaction was separate, and therefore unknown to specialists in other areas. . . . The things I was learning hadn't even been hinted at in my medical education."

After implementing the Simonton/Matthews visualization techniques in his own practice, Siegel found that drawings in which patients projected their unconscious feelings were as useful as lab tests for assessing their prospects. More surprisingly, he came to believe that the doctor's attitude was almost as important as the patient's in promoting or preventing cure. "If nine out of ten people with a certain disease are expected to die, supposedly you are spreading 'false hope' unless you tell *all ten* they'll probably die."

In Siegel's opinion, about three-quarters of the negative side effects of radiotherapy and drugs are fostered by doctors who signal their pessimism. As an example of this negative conditioning, he cites a study in which 30 per cent of patients lost their hair after taking a harmless saline solution they thought to be chemotherapy. "Many people are dead today because they lived out their doctor's prediction."

Though Siegel anticipated other doctors would be excited by his discoveries, his submissions to medical journals were rejected with the suggestion that he try psychological journals. This paralleled the experience of Wallace C. Ellerbroek, a surgeon turned psychiatrist who could not get an article on the mind's role in cancer published until he changed its focus to acne.

Such resistance, Siegel discovered, was mirrored by patients themselves. In findings that echoed those of Wilhelm Reich, Siegel defined the cancer-prone as persons who grew up feeling unloved and who later buried their personal needs in the needs of others. Eventually, disease became their way out, allowing expression of pent-up feelings of despair while garnering emotional nourishment from family and friends.

According to Siegel, 15 to 20 per cent of cancer patients consciously or unconsciously wish to die, while another 60 to 70 per cent perform to satisfy their physicians, preferring radical physical treatment to changing their self-images and lifestyles. Only 15 to 20 per cent were willing to re-educate themselves in an all-out attempt to get well. He described such patients as complex, independent, open-minded and imaginative people who asked questions, vented their feelings, disagreed with aspects of their treatments and often had a prickly relationship with their physicians.

Siegel's findings, linking personality and other psychological factors with disease, are supported by hundreds of studies:

•In 1975, S. Greer and T. Morris at King's College Hospital in London reported that women with breast cancer were unusually submissive and inhibited, especially in their expression of anger.

•In a mid-1970s study, Vernon Riley of Seattle's Pacific Northwest Research Foundation discovered that malignancy in mice bred to be susceptible to breast cancer could be varied from 7 to 92 per cent through stress.

•Using Rorschach tests in the 1950s, psychologist Bruno Klopfer found himself able to predict the rate of cancer growth in patients he had never examined: those with the fastest growth hid deep conflict with a smile, whereas those with slow growth were either well balanced or had severe conflicts they didn't repress.

•In a recent study of two hundred patients' drawings, psychologist Jeanne Achterberg predicted, with 95 per cent accuracy, who would be dead within two months and who would be in remission.

•Beginning in 1946, Dr. Caroline Bedell Thomas of Johns Hopkins University Medical School tracked the mental and physical health of 1,337 medical students every year for decades. One "striking and unexpected" result: the traits of those who developed cancer were almost identical to those who committed suicide. Typically, this involved the repression of aggressive emotions related to their own needs. She also found that by using only one drawing associated with one test she could predict what parts of their bodies would develop cancer.

•Calling upon his clinical work with nine hundred lung-cancer patients, Dr. David Kissen characterized them as having "poor outlets for emotional discharge." On discovering the same patients to be prone to peptic ulcers, rheumatism, dermatitis and certain neuroses, he concluded their psychological condition to be the true cause of their disease, which shifted from one set of physical symptoms to another.

Other research links positive emotions with positive effects:

•A 1982 study by Harvard psychologists David McClelland and Carol Kirshnit showed that movies about love increased levels of immunoglobulin-A in the saliva, the first line of defense against colds and other viral diseases.

•Drs. Walter Smith and Stephen Bloomfield reported in 1979 that people who cry freely catch fewer colds.

•A 1979 study by Dr. Fred Cornhill and Murina Levesque of the Ohio State University College of Medicine indicated that loving care halved the risk of heart attack in rabbits fed large amounts of cholesterol.

Such findings, along with Siegel's clinical experience, have persuaded him that all disease springs ultimately from lack of love—a conclusion that does not always go down well in medical strongholds. Soon after Siegel posted, in a Yale doctors' lounge, a double-blind study by a San Francisco cardiologist validating the benefits of prayer, someone scrawled across it: "BULLSHIT!"

THE LAYING ON OF HANDS

OCTOBER 1977

After the surgical removal of a large piece of gangrenous intestine, my Siamese cat returns from the vet in a wasted, listless and precarious state. My attempts to forcefeed her over the next few days, during which she refuses all food and water, prove extremely stressful and of limited value. On impulse, I decide to faith-heal her—not because I'm a believer but because I'm desperate.

I perform an interdenominational service, incorporating every piece of wizardry I've ever absorbed from pulpit or TV: prayer, chanting, laying on of hands, hypnotism, commands to heal, the lot. Even so, the ceremony is a short one, with fervor braked by feelings of foolishness.

Reluctantly, I keep a dinner engagement, fearing my cat may be dead on my return. However, as I open the front door, a giant furball hurtles at me from the darkness. The cat, who hours before was too sick to raise her head, is now swinging on my skirt and clawing my legs, shrieking to be fed. Though she doesn't retain this frenzied level of energy over the next few days, she does continue to eat with gusto, leading to rapid recovery.

Had I performed an act of psychic healing or just enjoyed good timing? Unfortunately, I've felt too rational to retest my skills. Maybe I'm afraid they wouldn't work. Maybe I'm afraid they would.

In Western culture, psychic healing is usually religiously inspired: through the laying on of hands, a charismatic individual becomes the channel for God's healing power. This tradition, with healing based on faith and performed by the holy, was practiced by the ancient Chaldeans and Babylonians, as well as by initiates of the Greek temples of Asclepius. After restoring sight and curing the lame, Jesus told his followers: "These things that I do, so can ye do and more." Among early Christian cults, healing was an ordinary part of preaching, often utilizing holy water and oil. At a time when European kings, like England's Edward the Confessor, claimed rule by Divine Right, they also exercised "the Royal Touch" to heal their subjects. Even Napoleon was said to have tried out his skills, to little avail.

Today, faith healing is endorsed with caution by the Roman Catholic Church. It is also a populist byproduct of TV evangelism— the medicare of the poor, the lonely and the dotty. However, because of the diceyness of such cures—their unpredictability, instability and appeal to charlatanism—any attempt by doctors to induce them has usually led to ridicule, banishment, imprisonment and even death. Yet through the ages some European physicians have dared to note the healing power of human touch, which many attribute to natural rather than to religious or magical forces. The ancient Egyptian *Ebers Papyrus*, dated about 1550 B.C., describes the laying on of hands as a medical procedure, and Hippocrates was also moved to remark, "It has often appeared, while I have been soothing my patient, as if there were some strange property in my hands to pull and draw away from the afflicted parts aches and diverse impurities." A curative power was also attributed by the ancients to iron magnets, which they stroked over the diseased organs.

In the sixteenth century, Dr. Theophrastus Bombastus von Hohenheim—better known today as Paracelsus—combined these two traditions in his description of a magnetic healing force, which he claimed swept in waves throughout the Universe. Alternately absorbed and exuded by humans, this solar power radiated around the body in a luminous shield, and could even be transmitted at a distance. As Paracelsus enthused: "Man is not body. The heart, the spirit, is man. And this spirit is an entire star, out of which he is built."

Inspired by Paracelsus, eighteenth-century Dr. Franz Anton Mesmer passed magnets over his patients to cure them by stimulating their "magnetic fluids." When he found he could create the same twitching and convulsing movements in their bodies through passes with his own hands, Mesmer dispensed with the magnets. Though credited with many startling cures—like ridding a scientist of paralysis and a professor of blindness—Mesmer was eventually driven out of Paris to his Swiss birthplace, where he devoted himself to treating the poor. When his disciples, experimenting with his techniques, discovered hypnotism, science declared Mesmer's cures—and all faith healing—to derive from the power of suggestion. Today, Mesmer is largely remembered through the word *mesmerize*, with its connotation of undue influence, just as Paracelsus has been negatively immortalized through the epithet "bombastic," derived from his birth name Bombastus.

Over the next century, a universal energy with magnetic properties was allegedly rediscovered over and over in laboratories across Europe. An early experimenter with electricity, Italian anatomy professor Luigi Galvani wrote in 1791 of a life force, similar to electricity and magnetism, that seemed to derive from the sun, had an affinity for metal, water and wood, permeated everything, pulsated through the human body by means of the breath, and exuded powerfully from the fingertips.

In the nineteenth century, German scientist and industrialist Karl von Reichenbach risked his reputation as the discoverer of creosote and several other chemicals when he declared evidence for a new universal energy, which he called od after the Viking thunder god, Odin. Od existed everywhere, in free circulation, and permeated everything; it radiated in a luminous glow from the human body and was vital to health; it was concentrated in iron, magnets and crystals, and conducted by metal, silk and water. Though confirmed by researchers in Britain, France and Calcutta, od was dismissed by orthodox science as a blemish on von Reichenbach's otherwise outstanding reputation.

In 1903, French physicist René Blondlot claimed to have discovered a vital force, both biological and universal, which he called N-rays. This finding was confirmed in experiments by other French researchers, who noted its many similarities to od and animal magnetism. Like other discoverers of a universal energy, Blondlot was held up to ridicule by orthodox science.

By the 1930s, the concept of energy fields was beginning to seep from subatomic physics into biology. Otto Rahn, a bacteriologist at Cornell University, noted a biochemical radiation from living cells that played a significant role in growth, cell division and wound healing: "It may be surprising that radiations have not been recognized and proven conclusively before this. The reason may be sought in their very low intensity. The best detector is still the living organism." Similarly, biologist Harold Burr of Yale demonstrated that all living systems have electrodynamic force-fields that respond to electrical fields from within and without, showing cyclical influences of the moon, of sunspots and of the seasons. Burr's colleague, Dr. L.J. Ravitz of Virginia, extended these findings to demonstrate that emotion was energy in motion, as Wilhelm Reich had once proclaimed. Like Reich, he found a connection between low energy states and diseases such as cancer, asthma, arthritis and ulcers. However, Ravitz believed himself to be working with electricity and not a new form of energy.

Though biology was only a couple of decades away from a time when a few of its most prestigious figures would dare to speculate on psychic blueprints and cosmic consciousness, medicine remained resistant to field theory. The success of such microbe hunters as Robert Koch, Louis Pasteur and Jonas Salk in isolating toxins responsible for infectious diseases, along with the drugs and vaccines to counter them, had reinforced the concept of the body as a passive battlefield on which armies of "good" microbes fought armies of "bad" ones for a disputed organ. By contrast, energy fields did not respect the political boundaries according to which medicine was organized and taught. They did not yield high-tech products that could be patented, packaged and promoted. The word *psychic* was particularly offensive, since it meant something unpredictable that might be possessed in greater abundance by a street-sweeper than a surgeon-psychiatrist.

After the professional crucifixion of Wilhelm Reich in 1957, it took a brave researcher to reopen the case for healing based on the existence of a universal force. Dr. Bernard Grad of McGill University in Montreal not only successfully replicated Reich's orgone treatment of cancerous mice but also embarked on experiments featuring the laying on of hands. After dividing a batch of mice with induced goiters into three groups, he instructed psychic healer Oscar Estebany to handle the first over forty days, while the second was treated with the heat equivalent of being touched and the third was left untreated. Although all the mice developed goiters, those handled by Estebany did so at a significantly slower rate. Grad ruled out the placebo effect on the grounds that the mice, being mice, were not psychologically suggestible.

To see if Estebany's hands emitted a force, Grad exposed some mice to scraps of cotton and wool Estebany had held in his hands, while a control group was exposed to untouched scraps. Again, mice in contact with the healer-treated scraps showed a significantly slower rate of goiter formation, implying that Estebany's hands had transmitted energy.

When biochemist Dr. Justa Smith of New York tested to see if psychic hands produced healing by speeding up the catalyzing activity of enzymes, she discovered they did: the longer Oscar Estebany held a test-tube containing a solution of the digestive enzyme trypsin, the faster it catalyzed; however, when Estebany held other enzymes, Smith found their reaction rate decreased. Employing other psychic healers, she confirmed this finding: some enzymes were always accelerated while others were always slowed. This perplexing result made no sense until Smith realized a unifying factor: the direction of enzyme activity always corresponded to the greater health of the organism, as if the force exuded by the healers had innate intelligence.

In studies by Dr. Dolores Krieger of New York University, the blood of sick persons whom Oscar Estebany treated by the laying on of hands showed a significant increase in hemoglobin when compared with the blood of patients in a control group. This was true even of cancer patients simultaneously treated with drugs known to induce anemia. More striking was the improvement or disappearance of brain tumors and gross symptoms of such diseases as emphysema and rheumatoid arthritis.

Inspired by these results, Krieger devised a technique she called Therapeutic Touch, which she taught to nurses in hopes that psychic healing was an acquirable skill. Controlled experiments indicated that it was, with ability enhanced through confidence and use. Over the past twenty years, this technique has been taught to more than twenty thousand North Americans, many of them professional caregivers. Though little actual touching was involved, subjects reported sensations of heat and tingling; the hands of some highly charged healers even produced electric shocks. When asked what they believed they were doing, most "touchers" claimed to be projecting psychic energy onto their subjects in hopes of activating their subjects' inner healers.

By contrast, Grad conducted an experiment in which first-year medical students, skeptical of psychic healing, laid hands on surgically wounded mice. Their rate of healing was *consistently below* that of a control group of mice who received *no* laying on of hands—a confirmation of the *nocebo* effect, in which a treatment fails because of the doctor's negative attitude.

Despite their unorthodox premises, all the above experiments proceeded along traditional scientific lines: an attempt was being made to explain the mysterious in terms of ordinary cause and effect. However, chemist Robert Miller pushed psychic healing back into the occult when he tested a theory held by both Paracelsus and Mesmer: that healing power could operate at a distance.

Using an electromechanical transducer to measure the growth of rye grass locked in his Atlanta laboratory, Miller instructed psychic healers Olga and Ambrose Worrall, six hundred miles away, to hold the plants in their thoughts during their usual nine o'clock prayer time. For several hours before the experiment, the transducer had registered stable growth of 6.25 thousandths of an inch per hour, creating a graph with a steady slope upward. At exactly nine o'clock the seedlings' tracing began to deviate upward;

by morning, it registered 52.5 thousandths of an inch per hour—an increase of 840 per cent! When the Worralls were asked how they had accomplished this feat, they said they had visualized the plants as overflowing with light and energy.

This apparent ability of the Worralls to telepathically project healing power verged on the miraculous. Yet their skills were topped by a Kentucky farmboy whose psychic mind seemed to know few physical bounds.

Born in 1877, Edgar Cayce (pronounced Casey) was a stationery salesman with grade-nine education when he suffered laryngitis that left him speechless for a year. Under hypnosis, it was suggested to him that he diagnose his own condition. In a normal speaking voice, Cayce described vocal-cord paralysis due to blocked circulation. When his hypnotist suggested he heal himself, Cayce's throat flushed crimson, as if blood were rushing to that location. On awakening, his laryngitis was cured. In a followup reading, Cayce even diagnosed the hypnotist's stomach ailment!

Though Cayce fought against what seemed to be a unique talent for diagnosis, time and again illness in his family forced him to put aside the photographic career he was trying to launch to utilize his skills. After doctors estimated that his wife, suffering advanced tuberculosis, had only a week to live, one suggested: "If there's anything in your monkey business, you'd better try it." Putting himself into a trance, Cayce detailed his wife's condition, then prescribed drugs that seemed toxic, along with the inhaling of apple brandy fumes from a charred oak keg. An attending specialist remarked, "Most wonderful discourse I've ever heard on tuber- culosis, but I don't see how she can be helped." Within months, Gertrude Cayce had made a complete recovery.

When Cayce's young son's eyes were damaged by a powder explosion, his doctor advocated removing one eye while offering no hope for the other. Refusing to accept this grim verdict, the "sleeping" Cayce prescribed dressings soaked in strong tannic acid. When the boy's doctor protested that this would damage the eye tissue further, Cayce tartly demanded, "Which eye? The eye beyond hope or the one you want to take out?" Twelve days later, when young Hugh Lynn's tannic-soaked bandages were removed, his vision was normal.

One of Cayce's first public readings was for five-year-old Aime Dietrich, severely retarded since age two, apparently as the result of influenza, accompanied by up to twenty convulsions a day. Putting himself in trance, Cayce traced the child's trouble to a spinal injury caused by a fall from a carriage. After Aime's surprised mother confirmed this forgotten incident, an osteopath made the spinal adjustments detailed by Cayce, thus relieving pressure on some nerves. Immediately, the convulsions ceased and, within three months, Aime had mentally caught up to her peers.

By the time Cayce died—some say of burnout—in 1945, he had provided about nine thousand diagnoses, often later confirmed by x-rays and medical tests. During these, he described human anatomy in astonishing detail, using clinical terms unknown to his waking mind. Drawing from traditional medicine as well as from psychology, homeopathy, osteopathy and herbal remedies, Cayce prescribed diets down to the last vitamin, detailed precise spinal manipulations and the preparation of compounds with obsolete and arcane ingredients.

When no druggist had heard of clary water, the rheumatic patient for whom Cayce prescribed it advertised in a trade paper. From Paris, he received a letter from a son of the chemist who had invented the product, discontinued nearly fifty years before. Enclosed was an old prescription—exactly the same as Cayce had, meantime, dictated in another trance.

Astonishing as these talents were, Cayce was employing only a fraction of his unique powers. Buoyed by simple Protestant faith, he found he could treat strangers at a distance. While he was lying on a couch in self-induced trance, his wife would announce the name and address of a patient anywhere in the world. Cayce would begin: "Yes, we have the body here . . ." With his secretary taking shorthand, he dictated his medical reading in formal, oddly convoluted sentences unlike his normal speech

In a typical case, occurring in October 1940, Cayce was asked to diagnose for a patient in a Kentucky hospital who had spilled scalding water over more than half of her body. Even if she lived, her doctors assumed she would be badly scarred and perhaps blinded. Eight hundred miles away in Virginia Beach, Cayce did an emergency reading without even knowing it was for a one-year-old. After the reassurance—"We do not find the injury to the eyes but rather the lids"—he again outlined the use of tannic acid, camphorated oil and other unguents, combined with eliminants to purge the body of toxins. Although his prescriptions were unusual, the child made a complete recovery except for a small scar, eliminated after another reading two years later.

In followup readings, Cayce usually picked up where he had left off and, if his instructions had not been impeccably adhered to, stated so. Though he spoke only English in his waking state, he sometimes diagnosed in other languages, perhaps two dozen in all. Just as amazing, Cayce often described what the patient was doing at the time of the reading, how the patient was dressed, what the weather was like or would be like: "Mighty fine looking cat you've got there"; "The radio's turned on to Detroit." When the patient was not at the expected locale through misunderstanding or accident, the projected eyes of Cayce sometimes went in search: "The body is just going down the elevator . . ."

On two occasions, Cayce found himself threatened by the law—once for practicing medicine without a licence and once for "pretending to tell fortunes."

Known scornfully among Kentucky doctors as The Freak, Cayce was examined by a medical committee that challenged him to prescribe for a woman, bleeding internally, whom they had agreed, among themselves, needed an operation. The entranced Cayce's correct measurement of the woman's pulse rate and temperature so outraged one physician that he ran a hatpin through Cayce's cheek to make sure he was really comatose, while another peeled back a fingernail, which later became infected. It was only when Cayce prescribed long walks for the patient, plus a raw, salted lemon, that anger gave way to laughter. However, after three weeks on Cayce's regimen, the woman was not only cured but robustly hiking ten miles a day!

A counterchallenge—issued by a doctor friendly to Cayce—
offered to pit Cayce's diagnostic talents against the committee's on
six cases of their own choosing; it found no takers. However, a
convention of lawyers from Kentucky, Tennessee and Indiana
decided to test Cayce in a way that would cause them no professional embarrassment: by presenting him with a list of personal
questions to which only they could know the answers. Cayce's
intimate knowledge of their affairs so shocked them that pending
charges against him, and doctors associated with him, were
dropped. As the attorney general of Kentucky, who witnessed the
display, philosophized: "It's not very far, you know, from here to
What's Over There, and Cayce falls through somehow."

Cayce's arrest for fortune telling—described by him as one of
the lowest points in his life—occurred in New York after a
plainclothes policewoman received a reading, then charged Cayce,
his wife and his secretary. After hearing Cayce and his character
witnesses, the judge quoted Shakespeare—"There are more things in
heaven and earth, Horatio, than are dreamt of in your philosophy"—
then dismissed the case on the grounds that the trio were sincerely
expressing the beliefs of "an incorporated ecclesiastical body." The
judge was referring to the Association for Research and Enlightenment, a non-profit organization Cayce and his coworkers had
formed to raise money for a hospital that was to offer healing based
on his readings. When Cayce asked himself in trance why his
clairvoyant powers had not warned of the police trap, he received
the enigmatic answer: "A certain amount of scouring was essential
for the better development of the soul." Cayce took this to mean that
he had been wrong to use his gift to raise money, even for the
hospital. As his equally devout wife reminded him, "Once you get
away from helping people it always makes you ill."

Though examined many times during his life by highly
qualified psychologists and other investigators, Cayce has never
been discredited. Today, an average of two thousand people a month
visit his memorial archives in Virginia Beach, which house fifteen
thousand readings on a variety of topics, along with a library of
supporting material. Among health-care professionals, his stature

grows as Western medicine catches up with him. According to verbatim records, he was ahead of science in suggesting disease diagnosis from blood analysis, the healing properties of gold chloride, the use of vitamin C to alleviate symptoms of leukemia, the potential of iodine as an inhibitor of polio (which he described in 1936 as an infectious disease for which some people were carriers), the description of sick organisms as having systems too alkaline rather than too acid, the use of rabbit serum for some cancers, the need not only to break down tumors but to eliminate their dead tissue.

In a 1950 survey, five years after Cayce's death at age sixty-seven, physicians who had treated patients according to his instructions were contacted by Sherwood Eddy, the international leader of the YMCA, who had become interested in Cayce's work. Estimates of both the accuracy of Cayce's diagnoses and the success of his treatments ranged from 80 to 100 per cent, for an average of 91 per cent. In all but one case of cancer, physicians noted that faithfully followed instructions produced definite, sometimes remarkable, improvement.

Health, in Cayce's philosophy, consisted of the harmonious interaction of blood, lymph, glands and nerves. He believed the body to be a self-healing organism, in which each cell had its own consciousness. He also believed nature to be a system in which every disorder had its counterbalance. His ability, which he claimed everyone possessed, was to tune into the collective subconscious, described by him as a vast river of thought flowing through eternity. After questioning a body's cells as to their needs, his subconscious self would then rifle through humanity's collective knowledge for the antidote.

So original and far-ranging were Cayce's reputed psychic talents that they present a greater challenge to the open-minded than to skeptics, who have only to dismiss him. Not only did this untutored farmboy dazzle specialists with his medical knowledge but he also successfully predicted earthquakes, World War II, the 1929 stock-market crash and other historical events. More problematic: he declared his belief in Atlantis, which—like Plato—

he described as having sunk through natural cataclysm into the Atlantic; he also provided two thousand reincarnational readings, which ran counter to his waking Christian views, but which he came to accept as authoritative.

Yet skeptics also have a difficult task. Not only does the sheer mass of archival material rule out systematic fraud, but Cayce's lifestyle presents them with the difficulty of solving a motiveless crime. Since he charged no fees beyond a strictly volunteer donation, he and his family lived much of their lives in deprivation. A humble yet complex man, often burdened by his talent, he filled his waking hours with Bible-reading, fishing and gardening. He shunned publicity, and never used his psychic power to make money for himself, although he proved—in advice occasionally given to others—that he could read tomorrow's stock market as easily as yesterday's newspaper. In his desire to be helpful to those petitioning him at the rate of up to two thousand a day, he increased his daily readings from two to eight, almost certainly hastening his death at age sixty-seven.

Typical of many doctors, Cayce did not follow his own advice—repeatedly received in trance—to slow down. Typical of history's reputed seers, he prophesied the manner of his own death. Twenty years in advance, he predicted he would die immersed in water while trying to resist pain. The medical cause of his death, on January 3, 1945, was pulmonary edema: Cayce drowned in his own body fluids.

Edgar Cayce cannot be explained, or explained away. If literature has its Shakespeare and music its Mozart, perhaps the psychic world can be allowed its Cayce. As one British wit quipped, "I am too much of a skeptic to deny the possibility of anything."

Holistic Healing:

IN SEARCH OF
THE FOURTH MONKEY

"I am not a mechanism, an assembly of various sections.
And it is not because the mechanism is working wrongly,
that I am ill. I am ill because of wounds to the soul, to the deep
emotional self and the wounds to the soul take a long, long
time, only time can help . . ."

—D.H. Lawrence

1985–1987

While writing My Father's House, I am plagued by itchy, swollen eyes diagnosed as an allergy to feathers and dust. When the book is published, I experience an ear blockage causing dizziness and nausea. Throughout the promotion of the same book, I am beset by laryngitis, which robs me of my voice. In each case, I am given pills and soothing unguents for which I am grateful. However, I perceive that my three sets of symptoms—targeting eyes, ears and throat—have a common cause. On the console radio of my natal home sat a statue of three squatting monkeys—See No Evil, Hear No Evil, Speak No Evil. Symbolically, that statue was my family's coat-of-arms. In writing my incestuous story—unspeakable, unbalancing and to which I have been deaf, dumb and blind—I have again fallen under its spell.

More precisely, I have fallen under the spell of the fourth monkey. In the original Indian symbol, four monkeys sat side by side. The fourth was lopped off when that statue was imported as a trinket by Victorian society. The fourth monkey had its hands over its genitals. By eliminating the fourth monkey, Victorian society did not eliminate sex but only public acknowledgment of it. The missing monkey fell into the unconscious, where it acquired almost unlimited psychic power, visible only through its mysterious and distorting effects. The fourth monkey—whose name was never spoken aloud—was the true ruler of the psychic life of my family and probably of Victorian society.

Everyone has a fourth monkey-on-the-back, as does every family, institution and society. The fourth monkey represents that which we repress out of ignorance or convenience or fear, exaggerating its power both to help or to harm.

After detaching itself from all things psychic, European medicine expanded zealously into the field of the body, aided by brilliant inventions like the microscope. Advances in microbiology transformed the G.P.'s black bag from a homey hodgepodge of suppositories and cough medicines into a lethal drug arsenal, while the surgeon's scalpel was marvelously extended with laser rays and ultrasound.

So dazzling was this high-tech world of wonders and the expertise required to operate it that the medical profession was taken by surprise when their once worshipful patients grew skeptical, disgruntled and even hostile. At a time when Western medicine was being hailed worldwide for its miracles, why were so many home-grown patients complaining as much about their treatment as their symptoms? Why was the feeling developing that Western medicine itself was unwell?

In my story of the four monkeys, it was the missing one that provided the clue for what ailed me, my family and the society that bred us. Because Western medicine devoted itself exclusively to the pursuit of the technological, its fourth monkey grew to contain all that is emotional, intuitive, psychological and mystical. Since humans are all these things, Western medicine became an incomplete system for large numbers of its clients, who increasingly held values different from those of their doctors. As dissatisfied shoppers, they began poking into moldering home-remedy books and dabbling in exotic cures from other cultures, with the result that today every Western city does a flourishing trade in yoga, native drumming, floral essences, crystal healing, acupuncture, herbalism and updated versions of the laying on of hands. Even in Canada, where medical treatment is government-supported, many quite sane people would prefer to pay fifty dollars to a native shaman or Chinese acupuncturist in a third-floor walkup than to visit a free specialist in the spiffiest medical center.

Central to these imported healing techniques—often eccentrically interpreted by homegrown converts—is the belief that healing is an art as well as a science; that body-mind-feeling-spirit create one holistic unit, and that to treat one is to treat the others. Curiously, the English word *health* is based on the Anglo-Saxon word *hale*, meaning whole. So is the English word *holy*.

SHAMANISTIC HEALING

JULY 1967
I visit a witchdoctor named Baranabas in a mud-hut village, nestled in a blaze of poinsettia bushes near Nairobi, Kenya. Several

people sit in his waiting room, including a woman with face decorated by zigzag scars. As my Swahili guide explains: "You slit the skin with a razor then rub in charcoal. It is very painful but it shows her people are brave."

Baranabas ushers us into his dispensary, a squat room with six steaming cauldrons of liquid in bright colors like Easter egg dye. What is my problem: stomach-ache? sadness? sterility? fear of baldness?

When my guide informs him that I am just a curious Canadian journalist, he explains a few of his medicines to me. Most are of powdered bark and roots, mixed with water, milk or blood. Some he grows himself, some he imports from India.

"Can you cure mental disease?"

"Spirits of the head? Yes, that will be the green liquid."

"What about sterility?"

"Much more complicated—the green, the blue, the yellow and no guarantee."

"How about a love potion?"

"I don't work spells. I'm a white witchdoctor."

Afterwards, a Canadian physician who is in Africa under joint-government sponsorship tells me: "One of my patients lay in bed for weeks with the covers over his head, afraid to come out because of spirit voices. Finally, I suggested his brother take him to a witchdoctor. He's still as crazy as a coot but at least now he's walking around, he's eating. I suspect witchdoctors here have about the same incident of cure as psychiatrists back home. Some of their medicines are pretty good, too. The only problem comes when they try to treat infectious disease with spells. The delay can be fatal."

Later that day, I visit a Masai encampment on the flat yellow East African savannah, fenced with thornbushes to keep out maurauding lions. Since its huts are constructed of dried cow dung, the odor is like a dull pulsation in the hot, dry air. Wreaths of flies halo the heads of the warriors—spear-thin and well over six feet tall, with their elaborately plaited hair drenched in red ocher to match their loincloths. Though many of them, as well as their wives and children, have open sores on which flies frenzy-feed, on no occasion do I see a Masai shoo them away.

By chance, I have come upon this tribe as its members are about to hold a celebration. On a clearing outside their circular *encampment, embracing some twenty families, the drumming, shrieking, clapping and chanting begin. Fortified by swigs from gourds containing blood, curdled milk and cow urine, two dozen spear-carrying warriors perform a flat-footed, head-jutting, body-jarring dance, with seven-inch dangling earlobes, stretched by the insertion of Coke tins, dancing independently across their shoulders. Spears held stiffly at their sides, they jump ever higher—two-foot vertical leaps, made more dazzling by their extraordinary height.*

A wizened old lady with shaved head typical of Masai women grabs my hand and, suddenly, I am dancing. As I thump thump thump on the sun-baked clay like an India rubber ball on concrete, compelled by the drumbeat, swept by feelings of non-reality, exhausted yet unable to stop, I confirm what I already know: Africa is not a geographic location but an altered state of mind. What I have yet to grasp is that this ceremony—noisy, hot, dirty and fly-infested—might be equivalent to a preventive trip to a Western medical clinic.

"Witchdoctor" was the label eighteenth-century Europeans used for Africans who invoked the supernatural to heal or to harm. By contrast, *shaman* is a Siberian word that means to shake with frenzy. It suggests the divine possession that is said to underlie the tribal healer's art. Today, it is used interchangeably with *witchdoctor*, the Aboriginal term *clever-man* and the native American term *medicine man* for healers who possess a close affiliation with nature.

Whereas Western medicine divides diseases between the physical and psychological, tribal medicine classifies *the healers* according to whether their abilities are physical or psychic. In practice, this means a division between herbalists, such as Baranabas, who prepare medicines like a pharmacist, and diviners, who diagnose and treat, often through inducing altered states.

Over the centuries, herbal lore was accumulated on all continents, by human trial and error and by the observation of sick or injured animals as they cured themselves from nature's dispensary. Apes stanch blood with astringent leaves; bears use spruce resin; woodchucks smear their wounds with hemlock gum, which doesn't dissolve in water. Elderly herd animals munch on cowparsnips for aching teeth and joints; dogs and cats nibble grass as an emetic; mongooses arouse themselves for battle with snakes by chewing the aptly named snakeroot; woodchucks have been observed wrapping broken legs with fiber-reinforced clay.

Though the diviner's function is sometimes hereditary, more usually a candidate is selected through omens, birthmarks, disabilities like blindness or visionary dreams induced by a personal crisis. Apprenticeship involves trials of endurance: fire walking, prolonged submersion in freezing water, exposure to wild animals, isolation, hunger and thirst. Not only do these select for bravery but their pain is said to transport the shaman's spirit into occult realms of higher power, perhaps by cutting down on other sensory information.

In tribal cosmology, the Universe is made up of three planes, with humans occupying a middle zone between sky-spirits and those of the underworld. In the shaman's trance-voyage of initiation, he or she descends to the lower zone by a sacred ladder, or the World Tree, common to early mythologies. After hideous psychic ordeals, such as being devoured by wild animals, the shaman ascends by rainbow or cosmic mountain or high altar into the celestial light of the sun. There he receives his healing powers, often including those of the animals who tore him apart.

Though most anthropologists judge the shaman's journey to be a psychic projection, some accept it on its own terms. As testified by American anthropologist Michael Harner, "Just like the scientist, the shaman depends upon first-hand observation to decide what's real. If you can't trust what you see yourself, then what can you trust?"

Whereas a Western doctor diagnoses according to materialistic principles of cause and effect, then prescribes drugs or surgery, a shaman confronted with the same symptoms is likely to diagnose soul sickness, requiring atonement. If the shaman does prescribe drugs, *he* is likely to take them rather than the client, to enhance his healing abilities.

For at least three thousand years, Mexican and South American natives have used "sacred" plants containing hallucinogenics to facilitate healing. In words that echo those of Edgar Cayce, Peruvian shaman Eduardo Calderon explained: "The subconscious is a superior part . . . a kind of bag where the individual has stored all his memories. . . . By means of the magical plants and the chants . . . the subconscious of the individual is opened liked a flower."

Anthropologist Douglas Sharon, who became an apprentice to Calderon, verifies: "The hallucinogenic San Pedro cactus is experienced as the catalyst that enables the *curandero* to transcend the limitations placed on ordinary mortals; to activate all his senses; project his spirit or soul; ascend and descend into the supernatural realms; identify and do battle with the sources of illness . . . 'to see.'"

Whereas Cayce and other Western practitioners treat their clients one-on-one, the shaman is likely to draw upon the psychic energy of a whole group. Placing his sick patient in a circle of drumming, chanting, clapping tribe members, the shaman may dance in the mask and skin or feathers of his totem animal, imitating its voice and movements with uncanny accuracy, planing like an eagle, pawing like a bear, howling like a wolf, until he seems to become that animal. Then, he visits the lower and upper spirits to ask how they have been offended and what actions will restore harmony.

Despite the vast difference between injecting a patient with morphine to kill pain and placing him within a circle of drummers, the placebo effect makes the results more similar than might be imagined. Laboratory research also indicates that some shamanistic techniques, intuitively developed from culture to culture, of themselves induce physical healing. For example, fasting, deep breathing and drumming at 180 to 240 beats per minute alter brainwave patterns and activate the parasympathetic system, while excessive perspiration from dancing and sweat lodges rids the body of toxins.

The parallel between tribal healing and Western psycho-therapy is even closer. According to anthropologist Claude Lévi-Strauss, the latest visualization techniques, like those used against cancer by Dr. Bernie Siegel, are a traditional part of tribal medicine; so is dream analysis, as rediscovered in the nineteenth century by Freud, and cathartic release of emotions, as stressed by primal therapist Arthur Janov.

American parapsychologist Ronald Rose, who spent several weeks with the Australian aborigines, was particularly struck by the sophistication of their methods of hypnosis. Not only could clever-men induce deep trances by having their clients stare at polished "clever-stones" but they seemed able to both heal and kill at a distance. As he summed up in *Living Magic*: "It is certainly true that aborigines have not developed a mode of reasoned thought in any substantial way resembling ours. But could it not also be true that aborigines have plumbed depths of the mind, rich in their peculiar rewards, that we have left relatively unexplored?"

When a client gets well, both doctor and shaman credit their superior techniques, but researchers such as Dr. E. Fuller Torrey believe most healing to be the result of psychic imponderables. As Torrey stated in *Witchdoctors and Psychiatrists*: "If a person believes a mental disorder is caused by hormonal imbalance or a missing gene, then the therapy is automatically thought to be scientific, whereas if the theory of causation involves evil spirits, then the therapy must be magical. In fact, psychiatric therapies are very similar all over the world and are relatively independent of the level of technology, the education of the therapist, or the theories of causation."

Many studies support Torrey's contention that healing— whether physical or mental—is more about meaning than about fact, and that shamanic practices are often as effective as Western ones. While it is true that life expectancy in tribal societies is sometimes only half that for Western societies, the daily life of their members is also far more hazardous, including as it does attacks by wild animals, starvation, poor sanitation and infectious disease. Similarly, herbal medicines once effective in curing bodies nurtured on natural diets often can't counter the chemical pollutants in today's foods and environment.

In 1977, the World Health Organization recognized the value of traditional healers by recommending their worldwide integration with Western services. Stated the British medical journal *The Lancet* in 1980: "Even where modern health care is available, the people may still prefer to consult their traditional practitioners for certain troubles. This decision may be quite reasonable, because systems of traditional medicine often have a holistic approach to illness, in which the patient is seen in relation to the environment, ecological and social."

ORIENTAL HEALING

JULY 1986

To visit the Chinese city of Guilin is to be surrounded with visual magic. Set in the lushness of paddy fields and lotus blossoms, it is fairy-ringed by what appear to be mountains of vast height and distance. Yet, strangely, these conical outcroppings do not recede as one approaches. Only a couple of hundred feet high, they are entwined with ancient paths that lead the climber breathlessly to the top.

At dawn on the slopes of these outcroppings, Chinese of all ages perform the slow, stately tai chi exercises by which they balance their energies and reaffirm their oneness with nature. It is the same ritual they have performed for thousands of years in their fields or on the streets, even blocking traffic. To witness this dance of universal affirmation, without Western equivalent, is to be in the presence of the fourth monkey.

Traditional Chinese medicine is a way of life, involving diet, exercise and social and spiritual values. It is drinking green tea for breakfast and taking your bird for a walk in its cage. At its heart is the belief that spirit and body are indivisible, that good health reflects inner and outer harmony, that the organism is greater than the sum of its parts, and that every person contains the grandeur of the Universe, as microcosm to macrocosm.

When an individual falls ill, it is assumed that a block exists in the flow of vital energy connecting that person to the Universe. Traditionally, this means a visit to an acupuncturist.

My own experience with acupuncture began in Hong Kong and resumed ten years later in California. As I sit on the edge of a cot in a Chinese clinic in West Los Angeles, a team of elderly Chinese doctors, in standard medical garb, take my pulse, look into my eyes, study my complexion and occasionally ask questions. Afterwards, an intern imbeds steel needles in clusters across my anatomy, first stretching the skin with thumb and finger, then twirling each into place with a deft tap. This is to stimulate the flow of invisible energy called chi.

Some of the needles I don't feel; others create pulsations sharp enough to cause pain, though not always where they are imbedded. The effect of an hour's session is an upsurge of energy, which has the unforeseen effect of sending me on shopping binges. Friends attending the clinic report emotions ranging from euphoria through indifference to repugnance.

Also in California, I visit a masseur who has recently incorporated acupuncture into his practice. In his experience, it accomplishes in minutes what used to take hours of manual manipulation, with long-term effects saving months of treatment. To demonstrate, he inserts needles into my shoulderblades while using pressure-point massage for the rest of my body.

His assessment is correct: for weeks I feel the stretch of muscles, akin to a thorough workout, where he inserted his needles, which I now judge to be more effective than thumbs.

According to Chinese legend, acupuncture was discovered more than four thousand years ago by peasants who found they could relieve suffering by pressing wounds with sharp flints. The underlying principle was one also noted by Hippocrates: "The greater pain blunts the lesser." However, ancient doctors, called upon to treat wounded soldiers, reportedly discovered that an arrow piercing one part of the body might paradoxically relieve pain in another part.

Around 2600 B.C., the revered Yellow Emperor of Huang Ti laid the foundations of Chinese medicine when he stated that all living organisms are connected to the Universe through energy called *chi*, which enters the body via fine pores that connect to channels called meridians. Introducing metal needles in place of flints and fishbones, the Yellow Emperor charted 361 acupuncture sites, to which he gave such poetic names as Jade Court and Heaven Rushing Out. According to his teachings, not only do needles inserted at these sites stimulate the flow of *chi* along its meridians but they also balance its yang and yin—opposing forces that the Chinese believe permeate all of nature as male-female, positive-negative, active-passive, light-dark, sun-moon, life-death and so on.

Until the 1970s, Western doctors ranked Chinese meridians right along with Martian canals in credibility: what could not be seen or measured did not exist. Then, the Communist government stunned the Western world with the news that eighty thousand operations had been performed during a dozen years using acupuncture instead of analgesic drugs. Of this group, 75 per cent of patients were said to be pain-free and less than 9 per cent required general anesthesia for extreme pain.

What was still missing to the Western scientific mind was any information about *how* acupuncture worked. Then, in 1973, Shanghai experiments with rabbits indicated that acupuncture stimulated the production of pain-killing substances, which scientists labeled endorphins. Also in the seventies, electromagnetic monitors demonstrated that acupuncture sites possessed lower electrical resistance from surrounding skin at a factor of ten to one. Later, a body-scanning process known as electronography, developed by Rumanian physician Ion Dumitrescu, showed that acupuncture points along the meridian of a diseased organ glowed abnormally, corresponding with the acuteness of a disease. More recently, a German laser device has been invented that emits an audible signal at the exact position of an acupuncture site.

Though skeptics still refused to believe that a needle inserted into the hip might affect a knee joint, evidence was mounting that it did. In a study by Dr. Janet Travell of George Washington University, massaging tender muscles in one area was found to relieve chronic pain in a seemingly unrelated area. When British doctor Alexander Macdonald examined Travell's drawings, he determined: "All but one of the tender muscle regions (or trigger points) in these drawings appear to correspond with the location of acupuncture points seen on the various Chinese charts. Furthermore, in all but four of the drawings, the trigger points and the referred zones of pain appear to be linked by the imaginary paths taken by the Chinese channels or meridians."

Such laboratory results offset the confession by the Chinese, after the Cultural Revolution, that earlier triumphs using acupuncture for major surgery had been exaggerated for political gain. As Macdonald concluded in his book *Acupuncture*, needling is suitable only for about 10 to 15 per cent of surgery; however, where it can be recommended, such as with tooth extractions, it is safer than drugs and creates fewer postoperative complications.

Needling is most effective in providing relief from muscular pain and arthritis, as well as from symptoms of migraine, asthma, allergy, eczema, addiction withdrawal, bronchitis, peptic ulcers and hayfever. That this relief can be dramatic and long-lasting is indicated by a 1975 experiment in which Professor Karel Lewit of Prague inserted acupuncture needles into 312 chronic-pain sites possessed by 241 patients. At 86.8 per cent of the sites, pain was immediately relieved, and in 37.5 per cent of those it never returned.

Recently, the effectiveness of acupuncture as a painkiller has been enhanced by the use of electric needles. A portable machine called a codetron even allows self-treatment by replacing needles with electrode pads that can be laid on the skin over the acupuncture points. In one eight-month study, conducted by co-inventor Dr. Bruce Pomeranz of the University of Toronto, 131 persons with chronic pain reported an average 90 per cent improvement after daily thirty-minute treatments. In an Israel study by Dr. Avraham Pavlotsky, fifteen out of nineteen cancer patients for whom pain medication was not effective reported codetron allowed them to carry on normal activity, with good quality of life, for six to ten months.

Despite growing verification by Western science, Chinese doctors might complain that Western acceptance—like Western rejection—merely reflects Western bias, which is to believe only what can be seen and measured, to perceive health almost exclusively from the point of view of disease, and to deal in parts of bodies rather than with the whole.

INDIAN HEALING

1980s–1990s

I and a dozen others sit crosslegged in sweatshirts and bare feet before a bearded young man in white turban, Indian tunic and leggings. Though Canadian-born, he is now a Sikh with an Indian name, trained in kundalini yoga. As a student, I take exercise and meditation classes from members of his ashram (community) without the more rigorous commitment of vegetarianism and religious practice. Founded by an Indian guru now resident in California, this ashram takes its inspiration from the humility and mysticism that inspired its fifteenth-century founder, Guru Nanak, with no reference to later militant and political elaborations.

We begin, hands folded, eyes closed, attention focused inward on "the third eye," chanting Indian prayers, chosen by sound to resonate through our bodies as if they were musical instruments. In this way we attempt to tune in to our bodies and, through them, the Universe.

The next fifty minutes are devoted to stretching and balancing exercises designed to increase spinal flexibility and deepen breathing. Our intention is to move kundalini *(sexual energy, said to be coiled like a snake at the base of the spine) up from the lower* chakras *(energy centers) to the more spiritual* chakras *in the head. Many of the exercises have self-descriptive names: bow pose, camel, frog, crow, chair, archer, butterfly. Some of the postures are almost impossible to assume let alone to hold for the suggested one to three minutes. Others seem deceptively easy until limbs begin to shake, muscles shriek and lungs explode. Some require long, deep breathing; others, the held breath; still others, the short, rapid "breath of fire."*

Like the Eastern proverb that states that the space between the spokes is necessary to create a wheel, so the space between the exercises, during which we lie on the floor experiencing their effect, is equally important. At first, yoga left me dizzy and nauseated. Apparently, I reverse-breathed by sucking in my diaphragm instead of expanding it. This posture, along with locked knees, high shoulders, pulled-back arms, stiff neck and forward-staring eyes, was standard issue during 1940s gym classes. Based on the military model, it was— as Wilhelm Reich also noted—effective for rendering an organism receptive to taking orders by repressing emotion but not conducive to health and happiness.

When I rehabilitated my breathing, the increased oxygen left me giddy, ecstatic, spacey, weepy. Now, after seven years of sometimes faithful, sometimes neglectful practice, the immediate effects of an exercise set are total relaxation and tingling limbs—again, what Wilhelm Reich called streaming. Long-term, the result has been improved vitality, flexibility and blood circulation, the lowering of tension, and greater harmony of mind and body. Yoga has also introduced me to transcendental practices which, without burdening me with a new ideology, have demonstrated the narrowness of the one I inherited.

Like Chinese philosophy, the older Indian system describes all organisms as being connected to the Universe by energy fields.

According to its five-thousand-year-old teachings, the human body is the physical manifestation of an invisible etheric body, which extends beyond it in an aura. This energy field sustains the body's form, allowing it to interact with the material world by means of the five senses.

The etheric body also connects the physical body to five higher, ever subtler planes of energy: the astral, the emotional, the intellectual, the spiritual and the divine. In birth, the soul is said to travel downward through the fields of ever-denser energy until it materializes in flesh and bone. In death, it reascends to the highest plane. And just as birth was completed by cutting the umbilical cord, so death is said to be finalized by severing what ancient texts, including the Bible, refer to as the silver cord, connecting soul to body.

To psychics with supersensitive vision, the etheric body appears as a fine web of tubular channels, shimmering with golden light. These carry *prana*—life energy that is drawn into the body from the sun through the breath. Where densely crisscrossed, the channels create seven spinning energy wheels. Roughly located up the spine, these wheels are known as the *chakras*.

On the material plane, the *chakras* are said to externalize as the seven glands of the endocrine system. The lowest and slowest in rotation is the root *chakra*, at the base of the spine, manifesting itself in the adrenal glands and governing the will to survive. The second *chakra* externalizes as the gonads, controlling the reproductive organs and the sex drive. The third or navel *chakra* externalizes as the pancreas and governs the digestive system and the power drive. The fourth or heart *chakra* manifests in the thymus and controls the circulatory and immune systems and is central to issues of love. The fifth or throat *chakra* externalizes in the thyroid gland, governs the lungs and is the focal point of creativity. The sixth *chakra*, between the eyebrows, externalizes in the pituitary gland and governs the nervous system.

Because of the pituitary's location between the brows, Westerners have often mistaken it for what esoteric texts call the third eye; however, the third eye is actually the seventh or crown *chakra* on top of the head, which manifests in the pineal gland, governs the upper brain and is described as the seat of consciousness through which humans contact the Divine.

Although the Indian medical model seems bizarrely at odds with the Western one, U.S. mythologist Joseph Campbell has brilliantly pointed out parallels between the *chakras* and various schools of Western psychology. The behaviorists with their emphasis on stimulus-response occupy the lowest *chakra*, having to do with basic survival. Freud and Reich were fixated on the second *chakra*, pertaining to sex. Alfred Adler emphasized the will to power, corresponding to the navel *chakra*. Though Campbell didn't complete the comparison, I would suggest Arthur Janov's primal therapy, dealing with emotional issues, corresponds to the heart *chakra*. The transcendental psychology of Abraham Maslow, emphasizing self-actualization and peak experiences, draws on the creativity of the fifth *chakra*, while Jungian philosophy, focusing on spiritual quest, reflects the imperatives of the higher two *chakras*.

As with Chinese medicine, the Indian system describes disease as a blockage in the energy system that later manifests on the physical plane. Healthful stimulation of the *chakras* is aided by deep breathing, meditation, diet, appropriate exercise and vibrations from chanting or music. However, in Eastern mysticism the ultimate function of the body's energy system is not physical health but spiritual Enlightenment.

Until recently, few Western scientists knew, or cared about the Eastern energy model. When healers such as Paracelsus, Franz Anton Mesmer and Wilhelm Reich claimed to have discovered an energy system linking the human body to the Universe, they were persecuted as quacks. Yet the connection between Indian *prana*, Chinese *chi* and the vital energies hypothesized by these Westerners is obvious.

Even in practice, Reichian therapy and Indian yoga have much in common: both emphasize breathing to circulate energy (orgone/*prana*) through the body; both define disease as blocks in that energy flow; both use relaxation techniques to engage the body's parasympathetic and immune systems for natural healing. Both systems also seek to arouse sexual energy for therapeutic purposes; however, whereas Reich brought energy down the spine to the genitals for active sexual release, yoga moves sexual energy (*kundalini*) up the spine for spiritual Enlightenment.

Despite the general disdain of Western medicine for the Eastern system, a few intrepid scientists have attempted to verify the etheric body through its aura—the radiation said to extend about six inches beyond the skin. Employing such devices as an ultraviolet camera, radio electrometer or Geiger counter, a string of researchers have found evidence that the body does radiate an energy that pulsates, flares and changes color. Strongest around the head and fingertips, it is said to intensify with mental activity, to reflect the organism's health, and to be affected by electricity and magnetism.

Using Kirlian photography—a process whereby high-voltage electricity is sent through an object in direct contact with film—beautiful pictures have been produced of organisms emitting colorful coronas. According to Russian inventor Semyon Kirlian, a healthy leaf radiates dynamic flares, a dying one only dim effects, and a dead one none at all. Pinpricks of light correspond with acupuncture sites, and plumes shoot from the fingertips of psychic healers during the laying on of hands.

Though these results have been replicated around the world, critics—not unreasonably—attribute the corona to ionization, ultraviolet rays, aberrant electrical effects and so forth. For now, the best evidence seems to be human—the persistent testimony of generations of Western psychics and Eastern seers, along with centuries of art, from China to Peru, depicting saints and magicians and shamans enshrouded in light or radiating halos. As Toronto sociologist Dr. Edward Mann, who has written extensively about life energy, has stated: "From American Indian shamanism to esoteric Judaism, this concept had predominated for millennia. As it has now become clear, Western civilization is virtually unique in history in its failure to recognize each human being as a subtle energy system in constant relationship to a vast sea of energies in the surrounding cosmos."

BRIDGING EAST AND WEST

OCTOBER 1976
I am jammed into a commuter train, originating in Calcutta. Though I am short for a Westerner, I tower over many of the sari-clad Indian women around me even with parcels on their heads. This

unusual experience proves my downfall, for just as we are pulling out of Chandernagore station, I notice decorations indicating a festival in progress. For weeks I've watched locals here and in Egypt jump on and off moving public vehicles. Now, on impulse, I leap onto the platform just as the train gathers speed—a stupid stunt as I realize even while in midflight.

The next sound I hear is that of something overripe and pulpy smashing against concrete. It is my head. Lying in shock, I gaze up at a ring of sober Indian faces. Even amidst fears of paralysis, my most prominent emotion is that of embarrassment. I force myself to stand, then I hobble half a block before collapsing behind some bushes.

Since I am traveling around the world by happenstance, no one even knows I'm in India. From the practical viewpoint, it is unthinkable for me to be ill or incapacitated. I repeat, as if saying a rosary or mantra: "I am well. I am not injured." Eventually, I pass out.

Perhaps an hour later, I awaken. Through willpower I drag myself to my feet. The whole right side of my body throbs; the right side of my cotton skirt is burned through; my right leg is scraped and bleeding; the color is peeled from the right sides of both shoes. On the back of my head I find a free-standing lump literally the size of a hen's egg. Nonetheless, I again force myself to walk, impelled by that one powerful thought: "I am well. I am not injured."

Glimpses of papier-mâché effigies and other elaborate decorations tell me that I have, indeed, hit upon an important celebration. Despite my injuries, I shuffle into step behind a procession bent on ceremoniously dumping a seventy-foot image of the mother goddess Durga into the Hooghly River. Then, caught up in the euphoria, I watch another spectacle involving officials on a platform. For reasons I am at a loss to explain—perhaps because I am the only foreigner—I am invited up onto the dais. When torches accidentally ignite its silken draperies, I watch mesmerized as flames lick up one side and across the top while young boys beat them with their bodies. Though we are now framed in fire, the ceremony continues unabated as spectators—eyes now on the young flame-beaters—make no effort to escape. In fact, they can't. All are imprisoned by other bodies, packed solid.

Against all odds, the flames are smothered. When I try to return to the train station, I find I can move only with the crowd, now pouring away from it. For hours I try to travel five blocks, only to be swirled backward as part of a human river driven by unfathomable currents through unpaved streets as wide as a four-lane highway. Half of Calcutta seems to be here, shoulder to shoulder and thigh to thigh.

Now I find myself pursued by giant trucks, mounted with three-storey figures outlined in wire and blinking white lights. No question of stopping to watch the parade. I am the parade! Along with everyone else, I must keep walking at the same stately pace. To stop or to slip means to be crushed. No North American crowd could stand this tension or this enforced closeness, but by now I am a will-less part of this human floe with pain acting as an ego-dissolvant binding me to the rest.

A few minutes before midnight, the crowd impulsively surges back to the station, pitching me onto the last train back to Calcutta. As I step out of my cab in front of my hotel on an unlit street, I have the powerful urge to look downward, as if someone has tugged on my skirt. Inches below my extended foot I see a square aperture somewhat inkier than the rest of the road surface—an open manhole!

When I awaken next morning I have trouble remembering where I am. As consciousness returns, I explore my arms and legs, hoping I'll be able to crawl out of bed. To my astonishment, I am pain-free. What is more remarkable: I bear no bruises or abrasions of any kind. Even the scrapes have disappeared from my right arm and leg. In fact, I have only two souvenirs: my ruined clothing and a tiny scab where the lump on my head used to be.

How to account for my "miraculous" cure? Had I healed my body through the power of suggestion? Did the trance-like state in which I wandered through the spiritually drenched Indian landscape aid in my cure?

Though psychic healing in the West is considered a rare and suspect talent, Eastern mysticism urges every person to seek the natural healing power within. When Western medicine shifted from the idea of germ-caused disease toward that of immunological breakdown, the gap between the two healing systems started to close. Simultaneously, a few doctors with experience of each other's cultures began to see provocative and exciting connections.

One of these bridge-builders is Dr. Deepak Chopra. Born in India, Chopra received his medical education in the United States, where he specialized in endocrinology—a choice connecting

Western hormonal knowledge to Hindu belief in the glandular system as the physical manifestation of the *chakras*. Though Chopra began his American practice using Western methods, he was disturbed—as Wilhelm Reich was before him—that Western texts were written from the standpoint of disease and dissection of the dead rather than from the study of healthy humans.

Chopra was especially troubled by Western treatment of cancer as a game of deadly assault: poisons are released like napalm into the body in the hope that cancer cells, which typically grow faster than normal ones, will ingest more toxins and die soonest. However, if all cancer cells are not killed off, they multiply anew—perhaps more virulently as a result of survival of the fittest. Even when the poison war does succeed, the body's immune system may be so depleted that it falls easy prey to other fatal disease.

By contrast, Chopra—like Bernie Siegel—became fascinated by the 1 per cent of patients with "incurable" diseases who somehow cured themselves. In his opinion, cancer remission was no more miraculous than the body's ability to heal a cut or a broken bone: neither mystery could be explained by science. As Hippocrates once had stated: "Doctors treat, nature heals." Yet Western medicine's emphasis on the mechanism of "how" had obscured the presence of that unknown process working behind the scenes, in the same way analysis of a puppet's strings and joints ignores the hidden intelligence of the puppeteer.

As an endocrinologist, Chopra knew a fact startling to the layperson: chemicals produced by one's own body behave differently than *identical* chemicals that are injected. Whereas a host-produced chemical fits into a cell receptor, key into lock, a manufactured chemical floods cell receptors indiscriminately. As Chopra elaborated in *Quantum Healing*: "The living body is the best pharmacy ever devised. It produces . . . everything manufactured by the drug companies, but it makes them much, much better. The dosage is always right and given on time; side effects are minimal or nonexistent; and the directions for using the drug are included in the drug itself, as part of its built-in intelligence."

What the host-produced chemical possesses is know-how. By contrast, "a man-made drug is a stranger in a land where every-one else is blood kin. It can never share the knowledge that everyone else was born with." Without this inherent information, the foreign chemical can't be deployed by the brain to the right sites or coordinated with other processes. Like a deaf and blind percussionist who has blundered into a stringed orchestra, it bangs and thumps, drowning out the other players while the conductor struggles in vain to catch its attention.

Because of this chemical know-how, Chopra concluded that intelligence existed throughout the body and not just in the brain. Such a notion is not so farfetched when one realizes that every cell, whether brain or kidney, has identical DNA giving it equal capacities. The notion that organs other than the brain can "think" was supported by the surprise discovery of receptors for brain-chemicals in the kidneys. Similarly, receptors for imipramine, a brain chemical abnormally produced during depression, were found on the skin, implying that emotions were also in free circulation throughout the body. Thus, when the brain is sad—or happy—so are the skin and the kidneys and the liver.

Through such observations, Chopra concluded that the distinction between mental and physical disease was false; that healing was more mental than physical; that the healthy body probably cured cancer routinely as a form of early prevention; that on the cellular level feeling happy and fighting cancer were the same thing. Such findings dovetailed with those of Wilhelm Reich, who had determined that his cancer patients' cells were depressed, pleasure-starved and de-energized, placing the patient in a state of willful suicide. This information was also echoed in the personal testimony of Edgar Cayce, who believed each body cell possessed an awareness of its own needs. It was supported in the experiments of Dr. Justa Smith, who discovered that the force exuded by the hands of psychic healers seemed to display an innate intelligence.

Chopra was faced with the age-old question: how does the psyche interact with the body to produce healing?

As previously stated: more than two thousand years ago Greek philosopher Democritus intuited that everything in the Universe was composed of indivisible bits of matter, which he called atoms. It wasn't until the nineteenth century that physicists proved atoms existed; then, early in the twentieth century, they discovered they were not indivisible but had a structure.

Within each atom is a nucleus, orbited by negatively charged particles called electrons. If an atom were blown up to the size of St. Peter's Dome in Rome, its nucleus would be visible as a grain of salt while its electrons—at least two thousand times smaller—would be like specks of dust orbiting near the dome's outer edge. Yet even an atomic nucleus is not solid. It is composed of positively charged particles called protons and particles without charge called neutrons, all of which zoom around at velocities in the vicinity of 40,000 miles per second. Evidence also suggests these protons and neutrons are divisible into even more elementary particles—the elusive quarks, which haunt the imagination of modern physicists the way the unicorn taunted medieval naturalists. However, even if such elementary particles existed they would be so small with speeds so fast they would be only a blur.

Either way, physicists lost faith in the absolute reality of the sensory world: since every atom is more than 99.999 per cent empty space, physical objects only appear solid to our crude, unaided senses because the velocity of their particles creates that impression, much like the twirling blades of an electric fan appear as a disc. And since most particles live less than a millionth of a second before being annihilated by other particles, only the energy field itself continues to exist, not its individual parts.

That is the significance of Einstein's famous equation $E = mc^2$. Since mass and energy are equivalent, atoms are not pellets of matter but non-material packets of energy, called quanta. Tables and oranges are not "things" but only concentrations of energy. Stated physicist Henry Stapp: "If the attitude of quantum mechanics is correct . . . then there is no substantive physical world in the usual sense of this term. The conclusion here is not the weak conclusion that there *may* not be a substantive physical world but rather that there definitely is not a substantive physical world."

It seems that the whole Newtonian world of solid objects may be an illusion, albeit a useful and orderly one—what Hindus call *maya* and Buddhists call *avidya*. As stated by first-century Buddhist Ashvaghosha: "All phenomena in the world are nothing but the illusory manifestation of the mind and have no reality of their own."

If so, the body as a hunk of bone and flesh steeped in liquid is also an illusion. On the subatomic level, well below our sensory awareness, matter thins out to such an extent that body and mind dissolve into a single dynamic forcefield. Chopra describes their relationship as a river of atoms and a river of thoughts held together by an underlying river of intelligence. In his view, information both predates and outlives matter. Therefore, humans are not organisms that learned to think but thoughts that evolved bodies: "What is a cell, then? It is a memory that has built some matter around itself, forming a specific pattern. Your body is just the place your memory calls home."

This Platonic belief in the mental as being primary to the material is supported by other scientists in other fields. According to astrophysicist Sir Arthur Eddington, sensory objects are merely "fancies of the mind," providing a set of codes signaling something deeper. Stated astronomer Sir James Jeans: "The Universe begins to look more like a great thought than a great machine." Neurologist Sir John Eccles agreed: "I want you to realize that there is no color in the natural world and no sounds—nothing of this kind; no textures, no patterns, no beauty, no scent." As Eddington summed up: "The stuff of the world is mind-stuff."

If this mental model is a correct one, then Western medicine has devoted itself—albeit brilliantly—to the treatment of physical symptoms rather than to the cure of disease. Whereas the physical model defines cancer as a disease of runaway cells, Chopra defines it as a distortion in the body's underlying psychic blueprint, creating that wild growth. To eradicate cancer it is not sufficient to destroy the cancer cells, but instead you must excise the memory of the cancer from the psychic blueprint so that more wild cells don't replace those killed off. How can this be accomplished?

Chopra was intrigued by a study of cancer remissions by Elmer and Alyce Green of the Menninger Clinic. Each of its four hundred participants had only one thing in common: each had suddenly experienced a radical shift in attitude so that they knew they would be healed by an inner force not limited to the self. "At that moment, such patients apparently jump to a new level of consciousness that prohibits the existence of cancer." Either the cancer cells disappear, or the disease stabilizes without further damage.

Chopra compared this "new level of consciousness" to the "fourth dimension" regularly achieved by Buddhist monks and

Hindu yogis through meditation, fasting and other ascetic practice. It is reputedly the mystic state in which one experiences the interconnectedness of all things. As stated by a Hindu proverb: "Like a wave, the mind at rest discovers that it is an ocean."

How can those who have never encountered the fourth dimension know it exists? For hundreds of years people in the West heard fabulous tales of Eastern holy men who could endure mountaintop temperatures dressed only in loincloths, who could perform awesome feats of prophecy and telepathy, who could even be buried alive for hours and live to tell the tale. The more scientific the West became, the more exaggerated these stories seemed, the more fraudulent, the more illusory. However, invention of the electroencephalograph—the EEG—in 1929 by German physician Hans Berger allowed researchers to monitor the brain's electrical activity by attaching electrodes to the skull. Instead of finding three brainwave patterns defining three states of consciousness, researchers found four: delta waves, the slowest, indicating dreamless sleep; theta, associated with dreaming; alpha, characteristic of deep relaxation; and beta, marking rational thought.

Subsequent exploration of the alpha state, or fourth dimension, found it to be a rich source of creative, artistic and even paranormal activity. Whereas the average person could maintain this "dozing" state for only a few minutes, Eastern yogis and Buddhist monks could extend it for several hours. Scientists also found these holy men were able, as claimed, to control their heart and metabolic rates, along with other "involuntary" bodily processes. During one experiment, reported by neurologist Richard Restak in *The Brain*, a yogi remained in a sealed box for more than ten hours, voluntarily reducing his oxygen consumption to as low as 25 per cent of the theoretical minimum to sustain life. In such suspended states, these mystics could endure extremes of hot and cold, and even blot out pain till it became merely an opinion.

By EEG experimentation, it was also discovered that children aged three to eight had a predominance of theta and alpha waves, corresponding to their high scores in tests of telepathy. Pregnant women also displayed above average levels of alpha rhythms, as did Albert Einstein, who remained in alpha state even when working with complex mathematical formulas.

While EEG testing missed the point of what yogis were all about spiritually, it did establish in the face of extreme Western skepticism that these Eastern mystics could hold their own in science's toughest terrain: the laboratory. Eventually, their meditative techniques were taught to heart patients, enabling them to lower their blood pressure and activate their parasympathetic systems for natural healing. This process was welcomed into Western hospitals under the scientific-sounding name of biofeedback—a label that, typically for the West, glorified the machine that recorded the scores rather than the meditator or the technique responsible for them

Meditation supported by diet is central to Dr. Deepak Chopra's clinical practice. More radically, he treats specific diseases with "primordial sound," tuned to the ailing organ. According to Chopra, these vibrations—of which *Om* is the most primordial— alter heart rate and produce warmth, tingling and throbbing as an accompaniment to healing. On the mental level, they create harmonic fusion with the fourth dimension, allowing delusions like the crippling fear supporting the disease to be stripped away: what appears as a change in the condition is, in his opinion, just a reflection of inner change.

If all this seems too rarefied for Western consumption, Chopra reminds us that superstring theory—one of the latest attempts of physicists to probe to the deepest levels of reality—is also based on vibrations. Briefly stated: billions of unseen superstrings are hypothesized to pervade the Universe, with their different frequencies giving rise to matter, energy, time, space and so on. Since these strings originate in a reality with more than our four dimensions, they are abstractions that can't be visualized. Similarly, ancient Indian texts perceive the cosmos, metaphorically, as a gossamer mesh, woven out of billions of strings of intelligence. These are called *sutras*, which is Sanskrit for both verbal phrase and stitch. *Sutras* is also the root of the medical term *suture*, connecting mental vibrations to healing.

The use of sound, or vibrations, to promote healing has a five-thousand-year Indian history. It is central to tribal medicine, which relies heavily on chanting and drumming. In the West, its formal tradition stretches back at least to Pythagoras, who created a religion based on the harmony of music and numbers. According to

Pythagoras, every planet has a distinctive hum, and together they make up the harmony of the spheres to which each human soul resonates.

In his book *Sound Health*, New Age musician Steven Halpern stated that when two or more oscillators in the same energy field vibrate, they shift rhythms until their oscillations are the same. Thus, music soothes or activates through resonance. This balancing is said to occur through the seven *chakras*, which resonate to the musical scale based on the discoveries of Pythagoras, with the lowest *chakra* as C, the second as D and so on.

In Western science, limited experiments indicate that hens lay more and larger eggs when listening to Baroque music, that geraniums grow faster and taller to Bach's Brandenburg Concertos, that zoo animals are soothed by some melodies and enraged by others. Yet, once again, in assessing the healing potential of music on humans, perhaps it is wiser simply to call upon collective, intuitive wisdom: who has not felt the power of a symphony or a rhapsody or the song of a bird to strike deep emotional chords that reverberate through body and psyche? If the Universe was, indeed, created fifteen billion years ago with the Big Bang, as astrophysicists hypothesize, one could do far worse than to imagine ultimate reality to be the harmonic resonance from that first primordial OOOOOOOOOOOmmmmmmmmmmmmm.

The Self:

WHO IS THAT CROWD IN THE MIRROR?

"Man is a plural being. When we speak of ourselves ordinarily, we speak of 'I'. We say 'I did this' 'I think this' 'I want to do this'—but this is a mistake. There is no such 'I' or rather there are hundreds, thousands of little 'I's in every one of us."

—G.I. Gurdjieff

DECEMBER 5, 1984

Though I rarely visit psychics, I'm in the Toronto office of one named Vince Vanlimbeek, who scored a hit with me a year before when he predicted—against my total skepticism—that I would give up residence in Toronto. Now that unlikely event has come to pass: in my purse I carry a ticket for tomorrow's flight to California, where I plan an indefinite stay. But first, this last joust with fate.

Though Vanlimbeek is right on all counts as he reiterates some of the events of my past few months, I remain unimpressed. I am not here, in the midst of a blizzard, with my throat sealed by laryngitis, to hear things I already know. As my half-hour appointment draws to a close, I grow depressed, even unaccountably panicky.

The psychic falls silent. Then: "I see your father. Why does he look so downcast?"

Since this past year has been marked by the return of violent memories having to do with an incestuous relationship with my late father, I impulsively provide an illuminating answer: "Because my father sexually abused me until the age of—"

The psychic's response hits before I can speak the defining word: "It was a lot longer than that, wasn't it, luv?"

"No, it was only till age five. I know for sure because that's when all my other memories begin."

After a thoughtful pause, he continues: "I see you putting together a jigsaw puzzle. The picture is coming clear but some of the pieces are in wrong."

By the time I go to bed, I've all but forgotten these comments in the press of last-minute errands. Yet, somewhere in the tender hours of morning, I am awakened by what I can only describe with embarrassment as a gong going off inside my head. As I lie in bed in the fuzziness and confusion of foundering consciousness, a disembodied male voice resonates the words: "Your psychic powers will be returned to you." This enigmatic message is followed by feelings of fear, panic and—finally—a repugnant realization: I now know for sure that my sexual relationship with my father did continue long past age five, as the psychic suggested. Over the past year, I have been scrunching down the size of my child-self as she appears in returning memories to square her age with the demands of my logical mind. Now even this modest ground has been exploded from under my feet. In sexual scenes pushing into consciousness, I see myself growing taller like Alice nibbling on magic mushrooms. At last, I am forced to recognize a disorienting truth: my incestuous relationship with my father continued into adolescence, perhaps into my high school years.

How can this be? How could I be sexually involved with my father as a teenager and not remember it? That's as preposterous as if my shadow were suddenly to detach itself from my feet to confront me with a mocking face supposed to be my own.

As I toss in the beginnings of that cold December day, which will eventually take me into sunshine, I can think of only one station-stop between myself and insanity. Many years ago I saw the movie Three Faces of Eve, based on the real-life story of Eve White, a mousy farmwife who created a second personality named Eve Black to play out her repressed sexual fantasies. Before entering analysis, Eve White didn't know of the existence of the promiscuous Eve Black, whose presence she experienced only through blackouts and headaches. Eventually, the two Eves were joined by a third, more sophisticated personality named Jane. According to the filmmakers, these three were then integrated into a single self.

I, along with thousands of others, watched agog as actress Joanne Woodward switched back and forth between Eve's three identities, with their distinctly different gestures, desires, values and memories. Though sympathetically treated, this poor woman— diagnosed as having a multiple personality—was obviously as much a freak as a three-headed calf in a circus.

The 1974 Encyclopedia Britannica, which I consult at my earliest opportunity, does little to dispel the sinister melodrama clinging to me like a cowl. Multiple personality disorder is, I discover, an extreme form of dissociation in which traumatic experiences, cut off from conscious awareness, develop into one or more separate identities. In all the world's history, the Britannica claims only 100 cases have ever been found.

Only one hundred? Can I be one hundred and one?

Who, or what, is the self?

Aristotle identified it as an intelligent animal striving for earthly perfection during a single lifetime. Plato defined it as a psychic entity, which evolved from incarnation to incarnation in a spiritual journey toward the Good.

In Descartes' credo, "I think, therefore I am," the self was a thinking being whose proof of existence lay in an ability to doubt that existence—to self-reflect. Through an ecstatic dream vision, Descartes identified the physical focus of mind and soul as the pineal gland; thousands of years before, Eastern mystics had also fixed on the pineal, which they believed to be the center of a reincarnating soul, or *atman*. The Sumerians and the Assyrians chose the liver as the seat both of the soul and of consciousness. Some early Greeks, including Aristotle, physically located consciousness in the heart; Hippocrates and Plato chose the brain. Medieval painters illuminated both head and heart as having transcendental significance.

Charles Darwin addressed the riddle of the self through origin: consciousness was a byproduct of the evolution of the brain. Creationists insisted on adding "soul" to the mind-body equation, but weren't sure where to physically locate it. The new science of psychology represented the victory of physiology over philosophy: self was the biological product of heredity and environment. Behaviorist John Watson narrowed the circumference of self even further by defining it strictly in terms of physical actions: one was what one did. Defying fashion, William James identified the self psychically with "the stream of consciousness"— an eternally moving experience of "now," which was part of a larger cosmic consciousness.

While rooted in the Aristotelean belief that humans were thinking animals, Freud described our psychic component as consisting of three parts: id, ego and superego, representing the instinctive self, the conscious self and the prohibiting, moralizing self. To the idea of consciousness, he added that of the unconscious, which he described as making up 90 per cent of the human psyche.

Jung's psychic model was also threefold: the ego, the persona and the shadow, representing the conscious self, the mask each of us shows to the world and the repressed self, which contains the parts of the psyche each of us refuses to acknowledge. To Freud's concept of the conscious and unconscious, Jung added the collective unconscious. He also hypothesized a transcendental Self, which was more than the sum of all its integrated parts.

To the average person in an average moment of an average day, the self consists of what each of us is currently aware of, plus what we remember ourselves to be, contained by the body we see reflected in the mirror. Therefore, the discovery that a vital hunk of memory is missing is physically equivalent to experiencing the loss of a limb. In the case of a multiple personality, the problem is compounded: not only must one contend with the loss but one is left to wonder what mischief that missing hunk might have been up to while one's eyes were closed. For a multiple, the convention of a single self enclosed in a single body is forever shattered. To receive an accurate reflection, the multiple must step between two mirrors and dare to look both ways.

One of the first documented cases of multiple personality disorder was that of Mary Reynolds of Pennsylvania, the devout daughter of a Baptist minister. After nineteen-year-old Mary failed to return from church one Sunday in 1811, a search party found her unconscious in a meadow. When revived, she was deaf and blind, with no memory of what had happened.

Though Mary's hearing and sight returned over the next three months, she again fell into an eighteen-hour swoon from which she emerged like a newborn, with no memory, no recognition of her family, and unable to speak, read or write. After five weeks in which she rapidly relearned these skills, Mary fell into a third profound sleep. Now she resurfaced as her old self, astonished at all the changes that had occurred during what she thought to be a single night's sleep.

For seventeen years Mary alternated between her new and old selves, always changing during deep sleep and never remembering the previous state. Where the old Mary was studious, melancholy, repressed and judgmental, the new Mary was cheerful, fun-loving, passionate and creative. As summed up by Reverend William S. Plumer in *Harper's* magazine of 1860: "In her natural state the strange double life which she led was the cause of great unhappiness. She looked upon it as a severe affliction from the hand of providence . . . but in her abnormal state . . . she looked upon [reverting to her natural state] as passing from a bright and joyous into a dull and stupid phase of life." For her last twenty-five years, Mary stabilized as her new fun-loving self.

During the 1880s and 1890s, other cases of multiple personality were diagnosed—a modest trend culminating in the celebrated Christine Beauchamp case.

In April 1898, a prim young woman consulted Dr. Morton Prince in his Boston office because of headaches and insomnia. Under hypnosis she revealed a different personality from the stiff, priggish self who had minutes before entered the room. Prince called this second personality B2—the Sleeper—in comparison to B1, whom he dubbed the Saint.

During followup treatment, a third personality emerged— an amoral, quick-tempered woman whom Prince dubbed B3, the Imp. For years, the Imp had fought the Saint for control of the Beauchamp consciousness without the Saint's being aware of it. If the Saint went to church, the Imp punished her by getting drunk, then leaving her to suffer the humiliation and the hangover. As a perverse joke, the Imp would take the last bus to a remote spot in the country, then abandon the bewildered Saint to walk home in the dark. Since the Saint was terrified of spiders, the Imp arranged for her to receive a box of them. When the Saint tried to knit a baby's blanket for a friend, the Imp several times waited till it was almost finished, then unraveled it. On the final occasion, the Saint awoke to find herself tied in the wool and had to cut herself free.

After a year of analysis, a more balanced personality emerged, whom Prince coded as B4, the Woman. Wrote Prince: "These three personalities ... might serve as an allegorical picture of the tendencies of man. If this were not a serious psychological study, I might feel tempted to entitle this volume, *The Saint, the Woman, and the Devil.*"

Temporarily forgotten in Prince's description was B2, the Sleeper. Yet the doctor was to make a surprise discovery: B2 was the real Christine Beauchamp, the birth personality who had fallen unconscious at age seven from trauma connected with a brother's death. She had not awakened for eighteen years—when Prince hypnotized the Saint to discover the source of her headaches.

Through hypnotic suggestion Prince fused the Saint and the Woman, squeezing out the unruly Imp. Then, resurrecting B2, he suggested that she would now possess the memories of the other personalities. As he recorded this dramatic moment in *The Dissociation of a Personality*:

"'Who are you?' I asked.

"'I am myself.'"

"'Where is B1?'"

"'I am B1.'"

"'Where is B4?'"

"'I am B4. We're all the same person, only now I am myself.'"

After the Beauchamp case, little was heard of multiple personality until the 1957 movie *Three Faces of Eve*. MPD seemed doomed to a doubtful place as a psychiatric footnote—what many skeptics thought to be a freak of hypnosis rather than a freak of nature.

All this abruptly changed in the 1980s, when more than five thousand new cases were officially recorded in North America alone. An MPD specialist, Richard Kluft of the Institute of the Pennsylvania Hospital in Philadelphia, treated 130 himself, considerably more than my 1974 *Encyclopedia Britannica* claimed had ever existed. More astonishing, after studying 1,055 persons chosen at random, Winnipeg psychiatrist Colin Ross hypothesized that 10 per cent of the population suffers from a dissociative disorder, while one person in every one hundred has multiple personality: "Instead of being obscure or rare, this is one of the most common forms of mental illness."

What was happening?

In hindsight, the MPD blackout seemed to reflect the resistance of therapists to diagnosing the condition rather than any paucity of candidates. One reason was conservative backlash to the therapeutic use of hypnosis. Another was the unwillingness of many psychiatrists to accept such a bizarre model of personality so at odds with "common sense." A third was misdiagnosis of multiple personality as schizophrenia, a much severer disorder characterized by disintegration of personality rather than its division.

Yet amidst these explanations lurks an unsavory other: society's refusal to deal with the cause of 90 per cent of MPD cases:

childhood abuse, especially incest. Even in the sexually liberated sixties, U.S. psychiatrist Cornelia Wilbur could not get professional journals to publish her now-famous case of the multiple known as Sybil, whose personality splintered during years of sadistic torture by her mother. After Wilbur presented Sybil's story to a psychiatric conference, all papers were published but hers. Even today some psychiatrists refuse to believe MPD exists: what elephant in the bedroom?

CREATION OF A MULTIPLE SELF

MAY 1989

As nearly as I can determine, my personality divided into two about the time I was five as the result of my father's oral rape of me. From then on it was "my" job to take on the world while my Other Self did scary and repellent things in my father's bedroom. Thresholds were important to us. While "I" stood like a zombie, scuffing my foot across the brass strip marking my father's room off from the rest of the house, I ceased to exist and "she" was born anew. She was my inner shadow, whose presence I felt but whose face I couldn't see, like the light in a closet which illuminates only when you're inside with the door closed. Dreams were like the pages of her secret diary, which she left around for me to find, often appearing in them as a young savage, or a mute, or a retarded creature with bad skin and scraggly hair. When I wrote my 1987 memoir My Father's House, *I called this outcast the Child Who Knows. I thought "I" had created her as my dupe, my fallguy. However, the process of remembering is a dynamic one. Even while researching this chapter, I have an insight that shifts the ground on which I thought I was standing. It was triggered by two observations that suddenly step off the page and link hands. One was the discovery by Dr. Morton Prince that the "real" Christine Beauchamp was the birth personality who fell unconscious at an early age, "as frequently happens." The second was an opinion by Toronto therapist Adam Crabtree that typically one alter personality will be angry, perhaps acquiring the generic name of the Angry One.*

Of a sudden I know the "I" writing this book is not the original "me." Of a sudden I understand that when my psyche divided in two, it was my birth personality who became the Child Who Knows. It was my birth personality who drowned like the Beauchamp Sleeper in the tidal wave of unconsciousness flooding my natal home while "I," the Angry One, the impersonator, escaped to the relative security of the external world. The Child Who Knows is not a phantom of my dreams; I am a figment of hers. This explains why I can't remember ever having been held by my mother, although the photograph album tells a different story. It explains why my childhood memories begin so abruptly, and in anger. It explains "my" almost total lack of fear—fear belonged to the Child Who Knows.

Now, as I look out my window at blue sky and green grass, everything remains the same yet everything feels different. It's as if I have spent a lifetime building an elaborate house, choosing the wallpaper and the furniture with care, landscaping to taste, only to discover that I do not have title to the land it occupies. My birth property is off somewhere in the forest, a brambly piece of unmarked territory containing one child's untended grave.

Do other surprises lie locked in the yellowed pages of that Other diary?

Multiple personality is now viewed by specialists as a plausible, even creative defense of a normal psyche to pain that otherwise would kill or drive one crazy. No longer stigmatized as freaky, it is instead forcing psychologists to revise their view of "normal."

In an ordinary day each of us uses different parts of our personality for different tasks. To an observer, the company president coolly signing a million-dollar contract may seem at odds with the look-alike father playing with his children, the husband berating his wife for spending too much on lightbulbs and the dandy showering his mistress with gifts. What connects the president with the father, the husband and the lover is the conviction of each that they are the same, plus their residence in a single fleshy suit.

At night our sleeping minds transport us on fabulous journeys in which we play roles our waking minds may judge foolish or immoral. Again, all that makes these experiences part of ourselves is our willingness to connect them to the face in the mirror next morning. Further along the arc of multiplicity are alcoholics, who behave when drunk with a violence they fail to recall when sober. Often families of alcoholics treat these conflicting "selves" as if no connection exists, then deny the abuse to outsiders.

A typical case of MPD begins when a terrified child enters shock during sexual abuse the way a mouse freezes in the claws of a pouncing cat. If the abuser and the rest of the family pretend the abuse is not happening, the child is likely to record the pain in a separate memory bank. Eventually these memories may crystallize into a separate identity. This divided reality—a reflection of family normalcy—saves the child the burden of hating the parents on whom he or she remains dependent. If the family is functional within the community, it also allows the child to capitalize on outer stability to learn and to grow.

The first division of consciousness must occur while the psyche is still malleable, often around age three and not later than seven. Like athletes who psych themselves beyond pain in order to perform superhuman feats, the child hypnotizes him- or herself into a state of consciousness beyond the psychological reach of the abuser. Often an "alter" has its genesis in an imaginary companion or in wishful thinking: "If I were strong, nobody would hurt me …" It may emerge out of guilt: "If I'm being punished, I must be bad." Since an alter is self-created, it will often have more freedom than the birth personality to express emotions and to act out fantasies.

According to Adam Crabtree in *Multiple Man*, one alter in a male multiple will likely be pathological. In 1977, police arrested a frightened and very confused young man named Billy Milligan as the campus rapist of Ohio State University. Psychiatric investigation revealed Billy to be the meek and unaware host of twenty-three alters of both sexes and many ages. Most dominant was Arthur, an atheist and a capitalist who spoke with a British accent, could read and write Arabic and had extensive knowledge of physics, chemistry and medicine. The "keeper of hate" was Ragen, a karate expert and Communist who spoke English with a Slavic accent and was fluent in Serbo-Croatian. Though Ragen had committed the robberies of which Billy also stood accused, it was a lonely lesbian alter named Adlana who committed the rapes.

Billy's fragmentation had resulted from his stepfather's beatings and sexual torture. To demonstrate to Billy what would happen if he told, the stepfather had forced him to dig a grave and then had buried him for several hours with only a pipe for air. Before releasing Billy, the stepfather had urinated down the air pipe.

After a psyche has split once, it is likely to do so again even when the conflict is not life-endangering. Like a dog that has discovered how to dance on its hind legs under threat of the whip, the child is now a skillful dancer. Some alters don't differ greatly; others may be highly specialized in feelings and abilities. Once invented, they acquire an energy of their own as if a character had stepped from the pages of a novel, drugged the author, then helped himself to the contents of the author's closets and bank account.

If faced with annihilation through fusion into a single personality, an alter may plot and plead with all the eloquence and despair of a prisoner on death row. When the Beauchamp Imp discovered that Dr. Morton Prince planned to eliminate her, she stepped up her vendetta against the Saint and then, in a poignant about-face, attempted to upgrade herself by learning French. Because of the reality of these "deaths" to the personalities involved, today's therapists often counsel greater cooperation among the alters rather than fusion.

Even though alters share the same body, they can be of any age or either sex, and sometimes these imaginary differences are imposed on their bodies in ways both subtle and outlandish.

A pioneer in the physiological differences of alters, Dr. Frank Putnam of the U.S. National Institute of Mental Health, found that alters can have brainwave patterns as different as if they were separate people—same brain, different minds. When actors tried to simulate alters in control tests, no such differences were found. Similarly, alters of the same person may achieve widely varying I.Q. scores; one alter can be left-handed and another right; one can have allergies with symptoms of hives or nausea or sinus congestion that magically disappear when another alter emerges.

As explained by Putnam: "When you work with a patient you see a lot of dermatological manifestations. Weals and rashes that come and go with a surprising rapidity when the patient is reliving, in a vivid way, a past traumatic event." In one spectacular case, when a woman was re-experiencing a childhood incident in which her mother had plunged her hand into boiling water, the hand grew fiery red up to a sharp demarcation line on her wrist.

Administering drugs to multiples can be tricky, since an adult dose may prove toxic to a child alter who emerges while the drug is in effect. Dr. David Caul, a psychiatrist who teaches at Ohio University, treated a woman whose three personalities had three separate menstrual cycles within a month. And Dr. Bennet Braun of Chicago reported seeing a patient's eyes turn from turquoise-green to gray when she switched from a vivacious personality to a mousy one. "It took about five minutes after the personality switch. . . . I was amazed."

Alters may also require glasses with different prescriptions—a nuisance for multiples who have not learned to control the comings and goings of their alters. "Many patients have told me they have a drawer full of eyeglasses at home," stated Braun. "They never are quite sure which pair to bring when they go out."

A brilliant description of being a multiple was given by Arthur, one of Billy Milligan's alters, to several children sharing the same consciousness with him: "Think of it as if all of us—a lot of people, including many you have never met—are in a dark room. In the center of this room is a bright spot of light on the floor. Whoever steps into this light, onto the spot, is out in the real world and holds the consciousness. That's the person other people see and hear and react to. The rest of us can go about our regular interests, study or talk or play. But whoever is out must be very careful he or she doesn't reveal the existence of the others. It is a family secret."

The study of multiples has led some psychologists to suspect that the idea of a single self housed in a single body is a convention rather than a reality. Though MPD is usually described as the fragmentation of a single personality, Putnam suggests that all of us may be born multiple and that normalcy may consist in linking up the parts. Newborns may not understand that when they are laughing and when they are crying they are still the same baby; therefore, it is consistency of nurturing that allows the child to discover the "I" connecting each emotional state and to learn to transfer information between them. If a caregiver has a vested interest in reinforcing a division, more than one personality becomes a logical result.

Where do I fit on the graph of multiplicity?

To my knowledge only two of me existed during childhood— my birth personality who remained under house arrest in my natal home, and the alter who went to school and thought herself normal. I am also certain that once I left my father's house for college, only one of me maintained permanent control of a single personality. But what about the chaotic years between—the high school years? Did I create other "me's" to handle the heavier sexual caseload of teenage dating? Is that why my memory of that period is still so sketchy and confused?

One day in the summer of 1987 I notice I have doodled, with my left hand, on a notebook: "My name is Wendy."

Since I have been going to a hypnotherapist to probe still-dark areas of psyche, I am intrigued. Who is Wendy?

My only association for that name is the heroine of James Barrie's play Peter Pan. *Yet the more I ponder that connection the more fascinated I become. The villain of that piece is Captain Hook, so-named for the hooked hand he wielded as a weapon. Similarly, the villain of my autobiographical novel* Pandora, *written fifteen years ago, is Pandora's father, who also wielded a hooked hand like a weapon. I've already discovered* Pandora *to be a minefield of incestuous codes. Is this another? The congruity of the two names—Peter Pan and Pandora— suggests it might be. Is Wendy the name of an alter I once possessed?*

A few days later, I am traveling to the office of my hypnotherapist when I find, on the subway seat beside me, a Globe and Mail *newspaper dated August 1, 1987. Conspicuously featured is a story on the play* Peter Pan, *which is to premiere at the Shaw Festival in Niagara-on-the-Lake. According to the reporter, playwright James Barrie appropriated the name Wendy from a child who used to call him her "fwiendy." More relevantly, the article quotes from scholarly literature comparing* Peter Pan *"to the incubus, the medieval spirit that was supposed to engage in intercourse with sleeping girls." Apparently, the shadow Peter lost in Wendy's bedroom was a Jungian one!*

Half an hour later, when the hypnotherapist counts me down into a light trance, I hear a voice, sounding like me and issuing from my mouth, identify herself as Wendy. As she tells the story: it was her job, when I was a teenager, to deal with my father's sexual advances.

The therapist asks: "Were you good at your job?"

"No. I did as little as possible. It was a boring job like a lot of people's jobs."

"Why didn't you quit?"

"You don't understand. That's why I was created. My only reason for existence. It was what I was supposed to do. Not to do it was to die. . . . Sometimes I thought I would kill myself but always I found a reason to live one more day. Call it my sense of duty. I was a sexual drudge—somewhere between a social worker and a cleaning lady. It was just the way things were. I didn't set them up. Everything was in place when I started. I kept things stable so other people could stay sane. I was good at that."

What to make of all this? Since I'm familiar only with the Walt Disney movie of Peter Pan, *I pick up a copy of the original Barrie play. Though I remember Wendy as a glamorous creature who knew how to fly, in the Barrie version she is essentially the drudgy, caretaking female I produced under hypnosis.*

One riveting detail I can't help but notice: Wendy's father is named George. So is mine.

The following weekend, the Toronto Star *runs an article on the upcoming Shaw production. This one lists the real-life boys out of whom Barrie forged his lithesome hero: Peter, George, Nicholas, Jack and Michael. Coincidentally, my father's name was George Nicholas. However, what stops me cold is the genesis of Mrs. Darling, whom Barrie patterned on the real-life mother of the five boys. She, along with Wendy and Wendy's daughter, is essentially the same character through three generations. Her name: Sylvia. Therefore, we have George Nicholas and Sylvia.*

Later that day, while I am still talking myself out of making too much of these peculiarities, the telephone rings. Incredibly, a woman's voice asks: "Is that you, Wendy?"

Hastily, I reply: "You've got the wrong number."

I hang up. The phone rings again. The same woman and the same question: "Wendy?"

Feeling quite weird, I repeat more forcefully: "There's no one here by that name. You've got the wrong number."

Before I can hang up again, the woman insists: "But I know this is the right number." She reads back the digits she has dialed.

"That's the number you got, but it's a wrong number. There's no Wendy here."

"There has to be."

I am growing testy: "There isn't! My name's not Wendy. Nobody named Wendy lives here, not me and not the person from whom I'm subletting."

"Wait!" The caller bursts out laughing. "The house-owner— that's my sister! I didn't realize she was away this summer. She changed her name a couple of years ago. It used to be Wendy—still is as far as I'm concerned."

What to make of this crowd of Wendys suddenly closing in around me? Why did I doodle "My name is Wendy?" Did I, as a teenager, create an alter named Wendy out of an unconscious understanding of the shadow-side of Peter Pan? Was it because of possessing such an alter that I invented a hook-handed father in my novel Pandora? Conversely, did I simply conjure up Wendy, in present time, from information about the Shaw production of Peter Pan, afloat in the atmosphere around me? If so, why? What to make of the peculiar coincidences reverberating around the names Sylvia and George Nicholas? Also: what to make of my apparent ability to anticipate information just before encountering it?

Was this what the Voice that once awakened me meant when it announced: "Your psychic powers will be returned to you"?

THE NEURAL SELF

Multiple personality is a defense that, under extreme cir-cumstances, capitalizes on the natural divisions in the psyche rather than on its potential for harmony. Like a crystal struck by a hammer, the psyche may—though not always—break along its natural faultlines; therefore, when Christine Beauchamp's ego-self fell asleep, her unbridled id wandered off to become the Imp, while her judgmental superego became the Saint. In my own case, the "I" who operated outside of my father's bedroom identified with an achieving head, while the birth child was left with an abused body and a grieving heart.

But just as the psyche has its natural divisions, so does the brain. As already described, because of its evolutionary development, the human brain is actually three-in-one: reptilian, mammalian and *Homo sapiens sapiens*, roughly corresponding to functions of instinct, emotion and reason. Even more conspicuous is the vertical cleft, dividing the cerebral cortex into two hemispheres. As early as the fifth century B.C., Hippocrates had deduced that the right brain controlled the left side of the body and vice versa, with information routinely exchanged over a neural pathway called the corpus callosum. Because both halves looked alike, scientists assumed they functioned alike. However, after it was learned that for most people speech was controlled exclusively by the left hemisphere, Nobel laureate Roger Sperry began studying persons whose corpora callosa were severed to see how each hemisphere functioned in isolation.

What Sperry and others discovered, during experiments in the sixties and seventies, was that the two sides of the human brain typically operate in fundamentally different ways, often with conflicting perceptions and separate memory banks. Whereas the left hemisphere thinks in words, the non-verbal right thinks in images; whereas the left brain excels in analysis and linear logic, the right is a whiz at separating foreground from background, recognizing shapes and noting patterns in a welter of details. In communicating with another person, the left brain reacts to the person's words while the right brain reads body language and facial expressions, sometimes coming to different evaluations. With the corpus callosum intact, the two brains cooperate to produce a more or less integrated personality. With the corpus callosum severed, each brain is forced to cope in isolation.

In a typical experiment, a split-brain subject stared at a spot in the center of a screen while the picture of an apple was flashed onto the screen's left side. Since he could see the apple only with his right hemisphere while his verbal ability was exclusively in the left, he could not name what he saw; however, his left hand was able to select the apple from a group of objects, indicating that his right brain understood its shape. When the apple appeared on the right screen, the subject named the apple but couldn't recognize one by shape among other objects.

Similarly, when blindfolded and presented with scissors to his left hand, the split-brain subject indicated by making cutting motions that he knew through shape what scissors were for; however, his isolated left brain told the tester, "I'd use that to light a cigarette." When a split-brain subject was shown a split screen with a dollar sign on the left and a question mark on the right, then was asked to draw what he saw using his left hand, he drew the dollar sign but insisted that he had drawn a question mark.

If the left brain is damaged, personality changes are often drastic, including loss of speech. Damage to the right brain produces changes less obvious but more bizarre. Though the ability to verbalize is unimpaired, people operating only out of the left brain don't understand the metaphoric use of language, so that the question "How do you feel?" may elicit the humorless response, "With my hands." When shown a calendar they will understand the word "October" but may not be able to deduce the concept of "autumn" from the detail of colored leaves and pumpkins. They may not be able to recognize a friend who has shaved a mustache because they can't recognize the whole face amongst changed details. And because they no longer identify with their own left side, they may fail to shave that half of the face or forget to wear a left glove.

Yet researchers discovered another information system that continued to operate even after neural connections between the two hemispheres had been severed. When a subject's mute right brain was shown emotionally stimulating pictures, the subject experienced eroticism, or anxiety, or serenity, or horror, without knowing what aroused these feelings. Apparently, emotion could transport, either telepathically or in some other unknown way, even though verbal and visual information could not. In other words, though the bridge was out, carrier pigeons were still flying.

Because of this apparent ability of the right brain to influence the left emotionally in the absence of conscious information, some researchers have theorized that the unconscious may be located in the right hemisphere. Although this is a minority view, personal evidence suggests to me that the part of my own personality which knew of the incest with my father operated predominantly out of my right hemisphere, matching psychic division with a neurologic one. At least, whenever "she" attempted to communicate with "me" it was with right-brain language: the visual imagery of dreams, coded metaphors that appeared in my writing, and paranormal phenomena, only grudgingly accepted by my literal left brain. She had also leaked powerful emotions to the conscious me, devoid of verbal information, so that all my life "I" had been motivated by feelings that belonged to the memory bank, history and experience of "someone else." Again, though the drawbridge was raised, the wounded and bleeding carrier pigeons had kept flying.

Whereas divisions in multiple and split-brain people may be extreme, these splits operate to some extent in everyone, giving the human personality its great flexibility. Good mental health is not so much the elimination of divisions as it is the establishment of harmony between them. At the very least, multiple personality demonstrates the innate capacity of the human mind, when faced with the gravest of dangers, to invent a creative solution. Multiple personality also demonstrates the independence of mind over brain. That a person who wants desperately to be someone else can persuade neurons to produce the brainwaves of another personality, and eyeballs to produce the vision of another personality, and skin to react with the allergies of another personality, makes a mockery of the definition of mind as merely the brain's byproduct. Apparently, the mind can control brain tissue, even mold it to its wishes. Yet, with multiple personality, one still must ask: *Whose* mind? What part of the psyche orchestrates the whole? If the separate personalities are like rabbits conjured out of a magician's hat, what does the hat itself represent?

In the late nineteenth century, hypnotists discovered the existence of a caretaker personality beyond the waking and hypnotized selves. In a typical experiment, psychologist Alfred Binet falsely persuaded a trance subject that the room they shared was without furniture; Binet then planted the post-hypnotic suggestion that on awakening the subject would continue to believe himself in an empty room.

After coming out of a trance, the subject was instructed to cross the room; he did so, by maneuvering around all the furniture.

When asked why he had not traveled in a straight line, the subject produced lame excuses that did not acknowledge the presence of furniture. Who was the mysterious perceiver, inside the subject, who saw the furniture, directed the body around it, but kept the secret from both his waking and hypnotized selves? As Binet confessed: "I for one am completely in the dark."

Multiple personality also suggests the existence of a hidden observer. After a childhood of divided consciousness, I emerged as an adult with a fortunate and secure life. However, some part of me chose not to allow the rest of me to live in peace. At the very times when I should have been most content, despair would well up from that place in my psyche where secrets were still hidden. In retrospect, I see that all of my major adult decisions were aimed at healing the split inside myself—a split "I" did not know existed. Increasingly, I appeared to be working willfully, on the conscious level, against my own happiness, but "I" had no choice. A decision had been taken on a deeper level of self that knew everything, forcing the conscious "me" to dig through psychic block after psychic block to the buried child I had abandoned. Why such compulsion? Why not let sleeping dolls lie? Why was it more important for me to learn the truth of my past than to enjoy my present? What, or who, was driving me? Was it Jung's transcendent Self that is more than the sum of the psyche's parts? Was it the part of the psyche that Western religions call the soul? Was it the Hindu *atman*?

To echo Binet: "I for one am completely in the dark."

THE PSYCHIC SELF

DECEMBER 1983

When I tell my sister about my incestuous relationship with our father, she exclaims: "I always felt something strange was going on!" Her next words are more enigmatic: "Remember your convulsions? You used to fall on the ground, screaming and choking and vomiting, unable to catch your breath. I was supposed to run and get Mother before you turned blue."

Although these "fits" belong to that shadowy preschool world before my memories begin, my sister has referred to them over the years with excitement and indignation; apparently, they made quite an impression on her. According to family legend, they were temper tantrums in which I alternately screamed, held my breath and banged my heels to get my own way. However, some tell-tale sexual aura must have lingered, causing my sister to pluck these scenes, and only these scenes, from dusty obscurity to associate them with incest.

Now that she has mentioned them, I find this connection a provocative one, since convulsions also marked the return of my hidden memories. Usually I would awaken in the ebbtide of turbulent dreams, heart thumping, limbs thrashing, alternately shivering and sweating. This was a sign that another hunk of memory had dislodged itself from the reef on which my childhood had shipwrecked, and was surfacing.

As I now recall, my childhood fits were terrifying, involuntary attacks during which I struggled for breath as I submerged myself in unconsciousness: then I was trying to forget. My adult ones reversed this process: they were voluntary, even welcome events because of their rich harvest of fossilized memories cast up like sea-shells by a powerful, all-knowing tide. Out of this flotsam and jetsam I was reforging an identity.

Since mind and brain are, at the very least, lifetime partners, I began to wonder how my divided personality might have affected, or been affected by, my brain's neural wiring. Because my two selves seemed to share my "fits," that suggested a place to begin.

In 1870, the French doctor Jean-Martin Charcot diagnosed hysterical convulsions, for which no organic cause could be found, as being linked in some undefined way to the genital system. Two decades later, Freud formulated what he called his seduction theory, tracing all hysterical symptoms, including hysterical fits, to the trauma of sexual abuse before age eight. However, Freud later refused to believe that incest could be as rampant throughout middle-class European society as his clinical findings indicated, causing him to recant his seduction theory in favor of his now-infamous Oedipus complex. This held that the infantile sexual abuse, which had been so persistently reported by his largely female clientele, was not real but imagined; in other words, it wasn't parents who lusted in reality after their children, but children who lusted in fantasy after their parents. Through this reversal,

Freud realigned his thinking with the medical prejudice of his day: that hysterical seizures were attributable to erotic cravings.

After treating shellshocked soldiers during World War I, Harvard psychologist William McDougall reinforced Freud's *earlier* findings by tracing hysterical seizures to real rather than to fantasized events: in the case of his soldiers, it was to the trauma of battle. Without warning, a shellshocked soldier's repressed horror might break through its amnesia barrier, causing him to fall writhing to the ground in a replay of his battlefield experiences.

In *The Primal Scream*, Arthur Janov also connected seizures to actual traumas, often sexual: "Clearly one blocked feeling in one's life does not produce the epileptic syndrome. . . . But when years of repressing feelings are involved, one must conclude that there is an accumulation of tension beyond the capacity of the organism to withstand it." And again: "With a large trauma, like rape by the father, there may be great areas of memory missing, like a couple of years. . . . The memory is stored with the pain and is restored by feeling the pain."

Similarly, at a 1987 Toronto conference on multiple personality disorder, Frank Putnam cited a folkloric study linking epileptic seizures with incest in society after society throughout the ages and around the world. He hypothesized a link between incest and certain kinds of seizures of the temporal lobes—a part of the mammal brain associated with emotion and memory, which is especially prone to convulsions.

Though the above evidence was mixed in texture, flavor and color, like a bag of licorice all-sorts, I felt it indicated that my childhood fits were connected with sexual abuse. Curiously, crosscultural folklore also persistently connects such fits with paranormal experience. In ancient Greece, epilepsy was believed to bestow the gift of prophecy, which was why it was called the sacred disease. The revered Delphic priestesses issued their forecasts while in a state of trance brought on by fits both self-induced and spontaneous. This was also true of many shamans: drumming, dancing and hallucinogens induced altered states, often initiated by convulsions. The early Christian mystics were notably seizure-prone: St. Paul was hysterically blinded during a fit in which he perceived himself as having been struck down by God's lightning;

St. Catherine of Siena had convulsions during which she reportedly radiated light and fragrance; St. Joseph of Copertino, a simple-minded monk of the early seventeenth century, had fits of such intense ecstasy that, according to crowds of eye witnesses, he flew.

The poltergeist, or noisy ghost, phenomenon, in which loud rappings are heard and objects seen to zap about without known physical cause, has also been linked to persons with histories of seizures. The biography of Mary Baker Eddy, founder of Christian Science, combined hysterical fits, poltergeist activity, religious fervor, mediumship and psychic healing. Similarly, fits and paranormal activity are characteristic of many cases of multiple personality. Mary Reynolds underwent seizures for more than a year before her first personality switch. Though Christine Sizemore, on whom the movie *Three Faces of Eve* was loosely based, suffered migraine headaches rather than fits, she sometimes had striking paranormal experiences. On one occasion, when she persuaded her husband to stay home from work because she feared he would be electrocuted, the man who subbed for him suffered that fate. The Beauchamp Saint saw visions of the Madonna, while the Beauchamp Imp sometimes claimed to be a possessing demon rather than an ordinary personality.

Apparently, as a young child I used to point out shapes in the tea leaves as my maternal grandmother told fortunes, causing her to remark: "Sylvia is like me. She knows things. She has the gift." Was this the ability, referred to by the Voice that promised "Your psychic powers will be returned to you"? Was this a talent, inherited by me, that split off when "I" split from my birth personality?

In a modern study of 120 accounts of reincarnational experiences, San Diego psychologist Dr. Frederick Lenz noted that all were initiated by sensory phenomena similar to that signaling epileptic seizures—ringing in the ears, flashing lights, vibrations. Some involved actual temporal lobe seizures. More usually, his clients experienced vivid hallucinations of past lives at the point where an epileptic would have a seizure.

Other sensory effects, often accompanying both paranormal experience and the onset of epilepsy, include tingling, dizziness, goosebumps, shivers, a sense of unreality and auditory hallucinations, such as the hearing of bells, a gong or the voice of God; these effects are especially characteristic of seizures of the right temporal lobe.

In 1980, psychobiologist A. Mandell linked temporal lobe epilepsy to ecstatic religious experiences. Similarly, in a 1983 study, M. Persinger found a correlation between peak experiences during meditation and activity in the temporal lobes; in a 1984 study of four hundred college students, he also found a strong connection between what he judged to be the "temporal lobe function" and reports of paranormal experience. Other medical studies have connected the temporal lobes with high susceptibility to hypnosis and the ability to dissociate.

When neuropsychiatrist Dr. P. Fenwick studied the brain-waves of psychics, he discovered a high proportion had anomalous behavior in their right temporal lobes. Some were epileptics, while others had discovered their psychic talents after receiving blows to the head. Edgar Cayce was typical of the latter. After being struck by a baseball at age fifteen, he underwent a series of seizures that ended in a coma. Then, while unconscious, the "sleeping" boy told his parents precisely how to poultice his wound. Years later, this would be viewed as Cayce's first reading, though at the time it was regarded as an aberration best forgotten.

In 1943, a Dutch housepainter named Peter Hurkos struck his head after falling from a ladder and was rushed to hospital. As he shook hands with another patient on his release, Hurkos was startled to hear the man's voice in his head stating the location of a meeting of the Dutch underground, scheduled for that afternoon. Because Hurkos belonged to the resistance, he knew the man did not, leading him to suspect the patient might be a spy. He therefore alerted Dutch underground leaders, who canceled their meeting at the Amsterdam cafe, which Nazi soldiers had already surrounded.

Hurkos went on to become a psychic detective who, in one of his most famous cases, described the murderer of a Miami taxi driver as a man with a tatooed arm and a left-leg limp, perhaps a sailor who had killed before. After searching waterfront bars, police came up with "Lefty"—a tatooed man with a limp who confessed to the murder of the cab driver and one other person.

The association of paranormal events with blows to the head or seizures has allowed doctors and skeptics to dismiss the events themselves as symptoms of disease. This is like dismissing the art of Van Gogh as a symptom of *dementia praecox* or the writings of

Virginia Woolf as a manifestation of manic-depression. More insidiously, some doctors employ such expressions as "temporal lobe epileptic personality" to discredit much of what the epileptic does and says as a symptom of the disease. In fact, the medical literature goes so far as to define mystic and paranormal experience reported by persons who have never had seizures as ELTLA—Epileptic-Like Temporal Lobe Activity. In this way, they use their medical authority to deny the credibility of others by prelabeling them as sick. A parallel diagnosis would be to describe a teenage girl in the throes of her first crush as suffering from PLRSA—Pregnant-Like Reproductive System Activity; the frequency with which such a young girl would, in the course of her life, become pregnant would verify the "early-warning" diagnosis. Or, even more elegant, why not label birth itself as PDVSA—Pre-Death Vital Signs Activity?

It was just this sort of psychological jabberwocky surrounding our society's view of psychic and mystic experience that caused Jung to exclaim in exasperation: "The gods have become diseases!" For my own part, if dropping a TV set produces more channels, why not watch them?

THE SYMBOLIC SELF

JANUARY 1984

Just as my sister has zeroed in on my childhood fits as having incestuous significance, so I focus on her eyes. When she was about nine her vision had suddenly gone bad, requiring her to wear strong glasses. That more than vision might be involved was suggested by our family album, in which she—a friendly, freckled kid with auburn curls—suddenly converts into a frumpy, frowning child with skinned-back hair, hiding behind gold-rimmed glasses. Even that childhood term we both used for her eyes—"gone bad," suggesting something that had spoiled—seemed provocative.

I broach the subject with my sister as we crunch through snow in the stately farm community where she and her husband brought up their five children. Though she was raised as the good kid and I the bad, we always had the decency not to capitalize on each other's problems. For the most part we stood neutrally on either side of a four-year age gap, separated by an unacknowledged river of pain. Now, on these adult walks during successive Thanksgivings, Christmases and Easters, we come to discover how much we like and love each other. Our strengthening bond is our surprise awareness of how completely our assessment of the past—seen from opposite riverbanks—coincides.

Now I ask her: "Do you remember how your eyes suddenly went bad so you had to wear glasses? Do you think there's a connection between that and the incest in our house? Did you see something you didn't want to see?"

She slowly shakes her head in frustration. "I've tried to remember but I can't. All I can see in my mind's eye is that closed bedroom door with you behind it. I was jealous. I felt left out." A rueful smile plays over her face, whipped by January wind into a ruddy glow. "I'll tell you what I thought happened to my eyes. I was playing hide-and-seek one summer with a gang at Gage Park when one of the boys touched my breasts. In the fall, when I couldn't see, I thought it was a punishment."

My sister's sad little story, connecting her poor vision with sexual guilt, supported what I instinctively felt: that the incest in our family had affected her like a biblical mote in the mind's eye. What had she seen that she didn't want to see?

Some psychologists understand that a sudden change in a child's eyesight may reflect stress as readily as optical problems. The vulnerability of our eyes to symbolic use is demonstrated by the frequency with which multiples require different glasses for different personalities, not corresponding to different eyeballs but to different viewpoints. As Billy Milligan changed personalities, his eyelids fluttered uncontrollably; the Beauchamp Saint constantly rubbed her eyes, and the Beauchamp Imp always referred to her coming out as "when I got my eyes open." In a study of 185 multiples, Canadian MPD specialist Dr. Margo Rivera so frequently observed alters change personality by rolling back their eyes that she hypothesized: "The move from one state to another is connected with the optic nerve."

The drama of multiplicity is one that I, too, play out optically inside my own skull: almost alone among my peers, I don't need glasses for reading or long distance because I possess a short-range eye and a long-range one, corresponding to an intellectual personality who analyzes, and a more mystical, intuitive one who sees holistically with a wide-angle lens. Together, they fabricate normal vision in the same way that the separate personalities who once owned them simulated a normal childhood. I also note that when people have lop-sided vision or hearing, their loss usually corresponds to the side of the brain they don't value: the overly skeptical personality generally loses the capabilities of a left eye-ear while the overly credulous, ungrounded person generally loses the capabilities of a right eye-ear.

Even under ordinary conditions, neurologists have noted that persons indicate which side of their brains they are currently using by a shift of the eyes away from that hemisphere to the side of the body they are controling. Thus, the request for a right-handed person to spell a word would cause an eye shift from the verbal left brain toward the right hand, which would then inscribe the word. Pupils automatically expand when they see something appealing but contract to express repulsion. More poetically, the eyes are described as windows of the soul. Lovers stare into each other's eyes as if in search of a deeper, ever-more-privileged look into the other. Eastern religions also emphasize the third eye of the soul, while many tribal societies fear the evil eye as well as the eye of the camera, which they believe will steal their souls.

In Western culture, most of our language of understanding is visual. We "see" solutions, "look" for "flashes" of "insight," value "bright" ideas, search for "enlightenment," avoid "dull" people, turn a "blind eye" to our own faults, "close our eyes" to unpalatable truths and "lose sight" of goals. In English, the connection between "eye" and "I" is strengthened by their common sound. The word *eye* also resembles a face, with *e*'s for eyes and a *y* for a nose. It is a portrait of "I."

Symbolically, we are our eyes.

SPRING 1985

In the midst of what has developed into a twice-yearly visit to psychic Vince Vanlimbeek, he suddenly asks: "Where are you going in two days' time?"

"To my sister's."

"Are you concerned about her?"

"No. Should I be?"

"You're going to find something has changed there. You'll be sad about what's happening."

Two days later, my sister informs me that she has a spot of cancer on her left eye that must be removed by laser surgery. The story, as she relates it, is a cheerful one extolling the wonders of medical science: zap and it's done! Her vision isn't endangered. She won't even be hospitalized.

Despite my concern, the eye operation is a medical miracle as advertised—skill and technology at its twentieth-century best. However, during the next couple of years my sister must again undergo laser surgery on the same eye, this time leaving a bloody scar. Her doctors consider her condition very rare—one in a million. Though psychological factors are not considered, the question continues to buzz through my psyche: What did she see that she didn't want to see?

I again broach the subject with my sister, this time as we are kicking through fall leaves along the bank of a river. "That was an odd story you told me about why your eyes went bad."

She looks at me in surprise. "What story?"

I repeat the incident of the boy touching her breast in the park.

She seems perplexed: "That's not what happened."

Pausing to throw a stick for her black hound, dancing around our feet, she asks: "Remember John at St. Peter's?"

"Of course!" When we were kids he would beckon us with an arthritic claw from his wheelchair outside of St. Peter's Home for Cripples and Incurables (later euphemistically renamed St. Peter's Infirmary). Too polite to refuse, we'd stand twitching with anxiety while he spun his hoary tales.

"One day he touched my breasts. Afterwards when my eyes went bad I thought that was why."

Here was another story connecting loss of vision with sexual guilt—this one closer to home since it involved an older man living in the hospital where our father later died. Peculiarly, my sister doesn't seem to recall the first story. I attribute this to two frightening seizures she has suffered over the past ten years, diagnosed as temporal lobe epilepsy, physical cause as yet unknown, leaving her memory slightly impaired.

I ask: "Do you remember the last time we talked about your eyes?"

"Yes . . . You asked if I'd seen something I didn't want to see. That made quite an impression on me because a funny thing happened afterwards. When I went to my eye doctor expecting to have my prescription strengthened, he weakened it instead. For the first time in my life, my eyes had improved."

"What about your epileptic seizures? Do you think there might be some link between those and my childhood fits?"

Again the wry smile. "All I know for sure is that it's dangerous for me to do the laundry!"

That cryptic remark—recalling that both her seizures had occurred while she was doing laundry—twists in my psyche like a rusty key. From the first return of my incestuous memories I've had a suspicion that something quite horrible, as yet unremembered, happened in the cellar of our father's house. Under hypnosis I've descended those cellar steps several times. Always I was specific about what I as a child was wearing and of everything around me. I was especially obsessed by a door my father had constructed from my mother's fruit cellar into the unfinished dirt cellar. Even today, mystery lingers in my mind over the function of that new door. While cutting down on my mother's preserve shelves, it led to an unlit place in the cellar that was never used.

As I stated under hypnosis: "I can smell the fresh lumber. Though the door leads nowhere, my father is obviously pleased with himself. Shivering, I go through the door. The dirt under my bare feet is silky like dust. I can see my mother's washing machine with the old-fashioned wringer."

Then I block.

Though I had no trouble connecting my childhood fits to my sister's officially diagnosed epilepsy, the medical literature does.

A bioelectrical system of great complexity, the living brain has been described by neurosurgeon Wilder Penfield as vibrating like "a vast symphony orchestra while millions of messages flash back and forth to their target." When an electrical explosion occurs within that system, messages shoot out in every direction, causing limbs to thrash in the haphazard manner that characterizes an epileptic seizure. Medical texts connect these brainstorms to organic causes—infection, injury, tumors, strokes, meningitis and hormonal changes;

they distinguish them from what they describe as hysterical fits, traceable to emotional causes. This distinction is maintained even though both kinds of seizures often occur in the same family.

In "kindling" studies, researchers found they could induce seizures in rats by shocking them with a one-second electric current once a day. Eventually 15 to 20 per cent of the rats began to have spontaneous fits without the electric current; another group had only to see the apparatus to convulse. The younger the animal, the more easily it kindled (literally, ignited); yet no matter how strongly a rat was electrically shocked the first time, it did not have a seizure then. Apparently, it took time and/or repeated torture for the current to change neural cells in some way. In other words, though the spontaneous fits ceased to have an observable organic cause, they shared a common source and a common neurological base with the others. However, if researchers had seen only the spontaneous fits, without knowing of the previous shocks, might they not conclude those fits were hysterical?

According to Wilhelm Reich, sexual stimulation and orgasm create a measurable electrical charge. When this is combined with physical force, emotional trauma and conflicting messages to repress/record, could the shock be strong enough to overheat a child's immature neural system, causing changes deep in the temporal lobes so vital for processing memory and emotions? When the abuse is repeated, are the child's brain cells permanently altered in some way, as with those of kindled rats? When convulsions occur spontaneously, are they mistakenly called hysterical by observers who have failed to consider the process by which an egg turns into a chicken?

Is the neural-neurotic distinction in the diagnosis of epilepsy just another example of the Cartesian divide that yawns through the medical profession, down which patients slide to their deaths?

THE DREAMING SELF

MAY 1989
I am leaving a Detroit TV show on the initial stop of a publicity tour for My Father's House *when I receive the first in a string of nasty phone calls. It is from a niece who tells me that cancer has invaded the*

fleshy tissue around my sister's left eye so that she is now in danger of losing it. With each city stop the news from home worsens. By Atlanta, I learn that the best my sister can hope for is the loss of an eye. An emergency operation is scheduled.

Next time I see Irene she is wearing a gauzy eye bandage but is in good spirits: if losing an eye will give her back her life, she is happy with the barter. Her good eye is firmly focused on the future, especially on her youngest daughter's July wedding.

By now I know six people whose vision has been seriously threatened by disease that is not age-related. Four have something else in common: all are sisters of known or supposed incest victims. I am still brooding about this connection as I return to my Toronto home from the train station. Uncharacteristically, I flip on my TV set as I enter the door. It is tuned to a documentary about artist Elizabeth Layton, a woman who, I discover, was so depressed for thirty years that she took to living in a closet. Part of her self-cure was the compulsive drawing of self-portraits. As the camera plays over these densely knotted, black-and-white whorls, studded with intense green eyes, I find myself automatically diagnosing: sexual abuse. What did she see that she didn't want to see?

As I am castigating myself for tunnel-vision, in which all experience is but a dark projection of my own, the camera switches for the first time to the artist: she is wearing a black eye patch.

The reception for my niece's July wedding is held in my sister's spacious garden, decorated with pink and white streamers and balloons. My sister greets guests from a chaise longue, immobilized by a postoperative blood clot in her left leg. A wheelchair carried her up the aisle of the church. Now she sits in elastic stocking with patched eye, basking in her youngest daughter's happiness, but embarrassed by her own immobility. As the mother of five adopted children, including a set of triplets, she is not used to letting others wait on her.

The following Thanksgiving, my sister meets my train, using a cane and wearing her new eye prosthesis: a painted eyeball with socket, lid and lashes, created from the same fleshy material used in Hallowe'en masks. Though offering perpetual insecurity as to whether its glue will hold, it is well enough established to engender wry self-jokes about the shock of finding her asleep with one eye open.

My dreams over the next few months are full of menace and very vivid, as if some barrier were melting between two realities, as when Alice put her hand to her bedroom mirror and felt it pass through into the Looking-Glass World: "I am running through dark and dangerous streets to my natal home when I see a sinister man with unkempt hair and battered face. He scuttles past, apparently as leery of me as I of him. Giving him wide berth, I run home, then upstairs to my attic bedroom, where I fall asleep on a cot."

A resounding rap at the front door—originating in my dream, but seeming to reverberate in the bedroom where I am now lying. Though it awakens me from sleep, I continue to dream in a hallucinatory state: "My mother—dead for three years—calls up the attic stairs: 'Irene!' Helpless, I watch my sister obediently climb out of the bed beside me, then put on her turquoise mother-of-the-bride dress with black veil."

Now fully awake, I shiver convulsively, feeling the stranger's sharp rap still resonate through my icy bones. I know who he is. I know what he wants. I know his message, and it is a cruel one.

What are dreams, and who is the self that experiences them?

No one knows for sure, though each of us spends about ninety minutes every night in this timeless Daliesque landscape concealed from our conscious eyes like the moon's dark side. Scientists don't even know what sleep is. The assumption that it was rest was undermined when researchers discovered that parts of the brain are busier during sleep than waking. Was this activity just a matter of revving motors and pushing brooms like the cleanup tasks of a maintenance staff, or was something crucial happening?

In 1953, two University of Chicago scientists found that dreaming correlated with rapid eye movements (REMs) beneath their sleeping subjects' closed lids. When they discovered that this period produced its own distinctive brainwaves, they concluded that dreaming was a separate state of consciousness, apart from waking and sleeping. That the REM cycle was controlled by the brain stem suggested it to be a vital function. However, physiologists still could not agree about whether the dreams themselves were significant or if they were just the equivalent of a verbal snore.

Historically, dreams have been attributed to three sources: body, mind and spirit. Today, each of these explanations still possesses both expert and popular support.

Tribal societies revered dreams as communication with the spirit world. Since they believed the soul left the body during sleep to become a privileged wanderer in the upper and lower realms, dreams were thought to possess a greater reality than waking experience. The dreamer was not only responsible for what he/she did in his own dreams but what he did in someone else's dreams. Dreams offered personal guidance from the gods, while those of a chief or priest directed the life of the tribe.

Although biblical prophets also accepted dreams as oracles from God, the medieval Church discouraged them as a threat to its authority: if everyone could tune in to God every night on a personal hot-line, what need for papal intercession? Increasingly, dreams were interpreted as the work of the Devil—an emphasis that, combined with the Church's demand for chastity, ensured dreams would indeed be erotic, demonic and torturing.

Aristotle declared all dreams to originate with the body: they were random images created by the organism's subtle movements as it rehearsed and reviewed daytime activity. Similarly, a draft in a sleeper's bedroom might swirl through a dream as a polar wind. Elaborating on this theory, neurophysiologist Jonathan Winson of New York has suggested that the nocturnal brain, free of sensory bombardment, processes events for long-term memory. Though Winson believes dream images are just an accidental byproduct of this downtime activity, he concedes that the mind may mold them into meaningful stories that guide conscious behavior. However, radicals of this school dismiss all dreams as gibberish—the refuse of the rational mind.

Greek philosopher Heraclitus anticipated contemporary psychology when he opined that dreams sprang not from body or spirit but from a person's own psyche. Plato similarly foreshadowed Freud's belief that dreams were the result of repressed instinctual desires when he stated: "In all of us, even in good men, there is a lawless wild-beast nature, which peers out in sleep." The Koran also decoded dreams according to the dreamer's psyche and lifestyle; however, so dependent on their guidance did some followers become that Mohammed eventually forbade dream interpretation.

Though Freud did not discover the unconscious any more than Columbus discovered America, he did convince European society that these nocturnal fantasies—prohibited by the Christian Church, then dismissed by science—might be worth another look. According to his theory, dreams are the royal road to the unconscious. All are triggered by the previous day's events, and all are the expression of an infantile id wish plus the resistance to that wish. It is this censorship that accounts for the dream's obscurity. The wish, usually sexual, is symbolically disguised to hide its shameful content, resulting in dense and pithy layers of meaning, difficult to penetrate. Thus, dreams are guardians of sleep: without their sublimation, the intensity of our guilty, repressed desires would awaken us.

Like Freud, Jung believed dreams to be a nightly letter from the unconscious to the conscious self. However, he judged Freud's sexual interpretations far too pessimistic and narrow. Instead of hiding shameful material, Jung believed dreams highlighted repressed information that it was dangerous to continue to ignore. By providing insight into the true state of the psyche, dreams compensated and balanced the conscious state. They also increased conscious choice by providing a wider and deeper frame of reference.

According to Jung, the obscurity of dream symbols resulted only from our failure to understand them in all their nuances. To interpret the image of "gun" as a concealment for "penis," in the manner of Freud, debased the symbol. Though "gun," in context, might carry some of the significance of "penis," the image contained other relevant meanings and was not a simple equivalent. As stated in the Talmud: "The dream provides its own interpretation." A gun is a gun just as a rose is a rose. Similarly, to take an image out of context alters both the image and its context, in the same way that cutting a sunflower from Van Gogh's painting would alter both the flower and the painting.

While Freud labeled the contents of the unconscious as uncivilized, troublesome and nasty, Jung respected the instinctive inner self as having a wisdom and integrity equal to the conscious self. Not only do dream images draw experience from the outer world into our inner one but they create a two-way bridge over which we project personal meaning onto outer events. Therefore, dreams are a critical part of our psyche's self-regulating healing system, corresponding to the body's immune system.

Whereas "small dreams" with their familiar, banal content come from our immediate personal history, "big dreams," full of universal images, are "messages from the gods"—what Jung described as numinous, from the Latin *numen* for spirit or deity. These universal images, or archetypes, appear spontaneously in our dreams, whether or not we know their meaning, providing each of us with a visual language, intuitively understood from culture to culture, by which we can communicate with the world of spirit. They may include such personifications as the Wise Old Man, or the Great Mother, or the Magician, or the Magical Child, or more general symbols such as the cat (as the instinctive self) or the bird (as the intuitive self) or the fish (as the spiritual self). As distillations of human thought, feeling and behavior, archetypes provide signposts and reassurance during times of change or crisis, and enhance ordinary existence with transcendental meaning.

Dream interpretation based on the Freudian system is concerned with the relationship of the individual to society, but dream interpretation based on the Jungian system is ultimately concerned with the relationship of the self to the spirit world, where Jung believed the true key to identity lay. To believe otherwise is to cast one's lot with the drunk who searched for his house key under the streetlight—not because that was where he dropped it, but because that was where the light was shining.

That the dream world is a place of heightened creativity is attested to by artists in every field. Composer Richard Wagner, artist Paul Klee, poet William Blake, all have paid special homage to its inspiration. Samuel Coleridge seized his poem *Kubla Khan* fully developed from that womb, just as Robert Louis Stevenson conceived *The Strange Case of Dr. Jekyll and Mr. Hyde* there. Goethe claimed that his finest poems were written in a state of somnabulism. Mozart described his musical compositions as dreams that came to him independent of his will. Descartes' philosophy was inspired by three dreams punctuated by claps of thunder. Newton worked out his most complicated mathematical formulas in his sleep. Elias Howe literally dreamed up the sewing machine. German chemist Friedrich August Kekulé credits his discovery of the ring-like structure of the benzene molecule to his dream of a snake biting its tail. Physiologist Otto Loewi dreamed, but forgot, an experiment he knew would demonstrate the chemical mediation of nerve impulses; after successfully instructing himself to redream the solution, he won a 1938 Nobel prize. Even golfer Jack Nicklaus claimed to have learned in a dream how to improve his game by ten strokes.

In recent years, dream researchers have discovered that the period just before sleep and just after waking, when the mind straddles both states, is especially conducive to creative and paranormal insight. This is the alpha-theta state that Eastern yogis and Zen masters have learned to prolong. Western researchers label this wake-sleep period the hypnogagia state, and describe dreams that occur there as lucid.

In my own experience, lucid dreams usually happen on first awakening. Sometimes they are preceded by a loud knock, or a gong, or a bell, or some other noise that originates in the dream but jars me into hallucinatory alertness. Sometimes I dream that I have awakened, only to continue to dream in this heightened state. Always such dreams are characterized by their great psychic energy and their authority—one of Jung's "big dreams."

My dream of the sinister stranger, whose rap yanked me like a carrot from dark soil into sunlight, was typical of this special genre. Its shadowy, natal setting indicated that I, as the dreamer, was venturing into deeply repressed childhood territory. An event was to occur that involved my entire family, living and dead—me, my sister, my mother and my father, represented by the menacing stranger. Some door was to open, involving my father—perhaps some dark truth to be revealed. The key player would not be me but my sister, now preparing herself for transformation. She was to be the bride, the bride of the stranger who was not a stranger: the fatal bridegroom.

JANUARY 1990
After a Christmas in which everyone makes a special effort, I receive another nasty phone call: though my sister seemed healthy and happy over the holiday, brain scans reveal she now has several brain

tumors, inoperable and malignant. She is nauseated and in severe pain. No one expects her to live more than a couple of weeks.

When I ask Vince how long she has, he replies oracularly: "She will get through her first winter." Then: "She's letting herself go emotionally. Are you aware of that?"

"Not particularly. Except, of course, that she's dying."

"You will know."

My sister undergoes cobalt treatments, which leave her remarkably improved. Exhausted yet cheerful, she lies on her sofa, her now-bald scalp wrapped in a scarf, planning a trip to Wales. And why not? She has never smoked, doesn't drink, watches her diet and exercises regularly; both our parents lived into their eighties; other people have recovered. Why not her?

As we work a jigsaw puzzle—a family obsession, dating from childhood—my sister confides in an embarrassed, overly casual tone: "Oh . . . I had a strange dream. I guess you'd call it a nightmare."

"What about?"

"I was a child, lying in bed. . . . Someone was in bed with me—a man. I had to clench my jaw or blood would come spouting out of my mouth. I kept thinking: the bad seed! the bad seed! I also had to keep my legs tightly closed or blood would come hemorrhaging out of my vagina. Or maybe I was afraid of getting the bad seed inside me. It's very confused. . . . A black rod was also in bed, trying to get inside me. I had to keep my vagina away from it, even to the point of stuffing it with something. Then the rod broke, or went limp. The bed was all covered with seeds or black kisses. I woke up drenched in sweat. I couldn't stop shaking and sobbing."

We are still working the jigsaw—yellow on yellow, blue on blue—pretending this is an ordinary conversation. "What do you think it means?"

"I don't know," She fixes me with her one good eye. "That Father got me, too!"

"When did you have that dream?"

"The night I learned I had the brain tumors. It bothered me for quite a few hours, but when it was over I felt something had been resolved."

I return home feeling churned up and very angry. That my sister's tumors are connected to her seizures and her seizures to my fits and both to incest, I have no medical proof and no doubt: people don't fool themselves about such things when looking into the eye of death.

Unable to sleep, I flip through my sporadically kept dream file. On May 24, 1989, the night of my sister's eye operation, I read: "My sister and I are in bed with a man. Something about our fear of wetting the bed. We lie with our mouths tightly closed and our legs tightly crossed. The urine-soaked mattress is slimy with eyeless, gray worms. The bad seed! the bad seed!"

I am freaked by the repetition of that tell-tale phrase. I find it once more in the report of a hypnotic session in which I attempted yet another time to remember what happened in the basement of our natal home. "My father is calling me. I skip down the stairs, aggressive and full of self-hate, like Patty McCormack in The Bad Seed. I feel as if I possess some kind of psychic power, which I am struggling to contain. I don't dare unleash this power, catalyzed by rage, because it would be lethal. I am absorbing the evil in the house. Though it makes me feel evil, I know I am protecting the house and everyone in it, like a lightning rod. My father calls again. . . ."

I am violently ill for the rest of the night. By the time I finish retching, I have remembered what happened in the basement: my father sits on a cream-colored kitchen chair, trimmed with green, in sight of my mother's washing machine. His legs are splayed, his fly is unbuttoned. Beside him is his newly constructed door—an emergency exit into the fruit cellar.

I recall, with rage and disgust, my sister's words: "All I know for sure is that it's dangerous for me to do the laundry!"

THE DYING SELF

At the core of human existence is the restless, never-ending search for greater meaning. For our species, this journey probably began some eighty thousand years ago when Neanderthal tribes interred their dead with food and weapons, suggesting belief in an afterlife. This faith in "something more" reached an apogee around 3000 B.C. in the Sumerian city of Ur, when a hundred members of the royal court escorted their king's corpse into his tomb, quaffed poison, then curled in the fetal position in apparent expectation of group resurrection.

Such ceremonies are the reflection of an inner need for meaning, which I believe to be as much a part of each of us as our heartbeat. At its most basic, this drive is demonstrated by split-brain patients who are forced to deal with a divided reality. When one subject was instructed through his right brain to draw the picture of a fire and through his left brain to draw a house, he drew a building over crossroads, resembling the local firehall. When asked what he had drawn, his verbal left-brain—unaware of the "fire" instruction—changed the crossroads into tree branches so he could rationalize: "I've drawn a treehouse."

Similarly, a highly intelligent woman, who was hospitalized because of a brain lesion that interfered with her sense of place, believed herself to be in her own bedroom. When a doctor challenged her by pointing to the elevators and asking what they were, she replied: "Elevators. Do you know what it cost me to have those put in my house?"

What these poignant anecdotes demonstrate is the determination with which even grossly brain-impaired people struggle to make sense of their moment-to-moment behavior. As neuroscientist Michael Gazzaniga of Cornell University stated in *The Social Brain*, "The presence of beliefs in our species results from the way the human brain is constructed." To lack that meaningful connection is to cease to feel like a person.

At no time are we humans passive recorders of sensory data; instead, we are its interpreters. When our eyes, in accordance with the science of optics, present us with an upside-down image of a rose, we automatically invert it to harmonize our visual perception with our sensation of touch. Perhaps the smell of the rose will remind us of the sachet that a grandmother used to scent her handkerchiefs, embuing present experience with past memory. Perhaps the velvety petals will bring to mind a baby's skin or a favorite blouse. Perhaps in handling the rose we will prick a finger, reminding us of the story of Sleeping Beauty, or of Jesus and the Crown of Thorns, or simply of the maxim that beauty sometimes harbors treachery. If an artist is painting nearby, we are likely to recognize, in his slashes of color on canvas, the image of the rose against a backdrop. We are certain to recognize it in a photograph, in a reflection, even in a black-and-white outline.

If a canary should alight on the rosebush and begin to sing, we hear its separate notes as a melody. Their beauty may thrill us, deepening perceptual experience with emotion. If the artist whistles the same notes in a different key, we will recognize the melody even though none of the tones are the same. Perhaps we may even jot down their sequence, using musical symbols that we will later elaborate into a composition for flute.

As we leave the garden, we may not even be aware that our unconscious mind has also found solace in the rose as a universal symbol of the integrated self, or the garden as a symbol of human consciousness, created by subduing and enclosing nature. Perhaps this unconscious awareness may inspire our musical composition as it has the artist's painting. Yet what, in reality, was this walk in the garden? According to the latest theories of quantum physicists, just our meaningful interpretation of light, energy fields and vibrations.

It is our species' intuitive grasp of meaning rather than cleverness that separates our minds from artificial intelligence. A famous example of intuition-in-action occurred in the third century B.C., when Archimedes was asked by his patron to find out whether a certain lump of gold had been adulterated with silver. Archimedes knew he could answer that question by weight, if only he could determine the metal's volume. As he was lowering himself into his bath, the water level rose, as always; however, this time it caused Archimedes to leap from his tub and run naked through the streets of Syracuse shouting: "*Eureka!*"—"I have found it!" What Archimedes had discovered was that an object displaces its volume in water—an insight now known as Archimedes' Law.

By contrast, computers—no matter how fast or how informed—are manipulators of symbols according to rules, without any grasp of their inner meaning. Even if a machine could speak English or Chinese fluently, it would not understand that it was speaking a language as opposed to doing algebraic equations: for the machine, symbols are symbols, without inner significance. It is this lack of resonance that makes it impossible for a machine to break its own programming, like a Copernicus or a Newton or an Einstein, to discover a more comprehensive truth so as to create an expanded program for a new generation.

At a point when I was most obsessively engaged in my own subterranean journey into inner awareness, I remember fixing friends with the glittering eye of the Ancient Mariner and telling them that the spiritual imperative of the human species was to make the unconscious conscious: what we can do that no other species can do and, therefore, what we *must* do. Many years later, I was surprised to find this view expressed by such diverse people as Richard Wagner, Carl Jung and Edgar Cayce. In Jung's estimate, every human is a unique experiment in the process of consciousness, carrying the obligation to develop that potential. Cayce was even more prescriptive: "Mind is the builder. Knowledge not lived is sin."

Yet most of us most of the time are like subatomic particles orbiting around a nucleus: we find the path requiring the least energy and stabilize there. That becomes our steady state—where we park ourselves, going around and around in semiconsciousness till some event jolts us from our lethargy. Then, still like the particle, we seek a new orbit, reflecting our new energy state, where we stabilize till another crisis knocks us up or down. This crisis may be the birth of a child, or a new love, or a career change; however, in mid-life it is just as likely to be a life-threatening one. Overnight we or a loved one may be shaken from our sleep and set upon an intensified journey leading to premature death. Yet, often on this foreshortened journey, much spiritual growth takes place. Even in the midst of physical suffering and humiliation, the afflicted person may seem more alive, even happier, than ever before. What is happening here? Clearly something meaningful, but what transformation is worth the price of death?

We as a species seem to have been created as vessels of consciousness. Apparently, the deeper, spiritual journey is not requested of us but demanded, with the stakes being higher than earthly happiness and perhaps even life and death. Is death, as religions have always claimed, just another state of consciousness, as sleep is to wakefulness? That view is a natural and rational one in cultures that believe in the priority of psyche over matter. In Western society, where our "common sense" has been forged in a smelter rather than in a desert or on a mountain peak, such acceptance requires a blind leap of faith. However, in the world being birthed by modern physics, logic suggests that death may prove to be illusory: if energy underlies both matter and psyche, what happens to that energy on dissoluton of the matter-psyche union?

Materialists reject the spiritual interpretation because it can't be proven. What they usually mean is that it can't be proven within a materialistic framework and, like the machines they claim all living organisms to be, they can't break their programming in the interest of greater understanding. However, since the human mind can function only through meaning, the belief that life is meaningless reflects a consciousness as divided as the brain that has been surgically severed: literally, its left half doesn't know what its right is doing. As philosopher Alfred North Whitehead once wryly stated: "Scientists who spend their life with the purpose of proving that it is purposeless constitute an interesting field of study."

For self-consistency, such a skeptic would have to experience a flower garden as only vibrations and energy fields. Our brain creates meaning. That's what it does. To draw an arbitrary line between materialistic and non-materialistic meaning is to swallow a horse while choking on the horn that turns it into a unicorn. The honest skeptic is the one who doubts not only the unicorn but the horse as well: the material world as well as the spiritual one. That is a logical position, though a difficult one emotionally. Either to be a Platonist or an Aristotelean is to enter into a belief system, but the Platonist acknowledges that belief as a premise. The dyed-in-the-wool materialist usually insists he has no premise: what elephant?

MARCH 1990

Two days before her oldest daughter's wedding, my sister suffers a relapse. Though nauseated and in pain, she insists on attending the service. Her husband and I dress her, bald and one-eyed, moon-faced and smiling, like an ancient buddha instead of my fifty-nine-year-old sister.

She has passed into the next, more virulent stage of her illness. In hospital, friends and family visit in shifts. She has already outlived her doctors' most optimistic predictions, yet her determination combines with excellent care and previous good health to establish another plateau. Again, she is able to return home. Though forced to cancel the trip to Wales, she is now planning one to Newfoundland, for which she has brochures. Our walks are reinstated as a single, slow limp around one block.

My sister has told no one else about her nightmare. Since I believe the unresolved past to be the cause of her illness, I see the pathway into the unconscious to be the most likely cure. However, when I point out doorways down into this labyrinth, she doesn't enter them, so neither do I. As always, she opts for the high wide road. She makes no complaint about her illness, and never will. She doesn't mention death, and never will.

My sister suffers another relapse and is readmitted to hospital. She establishes another, weaker plateau and returns home, this time in a hospital bed. Now the visit to Newfoundland has been replaced by plans for a camping trip to Northern Ontario. Meanwhile, she needs a walker to get out into the backyard. Eventually, she will need a hoist even to be lifted out of bed.

My sister returns to the hospital because of pains, which she blames on attempting to crawl up the stairs. Now she must be hand-fed by her husband. Family and friends continue to sit vigil. Since she placed no value on the time she gave to others, she is amazed to discover how much we cherish our time with her. She never loses her good humor or her smile. She never loses her desire to live. Occasionally, under the influence of death and drugs, she does lose her line of rational thought. She tells me she's too excited to sleep because of the troupe of Balinese dancers next door. She tells me that she is the madam of a brothel. She tells me that she has been speaking to our mother, who sends her love.

In the past eight months, I've watched the landscape through the window of the train to my sister's transmogrify from hard white to dun to confident green. Successive ditches of yellow, pink and purple have rolled like spilled paint through gulleys and across fields, then receded, then rolled again.

This morning, September 14, I note a seasonal change: the foliage is a wet black with splashes of gold and red. Birds rise from cornfields, then sharply wheel. Everything speaks of endings. The hills are veiled.

My sister died in her sleep at 2:30 this morning. I had awakened before three and was lying in bed thinking of her when the phone rang. People do not call at 3:08 with good news.

For a week she lay comatose, hooked between an intravenous machine and a catheter, rehearsing death, her respite grown cruel, while I, like the rest who love her, stand on a trap door, waiting for someone to pull the lever. Now that that lever has been pulled, I remain peculiarly upright, standing calmly on air. It seems that my sister has already slipped like sand through my fingers. Mostly, I mourned her that summer on the wind.

Trains are said to symbolize death: vehicles on a fixed schedule and a fixed track whose drivers are unseen. It was a train whistle through the mountains that marked our father's death. Now, as I debark from this one, I see that the stormy autumnal day has grown darker instead of lighter.

I iron my sister's turquoise dress—the one I ironed for two weddings and now for her cremation, with her ashes to be blown over a forest near her home.

Most people will say my sister died of cancer. They will say that as-yet-unseen tumors caused her seizures then spread throughout her brain, and they will point to a stack of records to support their thesis.

I say that my sister died a biblical death. I say that she died of evil, too many generations old.

THE QUEST FOR THE FOURTH MONKEY

The Universe

COINCIDENCE:

THE SOUND OF
COSMIC LAUGHTER

"'You'll see me there,' said the Cat, and vanished. Alice was not much surprised at this, she was getting so well used to queer things happening."

—Lewis Carroll, *Alice in Wonderland*

MAY 1978

I am being driven to a party by a filmmaker and his historian wife, whom I scarcely know. Also in the car is an East Indian faith healer, imported by them to treat a dying friend.

The morning after the party, I receive a Bell Canada bill, charging me for a phone call to Delhi. As I am about to phone Bell Canada to complain, a ridiculous thought strikes me: I'll bet this is the call the historian made to import the faith healer. Immediately, I dismiss this as absurd. Given the populations of Delhi and Toronto, what are the chances that this particular call would end up on my bill?

The hunch persists. When I look up the historian's phone number, I find it is the same as mine except for the last digit—a zero instead of a nine. Further investigation does confirm that the call on my bill is the one the historian made to arrange the faith healer's visit.

Computerized equipment had quixotically reconnected four people who had been together the night before. Was this a random mistake, or could it have significance?

Though I was just an acquaintance of the dying woman, her husband's first wife was an intimate friend of mine. As the result of an explosive love triangle twenty years before, those three were still locked in acrimony. In the car, while the historian was describing her difficulties in contacting the Indian faith healer, I had been thinking about the first wife, then traveling in India, but had tactfully refrained from mentioning her. The bill for the Indian phone call brought into the open what I had been suppressing: my closeness to the situation through the first wife. It also foreshadowed a real-life role I would soon play: for a brief period before the second wife's death, I would function as a go-between for the three feuding parties. In effect, I would be their psychic switchboard. Thus, the short-circuiting of the bill through me by Bell Canada revealed a connection already present in the unconscious that was to be played out in the near future.

While these ricocheting connections may be difficult for most people to take seriously, the principle involved has blue-ribbon support in philosophy, psychology and subatomic physics.

Carl Jung used the word *synchronicity* to describe a coincidence in time involving events without causal connection but nonetheless linked by meaning. According to him, to ascribe such a happening to chance would violate its most salient feature—its significance. This would be like describing a rainbow without mentioning its color. Jung viewed synchronicities as the byproduct of radical inner change, marking such crises as death, birth, falling in love, psychotherapy and artistic creation. Like lava showers, they revealed the buildup of underground forces destined to erupt; therefore, they were psychic warnings to which everyone should pay strict attention. As he stated in *Synchronicity*: "In most cases they were things which people do not talk about for fear of exposing themselves to thoughtless ridicule. I was amazed to see how many people have had experiences of this kind and how carefully the secret was guarded."

In the Case of the Willful Phone Bill, the synchronicities were generated by the members of the triangle, who were undergoing a dynamic psychological shift because of the fatal illness of one of them. I was an incidental player; yet, binding me psychically to the event was my conviction, without evidence and against the odds, that the call on my bill would prove to be the one made by the historian. What had telegraphed this truth?

While driving to the party, I had related what I thought to be an amusing anecdote about my failed struggle, while in Calcutta the year before, to phone Toronto. After traveling half an hour by rickshaw to a long-distance center, I had found three operators at an antiquated switchboard placing calls for all of that city. Several families had been camped overnight on the floor, awaiting connections for places less than a hundred miles away. Whenever a call did get through, jubilant shouts would break out as if for a winning touchdown. After recounting this story in front of the faith healer, I felt guilty about its tone of smug Western superiority. It was this nagging regret that caused me to suspect, however irrationally, that the charge on my bill was for the historian's call from Canada. My inner ear had caught the unmistakable ripple of cosmic laughter.

In his autobiography, *Memories, Dreams, Reflections,* Jung related how a synchronistic event eroded the resistance of a patient to analysis. While she was reporting a dream about a golden scarab, Jung heard a tapping behind him. Turning, he saw a flying insect knock against his window. When he opened the window, the insect flew in, allowing Jung to catch it in the air. "It was the nearest analogy to a golden scarab that one finds in our latitudes . . . which contrary to its usual habits had evidently felt an urge to get into a dark room at this particular moment." So moved was the woman at this manifestation of her dream scarab, which is an Egyptian symbol of rebirth, that she allowed her own transformation to begin.

It was Jung's respect for psychic magic that triggered his break with the obdurately rational Freud—an event also underlined by synchronicity. While the two men were discussing the paranormal in Freud's Vienna office in 1909, Jung found it increasingly difficult to hold back the sharp retort Freud's airy dismissal of the subject aroused in him. As his diaphragm grew hot like a stove, both men were startled to hear a loud crack in the bookcase beside them.

"There, that is an example of a so-called catalytic exteriorization phenomenon!" exclaimed Jung.

"That's sheer bosh!" shot back Freud.

"It is not. You are mistaken, Herr Professor. And to prove my point, I now predict that in a moment there will be another such loud report!" Immediately, a second explosion occurred in the bookcase. As Jung later stated, "To this day I do not know what gave me this certainty. . . . Freud only stared aghast at me."

It could be argued that Jung's repressed fury created a buildup of psychic energy that found its expression in Freud's thundering bookcase; however, no causal relationship of any sort could have existed between my will and the phone bill, since the bill was in the mail before I'd even met the faith healer. That bill remains as mysterious as a letter delivered from the future, a strangeness enhanced by a psychic postscript: the chance recipient of the phone call in India had been none other than the first wife. As a guest at the residence where the historian phoned to ask for the faith healer's address, she had happened to pick up the receiver; she had even hand-delivered the invitation to the faith healer. Was it my friend's psychic traces, already on the transaction, that caused the bill to short-circuit through me?

JUNE 18, 1983

As I walk through Toronto's Annex neighborhood on my way to the reference library, I brood over the novel I am writing, set in Germany during World War II. It has just occurred to me that I should strengthen its historical spine by incorporating a real-life Nazi leader as a major character. The question remains, who? It is to find that answer that I am going to the library.

As I approach Avenue Road, my thoughts switch to a dream I had the night before, centered on a sinister character named Jerry Halle: Halle spelled with an "e," as my dream took pains to point out. A sudden insight—not Jerry Halle, but the Jerry from Halle! Since I've been researching from the German perspective, I'd forgotten "Jerry" was British slang for German soldier. Now that I've made that connection, I'm also sure "Halle" refers to the German city by that name. I can even guess who "the Jerry from Halle" is: Nazi SS chief Reinhard Heydrich.

Another thought strikes me with the force of revealed truth: "I'll bet Heydrich is a Pisces!" Since I have little interest in astrology, I can think of no rational reason why this matters; however, I also know my dreaming self sometimes passes important messages to me through persons born, like me, under the sign of Pisces (February 19 to March 20). I make a mental note to check this at the library.

I am now striding past The Book Cellar on Yorkville Avenue. Glancing in the window, I see a biography entitled Reinhard Heydrich*—the focal point of a triangle of books in an otherwise empty showcase. Inside, I discover this biography by Günther Deschner is two years old—not the sort to dominate the window of a trendy bookshop. Discounted down to $6.95, even the price is right.*

After purchasing the book, I check the text. Heydrich is, indeed, a Pisces, born on March 9 while I was born on March 8. With this biography so fortuitously in my hands, I have a strong hunch Heydrich is the high-ranking Nazi I need for my novel. In the days that follow, this proves correct. Heydrich will function as the dark foil for the fictional character most resembling myself. He is what Jung would call my Piscean shadow.

How to explain this string of coincidences? Since I had been researching German history, no doubt my intuition that Heydrich was a Pisces came from acquired information, unconsciously stored. However, what can be said about my dreaming of Heydrich the night before I discovered his biography; that I started to think of him more than a block from the bookstore; that his biography—though two years old—dominated the window; that it proved the solution to a vexing creative problem?

Those who reject synchronicity usually argue that, given the multiplicity of events happening every moment, surprise juxtapositions are inevitable. This view is enshrined in the belief that if enough monkeys peck randomly at typewriters for long enough, they will produce the works of Shakespeare. However, when Yale physics professor William R. Bennet, a designer of computer programs, put the monkey thesis to the statistical test, he discovered that if a trillion monkeys were to type ten randomly chosen characters a second, it would take more than a trillion times as long as the Universe has been in existence just to complete the sentence "To be or not to be, that is the question."

Intrigued by Jung's thesis, scientist-historian Arthur Koestler spent a lifetime collecting anecdotes featuring synchronicity. Under the heading "Library Angel," he filed stories similar to my Heydrich one, describing the canniness with which out-of-date or obscure material flows into the hands of needful researchers. Another classification, noted by Koestler and other coincidence-collectors, honors the persistence with which lost property sniffs its way like a bloodhound, across time and continents, to its original owner.

In *Incredible Coincidence*, parapsychologist Alan Vaughan told how actor Anthony Hopkins, after searching all day for the novel *The Girl from Petrovka*, found a copy on his way home—facedown on a bench in London's Leicester station. Because of many hand-written editorial changes, Hopkins mentioned this copy to author George Feifer when they met a year later, in 1973 in Vienna, to make the film. Feifer was astonished. This was an advance copy he'd lost a year before Hopkins found it, and for which he'd offered a reward!

In a similar example, Irving Kupcinet of the Chicago *Sun-Times* checked into London's Savoy Hotel to cover Queen Elizabeth's coronation. On opening a drawer, he found items belonging to a friend—Harry Hannin of the Harlem Globetrotters. Two days later, Kupcinet received a letter from Hannin, then at the Hotel Meurice in Paris: "You'll never believe this, but I've just opened a drawer here and found a tie with your name on it." Kupcinet had stayed in that hotel room a few months earlier.

As Koestler summed up: "Whether one believes that some highly improbable coincidences are manifestation of some unknown principle operating beyond physical causality, or are produced by that immortal monkey at the typewriter, is ultimately a matter of inclination and temperament.... I have found to my surprise that the majority of my acquaintances—among whom scientists predominate—are inclined towards the first alternative, although some are reluctant to admit it, for fear of ridicule, even to themselves."

COINCIDENCE IN WESTERN SOCIETY

JUNE 1990
As a child, I repeatedly dreamed of myself as a character called Sylvia Locke. Since part of my consciousness was, in reality, locked off from the rest by amnesia, this was an appropriate metaphor. However, recently I was surprised to learn that I had a great-aunt named Sylvia Key. She produced two daughters, one of whom was a Sylvia who married a Dr. Locke.

While researching this book, I discover that neurologists use the metaphor of lock and key to describe the process by which chemical transmitters pass information from brain cell to brain cell. If a chemical key is a precise fit for the protein lock of its target cell, then the message is passed on; if it is not, the message is blocked. I also learn that the brain fissure, separating the higher intellectual faculties from the more emotional, more unconscious experiences of the mammal brain, is called the Sylvian fissure. Therefore, the name Sylvia Locke is an apt choice, medically and metaphorically, to describe my amnesia, in which deep emotional truths were psychically severed from my intellectual understanding.

Was all this just coincidence, or did I intuitively latch onto this advanced medical information, also carved in a branch of my family tree?

Early societies lived in a synchronistic world in which eclipses, storms and aberrant animal behavior were routinely interpreted as tribal portents. It was this belief in the harmony of the cosmic and psychic worlds that drenched their days with meaning. Biblical scribes quite naturally linked the birth of Jesus Christ with the appearance of a traveling star in the same way Plutarch, Suetonius and Ovid connected Julius Caesar's assassination with howling dogs, bad auguries and weather disturbances. Shakespeare employed such portents, along with acausal effects like storms, to heighten psychological drama, knowing audiences would make the right gut connection. They still do.

As with most psychic mysteries, Western scientists took the position that synchronicities didn't happen because no one was able to explain how they could. How could names in a family tree correlate to brain structures, or Bell Canada's mistake in long-distance billing correlate to dynamic changes in a love triangle, or an author's need for a character in a story correlate to a store clerk's decision to put an out-of-date biography in a window?

During the seventeenth century, philosopher Gottfried Leibniz intuitively devised a model of the Universe in which all action took place according to the acausal principle Jung would call synchronicity. In Leibniz's Universe, everything both physical and mental was composed of an infinite number on non-material, non-extended, non-temporal units of energy, differing from each other only in the intensity of their charge. Instead of acting upon each other through cause and effect as in Newton's Universe, these "monads" only appeared to interact because the behavior of each correlated with every other, according to a blueprint for the whole contained within each. Leibniz compared this to an orchestra whose members seem to interact because they are playing from the same score.

In such a Universe, the pairing of a star with a savior's birth, or a comet with a ruler's death, was no less rational than the pairing of the moon with the rising tides. All these events occurred as part of a synchronistic, pre-established harmony, which Leibniz attributed to the mind of God.

Though Leibniz's monadic theory struck remarkably close to that of modern subatomic physics, seventeenth-century scientists overwhelmingly rejected it. For the next two hundred years, Newtonian physics, in which every physical effect is always preceded by a physical cause, became the touchstone against which all theories were measured.

In the eighteenth century, skeptic David Hume shocked scientists by demonstrating that Newton's linear causality was not a rule of nature but just a projection of the human mind. As Hume explained, we observe that one event always follows another and so we make a rule that insists it will continue to do so. For example, when one billiard ball strikes a second, we expect the second to move because it has always done so. Then we assume that the first event caused the second. However, that is just an inference based on experience, expectation and the association of ideas, which is projected onto the future.

Although no one could rebut Hume, the success of Newtonian physics in predicting events persuaded most scientists to forget Hume's objections. Only a few continued to interest themselves in synchronistic occurrences outside of linear causality. One was French astronomer Camille Flammarion who, in 1900, included this now-famous incident in his book *The Unknown*. As a boy in Orleans, a certain M. Deschamps was given a piece of plum pudding by a M. de Fortgibu. Ten years later, M. Deschamps attempted to order a second piece in a Paris restaurant but was informed that the pudding had already been claimed—by M. de Fortgibu. Many years later, at a dinner party, M. Deschamps was helping himself to yet a third piece of plum pudding when he thought to remark: "The only thing missing is M. de Fortgibu." Just then, the door burst open and in tottered a now aged M. de Fortgibu, who had come by mistake to the wrong address.

In 1919, Austrian biologist Paul Kammerer proposed an acausal theory to explain all coincidences. In his view, similar objects and events tend to cluster in patterns, the way asteroids drift together in space under the influence of gravity. Like Leibniz, Kammerer believed these coincidences to be the expression of an underlying harmony, as fundamental as gravity. For twenty years, he filled logbooks with banal examples gathered while sitting on park benches or on trams: the number of people who were hatless, who carried bundles, who wore the same colors. Though Einstein reviewed this work as "original and by no means absurd," Kammerer committed suicide in 1926 at age forty-five, hounded to death, in the opinion of biographer Arthur Koestler, for his unorthodox views.

Though influenced by both Kammerer and Leibniz, Jung had no interest in banal coincidences demonstrating a general principle but only in their meaningful and unique manifestations. In his view, evidence for these lay all about, smudged like psychic fingerprints across ordinary events, hinting at their unconscious depths. The more numerous and unusual these clues and the more meaningful their linkage, the more compelling the proof that synchronicity rather than mere chance was responsible.

The reverberating coincidence in Flammarion's anecdote about de Fortgibu and the plum pudding is so beguiling that one longs to know the psychic connection between de Fortgibu and Deschamps. What drama was happening in both lives that made the pudding its psychic repository? What hypnotic connection obliged de Fortgibu to stride through the years for this final date with destiny? Without such information synchronicity sits like an unemployed ghost at a seance—its presence distinctly felt but never materialized.

SEPTEMBER 1987

As I am completing my memoir My Father's House, *I learn of the sudden death of my former husband on January 6. Deeply grieved, I add a postscript to my book, beginning it with his death. Though I am as yet unaware of it, this postscript will end with another death—my mother's, precisely six months later, on July 6.*

My mother lived alone and died unexpectedly, yet her body is found the same afternoon by a neighbor, who notices that my mother's door has been wedged open for several hours by an uncollected parcel. That parcel is an early draft of My Father's House, *accidentally sent to my mother's address—the place referred to in the title.*

The book's publication date is set by my publisher for September 10—a fact that gives me some relief since it is a date of no significance to me and I am becoming spooked by too many coincidences involving names and dates. However, during the first week of September, my publicist phones to announce my book's launch date has been changed. It will now be September 22—both my mother's and my husband's birthdate.

When people of common sense reject synchronicity as too flaky, they usually believe themselves backed by the hard evidence of physics. However, the increasingly weird world that scientists discovered inside the atom has forced them to relinquish linear causality as an absolute principle, along with the existence of an objective world. In place of these two sacred cows, they have acquired two others of a distinctly purple hue: acausal relationships, and a web-like Universe of interconnected energy fields. Both acausality and an interconnected Universe are consistent with the cosmos described by Leibniz; they are also crucial to synchronicity.

As already discussed: atoms are not indivisible pellets of matter, as scientists first thought. Inside each is a nucleus, orbited by electrons, and inside that nucleus are other particles, and inside those particles may be other particles, opening like Chinese boxes into ever smaller universes. The vast emptiness within each atom, amounting to 99.999 per cent of its content, caused the sensory world of solid objects to dissolve under scientific microscopes like the Cheshire cat, leaving only its mocking grin. Yet it wasn't that dissolution that stunned physicists so much as the quixotic behavior of subatomic particles themselves. These quanta possessed a Jekyll-Hyde personality. If physicists set up their apparatus to track a particle, that was what they found; however, if they set up their apparatus to track a wave, that was what they found. How could something be both focused in space as a particle and spread over space as a wave at one and the same time? How could a tree simultaneously be a forest, or a mountain a mountain chain? Did the paradox lie in the nature of the particle/wave that was being observed, or were the observers shaping the events they were trying to objectively record? Physicist Sir William Bragg summed up scientific exasperation when he dryly noted, "Elementary particles seem to be waves on Mondays, Wednesdays and Fridays, and particles on Tuesdays, Thursdays and Saturdays."

An immediate casualty of the wave/particle discovery was the model of the atom as a tiny solar system that could be visualized. Instead of an object with moving parts, it was now known to be a chameleon with an abstract nature beyond the grasp of Newtonian physics, or human perception, or ordinary language, or classical logic. As American physicist Henry Stapp stated, "An elementary particle is not an independently existing unanalyzable entity. It is, in essence, a set of relationships that reach outward to other things." This was the beginning of field theory, in which processes replaced objects, and in which it became as meaningless to speak of the actions of an individual particle as to discuss the exploits of a particular curl of flame in a forest fire.

Physicists also began to ask such questions as: Does a particle/wave exist before it is observed, or is it our observation that brings it into existence as a particle or a wave? This was an update of the old philosophical quandary: Does a flower grow unseen? The Copenhagen Interpretation, forged in 1927 by an influential group of physicists, said, in effect, no it does not exist unperceived. Science is the study not of an objective world but of human experience.

Here was the end of Newtonian science as it had been practiced for two hundred years. Instead of observing some "thing" mounted on a glass slide, the scientist was deemed to be looking into a mirror and seeing some reflection of himself. As American physicist John Wheeler stated, "Nothing is more important about the quantum principle than this, that it destroys the concept of the world as 'sitting out there'. . . . To describe what has happened, one has to cross out that old word 'observer' and put in its place the new word 'participator.' In some strange sense the Universe is a participatory Universe."

Niels Bohr, one of the creators of the Copenhagen Interpretation, summed up its impact: "Those who are not shocked when they first come across quantum theory cannot possibly have understood it."

More shocks were to come. In 1931, Werner Heisenberg won a Nobel prize for demonstrating that individual events in the quantum world are spontaneous and cannot be predicted. As described by his Uncertainty Principle: If a particle is propelled toward a fluorescent screen, it is not possible to calculate where it will strike because you can't establish both a particle's position and its momentum at the same time. This has nothing to do with crude instrumentation or lack of knowledge. Greater accuracy in establishing the position creates less accuracy in establishing the momentum, and vice versa. The two are mutually exclusive, like trying to see directly before and directly behind your head at the same time. However, if very large numbers of particles are propelled toward a fluorescent screen, it is possible to predict a statistical pattern, indicating where all the particles will land according to the laws of probability. In the quantum world, individual causes don't produce individual events: it is the interaction of the whole field, in ways unknown and unknowable, that produces a probable result.

To help understand the implications of this, imagine a table covered with dominoes set on end. Should an experimenter push a domino, it will fall, toppling the one behind, and so on down the line in a curve or on a diagonal so long as one domino strikes the next. This is Newtonian cause and effect set within linear time. If the experimenter had taken the trouble to measure the distance between the dominoes, in advance, the effect would be predictable. Similarly, by afterwards examining the pattern and every physical element that went into its creation, the original placement of the dominoes could be determined.

Now, imagine the same table again set with dominoes. This time, when the experimenter pushes one, another several columns away falls simultaneously, without having been struck or physically interfered with in any way. Dominoes continue to fall at random across the table. When they have finished, no direct causal connection can be determined between the dominoes that fell and those that remain standing. However, the experimenter—an experienced quantum physicist—flashes a paper on which he has accurately predicted the number of dominoes that would fall, though not which ones. He does this over and over with great success. When pressed for an explanation, he is forced to admit that he doesn't know how this particular party trick works; it just does.

That was the situation summed up by Heisenberg's Uncertainty Principle. As he described the mental process leading to his unorthodox conclusions: "I remember discussions with [Niels] Bohr which went through many hours till very late at night and ended almost in despair; and when at the end of the discussion I went alone for a walk in the neighboring park I repeated to myself again and again the question: can nature possibly be as absurd as it seemed to us in these atomic experiments?"

Although it was Albert Einstein's study of light that had produced the particle/wave paradox, he refused to accept the implications of quantum theory: that events on the subatomic level occur spontaneously without local causes, or that the Universe might be created by the observer. This led to his oft-quoted statement, "I cannot for a moment believe that God plays dice and makes use of 'telepathic' means as the current quantum theory alleges He does."

Einstein maintained instead that the theory was incomplete and that greater understanding would restore the objectivity that was a hallmark of the Newtonian Universe. However, in 1965, Irish physicist John Bell successfully argued that either you could preserve the objective Universe by giving up local causation or you could preserve local causation by giving up the objective Universe; you couldn't preserve both. In devising what became known as Bell's theorem, he used the fact that electrons spin, rather like tops, either clockwise or counterclockwise around their own axis, and that two electrons can be put into partnership so that their spin in opposite directions always adds up to zero. Though the experimenter can't know in advance the precise spin of either electron, once the spin and axis of one of the pair has been determined by measurement, the axis and direction of spin of the other can accurately be predicted since together they always add up to zero. In other words, by measuring one electron you determine the rotation of *both*. Experimenters found this happened no matter how far apart the electrons were separated, confronting them with one of the most perplexing questions in quantum physics: How can a particle in London know, faster-than-light, the axis assumed by a particle in New York so that it will always spin in the opposite direction? As Bell's theorem implied: either the observer created the effect through measurement, proving that the Universe is without objective reality, or the effect was created instantaneously through non-local causes—the equivalent of telepathy or synchronicity.

Many physicists have attempted to theorize their way around the dilemma posed by Bell, but the riddle remains unresolved, demonstrating why weird, strange and bizarre have become part of the working vocabulary of particle physicists. Though Einstein believed till the day of his death that quantum logic was the grin of the Cheshire cat to which tomorrow's science would glue the rest of the beast, most physicists have accepted the anomalies of the field, like quirky rules of grammar, to be mastered and used. So what, if a particle/wave is some kind of spotted/striped cat that can't be visualized or followed down dark alleys so long as its behavior, in groups, is predictable enough to spawn thrilling inventions like the transistor, the laser and the microchip?

Of course, the discovery of the acausal principle or a mechanism akin to telepathy on the quantum level does not "prove" their operation in the ordinary sensory world; however, it does demonstrate that such principles are not abhorrent to nature. This, in turn, allows at least for the possibility that individuals or events might, under special circumstances, partake of this deeper reality, resulting in phenomena that may be judged paranormal.

FEBRUARY 15, 1992

I am sitting at my computer, dredging my mind for personal anecdotes that might demonstrate synchronicity in the observer-driven Universe. As I contemplate the many times in which synchronicities involving my name have proved significant to me, my eye happens to fall upon a book, facedown on the floor beside me. It is Colin Wilson's The Occult. *On the back cover a single blurb describes the work as "worthy to be placed on the same shelf alongside William James, F.W.H. Myers's monumental study of* Human Personality *and Frazer's* Golden Bough." *My mother's maiden name was Wilson; my maiden name is Meyers, and my married name is Fraser. By coincidence, the three surnames most significant to me are joined on a book jacket in easy view at the point of time when I am searching for just such a coincidence. Is this a chance happening without significance, or did the observer-driven Universe synchronistically provide me with the example I wanted when I wanted it? If so, what are the implications of such a Universe? Are we all living in a New Age boutique in which to imagine something is to take the first step toward producing it? Is each of us a character in a self-created movie in which we risk creating a hell out of our own answered prayers?*

The concept of an observer-driven Universe not only restored philosophic values to science but seemed to make them prior and pre-eminent. In a world in which absolute law and objective events do not exist, what is left for the participant except personal values like meaning and purpose?

In attempting to understand how information could travel so rapidly in the quantum world, as demonstrated by Bell's theorem, physicists began to speculate about energy that could somehow process information. Some hypothesized that particles might be conscious, or "idea-like" as well as "matter-like." Others described the particle/wave nature of phenomena such as light as reflecting not the properties of light but our experience of light, and even of light's experience of us.

A belief was growing among physicists that what was important in the quantum world was not the interaction of things but the *interactions*. Beyond the manifestation of waves and particles were cosmic codes, or ordering principles, which predetermined everything in the sensory Universe. Just as Rupert Sheldrake had looked beyond the petals of a flower to find morphogenetic fields, so physicists were looking beyond all matter to find abstract fields of information and organization perhaps reminiscent of Plato's Forms. And vital to the operation of these underlying patterns were not forces that pushed or pulled in causal chains, as implied by Newtonian physics, but the synchronicities of Leibniz.

One of the authors of this emerging view was Nobel physicist Wolfgang Pauli. In particular, he was fascinated by parallels between his own quantum theories and Carl Jung's description of the collective unconscious. Just as probes into matter had led to the discovery of a subjective principle in the form of the observer-participator, so the deepest study of human consciousness had led Jung to an objective principle in the form of his universal ideas, or archetypes, which structured human understanding. Thus, on the deepest levels of reality mind and body, matter and psyche, observer and observed, particle and wave seemed potentially linked by abstract codes and patterns. Though these could not be directly perceived, they could be deduced from their impact on more accessible levels and expressed symbolically. In the scientific field, the symbolism used was mathematics. In the field of consciousness, it was image and myth.

In 1952, Pauli and Jung collaborated in the publication of joint essays in which each described mind/matter as different manifestations of the same underlying order, which operated synchronistically. Events judged paranormal reached down into that deeper reality, providing a bridge between it and the sensory world; similarly, meaning provided a bridge between the sensory world and human understanding. According to Jung, the deeper a person repressed an inner conflict, the more certainly the external world would have to act it out in what appeared as Fate, often signposted by synchronicities. That was the explanation behind meaningful coincidences, such as the sudden appearance of a real scarab at the moment when a dream scarab was being discussed. Pauli concurred: "From an inner center the psyche seems to move outward, in the sense of an extraversion, into the physical world."

Together, Jung and Pauli had declared physics to be a branch of psychology, as implied by the Copenhagen Interpretation. In such a Universe, poets and muses and sages and philosophers and mystics become our guides, for without an objective sensory world, science is left without any content. Just as a generation once announced "God is dead," so a new generation might pronounce "Science is dead."

Because Einstein refused to accept such a possibility, he spent the last thirty years of his life in pursuit of a unified field theory that would bring all of science back under the same set of rules, thus restoring the Universe as objective and external. Newton also spent most of his life looking for a unified theory, but for an opposite reason: judging his own materialistic physics incomplete, he yearned for a grander truth that would embrace metaphysical values. Whereas Einstein looked to mathematical equations, Newton looked to alchemical ones. Today, physicists continue the search, but no one has yet solved the riddle: Who, or what, is in charge here?

Wolfgang Pauli made one more contribution to the concept of synchronicity through what became known as the Pauli Effect. Because of his distaste for laboratory work, it was claimed by colleagues that this brilliant theoretician had only to appear beside a piece of experimental equipment for it to malfunction. When an apparatus collapsed in Professor J. Franck's Gottingen laboratory, he wryly wrote to Pauli, exculpating him from blame on the grounds that Pauli was then living in Zurich. A chagrined Pauli wrote back to confess he had not been in Zurich at the time of the accident. He had been parked in a train in the Gottingen station en route to Copenhagen!

SYNCHRONICITY IN THE ORIENT

SEPTEMBER 16, 1986
    I have a single-event pass for the Toronto Film Festival. After poring over dozens of possibilities, I decide on Rouge, *a feature film produced in Hong Kong. As I sit in a near-empty theater at ten in the morning, reading subtitles, I ask myself what I am doing here when I have a film script of my own I should be writing.*
    Grudgingly, I become absorbed in the story: a female ghost has returned from the dead on the anniversary of her suicide to seek her lover. Since my movie script is also a love story, involving a recently deceased person, the film begins to reverberate through my psyche in disturbing ways difficult to articulate. Though I immediately note that March 8, the date of the woman's death and the proposed lovers' reunion, is the same as my birthdate, it is only after several repetitions that I notice the hour of her death also coincides with the hour of my birth: eleven o'clock. By the time I learn that the heroine died in 1934, while I was born in 1935, I'm not sure whether I'm relieved or disappointed that at least the last digit of the date is "wrong."
    Afterwards, as I sit in the darkened theater watching the credits scroll by in Chinese, I lecture myself about the dangers of narcissism in which every event is interpreted as just another excuse to send me a psychic message—at best, a shocking waste of universal resources. As I get up to leave, I stop. My eyes are now riveted on the only name in the credits that has been translated from Chinese— presumably, the name of the lead actress. It is Sylvia . . . Sylvia Lui.
    I walk up the aisle, feeling weird, as if I were stumbling through a carnival funhouse with each mirrored surface reflecting back some distorted image of myself, pursued by the sound of disembodied laughter.
    Before I reach sunlight, I have decided to write this book.

Though Western scientists have traditionally refused to believe events could acausally affect each other, Eastern scholars took it as self-evident that they did. In recording history, they probed for meaning by asking, "What tends to happen together?" The assumption was that every moment bore the complexity of all that happened within it, and that any one event was meaningless when separated from the whole. This is field theory, in which cause is not viewed as one domino striking another but as the whole field, manifesting in a particular pattern.

Explained Jungian analyst Marie-Louise von Franz: "If you read Chinese historical chronicles, they simply say in the Year of the Dragon so-and-so the empress went off with her lover, the Tartars overran the country, the crops failed, and in the city of Shanghai there was an outbreak of the plague. . . . Naturally Western historians . . . said it was just ridiculous to collect a few random facts and put them together, it was idiotic. But for a Chinese reader . . . that is complete information for the Year of the Dragon so-and-so; he has an intuitive picture of how time was constellated at that moment, and that all these things had to happen together."

As Jung summed up in a 1929 lecture: "Synchronicity is the prejudice of the East just as causality is the modern prejudice of the West."

This difference is reflected in a contrasting East-West view of numbers. In the West, numbers stand only for quantities, but in the East they are also qualitative, with a synchronistic meaning apart from their mathematical use. For example, the number four is considered bad luck in Hong Kong, causing savvy real estate agents as far away as Toronto to change house numbers to avoid it. In Hong Kong, avoiding the number is based on acausal principles that link it with bad luck. However, in Toronto, the same avoidance is causal: the "bad luck" would be in losing the sale to a prospective Chinese buyer who believed in synchronicity.

Pythagoras also believed numbers to be mystical entities with structure and personality. Like Plato, he thought they existed prior to, and apart from, physical things, which were but their outer garments. In the West today, the residue of this old number mysticism can be seen in our celebration of anniversaries and birthdays, and in the lingering belief that certain numbers are lucky or unlucky. It also manifests in expressions linking number with identity, such as "his number was up" and "I've got your number"; however, such beliefs are dismissed as mere superstition.

Von Franz demonstrated the East-West attitudinal difference in a story about eleven Chinese generals who had to decide whether to attack or to retreat. After a long strategic discussion, three voted to attack while eight voted to retire; therefore, they attacked. "You see, in China three has the quality of unanimity, and by the chance effect that three people were for attacking they hit the quality of the number three. . . . A Chinese might say perhaps that underneath, unconsciously, there was unanimity for attack, despite the fact that only three were consciously for it. . . . That is the twist in the Chinese mind and it is a good twist because it really shocks one out of the prejudice that number can only be a quantity."

With the failure of local causation on the subatomic level, physicists increasingly began to describe the Universe as a single, dynamically interconnected cosmic web, in which the whole determined the actions of its parts and the parts the whole. This was the Universe envisioned thousands of years ago by Eastern seers. In Buddhism, it is *Dharmakaya*, meaning the Body of Being. In Taoism, it is the *Tao*, variously translated as the Whole, the One Thing, the Way, or the Cosmic Process. In Hinduism, it is *Brahman*, meaning Big.

All of these Eastern religions described the relationship of the individual to the Whole as that of a microcosm reflecting and containing the macrocosm. In Hinduism, this was expressed through the pearl net of the god Indra, in which each pearl reflected every other as well as the whole net. Astrophysicist Sir Arthur Eddington made the micro-macro case for modern physics when he remarked, "When the electron vibrates, the Universe shakes." Similarly, Leibniz hypothesized a cosmos in which each monad contained the blueprint for the Universe. In Greek philosophy, this concept was expressed as the One in the many, which Pythagoras demonstrated with the image of the circle, created by joining an infinity of points equidistant from a single point. Similarly, William Blake marveled in his *Auguries of Innocence*:

> To see a World in a grain of sand
> And a Heaven in a wild flower,
> Hold Infinity in the palm of your hand
> And Eternity in an hour.

On the biological level, geneticists know that every cell of an organism contains the blueprint for the whole organism, encoded in its DNA. Neuropsychologist Karl Pribram of Stanford University, California, demonstrated that even brain processes such as memory might work on the micro-macro principle. After monkeys had learned to open a complicated latchbox containing a peanut, Pribram began cutting out parts of their cerebral cortex to test the effect on their learning. Though the monkeys' ability to open the box was unimpaired, the time they required to do so doubled or even tripled. From this and other experiments, Pribram concluded that a particular memory could not be removed by cutting out small pieces of brain, but that the total memory would be weakened. He therefore hypothesized that memory was spread across the entire brain, with each piece containing and reflecting the whole. This organization he compared to a hologram.

An increasingly popular concept in science, a hologram is created when an object is photographed, using a mirror and laser, so that a patterned blur appears on a photographic plate. If laser light is shone through that patterned blur, or hologram, an apparent three-dimensional image of the original appears in space. When a small piece of the photographic plate is destroyed, the whole object can still be reproduced, but the image is less detailed. Thus, the entire image exists potentially in every part, with each part enhancing the clarity of the whole.

In an attempt to find a theory that would unify all reality, physicist David Bohm turned, like Pribram, to the concept of the hologram. Describing the Universe as an undivided and unbroken totality, Bohm speculated that everything that we perceive—matter, psyche, space, time—was what he called the *explicate* manifestation of an *implicate* order, unknowable to us because it possesses many more dimensions than the four we humans can comprehend. However, the totality of the Universe was enfolded, like a hologram, in every part, so that just as every neuron of every brain reflected the whole brain, so every brain reflected the whole Universe.

The theories of both Pribram and Bohm lead to breath-taking speculations: If the human brain is a hologram of the Universe, does that explain how Western philosophers and Eastern seers were able to intuit, thousands of years before modern science, the probable nature of the Universe? If the human brain employs only 1 per cent of its DNA for its own complicated coding, does the blueprint for the Universe take up the other 99 per cent?

A student of Buddhism, Bohm not only believed that meditation was an effective way of accessing the deepest reality but he also maintained that this higher consciousness was, in turn, capable of altering the structure of our minds: observer and observed were completely interactive, with each being a dynamic reflection of the other in a self-conscious, changing Universe, from which the mind abstracted its own evolving reality. As described in the seven-thousand-year-old sacred Indian Vedas:

> There is an endless net of threads throughout the Universe.
> The horizontal threads are in space; the vertical threads in time;
> At every crossing of threads there is an individual, and every individual is a pearl.
> The great light of Absolute Being illuminates and penetrates every pearl.
> And also, every pearl reflects not only the light from every other pearl in the net,
> But also every reflection of every reflection throughout the Universe.

LUNAR MAGIC

1935–1943

As a widowed immigrant with scant education, my maternal grandmother used what talents she had to support herself: where other women of her generation might sew or bake pies, she told fortunes in a downtown Hamilton tearoom.

By the time I arrive on the scene, my grandmother reads only for friends around her folding table with the wobbly leg—tea leaves and cards, not the fancy kind where an upside-down Hanged Man means transformation, but the no-nonsense British sort where the Ace of Spades means death.

All this is hushed up even in our own house.

The occasional stranger—usually richly dressed and trailing perfumes—is whisked upstairs through a darkened passageway of closed doors to the dining room where my grandmother lays out her cards and serves tea and shortbreads at her round oak table with its perpetual arrangement of Japanese lanterns, silver dollars and bittersweets.

Those closed doors are to protect the sensibilities of my father. My grandmother is offending two taboos: earning money in a house that already contains a male breadwinner, and practicing psychic arts, which my father regards the way someone might view a cockroach belly-up in the bathwater. His work at the Steel Company of Canada is legitimate; my grandmother's is not.

On only one occasion do I learn what goes on around my grandmother's oak table when the doors are closed. Having laid the cards for a client, my grandmother has a fainting spell, cutting short the reading. As I later overhear her tell my mother: "All I could see was Death. That woman's future was as black as mine."

When my grandmother dies at sixty-nine, having outlived a husband, three of four daughters and a grandchild, it isn't so much that her heart has broken but that it has worn through, like the heel of a woolly sock exposed to too many abrasions. Her death—apparently predicted by her when her Christmas cactus bloomed out of season— means the loss of magic for the women in our house. From now on, we will have no other gods before my father and the male Trinity designated by the Protestant Church. From now on, spiritual feeling will have to struggle each Sunday against hard pews and long-winded sermons. All miracles—except those bearing the Crucifix trademark— are banned from my life.

Though I was not aware of it as a child, I may have just relived the history of Western civilization, in which a matriarchal society, which believed psychic truths to be more fundamental than materialistic ones, was replaced by a technological patriarchy.

Since the turn of the century, archeologists have been uncovering evidence of a widespread Euro-Asian prehistoric culture, which may overturn our notions about civilization and even the nature of reality. A matriarchy, this culture is believed by some archeologists to have invented agriculture, pottery and weaving, to have evolved the cart wheel from the potter's wheel, to have developed the lunar calendar from the menstrual cycle. As worshippers of the Great Mother, its inhabitants lived and breathed magic: everything in their world was bound synchronistically to everything else.

Clues to the existence of such a society persisted in the Great Mother myths of early Mediterranean societies: Nut and Isis of Egypt, Ishtar of Babylon, Demeter of Greece, Cybele of Rome. First archeological evidence consisted of an abundance of goddess statues, dating from 30,000 B.C., discovered in sacred caves and burial sites from France to Siberia and throughout the Middle East to India. Of clay, stone, amber and bone, they depict a woman's torso with pendulous breasts, massive thighs and distended belly. Dubbing them "Venuses," early researchers dismissed them as male pornography.

At the turn of this century, archeologists made a momentous discovery on the island of Crete: the ruins of a wealthy and artistic civilization, beginning around 6000 B.C., devoted to goddess worship. Here were sophisticated cities; villas and vast palaces with abundant gardens, labyrinthine courtyards and elegant colonnades; plazas overflowing with art—joyful, exquisite, fantastic, whimsical, not about war, hunting, sacrifice or death but about butterflies, birds and cosmic eggs, with the Maiden Goddess at play while the Great Mother cradled her child.

Curiously, the significance of this goddess culture seems to have been intuitively grasped by a few Western writers even before archeologists appreciated their find. While studying pre-Christian literature, poet Robert Graves became intrigued by references to an ancient moon goddess who ruled the world of magic, the unconscious, inspiration and intuition. With his own subconscious steeped in this occult lore, he suddenly found himself able to understand obscure Welsh riddles and symbols, including an arcane Celtic alphabet whose eighteen letters were synchronistically paired with a sequence of wild trees. Astonished by the richness of this lost world, Graves concluded: "The most important single fact in the early history of Western religion and sociology was undoubtedly the gradual suppression of the Lunar Mother-goddess's inspiratory cult, and its supercession . . . by the busy, rational cult of the Solar God Apollo who . . . initiated European literature and science."

During Graves's obsession with the White Goddess, he found his life haunted by mysterious coincidences: items with symbols representing the goddess kept falling into his hands in improbable ways—a ring given to him by a friend, an antique sculpture bequeathed by a neighbor, a brass box on his desk bearing an image that he found represented the African moon goddess. Similarly, good and bad luck, which he judged synchronistic, trailed his finished manuscript, entitled *The White Goddess*: the first publisher who rejected it died shortly afterwards of heart failure; the second, who spiced his refusal with a disrespectful letter, dressed himself in women's underwear and hanged himself from one of the Great Mother's sacred trees! Needless to say, honors and profit greeted the publisher who proudly presented *The White Goddess* to the world.

W.B. Yeats was another poet who fell under the spell of the White Goddess. His fascination also bred a symbolic system based on the moon. Similarly, in the first volume of the mythological *Joseph and His Brothers*, novelist Thomas Mann coined the expression "moon grammar" to honor lunar truths: "Things take on a different look beneath the moon and beneath the sun. And it well may be that to the Spirit the light of the moon would appear to yield the truer illumination."

As we in the West discover more about civilization's roots, a truth is slowly dawning: our cultural evolution, with its emphasis on ego-consciousness and technology, has not been the triumphant stride through time that we once supposed. To live in perpetual sunlight is to believe we exist alone at the center of an invisible Universe, but when the moon rises we see other planets, comets, stars, galaxies. We touch infinity.

My grandmother had to hide her lunar talents because they were not valued. Like most systems of divination, the two she used were based on synchronicity: cards were shuffled, or the remnants of unstrained tea were spun three times in an overturned cup. Then my grandmother studied the random cards, or tea leaves, for patterns and shapes that had meanings she would intuitively interpret. According to one theory, the cards and tea leaves—or lines crisscrossing a palm, or planets in the zodiac—simply focus the diviner's energy, unlocking psychic talents. However, according to my grandmother and most diviners, a genuine acausal relationship exists between the fortune and the one who casts it. Through ritualized concentration, diviner and client enter into a pact with random events to produce, or discover, a likely destiny.

Although divination has generally failed to make a case for itself in the West, it remains a respectable pursuit in China, where the word *suan-shu* means both mathematics and divination. Unique as an oracle, the ancient text known as the *I Ching* (pronounced *Yee Jing*) operates exclusively on the principle of synchronicity. According to tradition, it began with predictions made from the cracks in a cow's shoulderblade caused by ritual burning: certain charred patterns were interpreted as having certain psychic meanings. About 4,500 years ago, this system was transferred to the shell of a tortoise, for which the First Emperor of China was said to have composed meanings. Other sages, including Confucius, added their thoughts, resulting in a subtle, multilayered book of wisdom still revered by Eastern scholars, corporate presidents and peasants alike.

To gain access to the *I Ching's* knowledge, the quester thinks intensely about a question, then tosses three coins (or forty-nine yarrow sticks) six times. By following simple rules, one of sixty-four interpretations is achieved, indicating the auspices and outcome of the question. To the Western mind, this is the stuff of fortune cookies. Nor are bits of commentary, taken at random, reassuring. Number 30: "Brilliant Beauty. Perseverance in the right way brings freedom and success. Caring for cows brings good fortune." However, to the scholar the *I Ching's* words and images are said to be like pebbles cast up from an ancient sea, to be examined, polished, admired and shifted into patterns by the meditative mind. Always ambiguous and often poetic, the interpretations reputedly embody all possible cosmic and human situations, generated by the dynamic interplay of yin (negative) and yang (positive) forces. This is reflected by their names: Progress, Unity, Perilous Chasm, Decrease, Family, Sudden Encounters.

Some Western admirers have gazed at the *I Ching* and seen yin and yang as corresponding to the dynamic interplay of negative and positive quantum charges; or they have viewed the tossing of coins, using the head/tails principle, as a precursor to the 0/1 binary system used by computers. Leibniz believed the *I Ching* demonstrated some of the mathematical knowledge he employed in inventing the calculus. Other scholars regard it as a Rorschach inkblot onto which the quester projects unconscious intentions to create a possible future.

Carl Jung considered that last explanation too superficial to account for the uncanny way the oracle seemed to produce the most relevant meaning—loosely worded enough to suit a variety of circumstances but strict enough to astonish. As he confessed in his memoir, he would sit for hours beneath his hundred-year-old pear tree, as if engaged in spiritual dialogue with a wise master, alive within the pages of the book.

Did that pear tree, on those long afternoons, absorb some of the psychic energy of that buddha-like figure sitting beneath it? Perhaps, because two hours after Jung's death it was struck by lightning. Then, on the tenth anniversary of Jung's death, toward sunset of a blazing day, filmmaker Laurens van der Post was completing a documentary in that same garden when the heavens cracked open once again: "Out of the hot blue sky the thunder clouds tumbled without forewarning, as if in a great hurry. . . . When the moment came for me to speak direct to the camera about Jung's death, and I came to the description of how the lightning demolished Jung's favorite tree, the lightning struck in the garden again. The thunder crashed out so loud that I winced, and to this day the thunder, wince, and the impediment of speech it caused are there in the film for all to see."

The Future Foretold:

WARPS AND ALL

"It is believed by most that time passes; in actual fact, it stays where it is."

—Zen master Dogen

DECEMBER 1983

I visit psychic Vince Vanlimbeek, for the first time, on the recommendation of a friend and because I pass his office every day. Though I've usually found fortune tellers to be as bad at their jobs as the chefs in the worst restaurants, he proves to be an honorable exception.

Without asking questions or pausing to greet me, he slips a tape into his recorder, gazes absently into space, then begins his spiel. My occupation is accurately though vaguely described as "teaching, or the passing on of information." Later, he correctly asks: "Does this passing on of information involve the U.S.?"

After insightfully describing a couple of people in my life without precisely pinning them, he inquires: "Have you been twice in the hospital recently?"

"No, only once."

"Then you're going again. I see two hospital beds, but it will just be overnight. Nothing to worry about, just like a toothache." In fact, this has already happened but I have unaccountably wiped it from my mind.

Vanlimbeek then launches into what will prove his coup de grace: "Would it surprise you to know you're moving?" Since I have lived in the same duplex for twelve years and have no intention of leaving, indeed it would.

"You're going to. That will be linked with drastic change, but you're not going to stay there either. It will be a stepping stone. It's a work-related move, involving the U.S. I see you combining living and working space."

Later, he elaborates: "You're going to kiss Toronto goodbye. You're going to pack up or sell off everything you own, no question. I see lots of water. . . . Did you cancel a trip or not go somewhere you intended to?"

"No." In fact, I intended to visit a friend in California, then backed off. Again, this is something I have forgotten.

"Well, I want you to think about it. This is important. I see mountains—they're gorgeous. That's also the way you'll feel when you see them. The road will be clear."

Though the reading is intelligent and without the shallow guile typical of these ventures, I leave my appointment feeling unimpressed and even grudging. I am especially dismissive of the claim that I will soon be moving. However, within the week I receive notice that I must vacate my flat and, within the year, I do pack up or sell off everything I own and move to California. On replaying the tape months later, I am struck by how accurate it has proven and by how often I relayed false or misleading information—not intentionally but perhaps through some block that caused me to deny and misremember.

Since that initial reading more than eight years ago, I have visited Vanlimbeek at six-month intervals. His precognitive hits include a number of deaths, a number of moves, the purchase of a condominium, a legal action and my sister's tragic illness.

Vanlimbeek's skill at plucking unlikely images out of my future impresses me as much as his prediction of events. On one occasion he described me as sitting in a covered wagon, with my head poked out the back, smiling into exceedingly lush, green fields. Since I'm intending to visit Alberta around the Calgary Stampede, I vow that under no circumstances will I climb inside a covered wagon even though all I'd likely see out back would be prairie dust. However, to my surprise, I spend several weeks that summer in China, including the town of Guilin, where I go riding with friends in a bicycle-powered open cart. Almost immediately, it rains. When the driver pulls a canvas top over the cart, I automatically stick my head out back to see the intensely lush paddy fields. As I remember the prediction, my smile is an unavoidable reflex.

Is Vanlimbeek ever wrong? Yes. His timing is usually off, and he exaggerates good effects. He is far more accurate when volunteering information than in answering questions. He never provides specifics in the form of dates or names, and much of what he predicts could fit a number of scenarios. However, some of his shafts have been so striking that I believe he sees the future by appointment while I catch only unbidden glimpses in my reveries and dreams.

Although many Americans were dismayed to learn that Ronald and Nancy Reagan regularly consulted San Francisco astrologer Joan Quigley while occupying the White House, the president and first lady were merely following a political tradition. Toward the end of World War I, Edgar Cayce was summoned to Washington twice to give readings to President Woodrow Wilson and his wife, Edith. During times of stress, President Franklin Roosevelt sometimes requested his staff to "lay the cards for me" and, in November 1944, he summoned Washington seer Jeane Dixon to the White House to ask a question he had not asked his doctors: "How much time do I have to finish the work I have to do?"

Her prediction, "Six months or less," was fulfilled when the president died on April 12, 1945, of a cerebral hemorrhage.

Perhaps it is the loneliness of high office, combined with crushing responsibility, that sometimes causes leaders to bypass the savvy of their advisers for the intuitions of psychics. Perhaps the timing so crucial for political success selects for leadership from the ranks of the psychically attuned. During World War II, Canadian prime minister Mackenzie King regularly consulted with mediums and even believed he received advice from deceased relatives and politicians. Compelled by a dream warning, Adolf Hitler reputedly leapt from a World War I trench a split second before his companions were entombed by an exploding shell. Later, the Führer's "second sight" may have saved his skin several times when quirky changes in plans foiled assassination attempts. Though Winston Churchill routinely exposed himself to the London Blitz, he also displayed a cat's agility for zipping into shelters or spontaneously altering habits in ways his aides called guided.

President Abraham Lincoln, whose wife, Mary, was believed to have consulted spiritualists, may have caught chilly intimations of his own future in a dream he related to biographer Ward Hill Laman a few weeks before his 1865 assassination: "There seemed to be a death-like stillness about me . . . then I heard subdued sobs, as if a number of people were weeping. . . . I arrived at the East Room which I entered. There I met a sickening surprise. Before me was a catafalque on which rested a corpse wrapped in funeral vestments. . . . 'Who is dead in the White House?' I asked. 'The president. . . . He was killed by an assassin.'"

Jeane Dixon has a well-authenticated claim for predicting both the assassination of President John Kennedy and the murder of his brother Robert. As early as 1952, when John was still a thirty-five-year-old congressman from Massachusetts, Dixon was foretelling both his presidency in 1960 and his violent death in office. In a 1956 *Parade* column, Jack Anderson first recorded her prediction in general terms: a Democratic president, elected in 1960, would die or be assassinated in office, not necessarily in his first term. By 1959, Dixon was publicly naming Kennedy and predicting an assassination. After his election, she repeated her revelation with greater agitation, and several times tried to warn Kennedy through his family and entourage. She was urging him not to take a trip to the Southwest before his office knew he was intending to do so, and in the weeks, days and hours before that fateful November 22, 1963, friends claim she repeatedly spoke of seeing a shroud over the White House.

In predicting Robert Kennedy's murder, Dixon was only one of a crowd who sensed his doom; however, corroborators claim that two months previous, she picked California as the place. Then, on May 28, 1968, when Dixon was giving a speech in the Embassy Room of the Ambassador Hotel, she confided to a friend and former reporter: "I don't think I can keep my mind on my speech. All I can see is a black cloud of Bobby Kennedy's body going from here up through the ceiling." At that moment, she was seated directly in front of the kitchen door, where Kennedy was shot on June 5.

Another chilling detail: two years previous, Dixon informed friends that she feared Robert might commit suicide, because she kept envisioning a pistol behind his ear. During a post-murder NBC-TV interview, an attending neurosurgeon stated: "If we didn't know that somebody had shot Senator Kennedy, it looks like he could have shot himself, because the wound is in the back of the ear."

History's most famous seer, sixteenth-century astrologer-physician Nostradamus, also secured his reputation by predicting the death of his leader with impressive accuracy:

> The young lion shall overcome the old
> In martial field by a single duel.
> He will pierce his eyes in a cage of gold.
> Two wounds from one, then he dies a cruel death.

Shortly after Nostradamus penned that verse, King Henry II of France, the old lion, was killed by a Scottish knight in a tournament when a splinter from the young lion's lance pierced Henry's gold helmet, putting out his eye and penetrating his brain. Though Henry recovered, he again fell ill from his wounds, to die "a cruel death."

In the same cryptic verse, composed of 942 quatrains spanning five centuries, Nostradamus has been credited with foreseeing the rise of Napoleon, the French Revolution, the death of the Romanovs, the opening of King Tut's tomb, the tyranny of Mussolini and of Hitler (whom he named Hister), the Battle of Britain, the bombing of Hiroshima, the Nuremberg trials, the Hungarian Revolt, the rise of the United States, the Gulf War and— just over the horizon—the dawning of a New Age in August 1999, after a series of great catastrophes.

The denseness of metaphor in which Nostradamus couched most of his prophecies meant he could seldom be proved wrong, only right, and usually after the fact. This was not true of Jeane Dixon who, throughout her lifetime, spattered the tabloids with hundreds of improbable, totally wrong predictions, undermining her more serious claims to having foretold the deaths of the Kennedys, as well as those of astronauts Grissom, White and Chaffee aboard an Apollo spacecraft.

This all-too-common occurrence—forcing what may be a genuine psychic talent beyond its capacity—leads skeptics to want to wheel out the old statistical scoreboard: how many predictions did a seer get right, versus how many were wrong? In my opinion, that's applying a false standard. First, all predictions are not created equal: "It's going to rain tomorrow" hardly equates with the prediction of an assassination eleven years in advance, before the key player was even in office. Second, like violin solos, every detailed prediction deserves to be judged on its own terms: three inept concertos do not retroactively ruin the virtuoso one preceding, though they may persuade you not to sit through to the end of the concert.

DECEMBER 13, 1984
After several days spent looking for a flat in West Los Angeles, I have a list of some two dozen possibilities, culled from ads, bulletin boards, friends' suggestions, even from trees. The process of on-site

sorting is predictably discouraging—too expensive, too isolated, too noisy, too long a lease, too repulsive. As I trudge back after the third day, I spot a For Rent sign in front of a two-storey building with the stately lines of a manor. Though I imagine it will be beyond my price range, I wander through the center hall, looking for a superintendent's apartment. When I find none, I leave.

Halfway down the walk, I discover this flat is on my list—the only one marked with an X. Returning, I knock at random on one of a dozen doors. No answer. I am leaving again when a most peculiar feeling overwhelms me. As if in a trance, I return to the same door and try the knob—certainly not a thing I would normally do. The door cracks open onto an empty flat. I step inside. Instantly, I know this is my flat. Not that it should be or even that I want it to be, but that it is, as conclusively as if the deal has been struck. Even without opening the door to the rest of the place, I know what I will find—an eccentric layout but already oddly familiar.

This uncanny sense of things foreordained pervades my two-year stay in Los Angeles. The items I buy, even the people I meet, exude this quality of having been waiting for me to catch up, like shadowy footprints that form even before I extend each foot . . .

In my experience, intimations of the future are most often gentle things, like a doe that nibbles on grass at the edge of the forest, quick to bolt when a hunter appears. Most often, they come upon me spontaneously, in off-guard moments, as in my dreams or when thoughts drift unsorted like spring pollen through my mind. They are most reliable when something important is at stake, such as a death, or when nothing much is to be gained. They are least reliable in pragmatic situations where I very much want something specific to occur: then that admixture of wishful thinking causes me to see the future I want rather than to intuit the one that is about to happen.

Like noxious gas, skepticism or the demand for proof kills on contact. And what is the point? Either these intuitions happen, or they don't. Either they are useful, or they are not. Evidence need not be presented to the self as if to a court of law. As the White Queen opined in *Through the Looking-Glass*: "It's a poor sort of memory that only works backwards."

THE INVENTION OF LINEAR TIME

Does the future cast its shadow before?

Tribal peoples as separate as the Mayans and the Norse observed the alterations of light and dark, of winter and summer, and assumed time to be cyclical: just as the sun and moon and all vegetation died to be reborn again, so this world and everything in it would die to be recreated again and again. This view of cyclical time, wed to the more sophisticated belief that time itself was an illusion, is central to the great religions of the East. In Both Hinduism and Buddhism, the Great Wheel grinds each of us through thousands of incarnations until Enlightenment is achieved by abandoning the illusion of time for immersion in the eternal bliss of *nirvana*. As proclaimed by the great Buddhist scholar Ashvaghosha in the first century: "The past, the future . . . are nothing but names, forms of thought, words of common usage, merely superficial realities."

Pythagoras and Plato also believed that human experience of time was cyclical and illusory, and that every event that happened would be repeated in a distant future. Plato theorized that a cycle ended when all planets returned to certain key positions they had once occupied, and various of his disciples estimated this Great Year to consist of 36,000 years.

Linear time was a product of the Judeo-Christian religion, Newtonian science, Darwinian evolution and Western technology.

According to the Bible, Creation was a unique event with a historical beginning and a foreordained end. Galileo's proof that day and night were produced by the Earth's rotation led to the objectifying of time as matter in motion. The fact that this physical rhythm through space was fixed and predictable inspired Newton to describe time as absolute, real and flowing evenly like a river. With the replacement of sundials by increasingly accurate clocks, time became an industrial commodity to be bartered and sold. Time was money.

Darwin's evolutionary theory, tying human fate to that of the apes, pulled all biological events within the materialistic causal chain. Time meant decay and death to every individual organism; it was inevitable and irreversible. To an octogenarian in a wheelchair looking at a high-school photo of himself in a football uniform, nothing seemed more certain.

By the end of the nineteenth century, the concept of time as traveling like an arrow in one direction seemed self-evident to the Western world. However, seventeenth-century philosopher Immanuel Kant spelled out future shock when he argued that space and time were not properties of reality but only habits of the human mind.

To comprehend Kant's meaning, imagine yourself gazing at the world through a square, red-paned window, with the frame representing space and the red representing time. Of course, everything through the window would look square-framed and red, and since everyone else was gazing through the same window, predictions about the square, red Universe would seem accurate. However, what the viewer was seeing was not reality itself but the square-red structure through which reality was being observed—in this case, the space-time structures of the human mind. Therefore, inventions like Galileo's telescope and Newton's laws do not increase, deepen or expand our human ability to see what is there; they only help us to make our square-red space-time version of it more self-consistent and detailed.

Kant's once-radical theory is now an orthodox one. Thus, today's scientists don't just wonder *if* the future can be foretold, they theorize *how*.

JULY 1, 1986

While living in California, I purchase a July 1 plane ticket to return to Toronto for a month, with bookings for my two Siamese cats. A couple of weeks before my flight, I change my reservation to July 4 and arrange instead for someone to live in with my cats.

On the morning of July 1, about the time I would have been leaving for the airport, my three-year-old male jumps out of my ground-floor window for his early forage. Of all the cats with whom I have shared living space, this is my favorite. When he fails to return within a few hours, I grow anxious. By nightfall, I am distraught.

My cat never returns and I never feel so happy about this California flat again. Every time the blind rattles I turn, hoping to see him hop through the window. My grief seems to have permeated like a bad smell into the paint on the wall and then to have congealed into a sense of doom, as if something worse were about to happen. Several times during the following weeks I mention to my California friends that the loss of a cat in my life has always proved an omen for other loss or death or change.

Though winter is just beginning, I feel a sudden, compulsive need to return permanently to Toronto. While sorting through papers, I uncover my missing cat's vaccination certificate. As I rip it up, I notice his birthdate: January 6, 1984. Goosebumps shiver up my arms and I begin to shake. Since I have learned to respect such forebodings, I meditate on that date, asking myself what significance it might have for me.

It comes to me that January 6 is the birthdate of my late father-in-law. Therefore, I scrawl "January 6" on a piece of paper, followed by my father-in-law's name, which is also that of my former husband. Impulsively, I add "Canada," for no rational reason except that July 1, the date my cat disappeared, is Canada's birthday. Then: "Loss . . . Death . . . Change."

Putting aside the paper, I continue sorting.

In early December, I leave Los Angeles for Toronto. A month later, I am writing about my former husband in my memoir when the phone rings. A friend tells me that my husband died the previous day, January 6, age fifty-five, of a heart attack.

Electrified, I recall the words that I scrawled two months previous on a piece of paper, like a memo of where I must be, when, for whom, and why: "January 6, Russell James Fraser, Canada. Loss . . . Death . . . Change."

Like other paranormal experiences, precognition frequently occurs between strongly bonded persons during times of crisis. Death—especially when swift and tragic—seems to be the single shared experience that is abrupt and shocking enough to jolt us out of our habitual mode of tunnel-viewing. Sometimes this knowledge embodies a warning or answers a plea for help; sometimes, as with the death of my former husband, it is simply a preparation for "loss . . . death . . . change," honoring an emotional bond.

In my view, what raised this experience above mere chance was its detail, including a name, a location, a specific date and a prediction, plus my overwhelming sense of the uncanny, which enclosed the whole event in a black border. Although my defenses were too strong for me to immediately comprehend the message's import, the instant it came true I "knew" it had been a prediction. I also "knew" that unconscious knowledge of my former husband's death had impelled my abrupt return to Toronto, with the vaccination certificate acting as a focus for my surfacing awareness.

COSMIC TIME

Today's scientists routinely speak of five distinct kinds of time: time-before-time, cosmic time, Newtonian time, subjective time and quantum time. Time-before-time refers to that point of ultimate compression, or singularity, before the Big Bang created our Universe around fifteen billion years ago. Since neither space nor time existed, even the words *before, until* and *after* are invalid and the language of Genesis is as appropriate as that of science. The best both can do is to postulate primordial Nothing from which Something emerged. *In the Beginning* . . .

Albert Einstein introduced cosmic time in 1905 when he published his special theory of relativity. In charting the Universe, scientists had already noted circumstances in which Newton's gravitational laws did not work, such as in predicting the orbit of the planet Mercury. Einstein explained these discrepancies by two postulates. First, since nothing is ever absolutely at rest, all motion is relative to something else. Thus, if one train passes another at a constant speed in a fixed direction, passengers on each train will experience themselves as stationary and those on the other as traveling. As in those old Hollywood westerns shot cheaply in a studio: which was really moving, the horse or the painted backdrop?

Einstein's second postulate was that light always travels at an absolute constant of 186,000 miles per second with respect to an observer, regardless of the state of motion of the light source or the observer. In Newtonian physics, if two cars are traveling toward each other at 100 miles per hour, then each can be said to be approaching relative to each other at a speed of 100 + 100 = 200 miles per hour. However, if a spaceship is approaching a star at 100,000 miles per second, the light from the star and the spaceship are not approaching relative to each other at 186,000 + 100,000 miles per second; they are approaching at a constant 186,000 miles per second. If the spaceship speeds up to 150,000 miles per second, they are still approaching at a constant 186,000 miles per second.

This concept can't be further explained. It just is. Einstein conceived that light was different from other forms of motion when, at age fifteen, he asked himself what would happen if he were to move at the speed of light and look into a mirror. He decided he would see nothing because the light from his face would never reach the mirror. He also determined that, if he were to go faster than light, the electromagnetic fields melding his atoms would be left behind; therefore, the idea of anything traveling faster than light contained a contradiction.

Special relativity was the monkeywrench that wrecked Newton's clockwork Universe. Since all our observations depend on light, its constancy combined with the relativity of motion meant that events could not occur simultaneously in spacially separate places. Therefore, no point of time could be isolated as "now" for every part of the Universe. Einstein again demonstrated this to himself by imagining he was traveling as fast as light away from a giant Newtonian clock. When he looked back, he noted that its hands seemed to stand still, since no other lightwaves from the clock could catch up with him until he slowed down.

On planet Earth, where velocities are far below those of light, time discrepancies are small enough to be virtually unobservable. Whether we are in New York at noon or in London at teatime, we think we can pin down an instant called "now." Since light always needs some time to travel, this is a misassumption, but a forgivable one.

When we look into the night sky, we begin to come to grips with space-time anomalies. Because light takes eight minutes to zoom from Sun to Earth, when we admire a sunset we are looking back eight minutes in time, and when scientists gaze through telescopes they may be viewing galaxies as they existed billions of years ago. This concept of time-past as perceived by ourselves from the viewpoint of a stationary observer has grown familiar to us. However, if each of us imagines each star or planet to be a past or future event in our own life as we travel in a spaceship, we begin to conceive of time in terms of distance, speed and motion rather than as something absolute and objective. If other spacecraft are zipping back and forth across the cosmos at different speeds, we can imagine the great potential for mixing up time sequences. This is especially true if the pilots of these spacecraft are reporting their observations to us with no indication of speed or location.

Because of the vast distances across which light chugs at a constant 186,000 miles per second, the radiance from a nova star in one part of the Universe takes many light years to travel to another part. Therefore, to people in spaceships time becomes a point of view, and the concepts of "now," "then," "before" and "after" break down into questions about the relative position of an observer and the speed that observer is traveling. An event in the past of one observer may be in the future of another, and even the order in which each person experiences events may differ. Metaphorically, it's as if the Universe were a vast echo chamber in which each member of an orchestra, choir and audience were attempting to perform in unison while running around at different speeds, with each person's "now" note reverberating amongst all the others. How can the conductor, at any given point, hear the universal song? As in the cosmos, "now" does not exist except in terms of "here" to every singer.

The task of Einstein's relativity theory was to adjust all natural laws so that they would work for observers anywhere in the Universe traveling at relative speeds. As our metaphoric cosmic conductor, he postulated the principles that would bring order out of the cacophony of "now" notes by establishing the relationship of each singer to every other.

Special relativity states that when a body in motion approaches the speed of light, time slows down from the viewpoint of a stationary observer, although someone on that speeding body would notice no distortion. This is a real effect: time not only *seems* to slow down but does so in fact, as measured by both mechanical and biological clocks. This is demonstrated by the famous Twin Paradox: if a twin traveled from Earth to a distant star at a velocity of 87 per cent of the speed of light, not only would he experience time as passing half as fast as if he had stayed at home but his watch would register time as having passed half as fast and, on returning to Earth, he would discover he had aged only half as much as his twin because of the slowdown in his heartbeat and other biological processes.

Which twin experienced "real" time? That question can't be answered any more than a tailor can measure the "real" length of a shadow in order to fit it with a suit. A shadow is the reflection of a three-dimensional object in two-dimensional space: all its weird contractions and expansions are a logical result of that. The same is true of the time distortions described by special relativity: because of the limitations of our sense perceptions, we earthlings are observing the three-dimensional "shadow" of something that is four-dimensional, of which we have no direct experience. This was the great truth grasped by Einstein when he determined that time and space in the cosmos could not be separated any more than a donut could be separated from its hole. Therefore, Einstein postulated a four-dimensional continuum, which he called space-time. This replaced Newton's model of the Universe consisting of three dimensions of space and one dimension of time. While Einstein's space-time continuum is internally logical, it cannot be visualized by the human observer and leads to effects that "make no sense." These effects are as mysterious to us as the shadow cast by a giant would be to a tailor in a two-dimensional world. He sees the effect of the giant's movements in two-dimensional space. He may even learn to predict how the shadow will change according to changing conditions; however, he can't imagine the real shape of the creature that cast such a shadow because he cannot visualize girth.

According to the Big Bang theory of creation, the Universe is continuously expanding. Because of that explosive name, some of us may visualize this cosmic event as a firecracker going off, shooting debris into space. A better analogy, proposed by astrophysicist Sir Arthur Eddington in 1930, likens the exploding Universe to a steadily expanding balloon, with its surface painted with dots. The dots represent galaxies. As the balloon grows larger, the dots move away from each other. No matter on what dot you plant yourself, that dot will seem to be the center of the Universe while all the other dots will seem to be expanding away from you. These galaxies are not expanding into pre-existing empty space; rather, the space is being created by the expansion. Since this happens within time,

time is simultaneously being created with space, accounting for the inseparability of space-time.

The surface of the balloon represents what physicists call curved space. However, since it is two-dimensional while the curved space of the Universe is three-dimensional, the balloon analogy provides only an intuitive approximation and not a true visual model.

Einstein's special relativity dealt only with objects traveling in a straight line at a constant speed. His general relativity, published in 1916, extended that theory to embrace gravity. According to Einstein, gravity was not a force as Newtonian physics implied but a geometric effect. Specifically, it was the curvature of space caused by any massive object, similar to the way a bowling ball, held in a quilt, curves the quilt.

In an analogy, created by Bertrand Russell, which I have adapted: Imagine that you are an alien in a spaceship hovering over the Earth. The only illumination is that created by the headlights of cars driving across the Earth's surface. Since you come from a planet enveloped in water, you can't imagine why the lights don't always move in a direct line, assuming that the travelers are trying to get from one place to another as quickly as possible. Instead they twist and curve in a way that makes no sense, especially in one area where they all make a gigantic circle. The only explanation you can come up with is that the travelers are trying to avoid whirlpools of varying size that either repel them or threaten to suck them in.

When the sun rises, you see the strange landscape of this planet for the first time. The straight routes traverse plains, which look much the same as the oceans on your planet on a calm day. However, the curved routes circumvent structures you learn are hills, while the huge one sweeps around a mountain. Suddenly you understand that all the effects you observed can be explained by the geography of this planet. Though each car was always traveling the shortest route to its destination, it had to curve around invisible local landmarks. This had nothing to do with a force repelling or attracting them, but was a logical reaction to the terrain.

This is the meaning of gravity as geometry rather than as a force. Celestial bodies do not attract or repel but—like hills and mountains hidden by darkness—they alter the space around them in ways that can't be seen except through their effects. In our vicinity of space, the Sun's great size creates a major distortion, corresponding to the mountain in the metaphor. Because light consists of particles with energy, and energy is equivalent to mass, then light is influenced by gravity. Therefore, when a light beam is shot near a planet, it must bend to follow the invisible curvature of space created by that planet's mass; however, like the cars swerving to circumvent a hill or a mountain, the light beam is traveling by the shortest route.

Since space cannot be separated from time in the cosmos, gravity will distort time as well as space: the greater the mass, the greater the curve and the greater the distortion of time.

Though still only theoretic, black holes are believed to form when a star at least twice the mass of our sun collapses, growing denser and denser with a progressively stronger gravitational field that curves space-time so completely that not even light rays could escape. Under such pressure, time would slow so drastically that, from the point of view of an observer, it would seem to have stopped. If a spaceship were to pass the "event horizon" of a black hole, beyond which escape is impossible, that spaceship would appear to a distant observer to hang suspended for eternity though its occupants would experience time as passing normally until the ship itself was squeezed out of existence and space-time disappeared. Alternatively, they might find themselves spewed out into another universe, or into a different time and place in this one, along with everything else that had been sucked into the black hole.

Before Einstein, scientists thought that space extended infinitely. Now, most believe it to be both expanding and curved. In predicting the ultimate fate of the Universe, the crucial question is: How curved?

In 1949, mathematician Kurt Gödel theorized that the Universe contained enough mass to curve space into an enclosed sphere. If space were circular, then time—which is inseparable from it—would also be circular, as intuited thousands of years ago by Eastern mystics. To travel into the future, Gödel calculated that a spaceship would have to fly in the direction of the Universe's rotation at 70 per cent or better of the speed of light; to get into the past, it would have to fly against the Universe's rotation.

Such a closed, expanding Universe would one day reach its maximum and then begin to contract. According to one model, time would go backwards, light would shine from the Earth to the Sun, oaks would shrink down into acorns, the ash covering Pompeii would swoop back into the mouth of Vesuvius, coffins would rise from the ground, John Kennedy would back out of his Dallas limousine and resume his presidency, and no one would notice anything odd since everyone's thinking processes would also be reversed. Eventually, the Universe and time itself would end in the Big Crunch.

Would there be another Big Bang, producing another Universe, either like this one or with different properties? That is what scientists call the oscillating Universe—a model also envisioned by Hindu mystics. The ancient seers attributed it metaphorically to the great god Brahma, who opens and closes his eyes a thousand times a day for a hundred years, creating and destroying universes with each blink, till he himself dies to be replaced by another Brahma. In modern cosmology, astrophysicist Werner Israel of the University of Alberta substitutes a black hole for Brahma. According to his theory, the collapse of the Universe would leave a single stew of black holes with "inflated mass increased to infinity." Not only would another Big Bang be inevitable but it would create a Universe more massive than this one.

All the above drama of crunching and oscillating is based on the premise of a closed Universe. However, if our present Universe does not contain enough matter to curve it around on itself, nothing would prevent it from expanding infinitely in every direction, growing darker and thinner and deader. This, too, would lead to the end of time, but—in the words of T.S. Eliot—"not with a bang but a whimper."

SUBJECTIVE TIME

DECEMBER 1963

My husband and I drive along icy roads to a ski resort near Mont Tremblant, Quebec. Ahead of us is a right-angled corner leading onto a small bridge. Though my husband turns the wheel, the car slides perpendicularly across the bridge into a frozen river. Seemingly at leisure, he straightens the wheel, turns off the ignition, opens the power windows for possible evacuation, even lowers the power aerial as the car s-l-ow-l-y drops its own length to stick, nose down in ice and mud.

Years previous I was in another car accident, this time with a bus at an intersection: again, that interminable wait while the crash seemed to happen in slow motion. On a third occasion, I was asleep with my head on the back seat of a car that was rear-ended. That impact knocked me to the floor—a matter of inches, yet, from the instant my head left the seat until it hit the floor, I had a train of thought so pithy that it took me the rest of the journey to try to relate it. Literally, my life passed before my eyes.

What could account for these bubbles of eternity in which a single second seems to expand in proportion to the human need for more time?

Unlike time in the cosmos, the time we carry inside our minds is independent of space. In this private theater, our thoughts leap about from person to person and continent to continent as easily as they fix on our own face in the mirror. Events in the realm of consciousness are also independent of past, present and future: though "now" can't be found in the cosmos, that is all that does exist in our heads—one single, eternally moving, forever undefinable instant. However, because we humans are body as well as mind, with insistent physical desires, we routinely bind our consciousness of time to our body's experience of it. And because we are members of a very efficient and extroverted collective, we have externalized and quantified time so that we have only to look at the nearest clock—usually on our own wrist—to know what time it "really" is.

This Newtonian idea of absolute time flowing as a river is not entirely displeasing to our conscious minds. Because of a mysterious something called memory, we think of ourselves as living for a span of time, which we divide into past, present and future, equating with a riverboat passenger's concept of what he or she has seen, is seeing and will see. If activities aboard the riverboat were run on a rigid schedule, then all the passengers might experience the passage of time in approximately the same way: breakfast at eight, handicrafts at nine, aerobics at ten. Yet when each of us is left to our own meditative devices, our mind's experience of the flow of time is more likely to be that of a single paddler in a canoe, who sometimes shoots forward into the rapids, sometimes meanders through quiet lagoons, and sometimes even slides backwards into an eddy before again plunging headlong.

This frustrating clash between subjective time and Greenwich time is often expressed in our metaphors. We say that time hangs heavy on our hands, that it slips through our fingers, that it flies, that it never ends, that it is lost, that it drags its feet and even that it stops. Though this inner experience of time seems more real to each of us than the one advertised on the nearest clock, we constantly invalidate it by apologizing for any discrepancies, on the grounds that we are wrong and the clock is right.

Not only do members of our species experience time differently in different moods but we also experience time differently at different ages. When we were children, our two-month summer holiday beckoned to us like an endless pathway of green and gold. Recess, though only fifteen minutes long, provided time enough to choose a game, pick teams and play a round or two before the teacher blew the whistle. For the presiding teacher, that same period probably seemed scarcely worth the trouble of donning winter boots. Given what we now know about the plasticity of cosmic time, is it possible that subjective time truly is longer for children? Can people, at one and the same Earth moment, even while sharing the same region of space, possess a different quantity of inner time, perhaps corresponding to a different quantity of disposable energy?

Einstein's famous $E = mc^2$ demonstrated the equivalence of mass and energy. He also demonstrated a connection between the gravitational effect of mass on time, thus linking energy with time through mass. Perhaps the world of consciousness possesses a yet undiscovered equation connecting energy and time, so that humans with more energy actually possess more time. Perhaps students attacking the same exam with varying focuses of energy actually have differing lengths of time to complete it. Perhaps energy-time explains why some people are able to accomplish so much more than others—their moments are indeed longer. Perhaps having more energy means having more time.

Perhaps children have larger amounts of energy, for the size of their systems, giving them more time per second to accomplish the formidable task of absorbing an entire culture. Perhaps that is why they experience time as passing slower than do adults—each moment for them may in fact be longer, a plump grape instead of a wizened raisin. Perhaps death can be defined as loss of energy = loss of time: the organism runs out of energy and so, for it, time stops. Nothing moves, not even thought, because no time is left for something to move in.

How does a fetus experience time? In its development from floating, fertilized egg to duplicate human, some biologists believe it re-enacts the amoeba's evolution from ocean organism to land mammal. Does this drama, as experienced by the fetus, require "eons and eons of time," as once suggested by Scottish psychiatrist R.D. Laing? Perhaps that is why so many women declare their pregnancies to be the longest nine months of their lives: as a vessel enfolding this process, each tunes in to the fetus's protracted experience of time. Yet this persistent observation of slow time by mothers-to-be is routinely dismissed as a perceptual mistake, perhaps even a complaint about pregnancy's inconvenience. Has the snappy efficiency of pointing to a calendar or a clock blinded us to the deeper truths encoded in our tissues?

The very old often experience time with the same blurred disregard for its passage as the very young. The linear concept of past, present and future, so vigorously impressed upon us as growing children, seems mysteriously to come unlearned. Elderly minds wander in and out of the past without seeming to know they should be in the present. Specifically, they incline toward childhood memories, which grow increasingly vivid—a cyclical concept of time, symbolized by the ancient image of the snake swallowing its own tail. This preoccupation with the distant past persists, despite the alarmed attempts of middle-aged children—then at the height of their clockworthiness—to yank them back to reality as dictated by Greenwich.

Perhaps the elderly do not so much lose energy as rechannel it from active outer use to inner contemplation. Perhaps the wandering mind is already detaching itself from its atrophying brain, like a ripe fruit from a dying stalk, in preparation for a more spiritual phase of its journey. Perhaps time-energy is draining, like the sand in an hourglass, from one state of consciousness into another.

Not only is time different for different people, at different ages, in different moods, doing different things, but it is species-specific. An elephant lives in a different universe from an ant, in time as well as in space. As organisms get smaller, requiring less space, their life cycles seem to speed up, requiring less time. Thus, elephants have a longer lifespan than rabbits, which, nevertheless, dramatically outlive butterflies—a persistent though by no means exact relationship between mass and time *as seen from the human point of view*. How the organisms themselves experience time is another question. Since a boulder is a mountain to an ant, might not a minute be a month? If a person lives in a different time frame from the rabbit sitting on its lap, could an adult human live in a different time frame from the child on its lap? If we, as humans, shrank to the size of ants, would time for us speed up? More to the point, if our world shrank with us, how would we know it?

Before Einstein confirmed the unity of cosmic space and time, this intuitive awareness was enshrined in popular culture. The English language uses *long* and *short* to describe both cedar boards and vacations. A long sea voyage was the Victorian prescription for a broken heart, and authors still relocate in foreign lands to write about their own lives in hopes that miles will distance them from emotional events as effectively as years. Perhaps this space-time equivalent also provides a metaphoric clue as to how the future in the ordinary world may be foreseen. A human watching ants drag a dead beetle can predict that those ants will soon have to circle around a stone, visible a foot away. This is a prediction about time, based on a greater command of space, allowing the human observer to see both ants and stone in the same space-time frame. Before the ants reach the stone, the human may remove it, or a galloping horse may dislodge it, or a sudden shower may disperse the ants, or they may choose to reroute themselves. Therefore, the prediction is a probable one that depends on conditions staying approximately the same.

Perhaps in the world of consciousness a viewpoint exists from which future probabilities in the external world can be observed as clearly as the future of the ants dragging a beetle. The closer the event in time (corresponding to space) and the fewer the choices, the more accurate the prediction. For thousands of years, mystics have talked about "higher" consciousness, suggesting elevation in space. Can they, through mental discipline, reach some metaphoric plateau that allows a panoramic view of past and future?

The connection between an organism's biology and its experience of time is tied to its metabolism, which means its use of energy, along with its perceptual ability. For humans, visual time can be divided into increments of one-twenty-fourth of a second, which is the speed of a movie projector. Action faster than that is too fine for us to distinguish. However, a trout can perceive visual increments as fast as one-fiftieth of a second. Therefore, a trout can pack over twice as much visual information into a second as a human. For a school of trout, watching *Casablanca* might be more like attending a slideshow, with each frame distinct from every other.

During meditation, practitioners dramatically alter their consciousness by slowing down their metabolic rate. In altering their biology, are they also altering their experience of time, in a "real" rather than merely an experiential way, just like the space twin who aged only half as much as his earthbound sibling?

Whereas Kant spoke of time and space as projections of the human mind, physicist David Bohm described them as four-dimensional abstractions from a higher-dimensional reality. Both essentially agreed with Eastern seers: that time is illusory, suggesting the possibility that it can—at least in theory—be slowed or subverted. Traditionally, the Hindu yogi does this through intense concentration on the moment, reducing it to zero, whereas the Buddhist meditator achieves the same effect through detached awareness. Both approaches have their parallels in ordinary experience. The "cool" mind of the Buddhist is like that of the dreamer, who experiences paranormal effects when his/her rational guard is down, while the "hot" mind of the yogi corresponds to that of the person in crisis, whose attention is focused with laser-like intensity. When I received intimations of my husband's death, I was idly sorting papers in the "cool" detached Buddha state of mind; by contrast, when he and I were hurtling in our car over a bridge, we were in "hot" time.

In the heat of battle, soldiers have frequently reported pockets of eternity during which they casually loaded guns and fired while time seemed to stand still. Athletes have also described moments of heightened awareness during which they had endless time to aim then slam a puck—a subjective truth brilliantly imitated by TV's slow-motion replays. Not only are such moments exhilarating but they are also intervals during which much work gets done—work with observable results. In the case of my husband preparing his car for impact, or of a soldier loading his gun, that time distortion has obvious survival value. Can a threatened organism, faced with a foreshortened future, expand its "now" moment with the mental equivalent of adrenalin? Can, for example, a human so effectively utilize a second that he or she passes into "trout time," allowing for twice as many events to happen in that second? Is that how my husband could, seemingly at leisure, perform a number of physical tasks, within a time-suspended bubble, while our car plunged over a low bridge? Similarly, is it having *more time* to shoot a puck or fire a football that gives top athletes their competitive edge?

And what about the orderly way in which my life passed before my eyes while I fell from car seat to floor, as if I were sorting my mental baggage for what might prove a new journey? If life is meaningful, or continues after death, that response would have spiritual survival value.

IS THE FUTURE FIXED?

AUGUST 8, 1990

A friend I am visiting challenges me over breakfast: "Why didn't you tell me you flattened my bike tire?" As it turns out, she is just joking about something she dreamed vividly enough to mention.

I, too, have had a dream, still very much on my mind. Mine was about a mutual friend who approached me, waving a sheet of paper and exclaiming, "An astrologer told me someone was going to be killed in a car like mine. Who could it be?" What chilled me enough to awaken me was my conviction that this dream is precognitive and my friend herself may be in danger.

I am meeting that friend for lunch. While I am debating if I will mention my dream, she arrives, waving a letter and exclaiming: "A woman I know was crushed by a car."

"What kind of a car?"
"Like mine. A van."
    *Immediately, I tell this friend my dream, warning her that I
feel she, too, must be careful. I also invite her for dinner that evening.*
    *This friend arrives for dinner an hour late, appearing shaken.
Her van blew a tire while she was driving down a hill. She credits my
warning for the fact that she was traveling much slower than usual,
perhaps averting an accident.*

    In the above prediction, four minds seemed to be in
contact—my hostess who dreamed about a flat tire, our mutual
friend who had the flat tire, her friend who had an accident in a
van like hers, and my dreaming self who connected them. Though
all that I remembered from my dream was the image of my friend
waving a paper and two lines of dialogue, these identified the two
vehicles as similar, identified two persons as perhaps in danger, and
mentioned an astrologer, implying prophecy. My hostess's
contribution—about the flat tire—might have been coincidental,
since she associated it with a bike I had borrowed. However, that
she thought to mention this dream when I was brooding over my
own suggests some connection. My dream's prediction, that
someone would be killed, might have been an exaggeration to
underline the warning, or it might have been an outcome that was
averted. Significantly, I sensed in advance that the dream was
precognitive, that something "real" was at stake.
    After several studies of dream precognition, psychologist
David Ryback concluded that about one in twelve persons has
knowingly had at least one dream that came true. Though
prophecies of doom are often the most dramatic, they are difficult
to validate because, like remorseful thieves who replace the loot
and wipe away their fingerprints, they invite tampering with the
evidence to prevent a negative result. In his book *Dreams That
Come True*, Ryback cited the case of a Florida woman who dreamed
her brother had disconnected a rod in his stock car, then had
forgotten to rehook it. When he climbed into the car to drive, she
began to scream.
    Next morning the brother phoned his sister to report that
he had been awakened the night before by a dream in which she

had screamed a warning. After the sister related her dream, the brother checked his car, even though he had not been tinkering with it. Sure enough, he discovered his brake cable was broken—a problem he believed would have caused a crash. Did the woman's precognitive dream save her brother's life, or did she merely have a well-timed nightmare dramatizing fears about her brother's dangerous hobby?

One of the most famous examples of what might have been purposeful avoidance occurred on March 1, 1950, when fifteen members of a choir were due at 7:20 P.M. for a practice at their church in Beatrice, Nebraska. As reported in *Life* magazine three weeks later, everyone was late for ten separate reasons, so that when the church exploded at 7:25, no one was killed. Was this the result of precognition combined with group telepathy, reflecting the choir's close bonding? According to mathematician Warren Weaver, the chance-against-odds of ten reasons so fortuitously coinciding calculates at one in a million.

During a 1974 Noel Coward revue in London, Ontario, comedian Beatrice Lillie unaccountably repeated the second verse of "Britannia Rules the Waves." Before she finished, an arc light crashed to centerstage where the cast would have been assembled if she had been on cue. Was this a fortuitous mistake on Bea Lillie's part, or does it demonstrate the blessings of precognition? If the latter, how frequently do people protect themselves from danger without realizing it?

That was the subject of a 1960s study by U.S. mathematician William Cox. Targeting trains that had crashed or derailed, Cox compared the number of passengers in these coaches with those in other coaches of the same train for seven preceding days and on the same day for three preceding weeks. In every case, fewer passengers occupied the damaged coaches, with estimated odds-against of one in a hundred. This suggested to Cox that potential passengers, "smelling" danger, had practiced purposeful avoidance.

What about the other half of the equation: How frequently do people use precognition, in the guise of hunches, intuitions, gut feelings and lucky guesses, to secure good fortune?

In a study reported in 1974, parapsychologists E. Douglas Dean and John Mihalasky focused on successful corporate presidents, whom they defined as having doubled their companies' profits within five years. When challenged to pre-guess numbers that were being randomly generated, these men scored 43 per cent higher than non-doublers. Though the sample used by Dean and Mihalasky was too small to be statistically relevant, this and other related tests seemed to support the executive ESP hypothesis. Perhaps just as notably, the presidents themselves overwhelmingly believed in their psychic power, and freely admitted relying heavily on it.

As an example of gut instincts in action, Dean cited the case of New Jersey automobile dealer Lawrence Tynan who, in June 1971, compulsively ordered five times more cars than he had ever ordered before, even though his lot was full and no one was buying. As Tynan confessed to Dean: "I thought I had gone crazy." Then, on August 15, 1971, President Richard Nixon announced a 10 per cent duty on foreign cars, along with relaxation of the 7 per cent tax on domestically produced cars. Suddenly, buyers were flocking to Tynan's lot, and since he had the goods while competitors did not, he emerged a millionaire. Was this a lucky guess, or was Tynan a man who had sniffed out tomorrow?

An insider's view of "hunch" decision making was provided by the late hotelier Conrad Hilton, who attributed his good fortune to a four-step process: relaxing in an empty Roman Catholic cathedral, visualizing the problem facing him, listening for the answer, and acting upon it no matter how foolish it seemed. It is perhaps the last part that distinguishes the knowing prophet from the lucky profiteer.

READING TOMORROW'S NEWSPAPER

APRIL 11, 1983
I awaken at dawn with a piece of a dream lodged maddeningly in my brain like a fragment of food caught in the teeth. Still groggy, I write it down just to get rid of it: "Two condors have hatched. One is off somewhere, but the second flies awkwardly to a friend's slate roof where it perches." Since the comic, ungainly image of the bird is still so vivid, I take unusual care in its description: "It is fat and unbalanced, very immature, with stubby wings that barely allow it to fly, the shape

of a peahen with speckled down feathers across its behind, a bald head and oversized feet."

Since all I know about the condor is that it's a bird of prey, I check Webster's dictionary: "Condor—a very large American vulture found in elevated parts of the Andes. . . . see CALIFORNIA CONDOR."

Unwilling to pursue the matter further, I retrieve my Toronto Star from the doorstep to read with my morning coffee. Astounded, I stare at the photo on page two. It is a six-inch close-up of the ridiculous bird from my dream with a caption reading: "BEAUTIFUL BABY. Sisquoc, the first California condor ever born in captivity, is doing well at the San Diego Wild Animal Park. The 2 1/2-week-old rare bird now weighs 1 pound, 15 ounces. His younger brother, Tecuya, is also doing fine."

What amazes me is how precisely my dream image corresponds to that of the news photo: no mistaking that grotesque body or those silly protruding feet! Where had I acquired such a specialized image? Had I once seen a picture of a baby condor? Had I learned sometime during the past two weeks of the birth of these twins? On the off-chance that I did, what was the probability of my dreaming so vividly about this nestling minutes before finding its photo prominently displayed in my newspaper? Though the condor story was hardly the most newsworthy, it was the most eye-catching—the one item anyone flipping pages could hardly help but notice. And why did my dream so pointedly note the birth of two condors even though I saw only one—an anomaly paralleled by the photo and caption?

Then there was that ironic footnote. My Webster's had ordered: "See CALIFORNIA CONDOR." See it I had!

Parapsychologists are struck by how often people with psychic sensitivity to the future claim to have previewed tomorrow's newspaper or TV news. This is especially true when the event is a national disaster with extensive coverage. Instead of envisioning the tragedy from the point of view of its participants, these people anticipate it the way they will experience it through the media, thus preserving the well-noted egocentricity of dreams.

On the morning of June 1, 1974, Mrs. Lesley Brennan was watching the movie *The Nevadan* on TV when a news flash announced an explosion in a chemical plant at Flixborough, Lincolnshire, twenty miles away, with many people killed and injured. At noon, Brennan reported the tragedy to Janice and Peter East, and they watched the evening news together. When the announcer described the explosion as happening in late afternoon, Brennan was indignant: "Silly reporters! Got it wrong again." However, next morning's paper repeated that detail. Said Brennan: "I went ever so cold. I really went funny. We went out and got another paper and that said teatime, too."

In fact, the plant had exploded at 4:53 P.M., killing twenty-eight people and damaging nearly two thousand factories and shops—five hours *after* Brennan made her announcement to friends.

On October 21, 1966, Constance Milder of Devon had a vision of an old schoolhouse in a valley. Then she saw a Welsh miner, and an avalanche of coal hurtling down a mountainside toward a terrified little boy with a fringe of long hair. "He looked so grief-stricken I could never forget him, and also with him was one of the rescuers wearing an unusual peaked cap."

Milder reported her vision to seven friends the day before a coaltip crashed onto a school in Aberfan, Wales, killing 144, mostly children. Later, while watching TV, she saw both the terrified child and the rescuer in peaked cap.

Intrigued by the number of people who claimed fore-knowledge of this Welsh tragedy, British psychiatrist J.C. Barker investigated sixty claims. Though most subjects had never before heard of Aberfan, thirty-five satisfied his criteria for detail, accuracy and corroboration. Only one was by someone who died in the disaster. The day before, ten-year-old Eryl Mai Jones told her busy mother: "Mummy, you must listen. I dreamt I went to school and there was no school there. Something black had come down all over it!"

Fiction is also a rich source of precognitive material, perhaps because of the zeal with which authors mine the unconscious. In his 1898 novel, *Futility*, American author Morgan Robertson told how a monster ship, called the *Titan*—remarkably similar to the *Titanic* in length, tonnage, number of passengers, shortage of lifeboats and reputation as unsinkable—also struck an iceberg on her maiden voyage in April in the North Atlantic. Though Robertson was known to write in a near-trance state, with little research, skeptics dismiss the parallels as shrewd guesswork based on probabilities. However, it's hard to attribute Edgar Allan Poe's accidental prophecy in "The Narrative of Arthur Gordon Pym of Nantucket" to Poe's having his finger on the social pulse. Published in 1838, it told how three shipwrecked survivors, adrift in an open boat, killed and ate a cabin boy named Richard Parker. Forty-six years later, in 1884, three shipwrecked British sailors, rescued from an open boat, were tried by British courts for killing and eating a cabin boy. His name: Richard Parker.

Though the coincidence with the Poe story was mentioned at the sailors' trial, none claimed to have been causally inspired by it. Did Poe foresee the future?

QUIRKS OF TIME

OCTOBER 1983

I am dining at a Toronto restaurant with a friend who suffers chronic back trouble. For no fathomable reason, I hear myself tell him: "In India the trendy new treatment for back pain is to carry an elephant on your back. It's sort of a ritual. In Calcutta you can see whole processions carrying them through the streets."

Despite my companion's puzzled but polite skepticism, I persist: "Well, of course, I don't mean large elephants, I mean baby elephants. Indian elephants are much smaller than the African ones, you know."

By now I am suitably embarrassed for myself. Why am I saying these silly things? They aren't witty, just stupid. Yet, compelled by a now-vivid image of a turbaned Indian carrying an elephant on his back, I launch into a highly implausible, completely false explanation about how this treatment works by massaging the spine.

Four hours later, I am having coffee with this same friend outside another restaurant when I stare open-mouthed over his shoulder: there is my turbaned Indian, bent double under an elephant—a stuffed one!

Though it's one thing to pick up the vibrations of a national disaster or the death of a loved one, it's quite another to dream the birth of twin condors or to hallucinate an East Indian carrying a child's toy on his back. Nor were these isolated incidents. Shortly after dreaming of the baby condors, I had a second dream in which two enigmatic black shapes planed across the sky before crashing into a pool where a dead horse floated. That evening, when I turned on the TV, I was startled to see the same silhouettes, now identified as a pair of condors, with square-tipped black wings stretched across the sky. As I watched mesmerized, they swooped down to gorge on the carcass of a wild horse.

During this same period of queer coincidences I had a long, discursive dream in which I was looking for a ski run called the Rambling Rose. That noon, the soup-of-the-day chalked on the board of my local East Indian restaurant was Rambling Rose. When I asked the chef what had inspired the name, he told me it had just popped into his head because of the soup's rosy color.

In his book *Man about Time*, published in 1964, J.B. Priestley told of soliciting BBC listeners to the show "Monitor" to send in their precognitive dreams. Of more than a thousand submissions, nearly half were about tragedies, and most of the rest were about trivialities over which many expressed embarrassment. Conspicuously missing were premonitions about routine job activities and everyday family happenings, even though these occupy most of our waking lives.

One celebrated example of precognitive silliness, which was investigated and confirmed by the Society for Psychical Research, centered on a Mrs. Atlay, wife of the bishop of Hereford, who dreamed that she had entered the dining room of the bishop's palace, after reading morning prayers, only to find an enormous pig standing in front of the sideboard. So amused was she by this dream that she told it to her children and their governess before reading the morning prayer. Afterwards she led them into the dining room where they saw, standing saucily before the sideboard, a huge pig, which had escaped its sty during the prayers.

The standard explanation for precognitive quirks is leakage: just as police calls sometimes bleed through commercial channels— or, it is said, through bedsprings and teeth-fillings—so inconsequential psychic messages may sometimes, in off-guard moments, seep through the filters put up by our brains. My alternative explanation is that these psychic fleabites may have personal significance: just as the dreaming mind rifles through the preceding day for images to encode its messages, so it may, on occasion, also dip into the near future. On the level of precognition, my baby condor dream was of no importance. On the level of emotional truth, it packed a wallop: since it occurred just before my incestuous past emerged into consciousness, something large was indeed hatching in my unconscious.

Another oddity of precognition is the frequency with which provocative mistakes are made. David Ryback tells of a woman who awoke in agitation convinced that her father-in-law had died. Though her husband refused to phone his family on the grounds that her anxiety was silly, the father-in-law himself called that evening to reassure them that he was all right: the UPI wire service had carried his death notice, having confused him with another doctor of the same name, so that his obituary had appeared that morning in the *New York Times*.

Why did the daughter-in-law pick up the media mistake instead of the emotional truth of her father-in-law's health? Surely in the world of the unconscious that should have carried more authority than the *New York Times*!

QUANTUM TIME

OCTOBER 23, 1986
I am having breakfast with my husband on the patio of our Toronto apartment. He has the front section of the Toronto Star, while I have the Entertainment section. When I ask if he would like to see the movie The Accused, he replies: "If you don't mind, I'd like to drive over to Hamilton and visit Mom and Dad's grave." Though surprised, I consent. Then, noticing that we've run out of milk, I announce that I'm going down to the store to buy some.

As I step from the elevator into the apartment lobby, I stare nonplused. The lobby has been entirely renovated! Though the doorman is not at his desk, a newspaper lies folded on top. Feeling peculiar, I pick it up and open it. I see the same headline as on my husband's paper—something about freeing Nelson Mandela before Christmas. However, as I focus on the date—October 23, 1988—I remember, with a sickening jolt, that my husband died more than a year and a half ago. Involuntarily, I picture him lying in his coffin, chest unheaving. No mistake. Dead.

It occurs to me for the first time that I must be dreaming. This thought does not bring the usual flood of relief. Everything up to the point where I stepped into the lobby still seems entirely real. When I struggle to make sense of this conflict, the conviction strengthens that I have a choice: I can take the elevator back up to the apartment I just left and pick up the story with my husband where I left off without any knowledge anything is amiss, or I can open my eyes to my present home and the life I now know.

For seconds—perhaps minutes—I hang suspended between two lives, awestruck at the implications. In the end, a preference for one does not overwhelm a preference for the other. What tips my decision is the feeling that the person who would return to the apartment to greet the man "I" thought dead would be someone "I" no longer knew, whereas if I stay with my present life I at least will possess the memory of this conflict.

I open my eyes in my present home. On my bed-table is yesterday's newspaper—the same as in my dream, no mystery there. Resting on top is the milkweed paperweight that my late sister gave to me under special circumstances—a peculiarity, since this table is not where it belongs and I don't know how it got here. Beside the paperweight is a real milkweed parachute, another peculiarity since my window is closed. Yet these are small perplexities, like the stir of wind in an airtight room, in comparison to the perceptual enormity I am facing: did I stumble into a parallel world?

Of course, my rational mind tears up that thought as soon as it forms; yet, after more than three years, I can still remember the awe I felt on awakening. As the sage Chuang-tzu opined: "I dreamt I was a butterfly, but pondered on awakening if I were not now a butterfly dreaming it was a man."

Today, I still hold that paradox in my mind.

In the subatomic world, where particles swirl like snow-flakes in a storm, the idea of time is even more elusive than in the world of the cosmos. In the life of a particle, what is past and what is future? Since all subatomic processes can be reversed in time with no loss of significance, one can as easily look at a close-up photo of swirling snowflakes and try to determine which direction is up and which down.

In 1949, U.S. physicist Richard Feynman suggested that quantum physicists might be routinely observing time-travel into the past without realizing it. According to conventional theory, every particle has an anti-particle of equal mass and opposite charge; when they collide, they annihilate each other. However, Feynman hypothesized that anti-particles may be particles traveling backward in time. Since the annihilation and reverse-time theories are mathematically equivalent, only convention establishes one over the other. Thus, the same particle could theoretically zip back and forth forever, appearing in different places at the same time.

The strategies of a subatomic particle in search of a future are equally provocative. An electron's orbit around the nucleus of an atom represents its energy state at any given moment. When an electron loses or gains energy, it must find a new orbit, representing its new energy state. It does this by leaping over space rather than passing through it the way a golf ball would have to do. Metaphorically, it's as if one were to make a movie of an arcing golf ball, then to slice out some of the frames so that the ball seemed to dematerialize in one frame only to rematerialize several frames later, having missed some of the spaces between. This is known as a quantum leap—something new in physics, but a commonplace in science fiction, the world of the paranormal and creative thought. In science fiction, it is teleportation, as familiar to "Star Trek" fans as the command "Beam me up, Scotty!" In the paranormal, it is telepathy, in which an image contained in one mind suddenly appears fullblown in another, regardless of distance. In creative thought, it is known as an intuitive leap, in which a conclusion is reached without consciously passing through an intervening chain of logic.

In the quantum world, the process by which an excited electron finds a new orbit is even more complex, for instead of making a single quantum leap it makes several—not in succession but simultaneously. This means that the same electron will exist, for an exceedingly brief period, in more than one place at the same time—another impossibility in Newtonian physics. Even odder:

while occupying these temporary orbits, it will affect other particle processes from these positions, creating changes that remain in effect even after it has stabilized in a single, chosen orbit. Again, metaphorically, it's as if a shopper, energized by having money to burn, were to suddenly teleport into three changing booths at the same time, where he/she would simultaneously try on three outfits, tearing off a button in one booth, writing on the wall in another, forgetting a wallet in the third, then quitting the store wearing a single outfit, but leaving the staff to pick up a button, clean a wall and find a wallet in the abandoned booths.

As previously described: a particle is, at one and the same time, a wave. In coming to grips with that duality, physicists began to speak of a particle/wave as a "probability wave"—an abstract mathematical entity that expresses the particle's dual nature as well as its possible position and energy state. The key word here is *possible*, since these are not fixed properties of the particle but embrace a range of potentialities that *might* manifest themselves. For this reason, physicists have come to refer to a particle as having a tendency-to-exist and to engage in events that have a tendency-to-occur—rather like the shopper who had a tendency-to-exist in several booths at the same time while choosing a single outfit for an actual future.

Although events in the quantum world are too abstract to be visualized, physicists have learned to make meaningful graphs of probability waves. Thus, if a particle has the possibility of passing through one of two slits when fired at a fluorescent screen, the probability wave for that particle would be drawn with two humps. When the particle is observed to go through one slit as opposed to the other, the hump representing the unused potential collapses, leaving only the hump that was actualized. Again this is a quantum leap—the mystifying jump from several possibilities not quite existing to a single actuality.

Since physicists make graphs to describe many particles facing many possible futures in many dimensions, the above is a gross simplification. The point to be stressed is that quantum physics acknowledges a zone of probability where present and future intermingle in some real though unactualized way. This is a free zone, never before recognized by science but familiar to occultists, where the distinctions of time are blurred; it is a womb in which precognitive events, if they exist, are generated.

In 1960, psychiatrist Ninian Marshall theorized that our brains' neural circuits might, through resonance, pick up the mixture of possibility and actuality in probability waves as they sweep toward a future. This would be experienced, in the sensory world, as precognition. Cambridge physicist and mathematician Adrian Dobbs agreed. As he stated in a 1965 paper: "We have to consider the system as, so to speak, trying out tentatively all the possible potentialities out of which one actuality emerges."

Dobbs postulated a five-dimensional Universe, with two dimensions of time, of which the second was a free zone ruled by probability instead of linear causation. Anticipation of future events would occur in this fifth dimension ruled by probability waves that predisposed the future to occur in specific ways. He called the hypothetical messengers of this fifth dimension psitrons. Of imaginary mass and faster than light, they would interact with neural processes to telegraph "pre-casts" of a probable future. An especially sensitive brain, or one in a receptive state, might consciously tune in to swarms of them, receiving a vision of tomorrow.

This is but one precognitive model. Physicists who vote for an observer-created Universe are even more radical. They suggest that not only does each of us have the potential to perceive the future but we actively create it. To the question "What collapses a probability wave with its many versions of the future into a single, realized event?" they reply: observation and/or measurement. In other words, we do! As summed up by Gary Zukav in *The Dancing Wu Li Masters*: "Without perception, the Universe continues . . . to generate an endless profusion of possibility. The effect of perception, however, is immediate and dramatic. All of the wave function representing the observed system collapses, except one part, which actualizes into reality."

This suggests the Universe is like a giant mind, creating endless possibilities, based on past events, that only humans and other conscious creatures can translate into action on the physical plane. This is the model that supports the New Age concept of visualization, in which to imagine a cure for cancer, or winning a lottery, or even a free parking space, is the first step toward materializing it. It is the model that supports the power of prayer, with or without the concept of God. It is what meditators mean when they talk of putting themselves in tune with their deeper selves and the Universe.

But an even greater materialistic outrage was to come: physicist Evan Harris Walker has suggested that the act of foreseeing an event in a particular way might even have the power to reach into the past to "fix" a cause so as to produce the anticipated future. Thus, the active-observer not only invents the future but can also reinvent the past, the way a novelist who has changed the ending of a story might then revise the first chapters to correspond. Of course, in real life the "author" forgets the act of revision, so that past, present and future appear as a seamless whole.

Just as radical: physicists Hugh Everett and John Wheeler suppose that all the possibilities represented by a probability wave are equally real and remain so. According to the Many Worlds Interpretation, each time an either/or choice is made the Universe divides into a pair of parallel Universes so that all choices are realized. If a person has a choice of going to a party or not going to a party, the probability wave governing that choice does not collapse, favoring one decision. Instead, the person duplicates, so that one self goes to the party and one does not, with each self continuing to divide *ad infinitum* as other choices are made. Since every self coexists in a separate band of reality, never the twain (or multi-twain) shall meet—except, perhaps, paranormally.

The Many Worlds Interpretation is unwieldy only if one thinks in terms of physical worlds dividing in real time and space. As a psychic concept, it is little more than a reflection of our present model of consciousness, in which infinite numbers of possibilities can be simultaneously imagined by an infinite number of conscious beings. In fact, this happens every night when the sun goes down: each of us lies in bed, imagining ourselves in one scenario after another, with no sense of the airwaves being overcrowded.

For the physicist, the Many Worlds model solves the problem of what happens to the other humps in the probability wave: on the drawing board, all were equal, but in an objective world or an observer-driven one, only a single hump materializes. By contrast, the Many Worlds model is created entirely out of prophecy: no matter what future anyone envisions, some version of that person will live it.

The concept of parallel worlds received one of its first expressions in 1600, when Giordano Bruno was publicly burned in Rome for writing a book called *On the Infinite Universe and Worlds*. Today its various versions have modest but serious support among both quantum and astrophysicists. The former tend to invent their extra worlds out of the potentialities of consciousness, while the latter conjure them out of the material sucked into black holes, or from "lost" dimensions simultaneously created by the Big Bang.

To understand how these precognitive theories support and contradict each other, imagine an unsorted heap of Polaroid photos that picture all future possibilities, with those at the top most in focus and those at the bottom still in an undecipherable blur. Though Adrian Dobbs perceives the future as being generated from the heap of photos in an objective way, he hypothesizes that the photos at the top of the heap, most nearly developed, can be envisioned by the psychically aware brain as pre-casts of the future.

According to physicists who support the observer-created Universe, the future is determined not by the photos themselves but by the observers of the photos. As each of us examines one photo and then another, those photos develop by absorbing energy from our perception and expectation. As we fill in more and more details through our concentration, one particular photo clarifies. For an instant, it is framed in our consciousness as "now," only to be followed in quick succession by another "now" and another.

Perhaps each of us has complete control over selecting our individual futures, frame by frame, to be spliced together as our personal movie. Perhaps other people's needs and desires compete with our own to create a single master print. Therefore, as one of us reaches for the desired next photo, someone else may snatch it, forcing us to select another. Or perhaps some photos come in strips, so that by choosing one we automatically acquire a string of others.

According to movie director Evan Harris Walker, not only does each of us create our own film but we can discard and replace earlier sequences so as to make the future more to our liking. According to directors Wheeler and Everett, all of our leftover frames go to create other movies, starring various versions of ourselves, which we never get to see since they are available only in Other World video stores. However, through some sort of fluke, a video in which I was still living with my husband appeared at my local outlet. After I reluctantly returned it, I was left with more-than-a-dream-but-not-quite-a-memory of one sequence. Does that other "me" still exist somewhere in a parallel universe? Did she accidentally see a sequence from my life video and make a similar choice to stay in her own dimension? Does "she" remember the Sunday when I wandered into her life? Does she also possess more-than-a-dream-but-not-quite-a-memory?

Some fifty years ago, Air Marshal Sir Victor Goddard had an eerie adventure in which he might have visited a parallel universe. The calendar year was 1935, while Goddard was serving as a wing commander in Scotland. One day, as he was flying through mountains in an open aircraft without radio-navigational aids, he was overtaken by a storm, which whipped his craft into a spin. After almost slamming a stone seawall, he lifted the nose of his plane over the waves of the Firth of Forth, then headed for Drem, an abandoned airfield outside Edinburgh.

Suddenly, beneath him, Goddard saw Drem and its surroundings brilliantly bathed in sunlight. However, instead of the derelict hangars he had visited only the day before, he saw a line of refurbished ones. In spick-and-span order, on newly laid tarmac, were four airplanes: three Avro 504N biplane trainers and a monoplane of unknown type, which puzzled him since he knew the RAF had no monoplanes. All were a bright chrome yellow, although RAF craft in 1935 were exclusively aluminum-doped.

Mechanics were pushing a second monoplane as Goddard roared overhead, just clearing the hangar. "I must have been making a great deal of noise and, normally, this would have caused a con-siderable sensation. Zooming the hangars, as I was doing, was a court-martial offence!... None of them looked up." This struck Goddard as very strange. He was also surprised to see RAF mech-anics in blue overalls instead of brown. Just as abruptly, Goddard was again beset by deluging rain, turbulence and semidarkness.

Despite this renewed danger, Wing Commander Goddard returned to his base at Andover in a strange euphoria, and it was only the incredulity of officers to whom he described this miraculous new airfield that shocked him into realizing he must be hallucinating. However, four years later the Drem airfield was, indeed, refurbished the way Goddard envisioned it—as a training school, equipped with 504N biplanes and Magister monoplanes. Moreover, these planes were yellow—a 1939 innovation for training craft to increase their visibility. By that time, too, air mechanics were wearing blue overalls; however, the new hangars at Drem were of a different material and placement than Goddard had seen.

A peculiarity of Goddard's experience was that everything seemed so ordinary, except that the sunlight was "ethereal . . . brilliant and glorious," and the mechanics didn't react to his craft. "Evidently they neither saw nor heard me, but I could see both my airplane *and* them, at the same time. Afterwards I wondered whether, in the context, they were more real than I was! But . . . I was not disembodied. I was aware of . . . the noise that my airplane made, and I was aware of the appropriate sensations as I swooped out over the hangars. I had, however, been suffering from mental shock. . . . I had been really frightened by the loss of control in the cloud, by the near certainty of death."

Did Wing Commander Goddard, in the hallucinatory grip of fear, visit a probable future, possessing an airfield exactly where he wanted one? Did his precognition of a revitalized Drem help bring it into existence? Did an alternative plan ever exist to refurbish Drem precisely as he envisioned it? Did he pick up that plan telepathically? Does that Drem airport, just as Goddard believed he saw it, exist in a parallel universe of other choices? And what of the blue-overalled mechanics, pushing the yellow monoplane from its hangar? Were they, at the instant he saw them, working at an airbase they believed to be in the present?

In the new world, still on the drawing board, these are not irrational questions.

Friendly Ghosts and Soulful Journeys:

IN GOOD SPIRITS

"Soul is the last four-letter word left that is
unmentionable among the in."

—James Hillman

OCTOBER 1986

Along with forty others, I assemble in a Los Angeles conference room for what is billed as a "Clairaudience" by an "internationally renowned" psychic from England. For the next two hours a nervous man in his thirties relays to the audience messages allegedly whispered into his ear by spirits from the Other Side.

"Helen—I have a message for Helen."

When no Helen materializes, a woman puts up her hand: "My mother's name was Helen."

"I guess that's it! Thank you for speaking up." He cocks his head: "What's that, Mother?" He returns to the woman in the audience: "You've got to get some containers to hold things, don't you? Rice and things like that?"

"Well . . . I've got to get planters for some plants."

"Oh, I see. That must be it. You're having trouble with the color?"

"Yes."

"Mother's aware of that, you see. . . . Do you know any Browns?"

"No."

A man exclaims: "My mother was a Brown."

"Mother Brown is standing beside me, feeling a little self-conscious. . . . Are you wanting to get a Rolodex, then?"

"What's a Rolodex?"

"She's saying to me 'paper'. . . . No, wait. It's pepper. Do you like spicy food?"

"I avoid it."

"Ah, well, that's what it is! . . . I feel a lovely vibration around this woman over here. You're a healer, aren't you?"

"I'm an accountant."

"A healer with words. Someone keeps saying, 'I'm her father!' . . . Your father lived where it was cold in winter, didn't he? He seems to want to give you a gift of some fresh raspberries that he's grown. . . . Was your mother always having trouble with her doorbell?"

"Yes!"

"And you're thinking of getting a new bell?"

"Yes!"

"You have a daughter, don't you!"

"No, I'm single."

"It's so hard to hear. . . . Oh, she's referring to you as her daughter. . . . Oh, dear, someone else is trying to push in. They're all crowding around, you see. . . . You know something about child abuse, don't you?"

"Just what I read in the papers."

I decide to play the game: *"I know something about child abuse."*

"Do you counsel mothers?"

"No."

"But you have formal training?"

"No."

"Are you a writer?"

"Yes."

"Something has been published. . . . Do you know someone who committed suicide?"

"Yes."

"A man? He shot himself!"

"No. He hanged himself."

"This had a strong influence on the family. There was another suicide? A lady. One was a family member and one not."

"Both were family members."

"It was your mother's family. He had tremendous internal problems. He couldn't face up to his own family. I'm getting a William or a Bill."

"No." *In fact, the last name was Wilson, but I don't immediately think of that.*

"The power is dropping. In a public meeting it's hard to get any depth. They're telling me it's time to close."

What to make of this shifty mix of irrelevancies, shot through with good luck or good reception? Do spirits walk among us? Can they be lured into our parlors and persuaded to speak? Do they really care about Rolodexes, raspberries and new doorbells?

This was the sort of superstitious twaddle scientific Enlightenment was supposed to banish. Yet, on March 31, 1848, a peculiar incident occurred near Hydesville in upstate New York that actively split the Western intellectual community for the next forty years.

After Mr. and Mrs. John D. Fox had put their young daughters to bed, they heard unusual noises reverberating through their farmhouse. On investigation, Mrs. Fox imagined she heard a pattern in the rappings, indicating a desire to communicate. At her request, the rapper knocked out the ages of the two Fox children—Margaret, eleven, and Kate, nine. Then, through leading questions in which three knocks meant yes and silence no, the rapper identified himself as the spirit of a man murdered by a former tenant for five hundred dollars.

Driven from their farmhouse—not by the rapper but by hordes of the curious—the Foxes discovered the rappings had followed them. Apparently, the "haunting" centered around Margaret and Kate. Using an alphabetic code suggested by them, the rapper knocked out messages, purportedly from the dead. Had the Foxes created a psychic telephone to "the other side"?

In a public demonstration in Rochester, four hundred people paid twenty-five cents to see the Fox sisters perform. Though local reviews were scathing, Horace Greeley of the New York *Weekly Tribune* invited them to hold seances in New York. Afterwards he endorsed the "perfect integrity and good faith" of the Fox sisters. Other distinguished believers included a judge of the Supreme Court, senators, clergymen, scientists, writers and historians.

Now the Fox sisters embarked on an international tour, which included seances at the White House and for Queen Victoria. Suddenly, families all over the Western world were holding hands in the dark, attempting to contact dead relatives. During the next couple of decades, Spiritualism developed into a full-fledged religious movement that, at its peak, produced an estimated thirty thousand trance mediums in America alone.

In 1882, the British Society for Psychical Research was founded with a stated bias for interpreting psychic phenomena within a scientific framework. During the next two decades, Michael Faraday, discoverer of electromagnetism, proved that table tappings and apparent levitation could be ascribed to the unconscious muscle exertions of the sitters. Other SPR investigators exposed so many self-styled mediums as blatant frauds or the victims of schizophrenia and multiple personality that angry believers nicknamed them the Society *against* Psychical Research.

However, one medium consistently produced results that could not be explained away: Boston housewife Leonora Piper. As a child of eight, she had been playing in the garden when she felt a breeze on her right ear, followed by a whisper: "Aunt Sarah, not dead but with you still." A frightened Leonora confided in her mother, and shortly afterward they learned that an aunt named Sarah had died at that time.

Piper's next psychic experience did not occur for another fifteen years. Then, during a seance at which she was a guest, she had a vision of many faces bathed in a bright light. After falling into a trance, she wrote a message for a Cambridge judge named Frost, also in the circle. Much shaken, he testified it could have come only from his deceased son.

As Piper's fame spread, she attracted the attention of psychologist William James. After rigorous testing, during which Piper poured out encyclopedic and intimate details of James's life, he declared: "Taking everything that I know of Mrs. Piper into account, the result is to me as absolutely certain as I am of any personal fact in the world that she knows things in her trances which she cannot possibly have heard in her waking state, and that the definite philosophy of her trances is yet to be found."

In another study of Piper, ethics professor James Hyslop of Columbia University declared that 77 per cent of the 1,000 pieces of information she received during fifteen sittings were correct, with only 5 per cent definitely incorrect.

After an independent investigation, the SPR issued a report, edited by physicist Sir Oliver Lodge, classical scholar Frederick Myers and Dr. Walter Leaf: "On the more delicate and interesting question as to the origin of the trance-utterances we cannot unite in any absolute view. We agree only in maintaining that the utterances show that knowledge has been acquired by some intelligence in some supernormal fashion."

Still unsatisfied, the SPR's chief spirit-spooker, Richard Hodgson, personally undertook to expose Piper. During his extensive investigations, Piper began receiving messages from one of Hodgson's friends—a skeptical lawyer named George Pellew who had been introduced anonymously to a sitting and had dropped dead four years later. In one hundred and fifty sittings over the next six years, Pellew's self-proclaimed spirit recognized thirty of his friends, also introduced anonymously to Piper's seances. On one occasion, while Piper was speaking in the voice of a different spirit, her hand started twitching. She grabbed a notebook, scrawled, "Private," then indicated that the message was for James Howard, a close friend of Pellew's. Writing furiously, Piper finished a page, thrust it at Howard, then began another, then another. As Hodgson later testified, the material she delivered contained precisely the kind of test-information for which Howard had asked. Howard pronounced himself "perfectly satisfied, perfectly."

Though Pellew's family was never convinced of the authenticity of Piper's contact, Hodgson's conversion was total: "I cannot profess to have any doubt but that they [the deceased]...have survived the change that we call death, and they have direct communication with us whom we call living, through Mrs. Piper's entranced organism."

Curiously, as Hodgson and the other SPR investigators died off, they allegedly began corresponding through Piper and other mediums. In particular, Piper began to receive extracts from Latin poems, wordplays and literary allusions from Frederick Myers. These were part of an interlocking set of messages received by mediums unknown to each other all over the world. Called "The Cross-Correspondence," this international cryptogram, compiled over thirty years, is regarded by some researchers as the best evidence yet for communication from beyond the grave.

A refreshing aspect of Piper's case was that she herself was not convinced that her information came from spirits. As she described her trances: "I feel as if something were passing over my brain, making it numb. . . . I feel a little cold, too . . . as if a cold breeze passed over me and people and objects become smaller until they finally disappear; then I know nothing more until I wake up, when the first thing I am conscious of is . . . a very bright light . . . and I see, as if from a distance, objects and people in the room; but they are very small and very black."

Despite Piper's brilliant record, an event occurred on October 21, 1888, that threatened the whole Spiritualist movement with an abrupt and ignominious end. After forty years of rave performances, Margaret Fox mounted a pine table on a New York stage in her stocking feet and, snapping her big toe against its top, caused loud rappings to reverberate throughout the auditorium. Dancing and clapping in excitement, she exclaimed: "Spiritualism is a fraud from beginning to end! It's a trick. There's no truth in it!" Then she accused her older sister Leah of manipulating her and Kate to make money.

In a New York *Herald* interview, Kate Fox concurred: "Spiritualism is a humbug from beginning to end."

Long-time skeptics toasted the demise of Spiritualism, confident it had burst like the Hindenburg dirigible. Though it did hang on for another decade, the Fox charade combined with other showy frauds eventually killed spirits-on-demand as a respectable pursuit. It also severely damaged the reputations of such scientists as Alfred Russel Wallace, codiscoverer of evolution, who had been an enthusiastic convert. What gloaters failed to address was why so many stars of the scientific world, as well as ordinary folk, had succumbed in the first place. Could it be that materialism, with its arrogant assumptions and simplistic denials, was as much an insult to the intelligence as mediums who pulled gauze from their rectums, pretending it to be Uncle Harry's ghost? Nor could generous helpings of ridicule scotch the persistent belief, expressed by William James, in "the presence, in the midst of all the humbug, of really supernatural knowledge."

Despite Spiritualism's decline, Carl Jung conducted experiments in 1899 and 1900 using his fifteen-year-old cousin Helene as a medium. Psychic talent was deeply carved in the branches of Jung's family tree. His mother, Emilie, wrote in her diary of sitting behind her minister father, at his request, while he was composing his sermons, to shoo away pesky ghosts. Emilie's mother was also a "ghost-seer." As reported by Jung's assistant, Aniela Jaffé: "The family attributed this talent to the fact that, as a girl, she had been seemingly dead for thirty-six hours. Her abilities were remarkable, even in the light of careful judgement. She saw apparitions of persons unknown to her, but whose historic existence was later proven."

Nonetheless, Jung concluded in his 1919 paper *The Psychological Foundations of Belief in Spirits* that ghosts were merely human projections. He maintained this view even after occupying a country home, where he endured rappings, foul odors, rustlings and drippings, culminating in the apparition of a solid-looking mutilated female head, on a pillow half a yard away, glaring at him with one eye. Subsequently, he learned that the house had frightened away all other tenants, leaving him with a puzzle: If spirits were just unconscious personal projections, why had so many people experienced terrifying phenomena in the same place?

By the time Jung reprinted his paper in 1947, he had undergone a metamorphosis—as had science—causing him to add this footnote: "After collecting psychological experiences from many people and many countries for fifty years, I no longer feel as certain as I did in 1919. . . . To put it bluntly, I doubt whether an exclusively psychological approach can do justice to the phenomena in question."

The most accomplished trance medium of the last half-century is usually conceded to be Eileen Garrett, who divided her psychic career between London and New York before her death in 1970. As an orphan growing up in Ireland, Eileen had three friends who were invisible to others—two girls and a boy, who spoke to her without words and seemed permeated with an ethereal light. She also saw all living things as if wrapped in a rainbow-colored "surround," which reflected their moods and health.

One day, while Eileen was sitting on her porch, she saw her Aunt Leone, who lived twenty miles away, coming up the walk carrying a baby. Appearing extremely ill, the aunt announced: "I am going away now, and must take the baby with me." After Eileen hastily fetched the aunt with whom she lived, Leone could not be found; next day, word reached them that Leone had died giving birth to a baby, which had also died.

Eileen was so harshly punished for having "willed" the tragedy that, in revenge, she killed her aunt's brood of ducklings. As she stared remorsefully at the little bodies, she saw a gray, smoke-like substance rise in a nebulous spiral from each, and then float away. This was a phenomenon Garrett would observe many times in her life, including at the deaths of three infant sons.

Until Garrett learned to control her psychic powers, she lived a chaotic life, beset by weird experiences and life-threatening illnesses. After some resistance, she gave herself over to parapsychologists to be trained as a trance medium. Although she was to give many virtuoso performances, the one that confounded the experts took place early in her career—on October 7, 1930, when she was being tested in London by the National Laboratory of Psychical Research. Shortly into the sitting, a voice issuing from her, in short, sharp sentences, identified itself as belonging to Flight Lieutenant Irwin, captain of the R101 airplane that had crashed two days before in France. The "captain" then described, in technical language, the exact circumstances of the disaster and the faults of design that had caused it. Extracted from pages of transcripts were such phrases as: "Whole bulk of the dirigible was too much for her engine capacity." "Airscrews too small." "Fabric waterlogged and ship's nose down." "Starboard strikes started." "Elevator jammed." "This exorbitant scheme of carbon and hydrogen is entirely and absolutely wrong."

During official investigations of the R101 crash, all of Garrett's details were proven accurate, or probable, while none were proven incorrect. No person but Flight Lieutenant Irwin could have known their total, since the plane's design had been kept secret. Though Garrett was closely interrogated by crash officials, no one could come up with an explanation, including Garrett, who, like Leonora Piper, refused to state categorically that her information came from spirits. Extensively tested on two continents, Garrett summed up her psychic ability: "I had the good fortune to enter it at an early age, when the mind, not too far removed from the mystery of birth, was able to accept wider dimensions in time and space. . . . What might be regarded as alien and dangerous by the adult world had no power to inflict doubt on the mind of the child."

SOME GHOST STORIES

FEBRUARY 1915
The footsteps always start at the bottom of the staircase—a child's footsteps, slow and definite, as if the child might be counting them: one . . . two . . . three. At the top of the stairs, the feet begin to skip. Abruptly, they stop as if the child is listening. Though the steps draw closer, they are now fainter. The child is tiptoeing. Again they stop—directly outside the door of the master bedroom.

That door is never opened from the hallway, though two people lie inside, waiting. When one of them answers it, no child is ever there.

Those footsteps continue to echo through the halls of that house, where a child has died, for almost six months. Several people hear them. Once or twice, crying is also heard. A decision to move is made. To a family that has left a homeland and crossed an ocean, what does another few blocks matter to ease the pain?

*All this happened to my mother's family twenty years before I was born. The wandering child was th*ught *to be my mother's sister Verna, who died in 1915, aged eight years and eleven months.*

Decades later, I related this story to a friend whose family moved into the same house—a friend, coincidentally, named Verna. She told me that she and her siblings had also feared the house was haunted—something not quite right on the second floor.

What are we to make of these ghost stories extending in an unbroken chain through all of known history and across every known culture? Orthodox scientists dismiss them as the product of wishful thinking, projection, gullibility, hoax, fear of death, love of the deceased, opportunism, imagination, hallucination, insanity or drugs. They also place the burden of proof on those who would believe.

However, theirs is an outdated view, based on a mis-assumption: that the clockwork Universe forged in Newton's name is a complete system. As almost a century of physics has shown, the concept of matter as the ultimate reality is like a white elephant pedaling in space, still unaware that the planks of its platform have all been sawed through, one by one. In a world in which the divisions between matter and energy, space and time, past, present and future are not real, why would the division between life and death be an exception to the rule of wholeness? At the very least the case for or against the spirit's survival deserves open-minded investigation, with the burden of proof on neither side. Not to grant that review is to side with the colleagues of Galileo who refused to peer through his telescope because to look was unnecessary: they *knew* the Sun orbited the Earth.

Though ghost stories have an impressive consistency from culture to culture, they often feature an ethnic twist. The ancient Chinese believed a ghost's chinless head materialized first, followed by the feet and then the body, while the Japanese expected to see their ghosts with disheveled hair. The Arabs feared a murdered man would rise from the dead where his blood was shed unless his specter was nailed to the ground. As people of large ambition, the Romans liked their spirits giant-size. One towering beauty, playing a reed pipe, was said to have prompted Caesar to cross the Rubicon. Another, claiming to be the Deity of Africa, urged Pliny the Younger to go to Rome, where he would achieve high honors. This the historian did, returning as a preconsul to Africa, where he eventually died—as she had also predicted.

One of history's first ghost-busters was philosopher Athenodorus of the first century B.C. When he inquired of an Athenian landlord why he was asking such a ridiculously low rent, Athenodorus discovered that previous tenants had been literally frightened to death by a hideous and uninvited see-through guest. Being low on funds, the philosopher rented the house anyway. On his first night, as he was absorbed in his studies, a persistent clanking at last broke through his concentration. Before him stood the grisly specter, manacled and chained, and as loathsome as advertised. Unruffled, Athenodorus tried to ignore it; however, its noisy distress, combined with its beckoning motions, compelled the philosopher to follow it into the courtyard. At a spot covered in shrubbery, the specter signed, then disappeared. Next day, Athenodorus fetched a magistrate, who ordered that spot excavated. A skeleton was discovered, bound in rusty chains. After its proper burial, the hauntings were said to have ceased.

By the twelfth century, the Christian Church was finding the concept of tortured souls, stuck in a purgatory halfway between heaven and earth, good for business. Portraits of half-rotted corpses became fashionable, and skeletons disinterred to make way for new tenants were often decoratively displayed. Given this morbidity, it was not surprising that apparitions began to appear to the living, often to beg for masses to atone for their sins. Abbeys were favorite haunts, especially the one at Glastonbury, once a pagan shrine and later the site of the first Christian church in the British Isles. Though the ghost of King Arthur was said to make annual Christmas visits, of greater contemporary interest is a group of thirteenth-century monks who apparently still inhabit the place.

Charged with excavations early in this century, archeologists Frederick Bligh Bond and J. Allan Bartlett decided to experiment with automatic writing, an occult practice in which spirits are invited to possess a subject's writing hand. On November 7, 1907, their first message came through: a floor plan signed *Gulielmus Monachus*—William Monk—along with specific instructions for digging, written in medieval Latin and archaic English. By following these, Bond and Bartlett unearthed a thirteenth-century chapel not shown in any records.

In the seventeenth century, ancestral homes took over from monasteries and abbeys as Europe's most haunted dwellings, especially in Britain. More worldly than their medieval antecedents, many of these phantoms seemed to have returned, like fussy accountants, to finish old business: rewarding their friends, spiting their enemies, revealing where they had stashed their loot and otherwise instructing, warning or chiding their heirs. Though skepticism was on the rise, Samuel Johnson probably spoke for the majority when he confirmed: "All argument is against it, but all belief is for it."

Urbanization brought hauntings into the cities, particularly into the theaters, where the untitled could enjoy them. A patron of London's Drury Lane Theatre Royal for two hundred years, the Man in Gray was considered an omen of good luck since he attended only plays destined to become hits—*Oklahoma, Carousel, South Pacific, The King and I*. After watching a midday rehearsal or an occasional matinee, he was seen to stroll from one end of the balcony to the other, in eighteenth-century powdered wig, tricorn hat and his trademark gray coat, before disappearing through the wall.

In the 1840s, a workman repairing the balcony in that area had discovered the skeleton of a man with a dagger between his ribs. Shreds of clothing dated the remains as eighteenth-century. Although these were buried with due ceremony, the Man in Gray seemed to have acquired a taste for Theatre Royal productions, and continued to visit the theater till his last sighting in the mid-fifties.

Throughout the centuries, war has bred a rich harvest of ghost stories, grim and heroic. According to Plutarch, Roman soldiers saw the legendary hero Theseus fighting for the Greeks after his death. The Greek victory over the Persians in 492 B.C. at Marathon was said to have left a legacy of screams and clashing steel and the smell of blood, with those who saw the ghostly warriors themselves doomed to die within the year.

At Edge Hill Field, Warwickshire, in 1643, Royalist forces under Prince Rupert fought an indecisive battle with Oliver Cromwell, leaving five thousand corpses. Months later, shepherds claimed to hear drums and cannon and to see fire and smoke. So insistent were these rumors that King Charles I sent a team to investigate. Not only did its members confirm the story but they testified that the apparitions were so distinct they were able to recognize some of the fighters. These included Prince Rupert, who had not been killed, leaving those who accepted eye-witness accounts to attribute the phenomenon to psychic energy created by the frenzied clash of emotions.

Phantom armies were also said to have refought the American Civil War battle of April 6, 1862, at Shiloh in Tennessee, where two days of combat had left a field strewn with twenty-four thousand corpses and a river that ran red.

In contrast to the discretion with which the British have handled their supernatural resources, the American media have so sensationalized promising sites, like the Amityville House, that any pale footsteps and gentle groans have long since been obliterated by trampling reporters and shouts of "That's a wrap!" Perhaps only the White House, where Abraham Lincoln's specter is said to work the night shift, has preserved its dignified claims. On the anniversary of his assassination, Lincoln's flag-draped funeral train is also said to slide noiselessly over black-carpeted rails, from Washington to his Springfield home, manned by skeletons.

Unlike the spiritually tortured ghosts of medieval times or the busybodies of the seventeenth century, today's specters seem motivated by sentiment. As "crisis apparitions," they appear to loved ones at the point of death or shortly thereafter to say goodbye, to express yearning, sorrow or regret. World War II produced a spate of these poignant farewells, usually of British sons to their mothers—perhaps reflecting the psychic unity of that civilian population, under siege, with its troops simultaneously facing death on foreign fields.

In 1944, Georgina Feakes of Kent was alone in her home when her cousin Owen Howison, recently killed in action in Italy, appeared to her in a golden mist. Though she could see his lips moving, all she could hear were his last two words: "Tell Mum." A few days later, Owen's specter reappeared. This time he explained, in a clear voice that his tank had been blown up but that he still felt very much alive. Again, he asked Feakes to tell his mother and to send his love "to poor Helen." When the spellbound Feakes blurted a request for proof of identity, the specter replied: "Watch!" From under his shirt, he produced a beautiful blue orchid, whose intoxicating scent drenched the room. Putting the flower back into his shirt, he repeated the gesture. "Tell Mum, please. Goodbye, dear cousin."

When Feakes reported this event to Owen's mother in South Africa, she received this reply: "On Owen's last leave he climbed Table Mountain and stole the blue flower which is protected by law and may not be plucked. He tucked it inside the chest of his shirt to bring home and had just taken it out to show (as I can't climb and had never seen one) when there came a knock. He was nervous of discovery (a heavy fine for picking it) and put it back inside his shirt, but it was only sister Cynthia. He showed me again, when the front door banged and he popped it for a second time into his shirt. This time it was brother Peter coming from work, so now I could really have a good look at this marvellous flower."

Owen's mother also testified that he had never mentioned the orchid to anyone outside the family for fear of prosecution. Similarly, none of Owen's relatives knew of his friendship with anyone named Helen. She introduced herself to the family only after this exchange of correspondence.

In some cases, the same spirit may appear to more than one person. In their 1886 publication *Phantasms of the Living*, the British Society for Psychical Research presented the following investigated story. Around nine o'clock on August 21, 1869, a boy of seven ran into his aunt's bedroom in Devonport, England, crying, "Oh Auntie! I have just seen my father walking around my bed." Since the boy's father was in Hong Kong, the aunt chided him: "Nonsense! You must have been dreaming."

When the boy refused to return to his bed, the aunt let him sleep in her room. Two hours later, as she herself was preparing for bed, she saw her brother, seated in a chair by her fireplace, his face ashen. Terrified, she put her head under the bedclothes. He called to her three times. Shortly thereafter, a letter from China confirmed the brother's death, of heat apoplexy, on the day of the visitation.

When today's spirits appeal to the living for help in righting a wrong, they usually seek justice rather than revenge. On October 12, 1907, Lieutenant James Sutton of the naval academy at Annapolis, Maryland, was found shot after a dance. The official story was that he had committed suicide in an irrational rage erupting from a drunken brawl. Even before this news reached Sutton's mother in Portland, Oregon, she had felt permeated by dread. Now, in shock, she experienced a vision of her son, who told her: "Momma, I never killed myself." He insisted that his companions had shot him during a fight, then covered up the murder as a suicide. For several months, the specter assailed Sutton. It reported details of the fight and described injuries, of which she had not been told.

The mother instigated an investigation, culminating in Sutton's body being exhumed. Its examination revealed many wounds not mentioned in the naval doctor's report but tallying with the specter's description. Other inconsistencies in the official story were also uncovered, although no murderer was ever apprehended.

Occasionally the appearance of a spirit body seems to represent nothing more than a glitch in the transport system, as if its former occupant carelessly abandoned it like an old overcoat on departing this earthly plane.

It was only after novelist Nathaniel Hawthorne saw the Reverend Dr. Harris sitting as usual by the fireplace in Boston's Atheneum library reading his Boston *Post* that he discovered the octogenarian had died a few days before. Yet for weeks Dr. Harris kept turning up in his same chair, looking quite solid. "At length, I regarded the venerable defunct no more than the other old fogies who basked before the fire and dozed over the newspapers."

When Dr. Harris failed to appear one afternoon, Hawthorne was struck by a second mystery. What had prevented him from investigating the phantom? The only excuse he could produce was a very human one: embarrassment. Talking in the Atheneum library was strictly forbidden, and he did not want to break that rule by seeming to address empty space.

SEPTEMBER 1976

While researching a novel at the British School in Rome, I spend most mornings and occasional evenings in its library—a cathedral-like room of shadowy nooks, spiral staircases and gothic galleries.

One evening, while in the school's dining room with British archeology students, I hear myself inquire: "Is there a ghost in the library?" After a collective intake of breath, the table explodes in high-tension laughter, leaving me to confront a disquieting truth: for two weeks I've been paralyzed with repressed fear over some cold, dead and clammy presence in the library, which, until I heard my question, I had blocked from awareness.

For my final week at the school, I work in my room, except for furtive day trips to the library to exchange books. Now that I have let my ghost out of the closet, what astonishes me is the sheer physicality of its presence. Some "thing" seems to be in the library, some mass-with-gravity that alters space in a palpable way, causing my nape hair to bristle, my heart to palpitate, and shivers to shoot up my spine—the whole repertoire of horrific responses, reported for thousands of years, and still a staple of supernatural tales. For a figment that is "all in my head," it has a startling effect on my viscera.

Now, fifteen years later, what continues to nag me is my failure to investigate my ghost. Perhaps I was inhibited because the school's staff did not speak English. Perhaps it was my embarrassment over that decidedly nervous dining-table laughter. Yet such rationalizations are equivalent to shouting: "Don't look! There's a flying saucer." Where curiosity is concerned, I've always been like Lot's wife—pure salt. Did the ghost put up a protective psychic shield—like the good ship Enterprise—blocking my inquiry? Was this the same mental strategy that forestalled Nathaniel Hawthorne in the Atheneum library?

In studying the phenomenon of ghosts, we usually ask: Are ghosts "real?" This question begs several others: Real in what sense? In the material sense? Then, surely, they aren't ghosts. Real to whom? To themselves? To the person viewing them? To the photographer who wants to snap them, carrying their heads or otherwise displaying their specialty? To the scientist who wishes physical evidence to show-and-tell his colleagues?

Perhaps a crisis apparition is a psychic postcard sent by the dead to the living—a concentration of dots and dashes that the receiver assembles, the way a computer makes photos of a satellite's blips from outer space. Perhaps the subtle body itself materializes in the same room as the receiver. If so, is this its last gasp, like a punctured tire spinning on momentum before collapsing, or has it become an independent energy form about to embark on a new journey?

And what can be said about pesky ghosts who, for centuries, seem to hang around the same places, banging the same doors, shrieking the same screams and clomping up the same staircases? According to folklore, they represent three types of persons: those who died violently and want redress or decent burial; those who died prematurely and cling pathetically to the sensory plane; those so set in their ways that even death and burial couldn't interrupt their daily routine. What these house-haunters seem to possess in common is their stupidity, leading to the conclusion that they are psychic debris, left behind by the departed who may, or may not, have something better to do and somewhere better to do it. However, crisis apparitions, like the one who presented the blue orchid, sometimes provide so much meaningful information that intelligence is indicated. When more than one person, separately or together, witness the same apparition, their agreement suggests an emanation from the sender rather than a projection of the receivers. *Suggests*, but proves nothing. What began as a strength of the Society for Psychical Research became its folly: defining itself in the terms of its materialistic critics. Eventually, its well-meaning search for irrefutable physical evidence encouraged mediums—some of whom might have possessed genuine talent—to manipulate their audiences with ever-grosser tricks, so that investigation of death, soul and God came to turn upon the concealed contents of a subject's bloomers. Yet, according to history's greatest seers, psychic phenomena are of little consequence unless related to spiritual development: the medium is *not* the message. Inner meaning is. *Why*, not how.

SPIRIT HELPERS

In 1971, a Welsh general practitioner named W. Dewi Rees asked 227 widows and 66 widowers if they had experienced hallucinations of their dead spouses. According to *The British Medical Journal*, almost half said yes. Though most found the apparitions comforting, they avoided mentioning them to friends for fear of ridicule.

In a 1982 Gallup poll, 43 per cent of Americans stated that they had had an unusual spiritual experience; 24 per cent said they believed it possible to contact the dead, and 14 per cent claimed to have seen a ghost. In another U.S. study in 1987 by A.M. Greeley, 50 per cent gave a positive answer to the question "Have you ever felt that you were really in touch with someone who had died?"

It seems that, independent of religious dogma and the disdain of orthodox science, large numbers of average people have arrived at an intuitive belief in spiritual continuity that, like coffee and their morning newspaper, sustains their everyday existence. Though common belief does not equate with truth, common experience comes closer to doing so: collective personal testimony, freely offered, without manipulation or reward.

Until recently, it was usually fright-night tales that Hollywood exploited for popular entertainment. Now, however, movies such as *Ghost*, *Always* and *Truly, Madly, Deeply* present the spirit world more cordially, rather like an upper-class suburb to which we can all aspire. This reflects occult mythology, in which spirit helpers have always been more numerous than ghosts who scare or pester. These include fairy godmothers, guardian angels, the little folk, muses, invisible companions, animals or birds that talk, genies who poof out of bottles, dead saints, even the beneficent Santa Claus and the tooth fairy.

According to esoteric writings of East and West, each of us earthbound travelers is guided by one or more advanced spirits who bear us unconditional love. Plato's teacher Socrates, declared by the Oracle of Delphi to be the wisest living person, had a disconcerting habit of wandering through the streets of Athens in apparent conversation with himself. By his own account, he was engaged with his *daemon*—an entity that, since his early childhood, had served as his moral guide. As he explained: "In the past the prophetic voice to which I have become accustomed has always been my constant companion, opposing me even in quite trivial things if I was going to take the wrong course." As to its origin: "When a good man dies he has honor and a mighty portion among the dead, and becomes a *daemon*, which is a name given to him signifying wisdom."

It was while Prophet Mohammed was meditating in a grotto near Mecca that the archangel Gabriel revealed to him that he had been chosen by Allah. Throughout the Old and New Testaments, God's senior angels ran a direct courier service to Moses, to Jacob, to St. Paul. A line of early martyrs claimed visitations by the risen Christ or the Madonna, then reportedly became visiting saints after their own deaths. In the first century, Augustine was turned from his debauched ways by an angel who solicited him in his garden: "*Tolle, lege!*" meaning "Take up and read." Opening a Bible at random, Augustine read: "Not in chambering and wantonness . . ." This led to his oft-quoted thanks to God for rescuing him from lust—but not too soon!

In the fifteenth century, Joan of Arc believed herself summoned to her heroic mission by the archangel Michael, who appeared to her in a form as solid as her eventual accusers. Napoleon Bonaparte also thought himself a host to guiding spirits—a shining sphere that encouraged, and a red dwarf who warned.

The eighteenth-century Swedish seer Emanuel Swedenborg claimed he could talk to any spirit he chose. In a well-documented story, Queen Louisa Ulrica of Sweden gave Swedenborg a private message with the light-hearted instruction: "If you should see my brother, remember me to him." When next at court, Swedenborg whispered a response into the queen's ear. Visibly shaken, she retired with the exclamation: "Only God and my brother can know what he has just told me!"

In another incident, also occurring in 1761, the Countess de Marteville consulted Swedenborg, greatly distressed because a silversmith was demanding payment for a bill she was sure her recently deceased husband had settled. Could Swedenborg contact her husband's spirit and ask after the receipt? Three days later, Swedenborg reported that it was in a certain upstairs bureau. When the countess protested that she had searched that bureau, Swedenborg described a hidden compartment behind one of the drawers. According to testimony from eleven sources, the countess recovered the receipt as Swedenborg indicated.

Like Socrates, Carl Jung relied on the wisdom of a spirit guide whom he called Philemon. When this figure first appeared in his dreams as an old man with horns and wings, Jung judged him to be a wise fragment of himself, which he had constellated. However, as Philemon developed in physical and psychological reality, Jung came to believe he was an outside independent force. At times, Philemon seemed so real that chatting with him in the garden was no different from consulting a living guru.

Edgar Cayce claimed to have been visited several times by a swarthy, white-turbaned figure who warned him when others were trying to exploit him. After the New York debacle in which he was arrested for fortune telling, Cayce was wandering through that city in shock when the white-turbaned stranger emerged from a crowd to kneel silently before him. This time, passersby apparently saw the figure. So many pressed in to observe the odd, perhaps surreal confrontation that Cayce had to be rescued by a policeman. When he looked back, the stranger was gone.

Among artists, Dante claimed to have been assisted by his inner guides Virgil and Beatrice. Robert Louis Stevenson assigned authorship of all his fiction to the "brownies" or "little people," and novelist Henry Miller complained that *Tropic of Cancer* had been dictated by an unseen power who showed no respect for his health or convenience.

In 1913, a "spirit" who called herself Patience Worth and who said she had lived in England during the seventeenth century, contacted Pearl Curran of St. Louis through an Ouija board. For twenty-four years, Patience dictated a large number of poems of reasonable quality, various philosophical discourses and five publishable novels. *Telka*, the most popular, related a tale of English country life, in an Anglo-Saxon dialect, using no words more recent than the sixteenth century.

Seven mediums were said to have seen the spirit guide accompanying Sir Arthur Conan Doyle, creator of Sherlock Holmes. Described by them as an elderly bearded man with tufted eyebrows, he was independently recognized by several as the deceased naturalist Alfred Russel Wallace. Though no evidence exists that Wallace aided Sir Arthur in his literary pursuits, Wallace's presence supported his own theory: that evolution was spiritually directed.

Many of the world's sacred texts are said to have been inspired by higher powers, either by a voice speaking through a human subject, or by spirit control of a subject's writing hand. These include the Koran, the Indian Vedas, the Book of Mormon and some parts of the Bible. George Fox, founder of the Quakers, as well as Protestant reformers Martin Luther and John Wesley, have all claimed God as their co-author. When Emanuel Swedenborg was asked how he could compile his erudite religious texts so rapidly, he replied that his angel dictated to him, "and I can write fast enough." After suffering through a clamorous period of poltergeist hauntings, Carl Jung thought he received a short text, *Seven Sermons to the Dead*, from the second-century mystic Basilides; however, he later dismissed it as a sin of his youth.

In the channeling frenzy of the seventies, a spate of quite ordinary folk claimed to have received spirit-dictated works, later published to notoriety and profit. Homemaker Jane Roberts had her garrulous correspondent Seth, who lectured on the spirit world, science and psychology. TV executive J.Z. Knight was guided by 35,000-year-old Ramtha, who dubbed himself the Enlightened One. Insurance-man Jach Pursel took his wisdom from the entity Lazaris, who tape-recorded healing wisdom, in a marbly accent, for New Age seekers. A current three-volume bestseller, *A Course in Miracles*, was channeled by psychologist and professed atheist Helen Schucman through an entity calling himself Christ. Despite the embarrassment of its authorship, many health-care professionals consult it with respect.

Even more idiosyncratic is the story of Rosemary Brown of London, who claimed to have been visited, from age seven, by the spirit of Franz Liszt, appearing as an old man. Eventually, he began dictating compositions to her, as did two of his friends—Chopin and Beethoven. Though Brown lacked musical training, she jotted the notes as fast as her pencil could fly, producing compositions that have been performed and recorded. Yet Brown's artistic performance was topped by Brazilian Luiz Antonio Gasparetto, who whipped off paintings in the styles of Matisse, Rembrandt, Picasso *et al.*, his brush allegedly guided by their spirit hands. Sometimes he painted with both hands, one canvas upside-down and one right way up. In a 1978 televised demonstration, he completed twenty-one pictures in seventy-five minutes. Like Brown, he demonstrated craft while lacking the genius of the masters.

Then there is the recent claim of a New York woman that she receives New Age recipes, featuring tofu and sesame seeds, from chef James Beard, who appears to her in his trademark white apron, looking only half his eighty-one-year age-of-departure.

Despite this giddiness, the experience of being guided— whether by one's own projection or a disembodied other—can be transformational. In *Love, Medicine and Miracles*, Dr. Bernie Siegel attributed his conversion to holistic healing to his inner guide, George, a long-haired, bearded young man in flowing white gown and skullcap, first contacted during meditation. To Siegel's astonishment, he found that a number of psychics could also describe George.

The feeling of being guided seems especially palpable during danger or isolation. When Charles Lindbergh climbed into the cockpit of "The Spirit of St. Louis" for his 1927 solo flight across the Atlantic, he was an atheist; by the time he touched down in Europe, he had become a mystic. Though Lindbergh had dozed off for long periods during his thirty-four-hour flight, he maintained that spirits, who seemed to pass easily through the walls of his plane, had advised and encouraged him in oddly familiar voices, "as though I've known all of them before in some past incarnation."

Similarly, during a 1933 solo assault on Mount Everest, Frank Smythe reported a strong, friendly presence that sustained him during his arduous journey. "Now, as I halted and extracted some mint cake from my pocket, it was so near and so strong that instinctively I divided the mint into two halves and turned round with one half in my hand to offer it to my 'companion.'"

Under ordinary circumstances, helpful spirits are said to prefer to exude goodwill, like the delicate scent of an invisible flower, without disrupting ordinary sensory experience. It was this kind of quiet but cataclysmic inner transformation that Tolstoy enjoyed one spring day in a forest, where he had gone to meditate on his quest for God. "'Why do I look further?' a voice within me asked. He is here: he, without whom I cannot live. To acknowledge God and to live are one and the same thing.... I was saved from suicide."

Psychiatrist Arthur Guirdham compared the atmosphere created by good spirits to that created by good people everywhere: "All of us recognize that there are some people with whom one has only to sit quietly for two minutes in order to feel better for it. . . . We do not even recognize that the reason these people make us feel better is because they emanate goodness."

Before he grasped this same subtlety, clinical psychologist Wilson Van Dusen of California had been puzzled about why his schizophrenic patients heard torturing voices five times more often than helpful ones. Then he realized that the loftier spirits preferred to communicate non-verbally so as not to cause a disruption. When they did manifest to his patients, they often appeared beautifully illuminated and presented ideas so edifying that their hosts had difficulty understanding them. One female spirit of great beauty showed a gaspipe-fitter thousands of symbols, indicating a vast knowledge of religion and myth, which he reported to Van Dusen with bafflement. Testified Van Dusen: "I couldn't help but begin to feel I was dealing with some kind of contrasting polarity of good and evil."

NOVEMBER 10, 1988

A California friend has sent me The Inner Guide Meditation *by Edwin Steinbrecher, outlining a ritual for meeting the inner guide whose task it is to enlighten me. After inducing a meditative state, I imagine a cave, as I have been instructed.*

My cave is conical and soaring, with a tear of sunlight about three stories up. When I enter, moss squishes under my bare feet. The air feels sensuous and thick, with a rotting, verdant smell. To the left I find a fold of rock through which I squeeze into a sunny, stony landscape.

When I call for an animal, as instructed, a white falcon banded with gold alights on a white branch. As I pursue it through a rock passageway, I see a pair of enormous, muscular feet, bound in reddish leather thongs. My eyes travel upward into the face of a Norseman, wrapped in reddish fur, with bushy red hair, beard and drooping mustache. Crinkly lines of great good humor slide down from deeply set eyes to a benevolent mouth. He seems as one with rock and soil.

The Norseman takes both my hands. Though he speaks no words, his touch exudes love, strength and patience. Still without words, he tells me that my task in this life is to explore death, for which he will be my anchor but not my guide. For that, I need a spirit of the night. He also tells me that, on returning home, I must discover his falcon's lineage.

When the Norseman withdraws his hands, I see two opals like teardrops in my palms. When I place them over my eyes, day turns to night. As I stare hypnotically at the full moon, it intensifies until it fills the sky. A Radiant Being steps down, shimmering with such iridescence I can scarcely make out her shape. Her touch is cool and compassionate, as she brushes my arm with one hand, while pointing to a large, still pool. I understand, without words, that the reflected moon is a door.

As I wade in, cold water slithers up my thighs. Stepping through the floating moon door, I swoosh downward, feeling the water slide over my head. Something dense cushions my fall. When I catch my breath, I am back in my own bed. It is then I have the experience, related in the introduction to this book, in which my former husband tells me I will see a pebble out of place at my cousin's funeral.

This story has two footnotes.

No. 1: On consulting a book of mythology, as my Norse guide instructed, I find the falcon to be sacred to the Egyptian god Horus, often depicted with hawk's head. Horus lost his left eye in battle with his wicked uncle Set, at the same time he deprived Set of a left testicle. This mythology seemed to foreshadow events that would occur within my family in less than a year: my sister's loss of a left eye also connected to an older man's testicles.

Footnote No. 2: When I relate the pebble story to the friend who gave me the meditation book, she informs me that the heroine of the novel she has just written also places pebbles on a grave—her lover's. Apparently it is an ancient custom meaning the dead will always be remembered.

SPECTERS OF THE LIVING

Most religions affirm that some part of the self remains after the demise of the physical body. In Eastern tradition, it is the subtle body, said to be attached to the physical body by a silver cord. On death, this nebulous self ascends through five increasingly finer planes of being—a reversal of its descent at birth. And just as birth was completed by cutting the umbilical cord, so death is finalized by severing the silver cord.

Even while a person is asleep, under anesthesia, in a trance or in shock, this double is said to be able to slip its fleshy mooring to wander about the occult world: a ghost of the living, sometimes haunting the dead. Many Eastern mystics claims they are able to travel at will, via the subtle body, to any place in the Universe. So do a few Western ones: witnesses testified to having seen Pythagoras in more than one place at the same time, and the Roman Hermotinus was so skillful at relaying information from distant places that his frightened enemies burned his body while it was comatose.

When Edgar Cayce entered trance, his vital functions slowed till he was in a near-death coma. By his own description, it was then that his "finer body" visited the subconscious of his clients to diagnose their ills. While in this altered state, Cayce forbade his attendants to pass anything across his supine body for fear of severing the invisible cord connecting it to his subtle body. On a couple of occasions, when this prohibition was accidentally breeched, he experienced near-fatal shock.

While out-of-body, Cayce claimed that dead spirits often pressed for access to his consciousness. He also spoke of passing through hierarchical planes of existence when retrieving reincarnational records. After he concluded his reading with the words "We are finished," it was necessary for his attendants to suggest, in a precise way, that all his vital processes be restored. More than once, when his body failed to respond to command, they were reduced to impassioned prayer. As testified by biographer Harmon Hartzell Bro: "His daily work was a kind of small dying."

Emanuel Swedenborg went into trance through fierce concentration that caused his breathing to all but cease. Like Cayce, his signal to proceed was an intense inner light, which to him appeared as a flame. Unlike Cayce, who never remembered what happened while he was comatose, Swedenborg claimed to have mastered the art of traveling at will between the spirit realm and this one while retaining full consciousness. He also seemed able to travel out-of-body to any earthly location, and to bring back verifying information.

Swedenborg's first public demonstration of his formidable powers occurred on July 17, 1759, during a party at the home of prominent Göteborg merchant William Castel. At six o'clock, Swedenborg grew pale and disturbed because a terrible fire was raging in Stockholm, three hundred miles away. Pacing in and out of the house, he described the fire in detail—where and when it had started, how it was now burning. Already, he lamented, the home of a friend, whom he named, had been reduced to ashes, and his own was threatened.

At eight o'clock, after Swedenborg had gone outside once more, he joyfully announced: "God be praised, the fire is extinguished, the third door from my house!"

Two days later, messengers from Stockholm confirmed every detail of Swedenborg's off-the-cuff reportage, attested by many witnesses. Even philosopher Immanuel Kant—the rationalists' rationalist, who conducted his own investigation—was impressed. As he agonized in a letter: "It will probably be asked what on earth could have moved me to engage in such a contemptible business as that of circulating stories to which a rational man hesitates to listen." In gross understatement, he concluded: "I am not aware that anybody has ever perceived in me an inclination to the marvelous."

In a 1766 letter, Kant was still brooding over the event, as well as on the paranormal in general. "While I doubt any one of them, still I have certain faith in the whole of them taken together." He went on to speculate that, in time, it would be proven "that in this life the human soul stands in an indissoluble communion with all the immaterial beings of the spiritual worlds; that it produced effects in them, and in exchange receives impressions from them, without, however, becoming humanly conscious of them, so long as all stands well."

Only lately and very reluctantly has Western science accepted the possibility that out-of-body experiences (OOBs) might be more than hallucinations. Since they occur spontaneously during sleep, they are even more difficult than most paranormal events to study in a laboratory. However, in a 1968 paper for the *Journal of the American Society of Psychical Research*, Dr. Charles Tart of the University of California reported on his experiments with a subject whom he called Miss Z. According to her own testimony, several times a week she would awaken to find herself floating near the ceiling over her physical body for periods lasting a few seconds to half a minute.

For four consecutive nights, Miss Z slept in Tart's laboratory with a random five-digit number positioned over her head so it could not be observed from the ground. If she floated high enough, she was to memorize it, then awaken herself.

On the final night, Miss Z correctly reported the five-digit number. However, after reviewing his procedures, Tart concluded that it might have been possible, through sophisticated cheating, to have discovered the number without elevating. Though he didn't distrust his subject, this proviso prevented him from considering his experiment conclusive. In support of Miss Z's testimony, Tart found she registered distinctive brainwave patterns during the time of her reported OOBs, similar to those noted by researchers monitoring Buddhist meditators.

On the second night of Tart's experiment with Miss Z, she had a nightmare in which she experienced a murder at a distant location. As she hastily jotted: "young girl (13 to 16?)—outdoors—stabbing, but not knife, more slender—head hurt (slapped?) not stabbed, surely—expanse of white, car white?—knew fellow." Simultaneously, a local sixteen-year-old girl was stabbed through the head with an instrument like an ice pick, then had her skull crushed. The murder was committed by her boyfriend in his white Thunderbird.

Years before, Miss Z had undergone a similar lucid dream, in which she was being chased down a dark street in her hometown. Since she was wearing an unfamiliar checked skirt, she felt herself to be in someone else's body. On awakening from her dream, in which her assailant raped then murdered her, Miss Z discovered that a young girl, wearing a checked skirt, had simultaneously been raped and stabbed to death in the same locale. However, since neither lucid dream was corroborated, Tart listed them as suggestive rather than conclusive.

JULY 15, 1987

Though I am suddenly wide awake, the dream doesn't seem to be over. As if clinging to a magic carpet, I swoosh down a chute, then up the other side. What makes the sensation of speed so realistic is the blast of wind whipping back my hair. I exclaim, "My God, I'm on the ceiling!" The instant I do, I find myself back in bed. My feeling is of exhilaration, as if I've just returned from some exotic place, outside of space and time, in which I possessed illuminations beyond remembering or expressing. I also sense this realm to be familiar—a place once accessible to me, perhaps as a child, with my passport later ripped up by my rational self.

I know what I have undergone is an out-of-body experience, in which my subtle body has supposedly separated from my physical one. Already suffering disbelief, I try to return to sleep. Again, some force seems to fling me to the ceiling, as if I were a beachball. A Voice commands: "Wake up! You'll forget, as you always do!"

I spend the rest of the night restlessly and obediently impressing these odd sensations onto my consciousness and trying—unsuccessfully—to repeat them.

ON THE OTHER SIDE?

Today, many people accept OOBs because of near-death experiences, during which they felt themselves to be hovering over their bodies while medical teams tried to resuscitate them. Gallup surveys indicate that more than one third of Americans who came close to dying have had this experience, independent of sex, age, intelligence, education or religion. Because of medical procedures that save victims from injuries that once killed, this amounts to an estimated eight or nine million Americans.

Remarkably homogeneous, near-death experiences (NDEs) begin with feelings of physical detachment, during which the comatose subject may witness procedures and hear conversations that, when reported, prove accurate. Washed by calmness, the patient then beholds a dark tunnel leading into supernatural radiance. Sometimes music is heard. Sometimes gardens or palaces are envisioned. Usually departed loved ones or saintly figures beckon. All this is infused with a rapture that ends when the patient is yanked back to normal consciousness.

Often near-death experiences produce emotions so exhilarating that values must be radically altered to incorporate them. After being seriously wounded during World War I, Ernest Hemingway told a friend: "I died. Then I felt my soul or something coming right out of my body like you'd pull a silk handkerchief out of a pocket by one corner. It flew all around and then came back, and I wasn't dead anymore." Shaken by the experience, Hemingway several times incorporated it into his fiction.

Despite the powerful persuasion of such accounts, cautious researchers stress that NDEs are not examples of persons returning from the dead but merely episodes in the process of dying.

In 1926, Dublin physician Sir William Barrett published *Death-Bed Visions*, in which he reported the paranormal experiences of his terminal patients. What impressed him was the frequency with which these apparitions contradicted his patients' conscious expectations: some saw relatives whom they erroneously believed were still alive; children were surprised to be greeted by angels without wings. He was also struck by his patients' exaltation, combined with their rational appreciation of their physical environments.

Building on Barrett's work, Dr. Karlis Osis undertook a large-scale survey of physicians' and nurses' deathbed observations in India and the United States. With questionnaires followed by interviews, he focused on 877 cases, about evenly divided between the two countries. Of these, 714 of the patients proved to be terminally ill, while 163 recovered. Approximately half of the U.S. sample was Christian, while half of the Indian one was Hindu, roughly reflecting the religious makeup of the two countries.

Visions were seen by 591 patients. In the United States, these usually were of dead relatives, in the following order: mother, spouse, offspring, sibling and father. In India, "welcomers" were more often religious personages. When these invited the dying to accompany them, 72 per cent consented, while 28 per cent protested or struggled. Curiously, all but one of the refusers were Indian.

Most visions lasted less than five minutes, but some continued for over an hour. Medical conditions usually conducive to hallucination, such as high fever, stress and morphine, had no effect or suppressed them. Unlike hallucinations of the mentally disturbed, deathbed experiences were visual rather than auditory, harmonious, consistent and similar rather than idiosyncratic. Contact with reality otherwise remained normal, and the patient was usually serene or enraptured.

Other studies support Osis's findings. However, while few critics doubt the vividness of the visions, they brand them as hallucinations without objective reality.

As tantalizing as having a near-death experience, flying out-of-body, contacting one's spirit guide or seeing a ghost may seem, the larger significance of these events lies in what they reveal about the Universe and our spiritual position within it. Like a single, enigmatic footprint in an expanse of sand, these mysteries lure us to search out a meaningful source.

Given the opposition of both science and the Christian Church to direct spiritual experience, Western occult writings have generally been scorned as the delusions of the ignorant. In this context, the revelations of Emanuel Swedenborg must stand as a brilliant exception.

Born in 1688, Swedenborg began his career by mastering all the sciences of his day. Still judged by many to have possessed more factual information than any other person in history, he wrote 150 scientific works in chemistry, physics, mineralogy, geology, paleontology, anatomy, physiology, astronomy, optics and so forth. These contained many original discoveries: he described the function of the ductless glands and the cerebellum; he originated the nebular hypothesis of the solar system; he suggested the particle structure of magnets. As an engineer, he built the world's largest drydock. As an inventor, he designed the first submarine, machine gun and pianola. As a mathematician, he compiled texts on algebra and calculus. He was also a musician, a watchmaker, a mechanic and an engraver; he was fluent in nine languages, and wrote his texts in Latin.

It was only when Swedenborg—like Alexander the Great—ran out of familiar territory to conquer that he turned his laser mind to inner space.

In the thirty-two religious volumes which Swedenborg wrote during the last three decades of his life, he described all of reality as a hierarchy of seven orders under God: three good and three evil, with humans occupying the free zone between. According to Swedenborg, as soon as a dying person's breath and heartbeat ceased, that person's soul began to awaken in the spirit world. Though the new arrival still felt alive, subtle differences accumulated, as in dreams, till the change of status became apparent. Then an angel instructed the initiate, with reference to the Book of Lives, in which every detail of that person's life had been recorded.

Since the spirit world was a manifestation of a person's inner feelings during life, with the physical and social coverings now stripped away, spirits soon found themselves face to face with who they really were. Eventually, they joined a society in one of heaven or hell's three bands of reality, chosen on the basis of like attracting like. Heaven was a place of unity, light and congeniality, with love of God as its highest value, followed by love of others. Hell was a place of self-love, disunity and discord, with the barrenness of one's own nature reflected in the barrenness of its atmosphere. Thus, evil and its punishment were as inseparable as one side of a board from the other.

According to Swedenborg, we humans are in direct contact with heaven and hell at all times through our minds, which reflect them as microcosm to macrocosm. Though usually unaware, each of us has two angels to guide us and two demons to distract us, with their characters complementing our own. Swedenborg claimed his knowledge came not from contemplation but from experience: guided by angels, he had rehearsed his own death several times.

While trafficking among spirits, Swedenborg lived a modest and scholarly life, making little show of his rumored occult powers. Though enemies attempted to have his work banned and him declared insane, he continued to enjoy robust good health, beset only by an occasional toothache, which he attributed to demons. Yet even here Swedenborg seemed able to command heavenly compensation: late in life, he grew a whole new set of teeth!

In February 1772, reformer John Wesley was surprised to receive a note from Swedenborg stating that the spirits had instructed him that Wesley wished a consultation. As Wesley later testified, indeed he did, but he had told no one. When Wesley suggested an engagement six months hence, Swedenborg replied that that date would not be convenient, since he himself would be dying on the twenty-ninth of the next month. He did—at age eighty-four, of a stroke.

Though Swedenborg's scientific fame was obscured by extreme disquiet over his religious writings, today, ironically, his scientific writings have fallen into obscurity while his religious ones are enjoying a revival, supported by Swedenborg Foundations in such cities as London, New York and Toronto.

SEEKING TRANSCENDENCE

SEPTEMBER 1986

It is my one experiment with LSD. While I chew a square of cardboard impregnated with acid, my companion informs me that my mind may seize upon one question as the theme of the whole experience. Since I am undergoing transition in every aspect of my life, I am curious as to which problem my hallucinating mind will consider primary. Will I tackle the creative questions posed by the book I am writing? Will I grapple with that ever-perplexing topic of "personal relationships"? Will I decide if, and when, to move back from California to Canada?

Shortly after the drug takes effect, I am astonished to hear myself ask some real or imagined higher force a question I've scarcely thought about since I graduated from philosophy, suffering from an overdose of metaphysics: "Who created the world?"

The answer from that higher force echoes the Protestant tradition in which I was raised: "God made the world."

I ask the second question from the Catechism I memorized as a child of seven: "Who made God?"

The answer is the orthodox one: "No one made God. God always was." Now comes the trick question—the one not inscribed in my little blue Catechism. The higher force demands: "Who's asking?"

Startled, I reply: "Who's asking who's asking?"

The reply: "Who's asking who's asking who's asking?"

Then again: "Who's asking who's asking who's asking who's asking?"

For several hours this question—unanswerable within the strictures of rational thought—reverberates inside my consciousness. It is the most remarkable dialogue of my life—certainly not because of the words but because of the spaces between them, during which I am invited to look successively deeper into myself in return for yet a deeper look into the reality of the higher force.

To the extent that an answer can be extricated, it is the clichéd one, found in a thousand illuminated texts: the self as microcosm of the Whole, the "i am" as the "I AM." However, the difference between these words and the experience is the difference between the letters spelling "sunset" and the miracle itself. For seconds, even minutes at a time, I am infused with the bliss of perfect love, of ultimate belonging—that ecstatic revelation so awesome, so astonishing, it keeps monks meditating for years in their temples, quenching their thirst in the fountain I barely taste.

Unfortunately, my frustration is almost as great as my joy, for after each shaft of revelation, my rational mind inevitably gasps with satisfaction: "Aha! Got it!" Since this is equivalent to leaping upon violinist Isaac Stern and claiming to have captured his melody, I lose what I thought I had, then try again, catch it again, then lose it again. Yet so powerful are my intimations of wholeness, truth and beauty that, more than five years later, I still carry within myself its never-to-be-forgotten afterglow.

As earlier mentioned, for at least three thousand years, Mexican and American natives have used "sacred" plants, such as psilocybe mushrooms, peyote and the San Pedro cactus, as an aid to exploring the spirit world. Known to scientists as hallucinogens, these plants contain chemical substances that produce visions most psychiatrists dismiss as crazy but which shamans worship as divine. To their users, the substances themselves are sacred, in the same way as Roman Catholics believe the wine and wafer of the sacrament transform into the actual blood and body of Christ. Far from distorting reality, magic plants are believed to fling open the door to the only true reality—not for escape, as in the Western tradition, but for transformation. As Mexican shaman Maria Sabina described her ceremonial intoxication: "I see the Word fall, come down from above, as though they were little luminous objects falling from heaven . . . with my hand I catch them, Word by Word."

Since hallucinogens are not part of Hindu or Buddhist tradition, Eastern seers employ diet, exercise and meditation to achieve their spiritual awakenings. They describe this process as the opening of the third eye—the pineal gland, said to be the physical manifestation of the crown *chakra*.

Located just above the brain stem, this tiny cone-shaped structure was described by fourth-century B.C. anatomist Herophilus as a sphincter regulating the flow of thought. In the seventeenth century, Descartes intuited—through inspiration received in a dream—that the pineal might be the center of consciousness by which the mind liaises with the body. Though this insight was to garner him the patronizing giggles of generations of college students, his dream-intuition—like that of Herophilus and the Hindu seers before them—contains an amazing truth.

In 1886, two simultaneously published papers—one in German by H.W. de Graaf, the other in English by E. Baldwin Spencer—confirmed that structurally the pineal body was a light-sensitive third eye. Once located on the head of the reptilian life-form that evolved into *Homo sapiens sapiens*, it had sunk as our brains had evolved to its present location just above the brain stem. Until 1958, many biologists thought the pineal to be a useless vestige. The discovery that it secreted the hormone melatonin, preventing sexual maturation before puberty, confirmed it was a functioning gland. Later it was found also to secrete serotonin, a hormone in common supply throughout the animal and vegetable kingdoms. The function of this substance was unknown in 1948, when Swiss chemist Albert Hofmann accidentally absorbed a minute quantity of a chemical compound derived from rye fungus. For the next several hours, he suffered delusions, mystical visions and terrifying hallucinations that convinced him he was insane. Hofmann had ingested lysergic acid diethylamide—LSD-25.

Though this chemical appeared to act on the nervous system to cause psychosis, later it was found to operate in the opposite way: LSD produced its hallucinatory effects by *blocking* the function of serotonin. This hypothesis gained confirmation when serotonin was found more prevalent the further one advanced up the evolutionary scale—from mammals to primates to humans—corresponding to an increase in ego-consciousness. Similarly, schizophrenics were found to be deficient in serotonin, implying their loss of an integrated self was equivalent to being under the influence of LSD.

The startling implication of all this is that our rational view of reality could be based on nothing more solid than the late evolutionary development of a hormone; if so, it might be argued that rationality is the altered state, while the one we label hallucinatory is prior, more universal and, hence, more "real." Because of Western bias favoring scientific progress, we have downgraded the past in favor of the present and intuitions in favor of physical facts. Yet it was through mystical visions that Descartes and Herophilus and the Hindus perceived thousands of years before science that the pineal was the chemical door between reason and other-consciousness.

Of course, both ways of viewing are invaluable: the rational providing the concentrated detail of a microscope, and the mystical providing the perspective of a wide-angle lens. For many psychedelic voyagers of the sixties, the sudden expansion of consciousness from micro to macro was as awe-inspiring as that experienced by the astronauts as they gazed back at planet Earth spinning majestically in space. Some of these voyagers groped their way over to the Eastern mystical tradition, perhaps surfacing years later as charismatic teachers. Others made a permanent commitment to radical politics, or to the healing arts. Most opted back into straight society as if their highs had been nothing more than Disneyland simulations. A very few used their drug experiences to deepen and broaden the psychiatric assumptions of their day.

One of these was Czech-born psychoanalyst Stanislav Grof, who had volunteered in 1956 as a test-subject for LSD. "I was treated to a fantastic display of colorful visions, some of them abstract and geometrical, others figurative and full of symbolic meaning. I also felt an amazing array of emotions with an intensity I did not know was possible." So cataclysmic were Grof's experiences that he converted from a Freudian atheist into a radical therapist with a profound respect for the mystical.

On emigrating from Prague to Baltimore in 1967, Grof met Abraham Maslow, who was then controversial for espousing a transcendental psychology based on what he called peak experiences. Defined by Maslow as spontaneous moments when the individual feels mystically fused with others and the Universe, they occurred during mountain climbing, or in a sacred place, or when touched by beauty, or creating art, or thrilled by love, or overwhelmed at the birth of a child. Like Jung before him, Maslow insisted: "Man has a 'higher nature' that is just as instinctoid as his lower animal."

Together, Maslow and Grof founded transpersonal therapy, aimed at *direct* experience of the sacred without the crutch of drugs: like Spiritualism in the Victorian age, this movement answered a secular call for "something more."

Because of his own thrilling adventures, Grof thought his task would be to intensify the spiritual lives of his clients. However, he found himself confronted with a brigade of sixties' "acid heads" who had chemically kickstarted their pineal glands and were now struggling to ground themselves in the ordinary. While other therapists viewed their drug-inspired hallucinations, often accompanied by paranormal experiences, as a dangerous distortion of reality, Grof saw them as the spillover from a too-sudden glimpse of a greater reality. In his opinion, his clients' biggest problem was Western society's denial of spiritual need till it had become a crisis, especially among the psychically gifted. As he stated in *The Stormy Search for Self*: "Many people in the midst of a peak experience have been sent to psychiatrists who gave them pathological labels, interrupted their experience with tranquilizing medication, assigning them the role of life-long psychiatric patients." Instead, it was Grof's aim to provide therapeutic guidance and support so his clients could emerge from their breakdowns radically transformed and more truly alive.

One of Grof's early emergencies was his future wife, Christina, triggered into chaos by the birth of her first child, closely followed by an auto crash in which she nearly died. "Suddenly I seemed to pass through an opaque curtain of death into a deep feeling of connection with everything in the Universe." Though Christina's near-death experience was an ecstatic one, she felt too overwhelmed to return to everyday reality. When confronted with other supernatural episodes, she tried to blot them out with alcohol.

Grof began to see Christina's need—along with that of his other addicted patients—to hit bottom with alcohol and drugs as a perverse re-enactment of the shamanic journey: like shamans, they descended into the underworld, where they were tortured by supernatural spirits before ascending into the light to be reborn. This connection between addiction and spiritual need had already been intuited by William James. As he stated in *The Varieties of*

Religious Experience: "The sway of alcohol over mankind is unquestionably due to its power to stimulate the mystical faculties of human nature, usually crushed to earth by the cold facts and dry criticisms of the sober hour."

Carl Jung had also noted the connection between alcoholic spirits and the sacred kind in a 1961 letter to Bill Wilson, co-founder of Alcoholics Anonymous. Comparing the craving for alcohol to a low-level thirst for union with God, Jung declared the antidote to be *spiritus contra spiritum*—Spirit against spirits.

Why spiritual need so often adopts what Eastern seers call "the vertical route to Enlightenment" is unknown. Perhaps it is because the underworld journey creates a healing fusion between the primal poles of human experience: life and death. Perhaps because it connects the known world with the unknown one. Whatever the reason, death and rebirth rituals were central to the initiation rites of Druid priests, the Gnostic Christians and celebrants of the Mystery cults of Egypt, Greece and Rome. As Roman statesman Cicero enthused after his own initiation: "Nothing is higher than these Mysteries. They have sweetened our character and softened our customs; they have made us pass from the condition of savages to true humanity. They have not only shown us the way to live joyfully, but they have taught us to die with hope."

To help modern questers to achieve direct mystical experience without drugs, the Grofs designed a technique they call Holotropic Breathwork, which—like yogic disciplines and the work of Deepak Chopra—combines breath control with the healing power of sound. In a safe group setting, individuals are invited to embark on fantasy trips, aided by music chosen to stimulate the *chakras*, from the lower sexual centers to the celestial ones of the head. Now an international movement, Holotropic Breathwork combines inspiration and therapy in equal parts: like the shaman's journey, like the ancient Mysteries, like early Christianity, it acknowledges the human need to aspire to spiritual realms.

NOVEMBER 11, 1990
Islands are places of convergence where water laps shore, where sun slides into water, where sky meets land. Insular and psychically intense, they are fit places for spirit to touch land.

Wards Island—a kilometer by ferryboat from downtown Toronto—is an eccentricity grown out of an anachronism. With its cluster of bungalows replete with treehouses, stone gardens, scrap-heap sculptures and plastic flamingos, it appears in winter to be an old-fashioned resort with smoking chimneys and woodpiles. In summer, drifts of cottonwood catch like snowflakes in the eyelashes, pile around lawn furniture, bury children's sandpails in a softly stirring whiteness even more anomalous. Across the windswept channel, in a portion of the sky featuring spectacular sunsets, looms post-modernist Toronto, so shockingly out of scale that it appears other-worldly.

We meet at the Harbourfront ferry dock at 8:15 A.M., cheerfully greeting those we know and easily identifying the rest by their tell-tale bedrolls.

"Are you going to breathe?" The quick smile, a little sheepish, a little superior, acknowledges this jargon like a fraternity handshake, sometimes extending it with a bit of belt-notching: "This will be my seventh."

The prow of our boat slides through ice pans with a slick, thrilling rush; or else it competes with yachts manned by suntanned sailors, massed like flotillas of ducks. Again on land we trek over an arched bridge that resembles the carved ivory miniatures in Chinese shops, through flocks of Canada geese and seasonal smells, along narrow streets where no cars drive. Our destination—a room in one of these bungalows—is already stripped to the rug, with windows blocked by blankets. We create nests from our bedrolls, stretched between four loudspeakers. One of each pair—the breather—climbs into the bedroll; the other—the caretaker—squats beside. In the afternoon we will exchange places.

Our host delivers the preamble—an inducement to relax, sometimes jazzed up with mention of inner guides and other commonplaces of the New Age, followed by instructions for deep, fast breathing. Music converts the room into an acoustical chamber, vibrant with contrasting rhythms: jungle syncopation, the radiance of violins, the deep-throated mystery of Gregorian chants, with each swatch chosen to appeal to a particular chakra. Sometimes the room erupts in groans and screams—primal feelings held tight, awaiting safe, shared catharsis, and often accompanied by thrashing limbs. For other breathers, the experience remains internal and blissful—a hallucinatory slide through swirling planets, perhaps touched with the awe-filled rituals of birth and death.

My own experiences have all been harmonious—guided fantasies in which I visit tombs of ancient ancestors, speak to my honored dead, participate as a monk in religious processions, swim with a pod of dolphins, give birth to a golden child, turn into a flock of fluttering blue butterflies, fly through space as a winged white cat. I explore the meaning of metaphysical paradoxes such as the One in the many, give thanks, problem-solve, check out my body for tension or disease. As the sonorous music washes through me, I heal.

Afterwards, each of us draws our impressions on papers already inscribed with a large circle, like a naked mandala. Some are pictorial and naive; others are wildly abstract. Using them as travel diaries, we share what we choose of our journeys, giving ourselves a spiritual history, creating our own myths.

Welcome the gods, and they will come. This simple house is one of their temples.

Possession:

THE DEVIL TO PAY

"The moment I choose, I can be rid of Mr. Hyde.
I give you my hand upon that."

—Dr. Jekyll

MARCH 3, 1990

A friend invites me to see the musical version of Phantom of
the Opera. *As we walk into the ornate Toronto theater, I think of some-*
thing psychic Vince Vanlimbeek predicted a week before: "You're going
to see a chandelier. It's gorgeous! It's goir g to be important to you. You'll
know what I mean." When I jocularly mention this to my companion,
who has seen the New York production, he replies: "If it's a chandelier
you want, you can't do better than the one you're about to see."

As we take our seats about eighth row center, I find myself
staring at a large heap on stage, covered by a dirty canvas bag. In case
I should miss the point, foot-high letters scrawled across the canvas
spell out: "CHANDELIER."

The musical begins with the auctioning of that chandelier from
the Paris Opera House, which the Phantom once haunted. Afterwards,
in a flashback, the chandelier is raised. It is, indeed, "gorgeous"—the
most striking image in a musical noted for lavish effects. At curtain
fall I sit shellshocked with the music of Andrew Lloyd Webber still
reverberating through me. As Vince predicted: "You'll know what I
mean."

The relevant plot of the Phantom *musical is as follows: when*
the father of opera apprentice Christine Daae dies, he promises to send
to her the Angel of Music as her mentor. Subsequently, the Phantom—
black-caped and middle-aged with a white mask hiding the right side
of his face—emerges from Christine's mirror. After teaching Christine
to sing, he attempts to make her the star of the Paris Opera by
sabotaging its current diva. The only other person to see the Phantom
is middle-aged Madame Giry. She tells Christine that the Phantom was
once a caged freak who escaped from a roadshow to live in the bowels
of the opera house.

Since the above story makes no literal sense, it begs to be
interpreted allegorically. Therefore, in my opinion: Christine's descent
into the Phantom's lair is a journey from light (symbolized by the
chandelier) into the labyrinthine darkness of her subconscious. The
Phantom—sent to Christine by her father on his death—actually is

her father. When he gives in to his lust for his daughter, his primitive self escapes its cage of restraint and his conscious self dies (symbolized by the mask covering the disfigured right side of his face).

Madame Giry functions as Christine's mother. As messenger between daughter and father, light and dark, she is a passive collaborator in Christine's seduction, but later aids in her rescue.

Christine's last exclamation is a cri de coeur for all who have triumphed over their own subterranean darkness disguised as the Other: "The enchantment is over!"

I was grateful to *Phantom* because it externalized, in full erotic dress, the incestuous conflict that had paralyzed me for too much of my life. What makes incest so insidious is that self-destruction becomes internalized and eroticized. Out of the seduced child's repressed sensuality, the Phantom lover is born—a haunting figure all the more powerful because he is partially masked behind revulsion. To free herself from possession, Christine (the female equivalent of Christian in *Pilgrim's Progress*) must conquer both horror and obsessional love for her idealized Phantom-father. For this, her reward is self-possession.

By contrast, the male struggle is against possession by one's own rapacious other self, as suggested by the Phantom's half-mask. In Christian demonology, Satan casts no shadow and has no reflection. However, what Satan has lost is not his reflection but his real self. He has become his own reflection, his shadow, his Other. In giving into incestuous lust, the Phantom loses his conscious self, symbolized by his now-masked right face, to become a moral outcast living in sewers.

This good-evil duality is also intriguingly explored in Robert Louis Stevenson's *The Strange Case of Dr. Jekyll and Mr. Hyde:* by unleashing his primal self, Jekyll turns into the monster he was Hyde-ing. In Mary Shelley's *Frankenstein*, a scientist creates a pillaging monster out of putrefying corpses—his own buried self, which he resurrects, then disowns. In Oscar Wilde's *The Portrait of Dorian Gray*, the licentious deeds of the protagonist deface a secret portrait, which is a mirror of his real self. Underlying all these struggles is the Faustian pact with the Devil—earthly booty in exchange for one's soul.

Often the battle between good and evil occurs in an isolated or self-contained place—a castle, a forest, an island or the Paris Opera House with its layers of reality and illusion. More recently, science fiction has projected this battle into outer space. However, in these intergalactic duels the evil alien is likely to be an unfeeling machine, reflecting man's new fear: that the price of repressing his beastly nature has become emotional deadness. This modern dread has heightened the attraction of the anti-hero, the rebel, the outlaw, even the gangster, who glamorously fights repression in its guise of law and order. It is also the theme of reconstituted westerns like *Dances with Wolves*, in which the white hero, who once conquered his savage nature by conquering the "redskin," now looks to his enemy for the instinctual self he has lost.

All these myths are easily analyzed in psychological terms— evil as the projection of one's Freudian id or Jungian shadow or Reichian inner deadman. The discovery that humans possess split brains, which sometimes oppose each other, makes it even more logical to define evil as a byproduct of our own conflicted minds.

This invisible inner split has been symbolized externally, from culture to culture, by the opposition of our right and left hands. In the Bible and the Koran, the elect are directed to the right hand of God while the damned are banished to the left. Allah has two right hands, and Christian saints-to-be were said to be percipient enough to suckle only from their mothers' right breasts. Muslim prophets and the Maoris of New Zealand believed guardian angels whispered into their right ears whereas demons whispered into their left. To worship Shiva/Shikta, Hindu god of destruction and death, meant to take the left-handed path. Medieval witches were left-handed and danced their widdershins to the left. In the Black Mass honoring Satan, the Lord's Prayer is spoken backwards, the equivalent of reading to the left.

This right-left dualism is universally ingrained in language. In Japanese, the word for left—*hiddarimaki*—also means crazy; in Italian, *mancino* doubles for dubious and dishonest; in Old English, *lyft* also means weak, worthless and womanish. As modern synonyms for left-handed, *Webster's* dictionary lists devious, indirect, oblique, clumsy, sinister, illegitimate, dubious, underhanded, inept and double-edged. The idiom "having two left feet" suggests awkwardness, while being "out in left field" implies foolishness. The French word for left—*gauche*—means both awkward and foolish in English, while the Latin—*sinister*—carries English connotations of evil. By contrast, the German word for right—*recht*—produces such noble English derivations as direct, erect, correct, rector, rectitude. The Greek word for right—*dexter*—becomes dextrous, decorum, decree.

We speak of restoring balance to an object as righting it. A law-abiding citizen is said to be upright, forthright and on the right side of the law. We give the right of way to the driver on the right just as we seat a privileged guest on the right. The best side of an argument is the right side and a person who wins it is in the right. A citizen in good standing has legal rights, birthrights, property rights, human rights. Political parties of the right define themselves as standing for law and order, and a courageous person is said to be composed of the right stuff.

In the West, this preference for right-wing values has even been projected onto the stones and spires of our cities. In Imperial Rome, state palaces and temples reflecting official wealth and power occupied what Romans called the right bank of the Tiber, while the Jews, artisans and Orientals lived on the left. Similarly, in Paris, the Left Bank of the Seine has traditionally been the haunt of artists and bohemians.

All this seems to reflect our guilty awareness that the Devil is none other than the reverse-handed person facing us each morning in our own mirror—the same image we see when we look at the Phantom with his masked right face becoming our masked left one. And yet, is it possible that evil consists of something more potent to which human wickedness merely attaches like feathers to invisible glue? Can alienation alone explain the sadistic glee with which the British Moors murderers, Myra Hindley and Ian Brady, recorded the death agonies of the children they brutalized and murdered? Or the mindset of Milwaukee misfit Jeffrey Dahmer as he drugged, sodomized, photographed and cannibalized his victims, saving their heads for his freezer and their genitals for his pickle jars? And what of the mesmerizing power of an otherwise petty talent like Adolf Hitler to inspire thousands to systematically kill in his name? As authors Subniv Babuta and Jean-Claude Bragard opined in their book, *Evil*: "Man has never been able to dispense with the notion of an external force of evil, possibly because he is aware that simple destructiveness does not encompass the range, breadth and—most important—the mystery of his experience of evil."

Does evil have supernatural power that is more than the sum of human causes? Ever since Freud introduced Western society to its id self, the official answer has been no: all evil could be attributed to humankind's untamed inner beast. Until recently, I was satisfied with that answer. But then, a sinister resonance in my life caused me to reopen the books and to ask the obvious question: If human evil is just the evolutionary residue from our bloodthirsty past, why is it so much worse than animal savagery? Where did our species acquire our will to evil, along with its pleasurable enjoyment?

I liken these questions metaphorically to the paradox posed by fifth-century B.C. philosopher Zeno: "If at each instant the flying arrow is at rest, when does it move?" Even if each individual act of evil can be traced to a human source, what gives evil its powerful trajectory? Could it be that there is a principle of Evil forever motivating the Faust in man?

CHRISTIANITY AND THE DEVIL

JULY 9, 1987

It is the night before my mother's funeral. What is left of our dwindling clan has gathered in my natal home. After hours of restless tossing, I awaken well before dawn, shivering in a room clammy with heat, awash in the wakeful expectancy I associate with the dislodging of real secrets. As I lie in that twilight zone between waking and sleeping, dream images slide through my consciousness, but so slowly each seems to surface through translucent jelly: "I am a child of eight, terrified to go down into the cellar. A baby is buried there—a boy. Something to do with a chipped enamel bowl my mother once used to drain dishes. Another dream fragment, this time about a girl in an old-fashioned dress with her hair in ringlets."

At daybreak I climb out of bed and creep downstairs into the basement. Passing through my mother's fruit cellar, I enter a portion of the basement, once dirt-floored, now bricked over. Fists clenched, shoulders hunched, using the short, determined stride of a child, I pace in the illumination of a single dangling lightbulb. Near the light I stamp my foot and announce in a child's voice: "This spot is bad." Then I move to a place near the stairs and stamp my foot: "This spot is bad." I prowl between them, still under the primal spell of my dream, repeating "bad bad bad bad bad bad," growing frantic, unwilling or unable to stop.

The two spots feel different. As I stare down through the bricks of the first, I imagine a male fetus curled in a shallow, scooped-out grave. The second spot is also a grave, but cold and deep and rectangular as in a cemetery plot—more a vision than a real part of this basement. It belongs to a girl, age eight or nine, in old-fashioned dress. I remember seeing such a child lying in her coffin—a photo of my mother's youngest sister, Verna, who died in 1915. I dismiss that association: Why would I dream of someone who died twenty years before I was born? Then I return my attention to the first spot, the "hot" one.

The sickening dread pervading my dream remains with me throughout my mother's funeral, like a bloated rat decaying in my belly. By day's end, I am agitated enough to want to tear up that cellar floor with my bare hands. In fact, it would require heavy equipment, and I am not that crazy. I am left with a mystery that seems unresolvable.

Over the next few weeks, my sister and I return several times to this nine-room house, where my mother's family lived for more than seventy years, to sift and sort. Toward nightfall, I grow uneasy. Since my mother's death, some undefinable shift seems to have taken place in the house's atmosphere. Something seems amiss, something nasty and tangible, seeping like poison gas from that tell-tale basement. Though I try to dismiss my anxiety as a byproduct of unhappy experiences here, it does not feel that way. Before, when recalling the past, I have always been a spectator, remembering fear; now I am undergoing it. As I lie in the dark, my skin a-prickle with sensations of the uncanny, I form the superstitious belief that Evil exists of and by itself as a force in this house, perhaps invoked by my father's perverted sexual practices. Through religious ritual my mother—a fervent Christian—kept it at bay. Now that she is gone, so are her checks and balances.

Next day, as my sister and I sort through layers of dusty accumulations, I confess these thoughts in embarrassment. Though I *expect* my sister to be politely dismissive, she instantly endorses my feelings. She, too, has experienced palpable fear in this house since our mother's death. She also reminds me of my childhood conviction that the house was haunted—how I would refuse to go down into the basement, or even up into our attic bedroom without a series of lights being turned on in sequence. On one occasion, when I had both hands full and could not manipulate the light on the staircase to the attic, she had called "boo" out of the darkness, causing such reflex fear that I flung two glasses of chocolate milk against the ceiling.

We both agree: under no circumstances would either one of us spend a night here alone.

A few weeks later, over dinner, a male cousin affirms his life-long fear of the house, centering on the basement. Later, I will learn from a nephew, who tended the house following my mother's death, of a sudden, icy terror that once caused him to flee the basement to my mother's bedroom, where he spent the night as if seeking protection. By then, I have also learned of a real-estate appraiser who—unmindful of the house's history—felt something baneful within its walls and could not wait to bolt the front door.

Six weeks after my mother's funeral, I have lunch with a female cousin in Toronto. In the midst of reminiscences, she mentions a maternal aunt who hanged herself fifteen years before. Even in a family of tortured lives and violent deaths, this aunt's story was an especially poignant one. As my cousin relates: "One day she came to visit me. She sobbed her heart out over so many things. One was the abortion she had at age sixteen. A friend of grandma's was a nurse, and she did it in the bathtub with a coat hanger, which was what they used in those days. The fetus was well enough developed to see it was a boy."

I shiver in the scalding brightness of that summer day. I have temporarily forgotten that for many years "my father's house" was my grandmother's house; therefore, it is ancient maternal secrets that the sighing house has released on the day of my mother's funeral.

That night I lie in the dark, eyes open, watching a re-enactment of the abortion that took place fourteen years before my birth, as if it were a Technicolor movie. Every action is precise and vivid, from the moment the nurse dons her brown rubber apron to her presentation of the fetus to my grandmother in an enamel bowl—the bowl that appeared in my dream, the chipped bowl I knew over a decade later as a dish-drainer.

Once more, against the odds, relevant information has found me. I believe some day I will also learn the story of the old-fashioned girl with the ringlets.

How did I acquire knowledge seemingly possessed only by the dead? How did my natal home acquire its negative charge so that even strangers could feel it? Did it possess memory? Did ancient secrets permeate its walls like psychic rot, recording the guilts and fears of those who lived there?

In the myths of most cultures, spirits of Light have battled demons of Darkness, imitating the alterations of day and night experienced on this planet. Since these spirits were thought to exist everywhere and to cause everything, early peoples tried to persuade, bribe, flatter, trick or coerce them into providing good fortune for themselves while visiting plague, drought and death on their enemies.

In the Nordic tradition, Loki the Trickster attacked Balder the Good in an attempt to destroy humankind. In ancient Egypt, the good god Osiris was beset by his Evil brother Set. In Persian Zoroastrianism, it was Ormazd the god of Light versus his Evil twin Ahriman.

Though the Olympian gods of Rome were more Freudian than spiritual, Christianity brought human conduct unequivocally back under divine jurisdiction, sternly refocused on Good versus Evil. Instead of a family of gods reflecting human passions, or twin gods of light and darkness, this new sect proclaimed that a single all-powerful God sat in judgement and He was perfect. His adversary was not His equal but His creation—a rebel light-bearer named Lucifer who, through free will, became Satan the Prince of Darkness. Though seldom pictured before the sixth century for fear of invoking him, Satan was described as horned, cloven-hoofed and shaggy-coated—an inversion of Pan, the Grecian god of procreation. His scepter was a pitchfork—the trident of Neptune, god of the sea, which is a universal symbol for the unconscious. He was also the demonization of the Great Mother goddess of procreation, whose sacred animal was the horned bull and who is also symbolized by the sea. This demonization of Pan, Neptune and the Great Mother indicated Christianity's prime targets: sex, women and humankind's deepest, most private thoughts.

As an inspirational religion, Christianity had preached love and ecstasy. However, after Roman Emperor Constantine banned all other faiths in A.D. 324, the Church began to trade off its spiritual riches for earthly power. Though angels as well as devils appeared in the Bible, the jealous Church fathers proclaimed the popular Greek and Roman *daemons*, of the sort who advised Socrates, to be demons. As a Greek word, *hairesis* had meant choice; now *choice* meant heresy—erroneous choice. Once a religion of the oppressed, Christianity had become a religion of the oppressors.

After Charlemagne's bloody conversion of the German tribes in the eighth century, their fierce forest gods were consigned to hell along with the more effete Olympian ones. With these snaggle-toothed monsters, leering goblins and lewd kobolds swelling his ranks, the Evil One now possessed more mystical power than ever before, thus presenting a new challenge to Church dogma: If God was all-powerful, all-loving and perfect, how could Satan be such a potent force?

It was this contradiction that the Cathars, a twelfth-century Christian sect of southern France, tried to answer. According to their Dualist creed, Good and Evil were two equal and primary forces—a return to the pre-Christian tradition. Fervent and high-minded, the Cathars also dared to believe in salvation based on personal revelation without the necessity for priests.

For two hundred years, the Inquisition confiscated Cathar property and burned adherents at the stake. By the fifteenth century, it had extended its persecutions to include witches—often healers and midwives, now branded as handmaidens of the Devil. St. Bernard spelled out this obdurate fear and loathing of women: "To live with a woman without incurring danger is more difficult than to resuscitate the dead." Medievalist Emile Mâle confirmed: "For the monk, woman is almost as powerful as the Devil. She is his instrument, and makes use of her to ruin saints. Such were the sentiments of the great abbots and reformers of the monastic orders. All were in fear of woman."

According to the Church fathers, witches sealed their pact with the Devil, now described as a two-faced black ram, by kissing his foul-smelling anal lips—a demonization of the vagina. A woman suspected of satanic practice was tossed into a river with limbs bound: if she drowned, she was judged innocent; if she survived, she was tortured until she confessed. This might include gouging out the "evil" left eye with which she was supposed to cast hexes; wielding burning pincers to yank off the left breast where she suckled Satan; driving nails through every inch of her body in search of the "Devil's spot" where she was said to feel no pain. A hundred witches might be burned in a single day, with their staked corpses strung from village to village like charred hydro poles.

In trying to repress the force of Darkness within an all-powerful, all-loving God of Light, the Church fathers became the demons they were opposing. And the more self-righteously they fought their inverted battle, the more European society became manipulated by Evil in the name of God and the Good.

Since Protestant reformers such as Germany's Martin Luther and England's John Wesley were equally in love with the Devil and damnation, the Reformation did not produce tolerance; however, it did fragment Christendom's secular power. That, plus the rise of science and the education of the middle classes, created revulsion for the religious orgy that had held Europe in thrall for so many centuries. Increasingly, Evil was stripped of its supernatural clout, its personifications and its status as a proper noun to become earthly, derivative and adjectival—the byproduct of all-too-human infamy, both personal and collective, for which modern society offered the only true exorcism: reason.

But could the supernatural be cast off as easily as a worn-out cassock? Did the Devil dissolve under Freudian scorn, or did he—like the Phantom—just escape down into the basement of the opera house?

In a recent Gallup poll, 86 per cent of Canadians said they believed in God, while 34 per cent said they believed in Hell, and 30 per cent confirmed belief in the Devil. In a U.S. Gallup poll, 95 per cent claimed belief in God or some kind of universal spirit, while 60 per cent said they believed in Hell.

Since 1974, when *The Exorcist* created some of the longest lineups in movie history, popular fascination with Satan has led to the recycling of demonic heroes, apparently as resilient as bubblegum. To Count Dracula, Frankenstein and the Wolfman, filmmakers have added a line of designer demons, marketed under brand names such as *Elm Street, Omen, Poltergeist, Entity, Hallowe'en, Prom Night* and *Stephen King.* Perhaps more insidious has been the influence of Heavy Metal groups like Judas Priest, Ozzy Osbourne, Motley Crüe and AC/DC (whose name is translated by some devotees as Antichrist/Devil Child). Their videos, celebrating blood sacrifice, necrophilia, violence and suicide, have been cited by police and the courts as providing inducements to crime. For example, self-styled satanist and serial killer Richard Ramirez, known as the Night Stalker, claimed to have been influenced by AC/DC's album *Highway to Hell.* Further blurring the lines between illusion and reality: the Church of Satan was founded in San Francisco by Anton LaVey, who played the Devil in *Rosemary's Baby.* The Process, another satanic cult, allegedly inspired Charles Manson and his gang of crazies to indulge in random murder aimed at hastening the apocalypse of Revelations. This included the 1969 slaughter of pregnant actress Sharon Tate, wife of Roman Polanski, who directed *Rosemary's Baby.*

More chilling than this lunatic violence are signs of satanic networks operating just under the well-scrubbed skin of middle-class North America. Often such cults begin with ritual sex and graveyard desecrations, then progress to animal sacrifice, rape and murder.

In July 1984, a Long Island teenager was fatally stabbed seventeen times in what his killers admitted was a satanic rite. Though David Berkowitz was convicted as a lone stalker in the Son of Sam killings, New York investigators have insisted, in a recent TV documentary, that he fronted for a tightly organized satanic cult. In 1986, in the rural Ontario town of Delhi, teenagers confessed to satanic animal sacrifices; in Verdun, Quebec, in 1987, police investigated the use of children in Black Mass and prostitution; in Chicago's O'Hare airport in 1984, a suspicious parcel from Miami yielded a dead fetus, a human skull and Hallowe'en masks.

In September 1990, a leaked Winnipeg police report named 150 residents, including a nurse, a restaurant manager and a bank executive, as belonging to five satanic cults active in this conservative prairie city of six hundred thousand. Allegations included ritual torture and slaughter of animals, indoctrination and use of children for pornographic videos; recruiting of female runaways for prostitution; ceremonial impregnation of a cult member, who was killed when she tried to flee with her newborn; the confession of an ex-member that she acted as sexual bait in the murder of three males.

Though the Roman Catholic Church has de-emphasized Satan for several centuries, he has remained part of Roman Catholic law. In a 1988 discourse on evil, Pope John Paul II warned that the Devil is so clever he can fool men into denying his existence in the name of rationalism. This sentiment was echoed by former Vatican official Monsignor Corrado Balducci in his bestseller, *The Devil Exists—You Can Recognize Him*: "There is nothing he likes better than to hear people say he is a figment of the imagination."

Legend holds that King Solomon rid the world of devils by imprisoning them in a black bottle, which he threw down a deep well near Babylon. After a couple of centuries of relative abstinence, Western society has uncorked that bottle. The Devil—real or metaphoric—seems to be enjoying a popular comeback.

DEMONS OF LEGEND

SEPTEMBER 1987
After the sale of my natal home, I seem to carry its sooty shadow back to the Toronto house I am subletting. Frequently, around three or four A.M., I awaken filled with the toxins of nightmares I can't quite recall. "Something" is hovering in the dark around me— something tangible and loathsome, requiring me to lie very still, silent and watchful so as not to materialize it. Logically, I assume I am still regurgitating memories of childhood abuse dislodged by my mother's death; however, my present terror feels like a product of adult wakefulness and not of infantile recall. Occasionally, I imagine I hear "it" breathe; certainly, the sound is not from myself, since I am holding my breath. As nearly as I can describe, I seem to be lying along the thin border between order and chaos. On the other side is freefall terror— Evil, dirty, bottomless and outside the rules. I do not believe the danger to be inside my own head. Rather, it seems that I stand at the gateway

of another dimension where my mind, though present, would be of limited use. I also have the disconcerting certainty that the physical world we humans assume to be real is just a serviceable illusion.

Though the possibility of traveling into this unknown dimension lures me, I don't feel sufficiently grounded to risk it. Instead, I grope backward into my ancestral past for the spiritual comfort of cross and candles. When preparing for bed, I also fall into childhood rituals— seeing that both shoes are placed precisely under my bed, rechecking doors and windows, traveling through the house by manipulating switches so I am forever walking in a path of light. Instinctively, I pray to my mother for protection and—hedging my bets—keep a butcher knife under my pillow.

I don't seek therapeutic help. The choice to cross the line or not seems mine. In fact, what probably prolongs my disorientation is my regret over drawing a psychic circle of safety around myself. In a reversal of my usual values, fear is my friend while my adversary— like Eve's, like Pandora's—is curiosity.

In occult tradition, the spirit world consists of a hierarchy of entities that, under normal circumstances, are veiled from us. During times of confusion, especially around death, this veil may be rent, allowing the riffraff of the spiritual world to spill through. In physical terms, this is like a lowering of the immunological threshold, leading to infection by germs.

Although the scorn of one's peers makes telling tales of spirit harassment risky and unlikely, in the early seventies folklorist David J. Hufford was fascinated to discover that 23 per cent of a sampling of ninety-three Newfoundland college students had experienced the supernatural entity islanders called the Old Hag. As Hufford described the phenomenon: a person awakens in the night, immobilized with terror. Often he/she feels a malevolent presence, followed by an intense pressure on the chest as if some "thing" were suffocating or strangling him. Either the person can't move or else he fears to do so. Often he believes he is dying. Newfoundlanders call this "being hagrid" or "having the Old Hag." Similarly, "hagging" means calling down the Old Hag on another by saying the Lord's Prayer backwards in the name of the Devil. Protection comes from leaving on a night-light, by keeping religious artefacts at hand and by hiding a knife under one's pillow—all responses I instinctively tried.

Though Hufford first attributed these findings to Newfoundland's cultural tradition, he later discovered a startling fact: 15 per cent of any random sample of one hundred North Americans, asked only to report on unusual psychic experiences, described the Old Hag phenomenon. Equally divided by sex, most had no history of paranormal events and otherwise appeared healthy. Sometimes several people suffered Old Hag attacks in the same location, indicating an infected atmosphere. Most occurred when a person was overtired and sleeping supine. Though often initiated by violent dreams, a disproportionate number took place during daylight naps. In either case, the victim was convinced he was awake and gave a realistic, finely detailed account of the experience. Hearing footsteps, frequently with a slushy, whooshy, "snurfling," shuffling or sliding undertone, was a common overture. So was the sound of an opening door. Less usual was hearing one's name called, along with grunting, moaning, laughter, scratching or bed-creaking.

The uncanny sense of a presence was repeatedly mentioned, as was the word *evil*. Sometimes the person saw a humanoid figure—a luminous white blob, a disembodied face with piercing eyes, a shape behind black veils, a murky or vaporous presence, a silhouette—often identifiable as one sex or the other. A few mentioned flickering lights, a foul odor, the banging of the bed, a sense of levitation, of being out-of-body, of being touched, of tingling or vibrating, of wrestling with something gelatinous. The attack ended when the paralyzed victim was able, or dared, to move a finger or an arm, or when someone intervened by shaking him. This last usually occurred when a friend encountered the victim staring wide-eyed and gasping in terror.

At the turn of the century William James provided a classic account of what Hufford would call the Old Hag phenomenon. He quoted "an intimate friend . . . one of the keenest intellects I know" in *The Varieties of Religious Experience*: "It was about September 1884, when I had the first experience.... A vivid tactile hallucination of being grasped by the arm, which made me get up and search the room for an intruder; but the sense of presence properly so-called came on the next night. After I had got into bed and blown out the candle . . . I felt something come into the room and stay close to my bed. . . . It stirred something more at the roots of my being than any ordinary perception. The feeling had something of the quality of a very large tearing vital pain spreading chiefly over the chest, but within the organism—and yet the feeling was not pain so much as abhorrence. At all events, something was present with me, and I knew its presence far more surely than I have ever known the presence of any fleshly living creature. I was conscious of its departure as of its coming: an almost instantaneously swift going through the door, and the 'horrible sensation' disappeared."

Almost a century later, a twenty-two-year-old American college senior reluctantly described the same phenomenon, after having been awakened in broad daylight by the inexplicable slamming of a door: "My roommate wasn't there and the door was still closed. . . . But—there was a murky presence that had just kind of materialized. . . . I felt this pressing down all over me. I couldn't breathe. I couldn't move. I was wide awake, you know. It was a fraternity house. I could hear everything going on all over the house. . . . And this murky presence—just kind of—this was *evil*." When the student succeeded in moving his arm, the apparition dissipated.

In the second century, the physician Galen ascribed these so-called supernatural assaults to physical causes—indigestion, poor circulation, asthma and sleep disorders. Predictably, Freud interpreted them as hallucinations connoting erotic desire. However, folklorist David Hufford was impressed by the homogeneity of the accounts; of their universality, affecting 15 per cent of today's North American population; of the conviction of each subject that he or she was awake and having a real experience. Though unwilling to postulate the existence of demons, Hufford refused to discount that possibility. As he cautioned in *The Terror that Comes in the Night*: "It was just such a rejection of untutored observation that delayed for so long the 'scientific' discovery of giant squid, gorillas, meteors. . . . Seasoned fishermen were said to mistake floating trees with large root systems for huge animals attacking their boats; farmers were said to have overlooked large iron-bearing rocks in the midst of their fields until they were pointed out by lightning; and in this case [of Old Hag attacks] 'children and savages' were said to have difficulty knowing when they were awake and when they were asleep."

Bearing a hissing, kissing kinship to Hufford's Old Hag was the incubus-succubus of medieval legend. A dwarfish, goatish male entity, the incubus raped, choked, suffocated and impregnated women during sleep; his female counterpart, the succubus, seduced men by riding them till they were "haggard." As St. Augustine warned in his fourth-century *City of God*: "It is widely credited, and such belief is confirmed by the direct or indirect testimony of thoroughly trustworthy people, that Sylvans and Fauns, commonly called Incubi, have frequently molested women, sought and obtained from them coition . . . the fact is testified by so many and such weighty authorities that it were impudent to doubt it."

More than a thousand years later, Pope Innocent VIII confirmed in his papal bull of 1484: "It has indeed come to our knowledge and deeply grieved are we to hear it, that many persons of both sexes ... have abused themselves with evil spirits, both incubi and succubi."

So prevalent were these alleged supernatural attacks that the word *nightmare*, in several European languages, derived from it. In Anglo-Saxon, Icelandic, Bohemian, Swedish and Old High German, *mara* meant one who crushes. In French, *cauchemar* meant the creature who tramples. In English, a night mare is a female horse who, by inversion, rides its victim through the night, while to be hag-ridden means to be incessantly "nagged."

When nightmares persisted through the day, the victim was diagnosed as demon-possessed, for which the cure was exorcism. Though descriptions of the evil invaders have changed with culture and fashion, this ceremony—going back four thousand years to the Babylonians—has remained basically the same. Employing incense, candles, chanting and water for purification, a representative of the forces of Light commands, frightens or induces the demon of Darkness to leave the body it has taken over.

Just as the Christian Church's recognition of Satan went underground for a couple of centuries, so did exorcism. Then, during a sermon in 1990, John Cardinal O'Connor of New York revealed that two exorcisms had been officially performed in that city in the past year. Another was televised in the spring of 1991, on ABC-TV's "20/20," hosted by Barbara Walters.

A 1967 case, with all the horrific frills expected by supernatural buffs, was described by Robert Pelton in *The Devil and*

Karen Kingston. After witnessing her mother fatally stab her alcoholic father, seven-year-old Karen was overwhelmed by debilitating fits of violence. When placed in a North Carolina state home, her condition deteriorated so drastically that by fourteen she was judged to have an I.Q. of only 45 and could not read, write or feed herself. Her body was covered with running sores; she exuded a stench, possessed coarse, lifeless hair, crossed eyes, a hunched body and a left leg two inches shorter than her right.

An exorcism was begun on April 13, 1974, by Reverend Richard Rogers and his wife, Ruth, assisted by Father John Tyson, a Roman Catholic priest, and Reverend Donald Sutter, a Baptist evangelist. Also in attendance were clinical psychologist W. Manley Fromme, psychiatrist Clarence Emory, general practitioner Julian Pershing, three nurses and author Robert Pelton. Though only Sutter and the Rogerses believed in demonic possession, in twelve sessions over three days Reverend Rogers allegedly expelled thirteen self-styled demons, each with a distinctive personality, manner of speech and specialized knowledge; eight also produced handwriting samples, which graphologist George D. Steinert testified could not come from the same personality. As each demon was expelled, the physical ailment for which it claimed responsibility was said to spontaneously disappear. On several occasions, Karen was reported to swell to three times her size. Holy water sizzled on her forehead, blisters appeared on her limbs, and her body gave off colored hazes. She reportedly levitated twice, once for seven minutes to a level of five feet, with two men trying to pull her down. Pictures were said to have fallen from the wall, cushions floated upward, a paper from which Father Tyson was reading a prayer burst into flame.

A day later, Karen was said to look like a normal adolescent. Her left leg had lengthened; her hair was a shiny reddish brown, her eyes were unclouded. Within a week her I.Q. measured 74, and two years later it was 110.

It is tempting to dismiss all such accounts as gross exaggeration or outright fraud due to religious mania, commercial opportunism, mental aberration or mass hysteria. Yet their undiminished popularity after three hundred years of scientific scorn testifies, at the very least, to their steely grip on the human imagination. William James was willing to go considerably further: "The refusal of modern 'enlightenment' to treat 'possession' as a hypothesis to be spoken of as even possible, in spite of the massive human tradition based on concrete human experiences in its favor, has always seemed to be a curious example of the power of fashion in things 'scientific.' That the demon theory...will have its innings again is to my mind absolutely certain. One has to be 'scientific' indeed to be blind and ignorant enough to suspect no such possibility."

Today, when presented with cases purported to be demon possession, most psychiatrists diagnose them as multiple personality, schizophrenia, temporal lobe epilepsy or the rare brain disorder known as Tourette's syndrome. In a 1982 study of this latter condition, which manifests itself in uncontrollable twitching and swearing, Drs. A. Shapiro and E. Shapiro stated that twenty-four of their Tourette's syndrome patients had undergone exorcisms by persons who thought they were demon-possessed, and that none had been helped. They also contended that William Peter Blatty's novel *The Exorcist* was based on such a case—a charge Blatty denies.

An alternative psychological view holds that patients with the above disorders are more vulnerable to demonic possession, in the same way an AIDs patient, with a weakened immune system, may contract pneumonia. Psychologists who accept this possibility see possession as operating on a continuum. Any close relationship may acquire numinous power, especially when an unnatural tie like incest is involved. On the death of the victimizer, what was domination by the living can slide over into possession by the dead. Similarly, in a tightly knit family or clan or cult, an individual may feel possessed by the group mind, sometimes represented or contained by a family dwelling. In extreme cases, some psychiatrists believe possession may be fueled by the supernatural.

A pioneer in this field, British surgeon-psychiatrist Kenneth McAll has stated his belief in possession by the living, by the dead and by demonic spirits. When the possessor seemed to be a dead person, McAll explored the victim's family tree to see who the disturbed soul might be. Then he used prayer and ritual to help that spirit find peace in its own realm. Afterwards he treated the victim for spirit-dependency in the same way he would treat an alcoholic for the underlying cause of his spirits addiction.

In his 1982 book, *Healing the Family Tree*, McAll also demonstrated how possession by the living can acquire a supernatural aura. After he diagnosed one woman as having a disturbed relationship with her son, she stopped for comfort at a church. There, a disembodied voice urged her to free her son by severing his umbilical cord. When she mentally manipulated scissors to cut the cord, she felt transformed by ecstasy. Simultaneously, her schizophrenic son felt a mysterious surge of release, allowing him to be discharged from the mental institute where he had been confined.

Using the same model as McAll, Toronto hypnotherapist Adam Crabtree has diagnosed some fifty cases of possession over the past seven years. Though Crabtree was not convinced he was dealing with the supernatural, he decided to treat each case *as if* it was exactly what it purported to be.

One young woman named Sarah complained of being possessed by the spirit of her late maternal grandmother. Under hypnosis, the grandmother confessed through Sarah that she had always felt guilty about her rejection of Sarah's mother. This neglect had motivated her to overcompensate with Sarah. After Crabtree explained to the confused spirit that her attachment was a hindrance, the grandmother became a benign influence on Sarah's life.

A more enigmatic case required Crabtree to analyze a self-styled sprite named Shamus, who spoke with an Irish brogue: "I had no difficulty in treating Shamus like a being, distinct from my client Mike. Shamus 'felt' like another person. But as distance from the work increases, the doubts grow. The evidence of the data has not changed but the passage of time of itself makes the extraordinary more unbelievable."

Though Crabtree hedged his bets, California psychiatrist Ralph Allison did not. A specialist in multiple personality, Allison began finding "alien" personalities, among the other split-offs, which made no psychological sense. As he stated in his 1980 book, *Mind in Many Pieces*, "Interestingly enough, such entities often refer to themselves as spirits. Over the years I've encountered too many such cases to dismiss the possibility of spirit possession completely."

When circumstances warranted it, Allison used exorcism as part of his treatment, as did British psychiatrist Richard Mackarness. Writing in the medical journal *The Practitioner* in 1974, Mackarness explained: "To me, demonic possession enters into the differential diagnosis of every disturbed person I see. . . . I do not claim to turn up many genuine cases, but when I do I have no hesitation in referring them for exorcism. To my critics I say that at worst it is a harmless form of mumbo-jumbo and at best it is life-saving and can mend broken lives."

A rarity among psychiatrists, Arthur Guirdham has claimed direct contact with the evil forces that bedeviled many of his patients. In his 1972 book *Obsession*, he described his first encounter, at age six, after an overwhelming sense of horror mesmerized him into opening his bedroom door: "His smile was not only diabolic but welcoming. . . . From head to foot he was covered with the same blue-grey pelt and everywhere a blueish aura emanated from him. . . . His legs tapered down to what appeared to be slender stumps, but I was so hypnotized by his face and his smile that I did not look closely at his feet. I know now that he had hooves."

Because of his own experiences, Guirdham refused to brand the night terrors so common to children as mere illusion. Instead, he analyzed them as evil, in ancient symbolic forms, beyond the child's ability to create; because the child's identity has not yet crystallized, he or she is more open to their presence. Guirdham hypothesized that the same "surreal lucidity" occurs during puberty, in psychosis and on the borders of sleep or death. He also maintained that places could become impregnated with an aura of evil, which sensitive persons could perceive. As an example, he cited a quite ordinary, even cheerfully decorated house, with a palpably bad atmosphere, in which five unrelated people of varying ages had committed suicide in rapid succession.

As a child, Guirdham's instinctive response to the presence of evil was to pray—an obsessional ritual inspired by free-floating guilt. He also suggested that children's games, like compulsive counting, rhyming, avoiding cracks and hexing, were attempts to ward off psychic awareness. Among adults, he included hand-wringing, sleepwalking, compulsive obscenity, workaholism, exaggerated punctuality and overrationalism. Physical symptoms such as eczema, asthma, migraine, allergies, tics and some epileptic seizures might also have this substructure.

Psychiatrists open to the diagnosis of demon possession report that it is often precipitated by dabblings in the occult. During the Victorian age, this frequently involved experimentation with seances; in the thirties and forties, with Ouija boards; in the sixties, with psychedelic drugs; in the seventies and eighties, with amateur hypnotism, witchcraft, crystal balls and mediumship.

In his 1990 book *Hungry Ghosts*, psychic investigator Joe Fisher related a cautionary tale in which he experienced himself as having been victimized by unsavory spirits. Intrigued by the skills of a Toronto trance medium, Fisher joined an occult circle that met weekly to converse with entities who allegedly spoke through her. One by one, members were paired with guides who chatted to them in distinct voices, presented detailed reincarnational histories, and seemed ideally mated to their emotional needs. "There were mother figures, father figures, quarrelsome eccentrics, big brothers and sisters, simple pals, gentle counselors, prattling comics. . . . And, in my case, a dream lover."

Giving her name as Filipa Gavrilos, she claimed to have been Fisher's lover in eighteenth-century Greece, but what hooked him was her intimate knowledge of his present life. Speaking in a heavily accented voice, she described the minutiae of his day and expressed private thoughts he had never uttered.

Thoroughly captivated, Fisher eventually went to Greece to authenticate Filipa's description of their last incarnation together. What he uncovered was a tapestry of partial truths, outright lies and painstakingly accurate detail interwoven with glaring anachronisms. Most intriguingly, a Greek linguist who analyzed Filipa's voice tapes identified her accent as that of a woman of northeastern Greece, whose idiosyncratic usage and pronunciation could be pinpointed to the years 1912 to 1920. Though still historic by Fisher's standards, that period was much later than the one Filipa claimed they had shared.

Who was Filipa? After sifting through the evidence, Fisher believes both he and the trance medium were duped by what occult tradition has described as hungry ghosts—insatiably greedy entities, depicted with tiny mouths, thin necks and gigantic bellies, who haunt the dead zone just above our earthly plane, like cons and hawkers eager to fleece the unsuspecting tourists.

It was this scruffy lot that clinical psychologist Wilson Van Dusen of California came to believe tortured his schizophrenic patients. Sometimes Van Dusen questioned "them" directly through strange voices that issued from his patients; at other times, the patients repeated their silent inner dialogues to him. With most, the initial disturbance happened suddenly: they heard and saw frightening things to which they adjusted with difficulty. All rejected the term *hallucination*, believing themselves in contact with actual beings from another dimension, which they labeled the Other Order, the Eavesdroppers and so on. Though some were helpful, most were louts, teasers, deceivers and scolds. Often of limited vocabulary and intelligence, they taunted their hosts with criticisms, obscene insults and plots on their lives. They would brag about producing the disasters reported in the newspapers, tempt their hosts to perform foolish acts and mimic their friends. Often they tried to possess some part of their hosts' bodies—an eye or an ear, which might suddenly cease to function. Some described themselves as demons, and all were anti-religious.

Van Dusen became fascinated at the correspondence between the hundreds of reports he collected from his patients and the occult writings of Emanuel Swedenborg. He also noted a parallel between the torturers of the lower order and the monsters of Freud's id, and between the guides of the higher order and the helpful archetypes of Jung's collective unconscious. In the end, Van Dusen concluded that his patients' experiences were a supernatural extension of normal experience.

MORE THAN PSYCHOLOGICAL?

1940–1984
The only other house I feared was the one in which my father was raised—a skinny, two-storey brick trimmed in lacy black iron like a witch's wedding cake. With its trap doors, sealed-off rooms and smell of secrets, it gave me goosebumps.

Most Sundays in the early forties my mother, father, sister and I went over to that other house to watch my grandmother die. My aunt Viola was my grandmother's full-time nurse—as thin as my father was fat. She and my father hated each other. At my grandmother's funeral, a quarrel of the "never darken my door" variety erupted. From then on my mother—a skillful mender of broken china—sent my sister and me alone to Aunt Viola's for visits several times a year. Our lunch—which my aunt made but never ate—was invariable: a tin of Campbell's alphabet soup, unheated and unthinned, divided between my sister and me, still in the shape of the container; a tin of creamed corn, also unheated; a platter of coldcuts, served with a half-basket of mashed potatoes, equally divided. Though criminally deprived herself, my aunt had picked up somewhere that children should be well nourished.

Long before that Everest of mashed potatoes made its appearance, I would start to giggle. By the time it had arrived, I would be choking with laughter—laughter devoid of merriment. Hysteria. As some deeply buried part of me already knew, my aunt had also had an incestuous relationship with my father. Aunt Viola, with all her peculiarities, was my future.

Eventually, my aunt inherited money. For months, she went on shopping binges in which she bought hats or gloves or shoes, to be laid out in rooms for people to view like gifts at a trousseau tea. All except for underwear, apparently preferring her tattered gray rags—perhaps a symbol of what could, and could not, be changed.

My aunt grew afraid of her natal home. On returning from downtown, she would sit for hours on her front steps, surrounded by her loot, afraid to go inside. Once inside she became afraid to come out. Eventually, she settled on fear of the outside world expressed in a fear of germs, especially on doorknobs, which she took to wrapping with Kleenex on her now-infrequent sorties.

The more that people tried to persuade my aunt to sell her house, the further into it she retreated. Other rich and distant relatives left her money. The gods, at first generous, had grown mocking. Now a crowded repository of treasures, her rooms had shrunk to passageways lined by cabinets that opened into other cabinets, and yet—for all her leatherbound first editions growing musty—only a single wood stove with pipes outstretched like supplicating arms heated the whole house. My aunt did not so much have a house as that house possessed a person. It, and the memories it contained, enthralled her.

Several things still afforded my aunt pleasure: a pile of National Geographics, which she read through an outsized magnifying glass, and her cat Mitzi, distinguished from all other cats who plied the back alleys by his fancy, store-brought dental work. My aunt was also a member of the Anglican Church and a generous donor until Mitzi—at last beyond the reach of medical science—was denied an Anglican burial. Deeply wounded, my aunt lavished her money on other more flexible faiths, still hopeful of the life to come while ever more careless of this one.

One morning in the fifties my mother phoned my aunt to say that my father was dying of pneumonia. Minutes later my aunt ran through the corridors of the hospital shrieking: "My brother is dying! My brother is dying!" When he didn't die, she became bitter toward my mother, who she felt had deceived her. Thereafter, whenever my mother—or, by extension, my sister or I—phoned her, she hung up, then changed her number.

Throughout the years I dreamed of my aunt—turbulent dreams that baffled my conscious self. Otherwise, I seldom thought of her. An exception occurred one day in June 1974, when I was visiting my eighty-two-year-old father at St. Peter's Infirmary in Hamilton. As I stood at his bedside, for what would be the last time, I suddenly found myself thinking, with great intensity, about my aunt Viola. What gripped me so fiercely that I felt close to passing out was a profound sense of identification: Aunt Viola was born on March 6; I was born on March 8. She was a Pisces, as was I. Our birthstone was the bloodstone.

Though I cared nothing for astrology I kept repeating these bits of nonsense like a litany until, at last, it was time to go. As I touched my finger to the back of my father's hand, he opened his eyes for the first time during that visit. Looking directly into my face, blue eyes vivid against the whiteness of flesh and sheet and hair, he spoke his last-ever words to me: "Thanks for coming, Vi." This message echoed through my psyche for a very long time.

Much later, commercial interests attempted to buy my aunt's house, but of course she refused. Still wed to her store of unhappy memories she instead hired two brothers to make the essential repairs demanded by the City. When a lawyer discovered the brothers had bilked her by enlarging the sums on her cheques, she was summoned by the police to identify them. Though she wasn't the only complainant, when those brothers got out of jail it was my aunt they came looking for. They entered her house through the cellar, using a crowbar. Too terrified to flee, my aunt typically buried herself deeper into the house.

The men emerged through the trap door into my aunt's kitchen. While my aunt cowered upstairs behind her double-bolted bedroom *door, the brothers made their way through the darkened house, in no hurry, ransacking as they went, as in the child's ghost story: "Now I'm in your living room, and I'm coming to get you! Now I'm on the staircase, and I'm coming to get you . . ."*

The brothers emerged on the second floor, ax and crowbar in hand. They easily discovered my aunt behind the only door that was locked. After pausing for a cigarette, they began to chop. Their ax had already splintered wood when the police arrived. A suspicious neighbor, whom my aunt had always refused to greet, had made a timely phone call.

Even then, my aunt had to be dragged from that house. This a step-niece managed, and here the story takes a welcome upturn. In leaving her ancestral home, my aunt dispossessed herself of her past. A spell had been broken. She began to eat and to live normally, even traveling to a few of the places she had seen in National Geographics *through her magnifying glass.*

When informed, in 1974, of her brother's death, her response was unequivocal: "Our bones will never lie together!" Thereupon she legally sealed the family plot, preventing his interment. She herself, aged ninety, was buried there ten years later.

Psychiatrists have convenient labels like paranoia and agoraphobia to describe my aunt's mental condition. However, to name a psychological state, or even to describe it by its symptoms, surrounds it with information without explaining it. What force kept my aunt imprisoned in her natal home for half a century in defiance of all the normal urges and passions for life? If her enthrallment was to her own projection, why didn't that follow her after she left? *She* was the same; only her location had changed.

Energy is the X factor in all stories of possession, of demonology, of inversion. What gives Evil its extraordinary psychic force?

That the Christian Church's centuries of persecution was about more than secular power is signified by the zeal with which its Inquisitors went about their God-appointed tasks. Like sadists who torture their victims into protestations of love before murdering them, they were not content just to kill the Church's designated enemies: they had to convert them first. A persecution was successful only if the heretic on the rack or the witch at the stake died begging forgiveness from an all-loving God. Those who refused were not just burned but gleefully mocked as they melted. Villages celebrated. They sang songs, chronicling the agonies of these women as they writhed and screamed.

Torturing a person into willful submission requires far more energy than running someone through with a sword. And this was done on an awesome scale, with modern kill-estimates running anywhere from several hundred thousand to nine million. The fifteenth century's notorious Jacob Sprenger saw to the torching of more than five hundred in one year. Summed up R.H. Robbins in his *Encyclopedia of Witchcraft and Demonology.* "Degradation stifled decency, the filthiest passions masqueraded under the cover of religion. . . . Never were so many so wrong, so long."

In modern times, the Germans were not seduced by a satanic call to Evil but by a savior's call to Good: the glorification of the Aryan master race (blond = light) through repression of what was judged to be its "dark" Jewish shadow. Even during the last bitter phases of World War II, when the Nazi state was struggling for survival, extermination of the Jews was accelerated—a suicidal commitment of troops and trains. What in hell fueled that baneful folly?

Perhaps an answer lies in the persistent connection between sex and religion. During ancient fertility rites, celebrants copulated in honor of the goddess of procreation—an ecstatic practice continued by the initiates to the Greek cult of Dionysus. An opposite form of worship elevated sexual denial. Apollo's Roman shrine was attended by Vestal Virgins, and the Roman Catholic Church is still served by nuns and priests who vow chastity. Pythagoras, who felt his mystic powers to be diminished by sex, advised its indulgence only in summer. By his own confession, Emanuel Swedenborg was an exceptionally randy man till age fifty-six, when he was flung from his bed by a blast of wind and a sonorous boom, which was followed by an illumination of Jesus Christ. That marked the cessation of his fierce sexual urges and the onset of his psychic power.

Both chastity and sensuality lost their innocence when yoked to fanatacism. By Roman times, the joyful revels of Dionysus had given way to the debaucheries of Bacchus, god of wine, symbolized by a giant phallus. In the fertility cult of the Persian goddess Cybele, delirious priests castrated themselves out of zealotry. Among early Christian martyrs, the purging of "sins of the flesh" inspired gruesome self-flagellations, along with the wearing of maggots as pridefully as pearls.

In India, Tantric yogis traditionally employed sex as their orgiastic rocket to ecstasy in rites celebrating the goddess Kali. More usually, Hindu yogis practice abstinence to coax *kundalini* energy up from the genitals to the third eye of Enlightenment. As already discussed: This third eye is said to manifest physically as the pineal gland, which has the structure of a primitive eye, and which even today functions in the human brain as a light sensor. The pineal produces two hormones—melatonin, a sexual regulator, and serotonin, a consciousness regulator. In the long days of spring, light decreases the production of melatonin, thus lowering sexual inhibitions and resulting in the restless malady known as spring fever. Fertility rites, marking the coming of the light, instinctively combined sensuality with worship. By contrast, festivals like Hallowe'en, honoring Satan as Prince of Darkness, traditionally took place at midnight, around or after the fall equinox. As celebrations of death and black magic, they exploited the depressive mood psychologists now diagnose as seasonal affective disorder (SAD syndrome), produced by light deprivation.

As biologist John Bleibreu summed up in *The Parable of the Beast*: "In modern usage the word [ecstasy] is commonly employed to describe a rapturous state of being in connection with either sex or religion. . . . It is becoming more and more difficult to avoid concluding that if ecstasy has any material biochemical basis in being, the biochemical substances controlling both its sexual and transcendental manifestations are probably manufactured in the pineal gland."

A hormonal link between sexual energy and psychic power may also be demonstrated by the noisy, ghost-like poltergeist that is said to cause plates to fly, windows to shatter, timbers to groan. Typically, such disturbances center on an adolescent, most frequently a girl, and often they cease with the onset of her menstruation. Stated Hereward Carrington, a pioneer parapsychologist of the 1930s: "An energy seems to be radiated from the body . . . when the sexual energies are blossoming into maturity. . . . It would almost seem as if these energies instead of taking the normal course . . . find this curious means of externalization." In describing the poltergeist as "a bundle of projected repressions," psychoanalyst Nandor Fodor agreed with Carrington's diagnosis.

In 1967, eleven-year-old Matthew Manning became the focus of poltergeist clamorings at his home in Shellford, England. Four years later in boarding school, the disturbances broke out in earnest. Broken glass and knives soared through the air. Coat hangers, squashed into balls as if by a giant fist, were hurled. Showers of pebbles fell indoors. Beds moved across the dorms; chairs danced. Spots of light appeared on walls, growing so hot the headmaster feared they would burst into flame.

Unlike most poltergeist generators, Matthew eventually learned to direct his excess energy into automatic writing and then into drawing. The result was a meteoric career as an artist, during which he produced works in the styles of Albrecht Dürer, Picasso, Da Vinci, Aubrey Beardsley, Paul Klee and even Beatrix Potter. Using ink, Matthew always started at the middle of the page and proceeded outward, without planning or correction. His Dürers and his Beardsleys fooled art experts.

When Matthew attempted to demonstrate his psychic talents on TV, cameras would break down and lights fuse. During extensive laboratory tests, it was found that he exhibited a unique brainwave pattern at the moment when he switched on his power. At the conclusion of one series, Nobel physicist Brian Josephson of Cambridge conceded: "We are dealing here with a new kind of energy."

It seems that humans may generate a life force that can make itself known through psychic phenomena. More normally, it is channeled for sexual or spiritual use; it can be catalyzed in the service of Darkness or of Light, and inverted through exaggeration or denial. In Christianity's founding days, it was a mystical faith in which ascetics channeled sexual energy for the life of the spirit. However, when the Church hierarchy embarked on its drive for power, it sought to control priests and laity through suppression of both their spiritual and their sexual drives. Obedience to the Church—body, mind, heart and spirit—not mystical union with God or joyous celebration of life, became the greatest Christian virtue.

Denied both sexual and spiritual expression, the repressed life force went underground, birthing a Satan bursting with numinous power—a Satan dynamic enough to create a four-hundred-year inversion, during which Good became Evil and Evil, Good. When questioning witches, it became routine to force them to confess to sexual intercourse with demons: no longer innocent victims of raping incubi, they were now judged active seducers. In the 1630s, the notorious Franz Buirmann of Cologne was one of many professional witch-hunters who worked out his sado-sexual desires by avenging himself on women who repulsed him. When a Frau Peller, the wife of a court assessor, refused his advances, Buirmann immediately ordered her head and body shaved, then oversaw her torture, which included allowing an assistant to rape her. The day's session ended, routinely enough, with Frau Peller being burned alive in a straw hut.

It was this constant connection between perverted sex and perverted religion that Freud noted in a January 1897 letter in which he compared the confessions of sixteenth-century witches to those of his sexually abused patients: "But why did the devil who took possession of the poor things invariably abuse them sexually and in a loathsome manner? Why are their confessions under torture so like the communications made by my patients in psychological treatment?"

If, as it seems, sexuality and spirituality are fueled by the same force, perhaps this energy is meant to be channeled into sex during the procreative years and into spiritual enhancement during the later years. This is the traditional pattern in Eastern societies, where elders often give up material possessions and their families for the begging bowl. However, through centuries of sexual and mystical repression, the Christian Church created a licentious, priggish and spiritually barren society, fatally fascinated with Sex and Sin—which of course combine in the worship of Satan.

The Saxons, who occupied what is now Germany, were fervent forest-worshippers till Charlemagne savagely converted them to Christianity. Given the now-inverted power of their gods consigned to hell, witch-hunting was bloodier, more imaginative and more prolonged in Germany than elsewhere in Europe. It was the surfacing of this repressed mysticism, in folk dress, that Hitler personified and catalyzed. Combining spiritual love of the Fatherland with high-minded puritanism, Nazi youths poured what Wilhelm Reich labeled "their orgiastic devotion" onto their Führer. This was symbolized by the swastika, which Reich described as being composed of intertwined bodies.

Given the West's repressive history, the connection between sex and spiritualism isn't one we intuitively comprehend. As materialists, we readily accept masturbation as the expression of a primal erotic drive but not prayer as the expression of an equally potent spiritual one; we understand the lust aroused by a *Playboy* centerfold as a sexual icon much better than the tears shed before a portrait of the Virgin Mary; we understand seduction easier than conversion; we understand the driving force behind rape more than the compulsion behind fasting and abstinence; we understand orgiastic ecstasy but not the visionary kind; we understand wars about oil more readily than wars about faith; we understand the highs of surfing but not of bathing in the River Ganges; we understand physical copulation leading to the birth of a baby far easier than mystical union with the Spirit leading to birth of the soul.

A life-long atheist, Freud interpreted religion as the sublimation of the sex drive. While overeating may also be a sex sublimation, no one suggests intercourse to be a replacement for eating. Both command their own primal territory despite that zone of interchange. The same, I believe, is true of spiritualism and sex. This is considered self-evident in virtually every culture but our own.

Part of the West's problem in understanding spirit is our false identification of dogma with the drive that produced it. In rejecting Mecca, Lourdes or the River Ganges, we also reject the force they are imperfectly expressing. In this we resemble a thirsty desert traveler who throws away a gallon of water because of its garish container. Another barrier is our justified revulsion for the horror wreaked, century upon century, by inverted spiritualism. Yet rape, cannibalism and necrophilia—however repulsive—have not caused us to reject sex. In fact, it could be argued that our sexual taboos spring not from fear of sex's abuses but rather from fear of its unbridled allure. I believe the same historical dishonesty lies at the root of Western society's rejection of mysticism: as members of a tightly structured, status-driven hierarchy, we fear its emotional, egalitarian appeal.

Western preference for sex to the exclusion of Spirit reflects the same temperamental bias that caused us to choose Aristotle over Plato. We are people of action. We understand what we can smell-see-hear-taste-touch. We crowd together in cities, which exaggerate our extroversion and eroticism, whereas mysticism is an introverted pursuit better served by the solitude of the desert, the silence of a forest, the exhilaration of a mountain peak. This is not to say that our society lacks spiritual values, but only that our pursuit of them has largely been delegated to our artists, whose inspired creations allow us to enjoy, even to purchase, spiritual feeling second-hand.

In North America in the sixties, sex and spiritualism finally exploded together in the service of a non-militant idealism. A generation of young people intuitively grasped not only their connection but also the creative force that synthesizes them: universal love, which they expressed in slogans like "Make love not war." The procreative urge, combined with callow sentimentality, soon tipped the balance in favor of the sexual and personal over the spiritual and universal. Whereas mysticism again submerged, the sex drive freed itself for sportive, joyful celebration. Three decades later, overindulgence and trivialization have brought about a predictable backlash. Fuelled by fear of AIDs, sex is again in danger of being realigned with prohibition and Evil. Sex + repression + death = Satan.

While today's demon movies seem to be about occult horrors, they are usually also about sexual perversion. Typically, little girls are portrayed as possessed by the Devil (*The Exorcist*), whereas little boys are the Devil incarnate (*The Omen*): like him, they possess their own forked instruments. In vampire tales, penetration of a sleeping virgin's throat to suck blood is obvious defloration. The Heavy Metal celebration of the midnight desecration of graves, enlivened by necrophilia, is an inversion of the ancient fertility festivals, marking the coming of Light. Ritual cannibalism and the drinking of blood to seal a Devil's pact is a debasement of menstrual blood, with its life-giving properties, as well as of Christian communion; eating feces (penis) and drinking urine (semen) is a perversion of male sexuality. Committing suicide in the name of the Devil is to offer one's self as his "bride" in Hell.

During the eighties, revolting sex-satanic rituals were alleged by hundreds of children in a spate of nursery-school and babysitting scandals across North America. Alarmed by what also seemed to be an epidemic of ritual abuse among multiple personalities, a Chicago psychiatrist conducted a 1986 study of 250 therapists working in this field. About a quarter reported that they had patients who were exposed to satanic rituals during childhood. Another study has estimated that 20 per cent of all cases of multiple personality disorder involve satanic ritual.

Does Satan exist as a supernatural force? In my view, he is more than a psychological projection but less than an entity. His forms, and those of his minions, are personifications born of the human imagination; however, the force that empowers these forms is real, universal and numinous. Though it may be morally neutral, once destructively catalyzed it becomes more than the absence of good in the same way a star that implodes becomes more than just the star's absence: it becomes a black hole.

Reincarnation:

SHADES OF THE PAST

"It is no more surprising to be born twice
than it is to be born once."

—Voltaire

SEPTEMBER 1982

I am driving through the deserted streets of old Montreal, very early one morning, in an eerie, cushioned silence created by foggy, low-slung clouds. As fall leaves gleam wetly in the blurred halos of old-fashioned streetlights, I remark to my companion: "This reminds me of Old Berlin . . ."

I pause, feeling peculiar. I've never been to Berlin, old or new.

When I do travel to that city a year later, I find its Eastern sector—virtually untouched since World War II—much the way I envisioned it that fall morning in Montreal. Its gaslit streets, its linden trees, its blank-faced, shrapnel-scarred stucco buildings, its grandiose baroque monuments, all seem oddly familiar. So does the rest of Germany, though I've spent only three days here twenty years ago. My grandfather, who emigrated from Bavaria to San Francisco in the nineteenth century, died when my father was six. The family's German past was scarcely mentioned. As a child, my one connection to things German was my obsession with Grimms' fairytales and the witches and demons of the German gothic tradition. Yet today I find alive in myself a Teutonic spirit, which manifests itself in everything from a fondness for the richer delights of German cookery to the mordant strains of Wagner. Ruined castles along the Rhine, a pantheistic reverence for the forests, all produce a baleful inner twang. Prussian authoritarianism, with its compulsion to play to rule, also runs a broad military stripe down my psyche.

Though I'm a bad linguist, after a few days in this country I even begin to dream in fragmentary German.

Déjà vu—that uncanny conviction of having experienced something before—haunts the psyche like footsteps that stop whenever you turn. As novelist John Buchan wrote in *Memory Hold the Door*: "I find myself in some scene which I cannot have visited before and which is yet perfectly familiar; I know that it was the stage of an action in which I once took part and am about to take part again."

Some physiologists dismiss this feeling as resulting from an eye blink: the mind exaggerates the time between exposures so that a scene observed a fraction of a second ago seems like a faded snapshot when compared with the present. Others simply deny any reality to the feeling: not to do so would open a Pandora's box of occult speculations about time and the nature of reality. How could anyone, after all, have memory about times and places never met?

Until recently, all branches of science considered mental processes confined to the brain, defined as a single organ spanning a single lifetime. However, disenchantment with Darwinism has led to psychological speculation over the existence of a collective memory bank to which each of us holds the psychic key: Jung called it the collective unconscious; James, the cosmic consciousness; Hindus know it as the *akashic* record or Great Library; Buddhists refer to it as the Great Mind.

According to another branch of speculation, the specific memories of one's ancestors are passed down in the genes of the DNA. Therefore, a tiny part of every cell of my body remembers everything my ancestors have experienced: wars, fires, festivals, births, plagues, rapes, beheadings, coronations, old London, old Athens, old Berlin—I was there!

If that glorious and arcane knowledge is, indeed, present in the cells that carry me on the Toronto subway or shopping for carrots, its presence is theoretic on most moments of most days. As with all memory, practical or inspiring, the trick is access. Yet occasionally, even in our own skeptical culture, some people insist they have, on occasion, acquired that access, as if, while browsing in a pawnshop, they were to open an antique locket and discover a faded photo of themselves.

A dramatic example of this kind of "memory" occurred on December 17, 1949, when Eva Hellstrom of Stockholm was en route to join her husband for a first-time visit to Cairo. In a hallucination, she envisioned a distinctive painting, consisting of four hearts meeting in the middle, against a rich pink background. Since Hellstrom was inexplicably convinced she would soon see the original, she sketched her vision, then showed it to several people, including a Swedish botany professor.

Twelve days later, Hellstrom visited Cairo's Coptic Museum which, she learned, was devoted to artefacts of Egypt's Christians. As soon as she entered the second room, the botany professor grabbed her arm and pointed to a stone slab: "Eva, there is your picture." All five others in the group agreed: here was the figure Hellstrom had sketched—a four-leafed clover in the shape of a cross. Though most of the paint was worn from the slab, the museum director confirmed the colors of the never-reproduced painting, which he called the Coptic rose, had likely been black on pink. Since these now-absent colors were the most striking feature of Hellstrom's vision, she had apparently hallucinated the original as it appeared a thousand years before.

At the same museum two years later, Hellstrom saw an Ethiopian bishop's robe with an intricate, multi-colored yoke that she had also envisioned and sketched before her first visit to Cairo. Though she had drawn two gold lions on the collar, that were not present on the original, these had symbolic significance, since the emperor of Ethiopia is known as the Lion of Judah. Had Hellstrom psychically projected a vision of the far past onto her own future, as if time could be collapsed as easily as a telescope? Had she somehow accessed the cosmic computer? Or did she have a genetic claim on ancient Egyptian history?

Dorothy Eady of Plymouth, England, had no trouble explaining the source of her "far memories."

When a child, Dorothy showed her parents a magazine photo of the temple at Abydos in Egypt, declaring: "Here is my home, but why is it in ruins and where are the gardens?" In 1956, after training as an Egyptologist, Eady journeyed to Abydos to help with the excavation of the 3,200-year-old temple. As reported on April 17, 1979, in the *New York Times*: "As soon as I saw the mountain, I knew where I was." Colleagues were astounded by her familiarity with the temple. Even in pitch darkness, she flawlessly described scenes she was seeing for the first time. She immediately revealed the location of the temple gardens, later confirmed by tree roots and ruined canals; she correctly estimated the original height of broken columns, and translated some of the more enigmatic hieroglyphics.

Though others were baffled by Eady's esoteric knowledge, she was not: ever since she had fallen on her head as a child and been declared dead, she was convinced she had lived at Abydos in a previous life, as an orphan adopted by the temple priests.

Defined by *Webster's* as rebirth into a new body or other life form, reincarnation is a traditional Eastern belief, which has been gaining Western converts. In a February 1969 Gallup poll, Protestants and Catholics in twelve Western nations were asked if they believed in rebirth. A surprising number did: Canada, 26 per cent; West Germany, 25 per cent; France, 23 per cent; Greece, 22 per cent; Austria, 20 per cent; United States, 20 per cent; Great Britain, 18 per cent; Norway, 14 per cent; Sweden, 12 per cent; the Netherlands, 10 per cent.

In a British Gallup poll ten years later, believers had increased to 28 per cent, with the greatest number in the 25 to 34 age group. A 1981 U.S. Gallup poll found 23 per cent believed in reincarnation for an increase of 3 per cent, while a recent U.S. college survey reported 31 per cent, perhaps indicating a trend.

Reincarnation appeals to the Western taste for moral justice: given the disparity in talent, wealth and beauty doled out at birth, how satisfying to believe in a Higher Bureau of Equal Opportunity to balance things in the next round. It also appeals to our intensifying quest for meaning: what's the point of experience if it's all to be chucked after three score and ten? And to the yuppie desire for more: is this all there was?

Some archeologists trace the idea of reincarnation back to the New Stone Age, circa 10,000 to 5000 B.C., when bodies were buried in the fetal position as if for rebirth. The shrouding of corpses is also thought to mimic the packaging of newborns in membranes. A popular belief of the Druids and the ancient Egyptians, reincarnation was central to the Mystery cults of Greece and Rome; it was embraced by Pythagoras, Socrates, Plotinus, poet Pindar, historian Plutarch, orator Cicero, and Plato, who stated: "Seeing then, that Soul is immortal and has been born many times, and has beheld all things both in this world and in Hades . . . to enquire and to learn are wholly a matter of remembering."

In A.D. 543, the idea of reincarnation was condemned by the Christian Council of Constantinople. Although persecution by the Inquisition destroyed popular Western support, it did not end its intellectual appeal. Subsequent believers included leaders such as Frederick the Great, Benjamin Franklin, British prime minister Lloyd George, Hitler and Napoleon (who claimed to have been

Charlemagne); men of affairs such as manufacturer Henry Ford, jurisprudent Oliver Wendell Holmes and General George S. Patton (who thought he had previously fought under Alexander the Great); writers such as Goethe, Blake, Wordsworth, Coleridge, Balzac, Flaubert, Hugo, Tolstoy, Emerson, Longfellow, Melville, Whitman and Thoreau (who thought he had lived at the time of Christ); composers such as Wagner, Mahler, Sibelius; painters such as Kandinski, Gauguin, Mondrian, Klee, Dali (who claimed to have been the mystic St. John of the Cross); philosophers such as Kant, von Schlegel, Kierkegaard, Nietzsche, Hegel and Schopenhauer, who stated categorically: "Were an Asiatic to ask me my definition of Europe, I should be forced to answer him: it is that part of the world which is haunted by the incredible delusion that man was created out of nothing, and that his present birth is his first entrance into life."

Typically, Western adherents marry reincarnation to the ideals of progress, reason, individualism, reward for virtue, even energy conservation. Plato declared that a wise person improved his lot from life to life while the sensuous or foolish one reincarnated sooner under worsening conditions, perhaps even regressing to a beast. A child of American pragmatism, Benjamin Franklin could not believe that God would waste millions of ready-made minds. Biologist T.H. Huxley believed that the theory of reincarnation offered the best explanation of physiological and biological phenomena, while William James thought that—unlike Christianity—it made moral and psychological good sense. Edgar Cayce believed that groups of people often reincarnated together in cycles, one of which was Atlantis, ancient Egypt, Rome, the Crusades and the early American colonial period. Immanuel Kant suggested that rebirth might continue from planet to planet, while some of today's astrophysicists speak of the death and rebirth of universes. Science writer Malcolm W. Browne elaborated this concept in the *New York Times* of February 10, 1981: "Some scientists develop personal preferences for one kind of *Götterdämmerung* or another. There are those who would prefer an open, one-shot universe, considering it to be consistent with biblical scripture. Some others would prefer a closed, oscillating Universe, aesthetically akin to the Hindu wheel of death and rebirth."

Hindus liken the oscillating universe to Brahma, breathing in then out. A Western metaphor compares it to the pulsations of a heart. Stated the *New Yorker* of July 17, 1965: many scientists "are coming around to the view that the Universe has a heartbeat. The cosmos expands and contracts much as a heart does, bringing to life a succession of universes with each lub-dub. . . . We congratulate science on finally beginning to discover its true identity, as an agent for corroborating ancient wisdom. Long before our century, before the Christian era, and even before Homer, the people of India had arrived at such a cosmogony."

Today reincarnation is embraced by more than four hundred million Hindus, Buddhists, Brahmins and Sikhs. It has wide currency among African tribes such as the Zulus and Bantus, as well as the aboriginals of Australia and the Americas. In tribal societies, the departed are usually thought to be reborn immediately into the same families, especially if the spirit is that of an abused or neglected child. Spirits are often said to lurk around pregnant women in hopes of entering them. Sometimes the dying arrange the deal while still alive; other times, they seek permission after death through dreams. Acceptance is sealed by naming the newborn after the departed.

In many societies the soul is thought to return as an animal, an insect or even a plant. Sometimes these animals are sacred to the society; sometimes they are the totem animals of the deceased. Snakes are popular recipients of souls, both in Africa and in China. Teutons and early Romans similarly welcomed house snakes as their ancestor-guardians, assuring their vilification by orthodox Christianity. Pythagoras, who was credited with the ability to communicate with animals, claimed to remember having been both an eagle and a bear, interspersed with a number of human incarnations.

Hindu scholars took an evolutionary view of reincarnation, stating that attainment of the human form required 8,4000,000 incarnations through plants, aquatic animals, reptiles, birds, quadrupeds and primates. Thereafter, the higher self or *atman* returns in a series of personalities linked by the law of *karma*, which guarantees that what a person sows in one life he will reap in another. Hindu theists believe this process is directed by the will of God, while non-theists consider *karmic* retribution the automatic expression of moral law. The goal is *gnosis*—an awareness that the separate personalities are illusory, leading to *nirvana*, a permanent state of oceanic bliss.

Buddhists regard God as an unnecessary complication, since the law of *karma* guarantees right and wrong will automatically reproduce themselves. Again, the goal is *nirvana*—an indescribably beautiful state of transcendence achieved by extinguishing the ego-consciousness, desire, ill will and ignorance, all of which keep one bound to the wheel of death and rebirth. Reincarnation is a collective human effort, with the successes and failures of one person affecting those of everyone else.

Hindus and Buddhists believe an Enlightened One can remember previous incarnations, and Buddha was said to have total recall of hundreds of thousands of them. Stated Lama Anagarika Govinda: "Because of lack of remembering, most persons do not believe there was a previous death. But likewise, they do not remember their recent birth—and yet they do not doubt that they were recently born. They forget that active memory is only a small part of our normal consciousness, and that our subconscious memory registers and preserves every past impression and experience which our waking mind fails to recall."

Whereas Western self-help books concentrate on getting the most out of life, ancient manuals like the *Tibetan Book of the Dead* teach how to get the most out of death through mastering the craft of dying and rebirth. Based on Indian Buddhist tradition, it was compiled orally over many generations, then committed to writing in the eighth century.

According to this sacred text, the *bardo* state between death and rebirth has three stages: illumination, illusion and pre-birth. At point of death, understanding is greatest and the light brightest, offering the initiate the greatest chance to escape the wheel of rebirth into the bliss of Enlightenment. If this opportunity is missed, the illusions of the second *bardo* begin. These include the self-projected *karmic* consequences of all the person's lives, played out like a magic show. Wonderment deteriorates into terror as the scenes grow more torturing. Although the dead person can still hack a path through illusion to the Clear Light, he or she is ever more likely to become entrapped in ego.

In the third *bardo*, the dead person falls prey to sexual fantasies about mating couples, and hungers for a new body. Eventually, a womb is entered, leading to rebirth, with past experiences forming the newborn's character.

Concluded W.Y. Evans-Wentz, editor of the *Tibetan Book of the Dead*'s 1927 English translation: "The field of the normal man's sense perceptions is, as can be demonstrated, narrowly circumscribed and extremely limited. There are objects and colors he cannot see, sounds he cannot hear, odors he cannot smell, tastes he cannot taste, and feelings he cannot feel. And beyond his work-a-day consciousness, which he assumes to be his only consciousness, there are other consciousnesses, of which *yogis* and saints have cognizance, and of which psychologists are beginning to glean some, but as yet very little, understanding."

PAST-LIFE REGRESSION

OCTOBER 1987
I visit a Toronto parapsychologist who uses hypnotism to regress clients to previous lives. Since my motivation is curiosity rather than belief, I joke to friends: "Just so long as I'm not from Atlantis!"

After the hypnotic countdown, I am urged to envision myself wearing a silver-belted robe and climbing seven steps to a beautiful white-marble temple: "Your feet are bare. Feel the marble. Count the steps. The temple doors open inward. You step inside. Now you are in a marble room, bright and airy. . . . You should see someone crossing the temple floor."

I envision a very tall woman with a mass of flowing white hair, dressed in a luminous white robe.

"Is she old or young?"
"It's impossible to say."
"What color are her eyes?"
"Diamond."
"Diamond?"
"Diamond."
"Where is she from?"

"Well, I'm a little embarrassed. . . . Atlantis."

"You shouldn't be embarrassed. All the Atlanteans are coming back today. I'm getting those by the dozens. I take it to be authentic. . . . Ask her to show you a past life she considers relevant to your present spiritual journey."

"I see a scribe, a little brown monk, in a desert setting, probably Mideastern. He's in a cave writing on scrolls. He's a functionary—a very boring little man. My habit of writing and recording has developed from that lifetime."

A second relevant life: "I'm a black-cloaked crone with sun-baked skin. I look like I'm ninety but that's just the climate. . . . My name's Mara."

"Go earlier in the life of that character."

"I'm about twenty. Redhaired. Voluptuous. A strong person—lots of willfulness, lots of power, not magical power though I pretend it is. It's a tribal situation. It's at night. I stand alone, always tending the fire, creating fear around me. Fear of my magic. . . . I sacrificed at least one baby into the flames. Later, when I was old and physically weak, I poisoned those who doubted my power or provided opposition. In the end, I just walked into the flames. . . . I'm an old woman covered in gray ash."

"What were your feelings about that life afterwards?"

"Horror. I can't understand how this cruel creature could have happened. I thought myself on the road to spiritual fulfillment."

"Why was this life lived?"

"I was an advanced Atlantean, very intellectual, supposedly learning compassion and humility."

"Is there any message of importance from anyone."

"Yes. That I have enormous inner power but my use of it is conflicted. The only real power is for good. Negative power is just apparent power because it creates nothing. I also have to link up with the monk. His prosaic qualities are valuable as grounding."

This exercise—much shortened here—was absorbing and even useful: the three storylines helped me to understand a wariness of my inner power that prevented me from using it as effectively as I might. Later, I was bemused to discover *Mara* to be the root of the world *nightmare*, referring to the medieval demon who brought night terrors, as well as the name of the evil adversary who tempted Buddha. However, nothing persuaded me that I had entered the skin of a past incarnation. What bothered me was how unskeptical my hypnotist chose to be.

Despite my personal reservations, thousands of other past-life regressions have been investigated with thought-provoking results. The most infamous began in Pueblo, Colorado, in the fall of 1952: amateur hypnotist Morey Bernstein put housewife Virginia Tighe into a deep trance and—to his startlement—invoked Bridey Murphy, an Irish woman who said she had been born on December 20, 1798, in Cork.

Almost four decades later I recollected this case as a hoax. However, re-examination suggests to me that Bridey Murphy's misfortune was to have been resurrected during a local newspaper war. Publications around the world reaped the fallout, gleefully hyping the story along with one newspaper one day only to righteously denounce it with another the next.

Critics were not hard to find. This was the fifties, when hypnotism was viewed as a tool of stage magicians and when behaviorism still held many psychologists in thrall: taught by John Watson to doubt the existence of their own consciousness, what were they to make of the consciousness of a nineteenth-century colleen addressing them through a Colorado housewife? One minister who tried to discredit Tighe later admitted to a Denver *Post* reporter that he had only pretended to know her as a Chicago schoolgirl "to debunk reincarnation because of its assault upon established religious doctrines."

In six hours of taped conversation, delivered with an Irish brogue, Bridey related a plausible though slight story of life in nineteenth-century Cork and Belfast. Most of Bernstein's interrogations were unsuccessful attempts to confuse her through repetition or to elicit facts that could be checked. This was hampered by Bridey's cloistered life, her near-illiteracy, the insularity of her times, her impatience and—oddly—airs of refinement that led one investigator to suspect her of exaggerating her family's prominence.

Though all Bridey's statements were contemptuously challenged, archival investigation in Ireland proved again and again that Bridey was right for her time and place while the experts were wrong. Evidence included the location of a district in Cork called The Meadows, where she claimed to have been born; her contention that tobacco was a crop grown in that area by her "cropper" father; correct references to a place called Mourne, no longer in existence, and to Bailies Cross (she called it Bailings Crossing), too small to appear on any map; to Farr's and to John Carigan's as grocery stores in Belfast; to the newspaper the Belfast *News Letter*; to two men who taught at Belfast's Queen's University—McGlone (McGloin) and Fitzmaurice; to the playing of the uilleann pipes at funerals—in this case, her own in 1864.

Bridey correctly described the contents of contemporary books, sang a song, recited a prayer and danced the Morning Jig, ending with a stylized yawn. She explained the currency of her day as well as a now-obsolete Blarney-stone kissing routine. Her colloquialisms included "Plazz" as a popular phonetic version of the Christian name Blaize; "the Orange," referring to an Orangewoman; "ditch" for bury, "tup" for chap, "slip" for child's frock, "linen" for handkerchief, "lender" for library, "flats" or "platters" for potato cakes, "leer" for lyre, "hut" for cottage, and "lough" for river (obsolete) as well as for lake, indicating her mother had rhymed it with "plow" (obsolete pronunciation) while her husband pronounced it to rhyme with "lock" (as today).

On the negative side: since Irish births, marriages and deaths were not registered before 1864, investigators were unable to confirm that Bridey (Brigitte) Murphy or her relatives existed. One investigator suspected a bookkeeper from the 1861–62 Belfast Directory might have been her husband, but her declaration (perhaps merely snobbish) that she was a barrister's wife prevented this conclusion.

Critics strove to attribute Virginia Tighe's Irish lore to outright fraud or to the influence of an Irish aunt. However, this aunt was born in New York and—according to Tighe—had no particular interest in her Scottish-Irish ancestry. Furthermore, they didn't become well acquainted till they shared a house when Tighe was eighteen. If this aunt *was* the source of the Bridey Murphy story, it seems that the process of acquisition was an unconscious one, with neither person having direct access to the arcane information that had been transferred.

In 1961, C.J. Ducasse, former chairman of the Department of Philosophy at Brown University and past president of the American Philosophical Association, extensively reviewed the Bridey case. Though he did not find the evidence conclusive, he proclaimed: "Neither the articles in magazines or newspapers . . . nor the comments of . . . psychiatrists hostile to the reincarnation hypothesis, have succeeded in disproving or even establishing a strong case against the possibility that many of the statements of the Bridey personality are genuinely memories of an earlier life of Virginia Tighe over a century ago in Ireland."

Ironically, Tighe herself was not convinced: "The thing that makes all this so difficult is that I'm not ready to say whether I do or don't believe in reincarnation. My husband and I have tried to keep open minds." Fiercely protective of her privacy, Tighe disliked being hynotized and refused to continue the tapings well before Bernstein went public with them. Both she and Bernstein reportedly turned down hundreds of thousands of dollars to appear on TV and, according to Bernstein, Tighe only reluctantly accepted a portion of the royalties from his 1956 bestseller, *The Search for Bridey Murphy*.

Twenty years after the Bridey sensation, Arnall Bloxham created another when, as president of the British Society of Hypnotherapists, he allowed several of his four hundred past-life regressions to be shown on BBC television. One featured Welsh homemaker Jane Evans, who claimed under hypnosis to have been Rebecca, a twelfth-century Jew living in York (which Evans had never visited). In a hysterical voice, Evans re-enacted the 1189 York uprising against the Jews, when Rebecca and her family were massacred in the crypt of a small church.

York professor Barrie Dobson, author of a book on the massacre, verified much of Rebecca's story, including the disputed fact that Jews had to wear insignias at that time in Britain. However, only the big Cathedral of York was known to have a crypt, and Rebecca denied this to be her sanctuary. Of York's forty other ancient churches, the likeliest candidate was St. Mary's, Castlegate. Amazingly, six months after Dobson's investigation a workman broke through its old flooring into what seemed to be a tomb. This last detail—unknown to any living person at the time of Evans's regression—ruled out telepathy as a source of information. It also seemed to rule out what Swiss psychologist Théodore Flournoy labeled cryptomnesia, meaning the regurgitation of unconsciously acquired information. Often used to explain away reincarnation, cryptomnesia may—or may not—be demonstrated by the following story.

While hypnotized by psychiatrist Reima Kampman, a thirteen-year-old Finnish student claimed to be the daughter of an English innkeeper, born near Norwich in 1138, and named Dorothy. Not only did she list places, along with their correct distances from Norwich, but she also sang what she called *Summer Song* in medieval English. Still intrigued by this case seven years later, Kampman again hypnotized the student to discover where she might have found such specialized information. Previous to the first session, the Finnish girl recalled having glanced through the book *The Story of Music*, by Benjamin Britten and Imogen Holst, which she had found on a library table. Inside was the rare *Cuckoo Song*, written in modernized medieval English. Though the Finnish student knew almost no English, she was now judged by Kampman to have memorized it at a glance—a stunning example of unconscious learning.

Yet nagging questions remain. Where did the thirteen-year-old acquire the rest of her very precise information about twelfth-century England? Why did she fixate on this material, and what caused her to mistake the song's title? Does a possibility exist—however remote—that the book refreshed rather than created the Finnish student's memory of *Cuckoo Song*? Did she reproduce it as *Summer Song* because that's how she once sang it as Dorothy the innkeeper's daughter?

Perhaps the most baffling reincarnation testimony ever recorded involves the possible rebirth of a group of thirteenth-century heretical Christians. In 1961, Dr. Arthur Guirdham, chief psychiatrist at Bath Hospital in England, acquired a patient in her early thirties so tortured by nightmares of being burned at the stake that she often awoke shrieking. During analysis, "Mrs. Smith" presented songs and religious rituals, written when she was a young girl, in what appeared to be antiquated French. Professor René Nelli of Toulouse University confirmed they were *langue d'oc*, the spoken language of thirteenth-century southern France. Nelli also declared them an astonishingly accurate description of ceremonies of the Cathars—a heretical Christian sect centered in Italy and southern France. One detail galvanized Guirdham: Smith claimed to have been imprisoned in a crypt that experts denied had been used for that purpose; however, subsequent research revealed that, on one occasion, prisoners had indeed been confined there.

Before meeting Smith, Guirdham had also experienced strangely compelling *déjà vu* feelings in southern France. Now he found they shared recurring nightmares, in which they were terrorized by a sinister figure identified by Smith as an enemy of the Cathars. Eventually, Smith also identified Guirdham as Roger-Isarn, her Cathar lover; this was beginning to sound like patient-therapist transference. However, in 1967 Guirdham visited the south of France to read thirteenth-century manuscripts, available only to scholars with special permission. These showed Smith to be accurate to the last detail in numbers and descriptions of people, places and events. Four songs she wrote out as a child were found word for word in the archives.

Other medievalists verified Smith's drawings of old French coins, jewelry and building layouts. She also documented a web of relationships between people too obscure for textbooks but traceable through dog-Latin records "owing to the ant-like industry of the Inquisitors and their clerks." One revelation confounded even the experts: as a thirteen-year-old in 1944, Smith said the Cathars wore dark blue robes, though historians insisted they wore only black. In 1965, Professor Duvernoy of Toulouse made public his recent discovery that, at one sitting of the Inquisition, the Latin record stated ten times that Cathar priests sometimes wore dark blue or dark green.

Subsequently, the vortex of the mystery shifted from Smith to "Clare Mills," an acquaintance of Guirdham's who compulsively related Cathar names to him, along with a nightmare in which she walked barefoot to a heap of faggots to be burned. En route, she was struck with a torch, corresponding to a blistery, real-life scar across her shoulders. She too had experienced powerful *déjà vu* feelings while visiting sites of Cathar persecutions.

Soon Mills was finding messages strewn about her home, written in her own hand, containing phrases from Cathar initiation rites and lists of names from Inquisition records. Though her French and Latin were of the high school variety, her notes were inscribed in thirteenth-century French and Latin. She also saw visions of an old Cathar lady and of two Cathar bishops, who provided verifiable historical details.

A circle of reincarnated Cathars began to assemble around Mills. Betty, a school friend Mills hadn't seen for years, informed Mills that her deceased husband had left a journal about Cathar life. Then Betty's seventy-year-old mother, Jane, sent Mills note-books filled by Betty, age seven, when ill with scarlet fever. One page, headed "Montréal 1204," contained nine Cathar names, listed only in the archives of the Bibliothèque Nationale in Paris. Jane also confessed, without prompting by Mills, that she had been haunted for years by visions of a monk in blue robes.

In the early hours of March 16, 1972, the anniversary of a mass burning of Cathars, Mills, Jane and Guirdham independently fell ill. Most severely stricken was Jane, who awoke with blistered legs.

Next, the husband of Penelope, a recently deceased friend Mills hadn't seen for ten years, brought Mills writings by his wife, containing Cathar references. He told Mills that Penelope had repeatedly dreamed of a hilltop castle containing blue-robed men. He was also troubled by dreams of blue-robed men and fragments of prayers.

After Mills had suffered an hysterical coronary attack, she was contacted by Kathleen, another friend she hadn't seen for ten years, who had been simultaneously hospitalized with coronary spasms. She told Mills of dreaming about their friend Betty, dressed in dark blue robes.

Testified Guirdham: "The whole experience has become so oceanic I can now do little more than record it."

If the Cathar story is a hoax, it is an elaborate one for little personal gain. If it is a group hallucination, it is supported by an astonishing array of paranormal phenomena—telepathy, precognition, synchronicity, genetic memory. If it is evidence for reincarnation, it confirms a common belief—group rebirth in which closely bonded persons meet again and again to work out a shared destiny.

PAST-LIFE THERAPY

In the past decade, emphasis in past-life regression has switched from attempts to prove the reality of the regurgitated information to its therapeutic use. By interpreting a client's far memories *as if* they are true, hypnotherapists trace a present-day fear, like claustrophobia, to a client's feeling that he or she once experienced death by suffocation; then, by reliving that trauma with vomiting, shaking, sobbing, convulsing, the client may cure the present problem through cathartic release. Thus, past-life therapy has incorporated the techniques of psychoanalysis and hypnotherapy, along with those of primal re-enactment.

As stated by Dr. Roger Woolger, a behaviorist who became a Jungian and then a past-life therapist: "It doesn't matter whether you believe in reincarnation or not. The unconscious mind will almost always produce a past life story when invited in the right way. . . . The unconscious is a true believer." In his book *Other Lives, Other Selves*, Woolger opined that analysts trained in Freudian and Jungian schools inclined toward the fantasy view, while hypnotherapists tended to believe these stories were authentic.

Said British psychiatrist Sir Alexander Cannon: "For years the theory of reincarnation was a nightmare to me, and I did my best to disprove it and even argued with my trance subjects to the effect that they were talking nonsense, and yet as the years went by one subject after another told me the same story in spite of different and varied conscious beliefs, until now, after well over a thousand cases have been so investigated I have to admit there is such a thing as reincarnation."

circa 1940
I sit on a stool with its seat patched from clothing of dead ancestors, in the gable of my attic bedroom, looking into the lighted window of the bungalow across the alley. As I stare, the bungalow walls seem to dissolve so that I see an old-fashioned kitchen. A peasant woman is standing at a wood stove, stirring a large metal pot with a wooden ladle. She is tall and stolid, perhaps in her sixties, dressed in a coarse floor-length skirt with loosely tucked blouse and a shawl—all

shades of blue faded to gray. On her head she wears a dustcap with strands of coarse gray hair streaking her plump, flushed face.

Only the area around the stove is lit—a buttery glow, probably of gaslight, shading into plank walls. The floor is also plank without rugs. I see a woodpile, a few heavy kitchen utensils, a roughly hewn table and a hand-made chair.

The back door opens. A workman enters in stocking feet, gray hair peaked as if he has yanked off a cap, his face like fissured clay, his body bent, his hands like roots. Without speaking, he sits at the table. The woman ladles stew from the pot into a wood bowl and sets it before him. Clasping a wood spoon, he begins to eat. The man and woman do not look at each other. They do not gesture, no word is said. Yet in the profundity of that silence I feel perfect understanding, perfect trust.

That is all. No matter how I yearn toward the comfort of that lighted window, I see no more: either the whole repeats—woman-stove-man-door-table—or it dissolves to black.

From childhood I have viewed that scene hundreds of times, usually when sweeping through farm country at night in a train. It is a scene bred by silence, an unfamiliar landscape and isolation—one single snapshot from the past, in tones of sepia, with no message scrawled on the back, drawing me to a door I can't open, a silence that I can't breach.

Is it a fragment of far memory from a life I once knew?

RESEARCH WITH CHILDREN

At age forty-eight, Montreal-born Ian Stevenson abandoned the practice of psychiatry to investigate reincarnation. From 1966 to 1977, he traveled an average of 55,000 miles a year to India, Lebanon, Alaska, exploring single cases over a period of several years and tape-recording dozens of interviews for each. As a professor at the University of Virginia, Stevenson became an internationally renowned authority on reincarnation, with more than two thousand cases in his files, one-third of which he or his investigators have declared authentic. Though controversial, Stevenson's work has been printed and praised in such professional publications as the *Journal of the American Medical Association*, which referred, in December 1975, to his "meticulous and extended investigations" where he "painstakingly and unemotionally collected a detailed series of cases in which the evidence for reincarnation is difficult to understand on any other grounds."

Stevenson specialized in cases involving very young children, thus minimizing the dangers of cryptomnesia. Typically, a child aged two to four mentions names and events foreign to his or her birth environment. At first, the information seems beyond the frustrated child's ability to express. With greater maturity, details proliferate, along with the child's insistence on their truth. The child also exhibits mannerisms and attitudes inappropriate to his age but consistent with the story he is telling. He may also possess untaught skills, which he claims belong to the other personality. He complains about the strangeness of being in a child's body and, most often, exhibits phobias having to do with a violent death.

When first taken to the places he has described, the child exclaims over all the changes since his death. He recognizes persons from his past life and artefacts he previously described. Stevenson maintains that some children have correctly identified sixty or seventy separate items, averaging 90 per cent accuracy. However, between ages five and eight, the child usually forgets the memories once so insistent.

In March 1964, Stevenson arrived unannounced at the village of Kornayel in Lebanon, where he had heard of a possible rebirth. Five-year-old Imad Elawar had talked since age one, both waking and sleeping, about a former life. His first words had been the names Jamileh and Mahmoud. Later he recalled being a member of the Bouhamzy family of Khriby, twenty-five miles away, where none of his real family had ever been.

In all, Imad mentioned fourteen names of people he knew in Khriby, including Jamileh, about whose beauty he raved. He spoke of his fondness for hunting, and claimed to have owned a rifle and a double-barreled shotgun, which he demonstrated by squeezing two fingers together. He also described his house, his dog, his yellow car, his bus, his truck that hauled rocks. One of his more traumatic memories was of a fatal accident in which a man had had his legs broken and his chest crushed. As Imad's family pieced together his story: he was Mahmoud Bouhamzy, who had been killed by a truck and who had a wife named Jamileh.

When Stevenson took Imad to Khriby, the child was overjoyed, but the trip proved a failure. Though they found a Mahmoud Bouhamzy, he did not have a wife named Jamileh and he wasn't dead. Nosing about on his own, Stevenson learned of a Said Bouhamzy fatally injured in a truck accident. Said Bouhamzy had a cousin named Ibrahmin who—to the scandal of the village—possessed a beautiful mistress named Jamileh. Not only did Jamileh dress as Imad had indicated but Ibrahim's house also matched Imad's description. It had been boarded up since 1949, when Ibrahim, then in his twenties, died of tuberculosis.

Though Imad's parents were embarrassed to learn of their son's scandalous past, they agreed to let him return to Khriby. Imad did not recognize Ibrahim's home from the outside, but inside one of his claims was soon confirmed: it did have two wells, one full and one empty—actually, vats for grape juice with mechanically controlled levels. Ibrahim also had had a yellow car, a bus, a truck and a dog, kept where Imad indicated.

When Ibrahim's sister and mother unexpectedly greeted Imad, he did not recognize his now elderly mother; however, he identified his sister Huda by name and his brother Fuad by an oil painting. Shown a photo of Ibrahim, he was asked: "Which was it, your brother or your uncle?"

Imad replied: "Neither. It was me."

His sister inquired: "You said something just before you died. What was it?"

Imad correctly answered: "Huda, call Fuad."

"How was the bed arranged when you slept in it?"

Imad correctly indicated that it was crosswise from its present position.

"In what manner did your friends talk to you during your last illness?"

"Through a window." Why? They were afraid of catching tuberculosis.

"Where did you keep your rifle?" Imad pointed to a compartment in the back of a closet, a secret known only to Ibrahim's mother.

According to Stevenson's report: of the fifty-seven claims Imad made before meeting his relatives, he was right in fifty-one.

Critics of Stevenson's work maintain that he was biased toward proving reincarnation; that he prettied up his cases; that he was gullible; that he failed to allow for the plasticity and imaginative powers of the human mind; that the child was reflecting the expectations of the adults around him; that the child must have received outside information or used telepathy; that the findings were culture-bound, since a past-life identity, for an Asian child, is the hallucinatory counterpart of a Western child's imaginary playmate.

In response, Stevenson pointed out that he was amassing evidence for reincarnation but not proof; that his critics could not explain away his cases' hard nucleus of fact; that many of his investigations began before the child in question had visited the past-life locale, thus minimizing on-site leakage; that many parents were hostile to their offspring's recall because of the belief that such a child would die young; that telepathy was an unlikely explanation, since it couldn't account for the child's obsession with one set of facts and complete lack of psychic ability in all other circumstances; that genetic memory was not a factor, since he chose only cases in which the child was not of the same lineal descent; that the immaturity of his candidates virtually eliminated cryptomnesia.

To counter the dearth of physical evidence supporting his work, Stevenson also collected cases in which birthmarks or deformities were said to correspond to the fatal injuries of the person with whom the child identified. In two hundred birthmark investigations, he obtained autopsy and other medical records supporting seventeen. For example, one Turkish child who claimed to have shot himself as a bandit by wedging a rifle under his right chin was born with a chin gash that an eye-witness said resembled the dead man's injury. Since consistency required an exit mark for the bullet, Stevenson asked the boy if he had any other birthmarks. He did: buried in hair on his left crown, aligned with the chin gash.

JULY 6, 1988
I awaken on the first anniversary of my mother's death, repeating: "Verna is dead. Verna is dead." As I lie in the twilight zone between waking and sleeping, I envision my mother's eight-year-old

sister, lying in a casket that has been lowered into a rectangular grave, her ringlets tied with a bow.

That Verna is the old-fashioned girl I also dreamed about on the night of my mother's funeral, symbolically buried in the basement of my natal home, I no longer doubt. Though the medical cause of Verna's death was pulmonary pneumonia, my conviction has grown, during this year of persistent dreaming, that the long-range cause of her death was sexual abuse. That is why I dream of her. That is why she haunts me. Her death within a year of my maternal family's emigration from England was like a spark plug that blew, exposing the family's faulty emotional wiring. Other tragedies rapidly followed: my grandfather, who hanged himself, age forty-nine, in the garage; my aunt, who had an illegitimate child, then died, age thirty-three, of what was described as a bungled gallbladder operation; another aunt, who died, age twenty-nine, cause unknown.

Within the week, a cousin who has been doing genealogical research phones me with a list of dates he has unearthed, including the birthday of the child Verna. It is March 8—the same as mine. She died on February 15, 1915, at eight years and eleven months in a house my mother's family rented on their arrival in Canada. The address is familiar—it is the home of a childhood playmate whose name, by coincidence, is also Verna.

That night I dream about reincarnation, though I can't remember the specifics—something about old birth records, having to do with paternity on my mother's side. When my clock radio switches on at six A.M., the topic under discussion is . . . reincarnation.

A couple of weeks later, I visit Vince Vanlimbeek for my biannual reading. He tells me: "I see an old-fashioned railway station. The fascinating thing is that it's empty. No trains, no people, no baggage. Everybody has gone. It's a place of putting to rest, of closing the door. . . . You're going to make a journey with a dual purpose."

I ask him a question that has been bothering me for quite a few months: "Was there sexual abuse in my mother's family?"

Vince looks quizzical for a few seconds before inquiring: "Your mother wasn't the only one in her family, was she? Wasn't there a child who passed over at an early age?"

"Yes."

"No doubt about it! That was sexual abuse."

Within a week, I am invited to London by my British publishers to promote their edition of My Father's House. I decide to combine this with a first-time visit to my mother's birthplace in Derbyshire.

The Alfreton train station proves a disappointment: of glass and brick, it is a 1966 replacement and not the gabled structure I fantasized. After depositing my bags at a Tudor inn, I make the two-mile hike through green fields, patched with February snow, to South Normanton. A coal mining village when my grandparents left in the spring of 1914, it has now acquired a few gaudy storefronts, even a suburb. Yet its central layout is the same; it is still authentically working-class, with row houses presenting a solemn, unbroken facade to narrow streets. Some are conveniently marked with their year of construction; others I learn to date through differences in trim.

Using an old surveyor's map gleaned from the local library, I peel off the seventy-five-year-old skin to discover the village as it used to be. I have another authoritative guide—a 1950 diary written by my mother on her return here after an absence of thirty-six years. She was fifty-one—four years younger than I am now. Its possession creates pleasant reverberations as I pass between rows of houses with identical chimneys, like crosses in a military cemetery, marching down a hill. There is the Picture Palace where traveling vaudeville shows were held, and the Leg O'Mutton Inn, boarded and soon to be demolished, and the jail now a clinic, and the Commons where the village children still play. The ancient cobbles are wet with occasional snowy patches. The air is February nippy. The chimneys puff acrid coal smoke into a hard blue sky—residue of South Normanton's colliery past.

Before me stands the staunch thirteenth-century Norman church where my mother was baptized and my grandparents were married. My mother's diary confides: "I could picture the years I spent there and the exact seat where I used to sit."

I am walking along Victoria Street when an elderly man in a cap stops me to inquire what I want. Apparently I look odd, or just too curious. When I tell him my family's surname, he points with his pipe to a house I have just passed. "But the last one died off years ago, ducks."

Again I must do cosmetic surgery—peel off the stucco and enlarged front window, add ivy, get rid of the house next door—to restore this modest ancestral home to the one made familiar by the sepia photo I am holding. Again, my mother's diary echoes in my ear, telling me of her last visit here: "Every time I look around I recognize a picture or an ornament, and of course every time one person remembers something another adds to it. We talk till our wagging tongues fall out."

I hike down the hill from South Normanton to a brook, then up the other side. It is Sunday morning. As I sit in the cemetery of yet another church on a hill, gazing back across meadows to the Norman tower of St. Michael's, I am caught in the resonance of two sets of pealing bells, as if the churches were exchanging Sunday gossip as their parishioners always do. I remember that churches are often built on the sites of ancient shrines, said to be connected by ley lines— invisible magnetic fields, radiating underground and outward. In Ireland, they are called fairy paths; in Australia, songlines or dreaming-tracks; in China, lung mei or dragon paths. Wherever they cross, that is said to be a psychic hot spot—Stonehenge, the monoliths of Easter Island, the Great Pyramid of Giza, the Oracle of Delphi.

I feel connected to my mother and to my ancestors in this place—a personal hot spot, connecting me through time, so that I understand what my maternal family gained by leaving and what it lost. My mother's diary whispers: "There were times when I felt I couldn't stand anymore. Of the six of us who left South Normanton in 1914, I am the only one left and no one to talk to about them all."

Again, I wonder what gave my grandmother the courage to override the wishes of her family, even the opposition of her husband, to emigrate. As a locally acclaimed psychic, she had already predicted her future: "Black, black, all I see is black."

Before catching my London train, I find an archival picture of the old station circa 1914—chimneyed, peaked and arched, as I had imagined it. One couple, formally dressed in black and almost invisible, stare stiffly at the vacant track, with the rest of the long platform strangely empty, no passengers, no trains, no baggage. "Everyone has gone. It's a place of putting to rest, of closing the door."

The caption on the photo reads: "Alfreton Station. Demolished in 1966. Note that the sign says 'Alfreton and South Normanton Station.'" While underlining the significance of the photo to me, this instruction is a curious one, since the pictured station doesn't have a sign.

Back in London, I must cancel my second day of media interviews because of laryngitis. As I gargle, steam, rub, dose, inhale, I intuit that I am choked with unexpressed grief for my mother. Her death was clouded by revelations of sexual abuse, anger and guilt. Now these are in perspective, permitting me to grieve as a child for the mother I lost; for the mother who betrayed me, who had been betrayed, whom I had betrayed; for the teenager who courageously abandoned her homeland; for the hopeful bride who dared not see the blackness of the shadow overtaking her . . .

I truly and deeply mourn, with grief that is primal, verbal and physical. Next day I have a voice, though not one in an octave I recognize as my own.

Seven days after returning to Toronto, I fly to the east coast for a nine-day reading tour. Again, on the second day, I lose my voice. My energy is high. I don't have a cold. My throat isn't sore. My sinuses aren't plugged. I just can't speak. The problem has slid deeper down my throat to lodge in my voicebox. What emotion have I left unexpressed? What can be deeper than mother-grief?

Suddenly, I remember: tomorrow is March 8, my birthday. It is also the birthday of the child Verna. I have just returned from South Normanton, the place where she lived most of her brief life. I arrived there on February 15, the anniversary of her death; yet, after a year haunted by visions of her corpse, I never once thought of her while in England. How odd! Too odd. Immediately, I begin to shiver, struggling against a weird concept that is fighting to gain credence. It isn't the first time I've wrestled with this idea, but I let it surface for the first time: little Verna and I are one and the same.

Now that the thought has materialized in words, I turn it around in my mind like a squirrel testing a nut for the best place to sink its teeth. Though skeptical, I allow myself to grieve as if I were Verna, spewing up the pain of a child who has been twice betrayed by the same people. My throat opens like a morning glory.

Six weeks later I return to England, this time to research my grandmother's two ancestral lines. The Derbyshire records are in the county seat of Matlock—a lovely town climbing two sides of a valley, cooled by the Derwent River and dominated by its own ruined castle. I move back in time through microfiche census records to parish registers, written on weathered parchments, dating almost to Shakespeare's time, their jumbled baptisms and deaths occasionally yielding a decipher-able ancestor's name.

All the occupations of my forebears are humble: coal miner, mill hand, hosiery worker, lace maker, cotton worker, farmer, laborer, railway worker, even pauper. The children, still unmolded, rate the tony sobriquet "scholar"—a genteel reminder of a world few are likely to experience. And yet one ancestor—my great-grandmother's brother—does manage to vault from tenth child of a canal boatman to become purchaser of the estate of the area's titled landowner.

I am astonished at how addictive I find all this: the piecing together of a verbal history as the social equivalent of getting my hands onto the genetic code. Through clues inherent in repeated names and occupations, I trace the Keys back to 1799; the Weightmans to the late 1600s. I never thought it would interest me to brood over graphs of names and dates, but now I understand that these are skeletons to which much flesh still clings.

I hike for ten or fifteen miles along roads, along lanes, along the mysterious paths still linking villages, over stiles, by streams, through flocks of sheep guarding their freshly dropped lambs, following maps that prove to be whimsically faulty, supplemented by a villager's arm pointing in one direction or another, counting on a providential bus to fetch me home by nightfall. The green fields—in this lucky spring—are as endless as the long days and blue skies, a solace for my spirit, which I know to be green-drenched: when deprived of vegetation for even a few days my eyes feel parched. Now the earth is a green aquarium. I plunge in.

These are not just hikes but meditations. In the aboriginal myths of Australia, the Ancestors were said to have crisscrossed the continent on invisible paths, singing out the names of everything they met, calling the world into existence. These songlines, or dreaming-tracks, made up of musical notes, are still used by the aborigines as lines of communication and of ownership. The man who goes "walkabout" is setting his feet into the prints of his Ancestors, participating in creation.

And so sing I. My feet connect villages with cemeteries while I ponder my numbered grids, connecting births with deaths, past ruminating cows, competing with sheep for right of passage.

The dominant figure of my maternal line is Great-grandfather Moses, who went down into the pits at age nine—one of nine siblings with biblical names. As stated in his 1932 obituary: "Being a keen traveler, he welcomed the advent of the bicycle and was the first to import the old velocipede cycle into Pennsylvania, if not in the whole of U.S.A. At first sight of him, the villagers were frightened and took shelter. Mr. Weightman covered many thousands of miles on the old solid and cushion tyred cycles, touring England, Scotland, Ireland and many parts of America. Later he took to motorcycling, which he continued until he was eighty years old. He retained all his faculties until the last few days. He was also an ardent lover and grower of flowers, especially roses."

Missing from this official prose was the fact that Moses was a spendthrift, a heavy drinker, a man notorious for his lust as well as his wanderlust. Wife Jane was prim, thrifty and long-suffering. If something spilled on the tablecloth before washday, she erased it with white chalk. Her favorite expression was the same as my mother's: "To turn a blind eye," along with "What the eye doesn't see, the heart can't grieve."

I believe that my grandmother had good reason to put an ocean between herself and her parents. I believe she did it to protect her daughters from her father, but that it was already too late. My suspicions are conjecture, only recently supported by incestuous hints from the living, sometimes later recanted. Yet I believe this explanation is the only one that makes sense of the behavior perpetuated in my family—the criminally privileged patriarch, the blind eye, the secretly grieving heart, the stains denied by white chalk. "Black, black, all I see is black."

In South Normanton, I visit Hamlet Lane—the Infants' and Juniors' School I know Verna must have attended. It is a gem of a building, molded out of softly glowing red bricks and overhung by blossoming trees, built on a scale that seems child-sized. As soon as I enter its front doorway my bones ache. I feel flooded with joy, which I am tempted to call nostalgia.

I collect bits of brick from the school, bark from a tree in the playground, wildflowers from the fields around South Normanton, leaves from the hedge by my ancestral home. I pack them in a small tin box, painted with the picture of an old-fashioned toy bear.

Back in Canada, I visit Hamilton Cemetery, looking for Verna's grave. I know I've been here once before—when I was eight, the same age as she when she died. We were in our Sunday best, which in those *days included hats. Mine, I believe, was blue with an elastic under the chin like a Girl Guide hat. It was probably spring, sunny but cool, with no leaves on the trees. Carrying a Sunday School paper and a Bible I had won for perfect attendance, I jumped around puddles, protecting my black patent shoes.*

I remember being intrigued with Verna's headstone, topped by a lamb in what my mother called "the children's cemetery." Later the adults paced between markers looking for Grandpa Tom's grave— unmarked because he had hanged himself.

Though I have no sense of direction, I feel confident as I now approach a sad little patch of cemetery with its small, broken tombstones. No longer just a children's graveyard, its liberal sprinkling of lambs makes clear that's what it used to be. As I look for my lamb amongst the flock, I grow unaccountably panicky: many are too worn or buried to read.

My lamb is sitting under a shade tree, sprawled on its plinth with a grace that eludes most of the others, its markings uneroded:

> *OUR DARLING*
> *VERNA MAY*
> *DAUGHTER OF*
> *Thomas & May*
> *WILSON*
> *AGED 8 YRS. & 11 MOS.*
> *Safe in the arms of Jesus.*

This elegance—more than an immigrant family could afford— pleases me. A tragedy has been well marked. Care has been taken, attention paid. I bury my little tin box in the difficult soil, crying out of gratitude that such communication is still possible.

This is a quiet story—no telling clues, no witnesses, no scars or birthmarks that can be seen. I have produced little more than a point of view with no supporting evidence—the interpretation of psychic ley lines, converging on an unlikely truth. Are Verna and I manifestations of the same spirit? All I know is that part of my mind has gone to some trouble to give me that impression. As stated by Dr. Roger Woolger: "The unconscious is a believer."

The night I return from the cemetery, I have the following dream: I am in a sepia landscape that is supposed to be England, following an old man through valleys, along creeks, over uneven ground. He is wearing a fedora atop longish, stringy hair, with shorts, socks, sandals and a walking stick to supplement his knobby legs—a venerable and certain figure. I am following him from village to village, each circled on a map, with those important to my family's history radiating lines of magnetism.

I recognize my guide. He is the legendary Old Man, the personification of age-old wisdom whom Carl Jung says appears when consciousness is overwhelmed with material that is being clarified, understood and newly assimilated. He appears in dreams to tell us we are on the right path. He is my Ancestor whose footprints I must follow, my creator of primordial song.

Summation:

THE NEW MYSTICISM

"My friend, all theory is gray and
the golden tree of life is green."

—Goethe, from *Faust*

Let me retell an old story:

Three blind men were arguing over an elephant. One, grabbing hold of the trunk, announced: "Elephants are long and round and muscular!" The second, who was feeling the side of the elephant, protested: "How absurd! Elephants are vast beyond comprehension and wrinkled." The third, grasping the beast's tail, shouted in triumph: "You are both fools. An elephant is small, tough and hairy!"

To settle the argument, they consulted a fourth man, sitting silently by himself with his eyes closed. "What is an elephant?" they demanded.

Without opening his eyes, he replied: "It is the idea of Elephant I carry in my own head."

Ten years ago, I attended a Toronto seminar by Joseph Campbell, who spoke about the power of myth to light a spiritual path. Although well known among Jungian scholars, Campbell was not yet the public figure he was destined to become. His daring message, delivered with passion, astonished me: Christianity is religious pathology.

As Campbell argued, in person and in his many books, religions traditionally claim authenticity for the Mystery that their myths enshrine, but not for the literal truth of the myths themselves. Like Plato's illustration of the cave, these myths are acknowledged to be metaphors illuminating a truth so large it can't be captured in words or reduced to historical facts.

At its founding, Christianity acknowledged this tradition by adopting a mythology common to many Mediterranean Mystery cults: the birth of a god on earth, his temptation by the evil one, his death and resurrection, all woven into a coat-of-many-colors of distinctive style and fit. However, with worldly success, the once-humble Christian cult created a Holy Roman Empire that was holy in name only, then viciously undertook to persecute all who did not believe its myths to be fact. Traditionally, to have faith meant to have faith in the Mystery to which the myths provided an ethnic gateway, but now Christianity insisted its mundane trappings were the Mystery itself. To confuse myth with fact is to debase myth by failing to appreciate its transcendental function as the bridge between the known and the unknowable: it is to turn true myth into false fact. This is the alchemy of converting light into lead because lead, being heavy and three-dimensional, seems more real. It is religious pathology.

For the medieval Church, the most dangerous heresy turned out to be the one espoused in 1543 by Copernicus—that the earth revolved around the sun, in defiance of Christian dogma. As science gained ascendancy with its arsenal of secure facts, Christianity scrambled to prove its spiritual beliefs in the same materialistic terms. Thus, its credibility came to hang upon convincing a now-sophisticated laity that the Garden of Eden really happened, and that Christ was a historical person who actually rose from the dead. This was equivalent to tying the relevance of Shakespeare's Hamlet to his having *really* been a Prince of Denmark, or the story of Little Red Riding Hood to authenticating a scrap of her red cape. And since Christianity had proclaimed itself the one true religion, when it failed to come up with the goods under the terms it had vain-gloriously approved, the supernatural itself seemed to have failed.

By the time I walked the earth, North America was completely dis-spirited. Religion meant moribund rituals and defensive sermons; ghost stories were the fodder of campfire tales; Ouija boards, once for communication with spirits, were children's toys; divination was the province of old women and lovesick adolescents. However, midway through the twentieth century, something marvelous began to happen. An elite of scientists who had once prided themselves on their acquisition of objective, value-free facts suddenly began to suspect a deeper truth: that, all along, they had been dealing in consensus rather than in fact. The English word *theory* derives from the Greek *theoria*, which has the same root as *theater*, meaning to make a spectacle. Like myths, scientific theorems didn't describe reality but merely organized observations from a particular viewpoint. They told a story.

With this realization, a scientific vanguard broke through the particularization of its own religion—that of materialism—to a new appreciation of universal Mystery. They became born-again questers, nurturing a sense of reverence for the Universe, more profound than that of many priests and preachers occupying Western pulpits.

Despite the zeal of this visionary few, the radical implications of the New Mysticism have been slow to seep down through scientific ranks into popular consciousness. Though possessed of awesome credentials, most scientists are creatures of habit who, like conscientious bus drivers, of necessity keep their eyes fixed on the traffic ahead instead of gaping up at the sky through their side windows. Many did not wish to see that the Universe they were creating, concept by concept, was a psychic one in which time and space had no more ultimate reality than a rainbow. While this was not a Universe that proved the existence of God, soul, immortality, spiritual values, higher meaning or purpose, it was one in which these concepts were perhaps more logical than illogical. And like the wise men who crawled out of Plato's cave of shadows into the bedazzling light of the Good, the greatest Western scientific minds did not shy away from such a connection. Stated Einstein: "Everyone who is seriously involved in the pursuit of science becomes convinced that a spirit is manifest in the Laws of the Universe, a spirit vastly superior to that of man."

Half a century later, American astronomer Allan Sandage expressed the same unselfconscious sense of wonder: "Here is a miracle that seems almost supernatural—an event which has come across the horizon into science through the Big Bang. . . . It still remains an incredible mystery: why is there something instead of nothing?"

Astrophysicists spoke glowingly of the thrill of star-gazing, not in search of hard data but as mystics unashamed to claim lineage to the astrologer-priests of Ur and Stonehenge. To honor that reverence, physicist and sculptor Robert Wilson used Beauvais Cathedral in France as his architectural model for the Illinois headquarters of Fermilab, a particle accelerator where scientists smash atoms to study their composition. Both structures, he explained, embody "an ultimate expression"; both probe to the core of the unknown—the one into spirit, the other into energy.

Nor did these scientists hesitate to draw parallels between such a Universe and the dynamic interconnecting web of life intuited thousands of years ago by Eastern mystics. Stated physicist Fritjof Capra in *The Tao of Physics*: "The two foundations of twentieth-century physics—quantum theory and relativity theory—both force us to see the world very much in the way a Hindu, Buddhist or Taoist sees it."

This is especially evident in the quantum field, where perceptual challenges send physicists rushing gratefully to the poetry and paradox of Eastern mysticism. More than one has compared the arcing and colliding of particles to the cosmic dance of Shiva, Hindu god of creation and destruction. As Hindu scholar Ananda Coomaraswamy said, "He rises from his rapture, and dancing sends through inert matter pulsing waves of awakening sound, and lo! matter also dances, appearing as a glory round about Him. . . . This is poetry, but none the less science."

Though it may offend some Western researchers to discover that, after three centuries of wonder and wizardry, the radial tire they have invented is no replacement for the Buddhist prayer wheel, the more thoughtful will appreciate that humans have need of both the sensory and the spiritual. Dispossessed of our spiritual territory, we in the West have made an adventurous loop through materialistic terrain back to our cultural beginnings, much the wiser for our journey. In completing this circle, we are ready to incorporate both halves of the human brain—the truths of Democritus and Aristotle and Newton and Darwin and Freud synthesized with those of Pythagoras and Plato and Augustine and Descartes and Leibniz and Wallace and James and Jung.

At the beginning of this book, I imagined that my life was a journey; if pressed for a metaphor, I might have envisioned myself in a canoe, paddling along a river. Now I know there is no canoe and no canoeist, only the river that for a few decades has imagined itself to be a woman. In another couple of decades, it will have another thought about itself in this part of the river, but I have not lost a canoe. I have gained a river.

For hardcore materialists, the dissolution of the sensory world as an objective and ultimate reality is as dismaying as loss of faith to a priest. Both find themselves deprived of what sustained them—the one solid ground underfoot, the other a set of wings. Yet the loss of Newtonian law is not a loss of physical order any more than the loss of Christian faith is a loss of spiritual feeling. Both disorientations mean only that understanding must be embraced on a higher level. We must tell each other greater myths.

Though Descartes could not prove the existence of the physical world, he accepted its reality because "God would not deceive us." To a second-year philosophy student, that seemed very lame indeed. However, now that I have divorced my idea of God from the Christian version, I believe I understand Descartes' deeper meaning—or, at least, a deeper meaning suggested by him. I believe Descartes' view to be equivalent to the one intuited by Einstein when he stated: "The most incomprehensible thing about the Universe is its comprehensibility." In other words, a curious "fit" exists between the way the cosmos works and the way the human mind perceives. This was a fit noted by Pythagoras when he found that the Universe could be described by mathematical equations, and it is still a source of amazement. Stated astronomer Allan Sandage: "Out of the Big Bang has come a nonchaotic system. . . . All students that ever study are mystified by the recipes that the great scientists have found, but the Universe works by those recipes."

The cosmos is orderly. Our minds understand that order. Some astrophysicists trace this connection to a common cause: since all the Universe, including ourselves, existed embryonically some fifteen billion years ago within a speck of energy infinitesimally small and infinitely powerful, we humans are womb-mates to the brightest quasars on the fringes of the known world. We understand the Universe because it is us and we are it. The *son et lumière* of the Big Bang was *our* birthday party too.

Universal orderliness and our understanding of it allows us to lead non-chaotic sensory lives. But, if the human mind can comprehend the physical Universe, why deny its ability to comprehend the psychic Universe of which it is more obviously a part? Through intuition, the human mind, from Neanderthal to Plato to Einstein, has sensed that life has meaning beyond human projection, and that the spiritual and the mystical exist as surely as the mental and the emotional. Despite the valuable role played by honorable dissenters, that is what human history tells us. For Western pragmatists to dismiss the spiritual as superstition is to throw out most of our own cultural heritage as well as everybody else's.

Part of the West's spiritual barrenness arises from our itch to define the mysterious in words reflecting our time and place. Thanks to our faulty Christian heritage, we have only a fuzzy grasp of mystical feelings while we gleefully haggle over precise expression of belief. By contrast, Eastern mystics have a profound impression of the mystical experience while settling for its vague and paradoxical expression. Stated the great mystic Lao-tzu:

> There is something formless yet complete
> That existed before heaven and earth.
> How still! how empty!
> Dependent on nothing, unchanging. . . .
> I do not know its name,
> But I call it Meaning.
> If I had to give it a name, I should call it The Great.

For the Universe to be meaningful to, or through, humans, it must be both intelligent and moral. Basic to most ethical systems is the Golden Rule: "Do unto others as you would have them do unto you." This respects one's self, one's neighbor and the collective. That is probably all of an ethic that is universally necessary; everything else is local interpretation or dogma.

The assumption that we are part of a moral, intelligent Universe based on some version of the Golden Rule is no larger than the assumption that we are not. It is certainly no larger than the assumption that has sustained Western science for several centuries: that a comprehensible physical Universe exists.

Eastern mystics put themselves in contact with the Great Mind through meditation. In the West, this intuitive connection has been lost through disbelief. To re-establish the link, we must enter a process of unlearning: the unlearning of disbelief. As Augustine stated, *Credo ut intelligam*: "I believe in order to understand." When I first encountered that statement, I took it to be an anti-intellectual one: faith versus reason. Now I see that it is not—or, rather, that the faith lies in taking the risk and not in the belief. The principle involved is that of leaping over a cliff to see if one can learn to fly on the way down. Pragmatists think that that is stupid; yet when they see someone flying, they sometimes grow wistful: "I wish I could do that."

The dilemma for the pragmatist is not lack of courage or even lack of spiritual will. It is an inability to challenge the causal chain, to put the cart before the horse. In their commonsensical view, you learn to fly and then you jump, but in an intuitive system you must leap first and then hope the proper causes and effects rush into place in time to prevent your crashing. You have to believe flight is possible and worth the risk without having tried it.

The same principle governs another kind of falling—falling in love. You fall in love, then you find out what love is. The faith is in the falling just as it is in the leaping. The faith is not in the love or in the spiritual belief: the existence of both becomes self-evident as a matter of experience. *Credo ut intelligam.* The same principle governs the creation of most art and even the discovery of scientific truths. First comes the vision or the theory, then the leap into the unknown, backed by techniques and procedures brought into place in hopes of achieving the motivating vision. First effect, then cause. The cart before the horse.

These are some of the great moments in my life: Biking through windswept Danish fields on the edge of a twilight storm, with the long grass standing on end, and hares hopping to and fro like newly landed Martians. Diving from a log sauna into the frigid waters of an Ontario lake, then looking up into the closing eye of an eclipse. Driving at night in a convertible through the Arizona desert, with every star accounted for, with Indian fires flickering from cliffside caves, and the still-balmy air so thick you could caress it in your palm. Scuba-diving off the Bermuda coast over the carcass of a wrecked ship, nudged by friendly schools of tropical fish. Watching a herd of Kenyan elephants dancing by moonlight in a salt lick of pink mud. Traveling by dogsled through infinite white, with sled-runners screeching like a cranky violin bow across the wind-packed snow, and with the air whipped by the primal song of the Inuit driver: "Eyiiooow, Eyiooow!"

When I review these experiences, I see they are both intensely sensuous and ardently spiritual. When immersed in them as in a baptismal river, I could not tell where spirit began and body ended, where the Universe began and I ended. Most occurred in unfamiliar places, when I was paying more than usual attention, or in the borderlands between light and dark, between water and air, or in a blur of windy speed. Sometimes I was alone, and sometimes I was not, yet always I was partly alone and always I was not. Always I felt healed, always I felt awestruck, always I felt as one with the Silence.

For most people, mystical experience is generated by meaningful moments brimming with universal love and a sense of wholeness. When these happen inside church or mosque or synagogue, they are more likely to be inspired by beautiful voices raised in song than by the mastering of some fine point of dogma. Most convincingly, religion is a feeling, not a set of beliefs or the egotistical hope for personal survival. The despair that scientific Enlightenment bequeathed to Western society was not the fear of ceasing to exist but a benumbing sense that the span each of us did possess was without meaning.

Though none of my above experiences occurred in a designated place of God, I have no trouble in calling them holy. By contrast, many of the most boring hours of my childhood were ones I spent in church. That enforced silence—unlike the silence of a forest—was truly empty. And yet, perhaps that empty space, where something should have been, preserved a place in my inner landscape where Spirit would want to be—a vacuum pleading for Silence.

Did God create humans or did we invent God? Are we his myth, or is he ours?

Materialists from Democritus through Darwin believe in a reverse creation: that we humans invented God to satisfy our needs and yearnings. This is the "bottom up" theory. By contrast, most religions take the "top down" view: first came God, from which all abundance flows. This is expressed most poetically in the form of the Hindu god Vishnu, who floats on the cosmic Milky Ocean, dreaming up the world. It is echoed by the Kalahari bushman who opined: "There is a dream dreaming us."

In classical philosophy, the big three arguments for belief in God are ontological, cosmological and teleological. God exists self-evidently through intuition: we know because we know—the same basis on which all knowledge ultimately stands. God exists through the demands of a first cause: no matter how far back one goes in the causal chain, one eventually comes to a Prime Mover, which we might as well label God. God exists through the evidence of universal design and purpose: the orderliness of the Universe, and the systematic way it unfolds, suggest an intelligent designer, in the same way a watch suggests the existence of a watchmaker.

This is the high ground occupied by most religions, philosophies and mystical systems. To the transcendentalist, such arguments are irrefutable; to the materialist they are irrelevant. However, during the last two centuries of Western culture, a new spiritual view has emerged that combines the bottom up view with transcendence. According to this theory, not only is human consciousness evolving but so is God's.

In the philosophy of Henri Bergson, evolution is a creative and dynamic process in which all of the past works on the present to produce an unpredictable future. Because of the dynamism of the life force, or *élan vital*, which drives evolution, tomorrow is more than the sum of all our yesterdays in the same way a tumbling snowball sets off an avalanche. Similarly, Hegel believed God, which he called the *Geist* or Absolute Idea, to be the totality of everything in the Universe, including our evolving selves. Through strife on the sensory plane, and especially through the clash and synthesis of opposites, we humans are ascending to ever-higher self-consciousness, allowing the *Geist* to realize itself through the collective human spirit. If God exists, even He doesn't know what will happen tomorrow. If God doesn't exist today, He may tomorrow.

This belief in the co-evolution of God corresponds to the co-development of space: just as the expanding Universe simultaneously creates space, perhaps expanding human consciousness simultaneously creates God. Stated Carl Jung: "As it gradually dawns on people, one by one, that the transformation of God is not just an interesting idea but is a living reality, it may begin to function as a new myth. Whoever recognizes this myth as his own personal reality will put his life in the service of this progress. . . Such an individual will experience his life as meaningful."

In ancient mythology, the Earth was personified as a living organism, usually as the offspring of Mother Moon and Father Sun. As a natural scientist, Aristotle also spoke of the Earth as a single organism; however, this concept was lost in the seventeenth century's fascination with the Universe as a giant machine. In 1785, geologist James Hutton revived the biological view when he compared the cycling of the Earth's elements to circulation of the blood, then opined that physiology was the proper discipline for study of the Earth. In recent years, British chemist James Lovelock has popularized this concept in a theory he called Gaia, after the Greek earth goddess.

Lovelock derived Gaia from biological evidence: the planet's ability, like a single organism, to modify its environment to its needs. For example, in the 3,500 million years of life on earth, the climate has changed very little, even though the Sun's output of heat has increased by 30 per cent; similarly, the composition of the Earth's atmosphere, soil and oceans has adjusted to favor life, in seeming violation of the rules of chemistry and chance. Lovelock attributes this to the planet's purposeful development of a self-sustaining web of species that harvest and support each other. In this web, the role of our species is as Gaia's mind—a concept that gains persuasion as sophisticated communication systems put each of us into instantaneous contact, like neural cells of the brain. Lovelock even speculates that Gaia may achieve, through us, the ability to self-reflect: "She is now through us awake and aware of herself. She has seen the reflection of her fair face through the eyes of astronauts and the television cameras of orbiting spacecraft. Our sensation of wonder and pleasure, our capacity for conscious thought and speculation, our restless curiosity and drive are hers to share."

Like the human brain, our Earth is culturally organized into halves, which we also call hemispheres. Historically, Eastern culture has been mystical, intuitive, holistic and synchronistic, while that of the West has been materialistic, intellectual, analytical and linear. Similarly, holistic Chinese characters are read from right to left, and Chinese maps traditionally placed south at the top. These mirror-like differences reflect the bilateralization of our right and left brains, suggesting that our globe may, indeed, have ambitions to evolve into a mind.

The well-known Chinese symbol of yin and yang consists of a circle divided by a curved line creating equal halves, like embracing embryos. One is black and the other white, yet each has an eye of the opposing color. This symbol stands for the conflict and synthesis of all opposites, with the potential for resolution contained in that single eye—the seeding of each half by its opposite. Through intensified global contact, East and West now seem to be in the process of synthesis, with the white eye of the East representing Japan's technological society, and the black eye of the West representing a revitalized native American culture. I see this integration as a possible next stage in Earth's adventure in consciousness—the equivalent of a split brain regenerating its severed corpus callosum.

What if webs of life on other planets in distant galaxies are simultaneously evolving into single brains? Would these new superminds be able to see the infra-red Universe to which we are blind and hear the Pythagorean harmonies to which we are deaf? Perhaps, many millions of earth years from now, Gaia will signal to these other minds, spinning through the once-silent Void. Perhaps these questing minds will discover themselves to be microcosms of an even grander macrocosm—the Great Mind some call Brahma and others call God.

All this is true. It is true myth.

Notes

INTRODUCTION

Page 18. J.W.N. Sullivan quote from *Churchill's Black Dog, Kafka's Mice*, Anthony Storr, Ballantine Books, New York, 1990.

22. J. Robert Oppenheimer as quoted in *The Tao of Physics*, Fritjof Capra, Fontana Paperbacks, London, 1983.

I. THE SELF

TELEPATHY

32–33. Wofgang Köhler research from *The Great Psychologists*, Robert I. Watson, Sr., Lippincott, Philadelphia, 1978.

34. Cyril Burt as quoted in *The Roots of Coincidence*, Arthur Koestler, Random House, New York, 1972.

35–36. Research and quotes by Drs. Maybruck, Trethowan, Hope and Chamberlain, *From Parent to Child: The Psychic Link*, Carl Jones, Warner Books, New York, 1989.

36–37. Ehrenwald research from *Mother-Child Symbiosis*, Jan Ehrenwald, in *The Signet Handbook of Parapsychology*, Martin Ebon, ed., New American Library, New York, 1978.

37. Ernesto Spinelli research from *Through the Time Barrier*, Danah Zohar, Heinemann, London, 1978.

37–39. Tom Bouchard research from *Twins*, Peter Watson, Hutchinson & Co., London, 1981.

40–41. Psi-trailing research from *The Study of Cases of "Psi Trailing" in Animals*, J.B. Rhine and Sara R. Feather, in *The Signet Handbook of Parapsychology*, Martin Ebon, ed., New American Library, New York, 1978.

41. Flak anecdote from *The Psychic Power of Animals*, Bill Schul, Ballantine Books, New York, 1988.

42–43. Watson research from *Supernature*, Lyall Watson, Sceptre Edition, London, 1986.

43. Flattid bug research from *The Occult*, Colin Wilson, Grafton Books, London, 1979.

44–45. Janet–Myers research from *Hypnotism and Psychic Phenomena*, Simeon Edmunds, Wilshire Book Company, California, 1961.

45–47. Gilbert Murray research and quotes from *The Roots of Coincidence*, Arthur Koestler, Random House, New York, 1972.

47. Schmeidler research from *Personality Differences in the Effective Use of ESP*, Gertrude R. Schmeidler, in *The Signet Handbook of Parapsychology*, Martin Ebon, ed., New American Library, New York, 1978.

49. William James as quoted in *The Science of the Paranormal*, Lawrence LeShan, Aquarian Press, Northamptonshire, 1987.

49. Henri Bergson quote, *ibid.*

52. Wallace–Darwin correspondence as quoted in *The Brain: The Last Frontier*, Richard M. Restak, Warner Books, New York, 1980.

53. Julian Huxley quote, *ibid.*

54. Washoe research and Eccles quote from *The Wonder of Being Human*, John Eccles and Daniel Robinson, New Science Library, London, 1985.

55. Penfield quote from *The Mystery of the Mind*, Wilder Penfield, Princeton University Press, New Jersey, 1975.

56. Arthur Eddington as quoted in *The Science of the Paranormal*, Lawrence LeShan, Aquarian Press, Northamptonshire, 1987.

56. Wallace–Darwin anecdote from *Toward a New Brain*, Stuart Litvak and A. Wayne Senzee, Prentice-Hall, New Jersey, 1986.

58. Iglulik hunter as quoted in *The Elements of Shamanism*, Nevill Drury, Element Books, Dorset, 1989.

58. Arthur Grimble anecdote from *The Occult*, Colin Wilson, Grafton Books, London, 1979.

58–59. Tomas Roessner anecdote from *The Elements of Shamanism*, Nevill Drury, Element Books, Dorset, 1989.

65. William James as quoted in *From Parent to Child: The Psychic Link*, Carl Jones, Warner Books, New York, 1989.

66. Carl Rogers as quoted in *Reincarnation*, Sylvia Cranston and Carey Williams, eds., Julian Press, New York, 1984.

PSYCHIC POWER

71–77. Wilhelm Reich research: see bibliography.

71. Friedrich Nietzsche as quoted in *Fury on Earth: A Biography of Wilhelm Reich*, Myron Sharaf, St. Martin's Press, New York, 1983.

72. Reich quotes from *Character Analysis*, Wilhelm Reich, Orgone Institute Press, New York, 1949.

74–75. Reich quote from *The Cancer Biopathy*, Orgone Institute Press, New York, 1948.

77. Janov quotes from *The Primal Scream*, Arthur Janov, Dell, New York, 1970.

85–86. Galvani, Von Reichenbach, Blondlot, Rahn, Burr and Ravitz research from *Orgone, Reich and Eros*, W. Edward Mann, Simon & Schuster, New York, 1973.

87–88. Grad research from *The "Laying on of Hands,"* Bernard Grad, in *The Signet Handbook of Parapsychology*, Martin Ebon, ed., New American Library, New York, 1978.

87–89. Smith, Krieger and Miller research from *Vibrational Medicine*, Richard Gerber, Bear & Co., Santa Fe, 1988.

89–94. Edgar Cayce research: see bibliography.

HOLISTIC HEALING

100. Michael Harner as quoted in *The Elements of Shamanism*, Nevill Drury, Element Books, Dorset, 1989.

101. Eduardo Calderon quote, *ibid.*

102. Douglas Sharon quote, *ibid.*

106. Codetron research from an article by Marvin Ross, *Globe and Mail*, January 19, 1991.

110. Mann quote from *Orgone, Reich and Eros*, W. Edward Mann, Simon & Schuster, New York, 1973.

115. St. Peter's dome analogy from *The Tao of Physics*, Fritjof Capra, Fontana Paperbacks, London, 1983.

115. Henry Stapp as quoted in *The Dancing Wu Li Masters*, Gary Zukav, Bantam Books, New York, 1980.

116. James Jeans as quoted in *The Roots of Coincidence*, Arthur Koestler, Random House, New York, 1972.

116. John Eccles as quoted in *Quantum Healing*, Deepak Chopra, Bantam Books, New York, 1989.

116. Arthur Eddington as quoted in *The Mythic Image*, Joseph Campbell, Princeton University Press, New Jersey, 1974.

THE SELF

127. Colin Ross research from an article by Janice Dineen, *Toronto Star*, January 19, 1991.

131–132. Research and quotes by Dr.'s Putnam, Caul and Braun from *Bizarre Diseases of the Mind*, Richard Noll, Berkley Books, New York, 1980.

132. Billy Milligan as quoted in *Multiple Man*, Adam Crabtree, Collins, Toronto, 1985.

139. Alfred Binet quote, *ibid.*

142. Dr. Frederick Lenz research from *The Search for Yesterday*, Scott Rogo, Prentice–Hall, Englewood Cliffs, New Jersey, 1985.

143. Mandell and Persinger research from *Pseudoscience and the Paranormal*, Terence Hines, Prometheus Books, Buffalo, New York, 1988.

143. Edgar Cayce anecdote from *A Seer Out of Season*, Harmon Hartzell Bro, New American Library, New York, 1989.

143. Peter Hurkos anecdotes from *Paranormal or Normal?*, Alan Radnor, Lennard, Luton, 1989.

144. ELTLA research from *Pseudoscience and the Paranormal*, Terence Hines, Prometheus Books, Buffalo, New York, 1988.

144. Carl Jung as quoted in *Other Lives, Other Selves*, Roger J. Woolger, Bantam Books, Toronto, 1988.

145. Margo Rivera research from an article by Marilyn Dunlop, *Toronto Star*, February 28, 1992.

148. Penfield quote from *The Mystery of the Mind*, Wilder Penfield, Princeton University Press, New Jersey, 1975.

149. Kindling research from *Epilepsy*, Dr. Alvin and Virginia B. Silverstein, Lippincott, Philadelphia, 1975.

152. Winson research from *Brain and Psyche*, Jonathan Winson, Doubleday, New York, 1985.

158. Firehall and elevator anecdotes from *The Social Brain*, Michael S. Gazzaniga, Basic Books, New York, 1985.

160. Edgar Cayce as quoted in *A Seer Out of Season*, Harmon Hartzell Bro, New American Library, New York, 1989.

161. Alfred North Whitehead as quoted in *The Science of the Paranormal*, Lawrence LeShan, Aquarian Press, Northamptonshire, 1987.

II. THE UNIVERSE

COINCIDENCE

172. William R. Bennett research from *Reincarnation*, Sylvia Cranston and Carey Williams, eds., Julian Press, New York, 1984.

177. William Bragg as quoted in *The Roots of Coincidence*, Arthur Koestler, Random House, New York, 1972.

177. Henry Stapp as quoted in *The Tao of Physics*, Fritjof Capra, Fontana Paperbacks, London, 1983.

178. John Wheeler, *ibid*.

178. Niels Bohr as quoted in *The Dancing Wu Li Masters*, Gary Zukav, Bantam Books, Toronto, 1980.

179. Werner Heisenberg as quoted in *The Tao of Physics*, Fritjof Capra, Fontana Paperbacks, London, 1983.

180. Albert Einstein as quoted in *The Cosmic Code*, Heinz Pagels, Bantam Books, New York, 1983.

183. Wolfgang Pauli as quoted in *The Dancing Wu Li Masters*, Gary Zukav, Bantam Books, New York, 1980.

183–184. Wolfgang Pauli anecdote from *Synchronicity: The Bridge Between Matter and Mind*, David Peat, Bantam Books, New York, 1987.

185. Von Franz quotes from *On Divination and Synchronicity*, Marie-Louise Von Franz, Inner City Books, Toronto, 1980.

185. Carl Jung as quoted in *Synchronicity: The Bridge Between Matter and Mind*, David Peat, Bantam Books, New York, 1987.

186. Arthur Eddington as quoted in *Quantum Healing*, Deepak Chopra, Bantam Books, New York, 1989.

187. Karl Pribram research from *The Brain: The Last Frontier*, Richard M. Restak, Warner Books, New York, 1980.

189. Great Mother research from *The Chalice and the Blade*, Riane Eisler, Harper & Row, New York, 1987.

190. Graves quote from Afterword to *The White Goddess*, Robert Graves, Faber & Faber, London, 1959.

191. Thomas Mann as quoted in *The Mythic Image*, Joseph Campbell, Princeton University Press, New Jersey, 1974.

193. Van der Post anecdote from *Jung and the Story of Our Time*, Laurens Van der Post, Vintage Books, New York, 1977.

THE FUTURE

198–200. Jeane Dixon research from *Jeane Dixon: The Witnesses*, Denis Brian, Doubleday, New York, 1976.

210. Kurt Gödel research from *Through the Time Barrier*, Danah Zohar, Heinemann, London, 1982.

211. Werner Israel as quoted in an article by Terence Dickinson, *Toronto Star* March 3, 1991.

219. Beatrice Lillie anecdote from *Incredible Coincidence*, Alan Vaughan, Ballantine Books, New York, 1989.

219. William Cox research from *Through the Time Barrier*, Danah Zohar, Heinemann, London, 1982.

219–220. Executive research from *Testing for Executive ESP*, Douglas Dean and John Mihalasky, in *The Signet Handbook of Parapsychology*, Martin Ebon, ed., New American Library, New York, 1978.

221–222. Mrs. Lesley Brennan anecdote from *Arthur C. Clarke's World of Strange Powers*, John Fairley and Simon Welfare, eds., Collins, London, 1984.

222. Aberfan anecdotes from *Through the Time Barrier*, Danah Zohar, Heinemann, London, 1982.

223. Edgar Allan Poe anecdote from *Incredible Coincidence*, Alan Vaughan, Ballantine Books, New York, 1989.

225. *New York Times* anecdote from *Dreams that Come True*, David Ryback, Ballantine Books, New York, 1990.

227–228. Orbiting electron research from *Through the Time Barrier*, Danah Zohar, Heinemann, London, 1982.

229. Adrian Dobbs research from *The Roots of Coincidence*, Arthur Koestler, Random House, New York, 1972.

230. Evan Harris Walker research from *Through the Time Barrier*, Danah Zohar, Heinemann, London, 1982.

230. Many Worlds research from *The Dancing Wu Li Masters*, Gary Zukav, Bantam Books, New York, 1980.

232–233. Victor Goddard anecdote from *Riddle of the Future*, Andrew MacKenzie, Arthur Baker, London, 1974.

FRIENDLY GHOSTS

239–240. Piper, James and Hodgson research from *Hypnotism and Psychic Phenomena*, Simeon Edmunds, Wilshire Book Company, California, 1961.

240. Leonora Piper as quoted in *Multiple Man*, Adam Crabtree, Collins, Toronto, 1985.

241. Margaret and Kate Fox as quoted in *A Skeptic's Handbook of Parapsychology*, Prometheus Books, Buffalo, New York, 1985.

241–242. Jung research and Jaffé quote from *The Psychic World of Jung*, Aniela Jaffé, in *The Signet Handbook of Parapsychology*, Martin Ebon, ed., New American Library, New York, 1978.

242. Garrett research from *Adventures in the Supernormal*, Eileen Garrett, Paperback Library, New York, 1968.

243. Flight R101 anecdote and Garrett quote from *Hypnotism and Psychic Phenomena*, Simeon Edmunds, Wilshire Book Company, California, 1961.

246. Bond–Bartlett anecdote from *Ghosts and Poltergeists*, Frank Smyth, Aldus Books, London, 1976.

246. Samuel Johnson quote as in *Ghosts*, Peter Haining, Sidgwick & Jackson, London, 1974.

248. Georgina Feakes anecdote from *Arthur C. Clarke's World of Strange Powers*, John Fairley and Simon Welfare, eds., Collins, London, 1984.

249–250. Nathaniel Hawthorne anecdote from *Ghosts and Poltergeists*, Frank Smyth, Aldus Books, London, 1976.

253. Emanuel Swedenborg anecdotes from *The Presence of Other Worlds*, Wilson Van Dusen, Harper & Row, New York, 1974.

254. Edgar Cayce anecdote from *A Seer Out of Season*, Harmon Hartzell Bro, New American Library, New York, 1989.

254. Patience Worth research from *Hypnotism and Psychic Phenomena*, Simeon Edmunds, Wilshire Book Company, California, 1961.

254. Arthur Conan Doyle anecdote from *Hungry Ghosts*, Joe Fisher, Doubleday Canada, Toronto, 1990.

256–257. Tolstoy as quoted in *The Varieties of Religious Experience*, William James, Longmans, Green New Impressions, London, 1937.

257. Guirdham quote from *Obsession*, Arthur Guirdham, C.W. Daniel Co. Ltd., Essex, 1972.

257. Van Dusen quote from *Hallucinations as the World of Spirits*, Wilson Van Dusen, in *Frontiers of Consciousness*, John White, ed., Julian Press, New York, 1974.

260. Emanuel Swedenborg anecdote from *The Presence of Other Worlds*, Wilson Van Dusen, Harper & Row, New York, 1974.

260. Immanuel Kant letter as quoted in *Natural and Supernatural*, Brian Inglis, Hodder and Stoughton, London, 1977.

261. Tart research from *Out-of-the-Body Experiences: A Psychophysiological Study*, Charles Tart, in *The Signet Handbook of Parapsychology*, Martin Ebon, ed., New American Library, New York, 1978.

262–263. Ernest Hemingway as quoted in *Reincarnation*, Sylvia Cranston and Carey Williams, eds., Julian Press, New York, 1984.

263. Osis research from *Deathbed Observations by Physicians and Nurses*, Karlis Osis and Erlendur Heraldsson, in *The Signet Handbook of Parapsychology*, Martin Ebon, ed., New American Library, New York, 1978.

265. Swedenborg research and John Wesley anecdote from *The Presence of Other Worlds*, Wilson Van Dusen, Harper & Row, New York, 1974.

267. Maria Sabina as quoted in *The Elements of Shamanism*, Nevill Drury, Element Books, Dorset, 1989.

268. Pineal gland research from *The Parable of the Beast*, John Bleibreu, Collier Books, New York, 1969.

269–271. Grof research from *The Stormy Search for Self*, Stanislav and Christina Grof, J.P. Tarcher, Los Angeles, 1990.

270. Abraham Maslow as quoted in *The Occult*, Colin Wilson, Grafton Books, London, 1979.

POSSESSION

284. St. Bernard as quoted in *The Mythic Image*, Joseph Campbell, Princeton University Press, New Jersey, 1974.

284. Emile Mâle quote, *ibid.*

286–287. Winnipeg police report from *Toronto Star*, September 19, 1990.

287. Monsignor Corrado Balducci as quoted in an article by Michael McAteer, *Toronto Star*, September 22, 1990.

292–293. William James as quoted in *Hungry Ghosts*, Joe Fisher, Doubleday Canada, Toronto, 1990.

293. Shapiro and Shapiro research from *Pseudoscience and the Paranormal*, Terence Hines, Prometheus Books, Buffalo, New York, 1988.

294. Crabtree anecdotes and quote from *Multiple Man*, Adam Crabtree, Collins, Toronto, 1985.

297. Van Dusen research from *Hallucinations as the World of Spirits*, Wilson Van Dusen, in *Frontiers of Consciousness*, John White, ed., Julian Press, New York, 1974.

302–303. Hereward Carrington as quoted in *Poltergeist Phenomena and Psychokinesis*, A.R.G. Owen, in *The Signet Handbook of Parapsychology*, Martin Ebon, ed., New American Library, New York, 1978.

303. Nandor Fodor as quoted in *Supernature*, Lyall Watson, Sceptre Editon, London, 1986.

303. Matthew Manning research and Brian Josephson quote from *Creatures from Inner Space*, Stan Gooch, Rider & Co., London, 1984.

304. Franz Buirmann research from *The Occult*, Colin Wilson, Grafton Books, London, 1979.

304. Sigmund Freud 1897 letter as quoted in *Ritual Abuse*, Kevin Marron, Seal Books, Toronto, 1988.

REINCARNATION

311–312. Eva Hellstrom anecdotes from *Riddle of the Future*, Andrew MacKenzie, Arthur Barker, London, 1974.

314. Arnold Schopenhauer as quoted in *Reincarnation*, Sylvia Cranston and Carey Williams, eds., Julian Press, New York, 1984.

316. Lama Anagarika Govinda quote from his introduction to the English translation of *The Tibetan Book of the Dead*, W.Y. Evans–Wentz, ed., Oxford University Press, Oxford, 1960.

321. C.J. Ducasse as quoted in *Hypnotism and Psychic Phenomena*, Simeon Edmunds, Wilshire Book Company, California, 1961.

321. Virginia Tighe, *ibid.*

321. Jane Evans anecdote from *Other Lives, Other Selves*, Roger J. Woolger, Bantam Books, Toronto, 1988.

322. Reima Kampman anecdote from *Arthur C. Clarke's World of Strange Powers*, John Fairley and Simon Welfare, eds., Collins, London, 1984.

322–324. Arthur Guirdham research: see bibliography.

325. Cannon quote from *Power Within*, Alexander Cannon, Dutton, New York, 1953.

326. Stevenson research from *Twenty Cases Suggestive of Reincarnation*, Ian Stevenson, University Press of Virginia, Charlottesville, 1974.

SUMMATION

342. Albert Einstein as quoted in *Toward a New Brain*, Stuart Litvak and A. Wayne Senzee, Prentice-Hall, New Jersey, 1986.

342. Allan Sandage quote from TV documentary "The Creation of the Universe," November 20, 1985, written and presented by Timothy Ferris.

344. Albert Einstein as quoted in *The Mystery of the Mind*, Wilder Penfield, Princeton University Press, New Jersey, 1975.

344. Allan Sandage quote from TV documentary "The Creation of the Universe," November 20, 1985, written and presented by Timothy Ferris.

348. Carl Jung as quoted in *The Creation of Consciousness: Jung's Myth for Modern Man*, Edward Edinger, Inner City Books, Toronto, 1984.

349. James Lovelock quote from *Gaia*, Oxford University Press, Oxford, 1982.

Select Bibliography

Allison, Ralph, *Mind in Many Pieces*, Rawson Wade, New York, 1980

Babuta, Subniv, and Bragard, Jean-Claude, *Evil*, Weidenfeld & Nicolson, London, 1988

Bernstein, Morey, *The Search for Bridey Murphy*, Doubleday, New York, 1965

Blakeslee, Thomas, *The Right Brain*, Doubleday, New York, 1980

Berrill, Norman, *Man's Emerging Mind*, Dodd, Mead, New York, 1955

Bleibreu, John N., *The Parable of the Beast*, Collier, New York, 1969

Bohm, David, *Wholeness and the Implicate Order*, Ark Paperbacks, London, 1983

Brian, Denis, *Jeane Dixon: The Witnesses*, Doubleday, New York, 1976

Bro, Harmon Hartzell, *A Seer Out of Season*, New American Library, New York, 1989

Brumbaugh, Robert S., *The Philosophers of Greece*, Crowell, New York, 1964

Cannon, Alexander, *Power Within*, Dutton, New York, 1953

Capra, Fritjof, *The Tao of Physics*, Fontana Paperbacks, London, 1983

Campbell, Joseph, *The Masks of God* [Vol. 3]: Occidental Mythology, Viking Penguin, New York, 1964

———, *The Mythic Image*, Princeton University Press, New Jersey, 1974

Chopra, Deepak, *Quantum Healing*, Bantam Books, New York, 1989

Christie-Murray, David, *Reincarnation: Ancient Beliefs and Modern Evidence*, Prism Press, Great Britain, 1988

Cirlot, J.E., *A Dictionary of Symbols*, Philosophical Library, New York, 1962

Copelston, Frederick, *History of Philosophy, Vols. 1 and 4*, Image Books, Doubleday, New York, 1963

Crabtree, Adam, *Multiple Man*, Collins, Toronto, 1985

Cranston, Sylvia, and Williams, Carey, eds., *Reincarnation*, Julian Press, New York, 1984

Douglas, Alfred, *The Oracle of Change: How to Consult the I Ching*, Penguin, 1972

Drury, Nevill, *The Elements of Shamanism*, Element Books, Dorset, 1989

Ebon, Martin, ed., *The Signet Handbook of Parapsychology*, New American Library, New York, 1978

Eccles, John, and Robinson, Daniel N., *The Wonder of Being Human*, New Science Library, London, 1985

Edinger, Edward, *The Creation of Consciousness: Jung's Myth for Modern Man*, Inner City Books, Toronto, 1984

Edmunds, Simeon, *Hypnotism and Psychic Phenomena*, Wilshire Book Company, California, 1961

Eisler, Riane, *The Chalice and the Blade*, Harper & Row, New York, 1987

Ellison, Arthur, *The Paranormal*, Dodd, Mead, New York, 1988

Evans-Wentz, W.Y., ed., *The Tibetan Book of the Dead*, Oxford University Press, Oxford, 1960

Fairley, John, and Welfare, Simon, *Arthur C. Clarke's World of Strange Powers*, Collins, London, 1984

Fisher, Joe, *Hungry Ghosts*, Doubleday Canada, Toronto, 1990

Finucane, R.C., *Appearances of the Dead*, Junction Books, London, 1982

Fraser, Sylvia, *My Father's House: A Memoir of Incest and of Healing*, Doubleday Canada, Toronto, 1987

Freud, Sigmund, *Civilization and Its Discontents*, Norton, New York, 1963

Gardner, Martin, ed., *The Sacred Beetle and Other Great Essays in Science*, Prometheus Books, Buffalo, New York, 1984

——, *Science, Good, Bad and Bogus*, Prometheus Books, Buffalo, New York, 1981

Garrett, Eileen, *Adventures in the Supernormal*, Paperback Library, New York, 1968

Gazzaniga, Michael S., *The Social Brain*, Basic Books, New York, 1985

Gerber, Richard, *Vibrational Medicine*, Bear & Co., Santa Fe, 1988

Gooch, Stan, *Creatures from Inner Space*, Faber & Faber, London, 1959

Grof, Stanislav and Christina, *The Stormy Search for Self*, J.P. Tarcher, Los Angeles, 1990

Guirdham, Arthur, *The Cathars and Reincarnation*, Neville Spearman, London, 1978

——, *The Lake and the Castle*, Neville Spearman, London, 1976

——, *Obsession*, C. W. Daniel, Essex, 1972

——, *We Are One Another*, Neville Spearman, London, 1974

Haining, Peter, *Ghosts*, Sidgwick & Jackson, London, 1974

Hall, James A., *Jungian Dream Interpretation* Inner City Books, Toronto, 1983

Halpern, Steven, *Sound Health*, Harper & Row, San Francisco, 1985

Hamilton, Bernard, *The Medieval Inquisition*, Holmes & Meier, New York, 1981

Hardy, Alister; Harvie, Robert, and Koestler, Arthur, *The Challenge of Chance*, Random House, New York, 1972

Hines, Terence, *Pseudoscience and the Paranormal*, Prometheus Books, Buffalo, New York, 1988

Hobson, J. Allan, *The Dreaming Brain*, Basic Books, New York, 1988

Hufford, David J., *The Terror that Comes in the Night*, University of Pennsylvania Press, Philadelphia, 1982

Inglis, Brian, *Natural and Supernatural*, Hodder and Stoughton, London, 1977

James, William, *The Varieties of Religious Experience*, Longmans, Green New Impression, London, 1937

Janov, Arthur, *The Primal Scream*, Dell, New York, 1970

Jastrow, Robert, *The Enchanted Loom*, Simon & Schuster, New York, 1981

Jaynes, Julian, *The Origins of Consciousness in the Breakdown of the Bicameral Mind*, Houghton Mifflin, Boston, 1982

Jones, Carl, *From Parent to Child: The Psychic Link*, Warner Books, New York, 1989

Jung, C.G., *Answer to Job*, Princeton University Press, New Jersey, 1973

——, *Dreams*, Princeton University Press, New Jersey, 1974

——, *Memories, Dreams, Reflections*, Vintage Books, New York, 1989

——, *Synchronicity*, Princeton University Press, New Jersey, 1973

Koestler, Arthur, *The Roots of Coincidence*, Random House, New York, 1972

Krüll, Marianne, *Freud and His Father*, W. W. Norton, London, 1986

Kurtz, Paul, ed., *A Skeptic's Handbook of Parapsychology*, Prometheus Books, Buffalo, New York, 1985

LaBerge, Stephen, *Lucid Dreaming*, Ballantine Books, New York, 1986

Lechtenberg, Richard, *Epilepsy and the Family*, Harvard University Press, 1984

LeShan, Lawrence, *The Science of the Paranormal*, Aquarian Press, Northampton-shire, 1987

Litvak, Stuart, and Senzee, A. Wayne, *Toward a New Brain*, Prentice-Hall, New Jersey, 1986

Lovelock, J.E., *Gaia*, Oxford University Press, Oxford, 1982

Lowen, Alexander, *The Betrayal of the Body*, Collier Books, New York, 1969

McAll, Kenneth, *Healing the Family Tree*, Sheldon Press, London, 1982

Macdonald, Alexander, *Acupuncture: from Ancient Art to Modern Medicine*, Unwin Paperbacks, London, 1984

MacKenzie, Andrew, *Riddle of the Future*, Arthur Barker, London, 1974

MacKenzie, Norman, *Dreams and Dreaming*, Vanguard Press, New York, 1965

Mann, W. Edward, and Hoffman, Edward, *The Man Who Dreamed of Tomorrow. A Conceptual Biography of Wilhelm Reich*, J. P. Tarcher, Los Angeles, 1980

Mann, W. Edward, *Orgone, Reich and Eros*, Simon & Schuster, New York, 1973

Marron, Kevin, *Ritual Abuse*, Seal Books, Toronto, 1988

Morris, Richard, *Time's Arrows*, Simon & Schuster, New York, 1985

Noll, Richard, *Bizarre Diseases of the Mind*, Berkley Books, New York, 1980

O'Connor, D.J., ed., *A Critical History of Western Philosophy*, Free Press of Glencoe, 1964

O'Connor, Peter, *Dreams*, Methuen Haynes, North Ryde, 1986

O'Grady, Joan, *The Prince of Darkness*, Element Books, Dorset, 1989

Pagels, Heinz R., *The Cosmic Code*, Bantam Books, New York, 1983

Peat, F. David, *Synchronicity: The Bridge Between Matter and Mind*, Bantam Books, New York, 1987

Pelton, Robert, *The Devil and Karen Kingston*, Pocket Books, New York, 1977

Penfield, Wilder, *The Mystery of the Mind*, Princeton University Press, New Jersey, 1975

Percheron, Maurice, *Buddha and Buddhism*, Harper & Row, New York, 1954

Prince, Morton, *The Dissociation of a Personality*, Meridian Books, New York, 1957

Radnor, Alan, *Paranormal or Normal?*, Lennard, Luton, 1989

Reich, Peter, *A Book of Dreams: A Memoir of Wilhelm Reich*, E. P. Dutton, New York, 1989

Reich, Wilhelm, *The Cancer Biopathy*, Orgone Institute Press, New York, 1948

————, *Character Analysis*, Orgone Institute Press, New York, 1949

————, *The Function of the Orgasm*, Orgone Institute Press, New York, 1942

Restak, Richard M., *The Brain: The Last Frontier*, Warner Books, New York, 1980

Robbins, R.H., *Encyclopedia of Witchcraft and Demonology*, Peter Nevil, 1959

Roberts, Harry C., translator and editor, *The Complete Prophecies of Nostradamus*, Nostradamus Co., Oyster Bay, New Jersey, 1947

Rogo, R. Scott, *The Search for Yesterday*, Prentice-Hall, New Jersey, 1985

Ryback, David, *Dreams that Come True*, Ballantine Books, New York, 1990

Schul, Bill, *The Psychic Power of Animals*, Ballantine Books, New York, 1988

Scruton, Roger, *A Short History of Modern Philosophy*, Ark Paperbacks, London, 1984

Sen, K.M., *Hinduism*, Penguin Books, Baltimore, Maryland, 1961

Sharaf, Myron, *Fury on Earth: A Biography of Wilhelm Reich*, St. Martin's Press, New York, 1983

Sheldrake, Rupert, *A New Science of Life*, J.P. Tarcher, Los Angeles, 1987

Siegel, Bernard, *Love, Medicine and Miracles*, Harper & Row, New York, 1986

Silverstein, Dr. Alvin and Virginia B., *Epilepsy*, Lippincott, Philadelphia, 1975

Sizemore, Chris Costner, *I'm Eve*, Jove Publications, New York, 1978

Smyth, Frank, *Ghosts and Poltergeists*, Aldus Books, London, 1976

Steinbrecher, Edwin C., *The Inner Guide Meditation*, Samuel Weiser, York Beach, Maine, 1988

Stearn, Jess, *Edgar Cayce—The Sleeping Prophet*, Doubleday, New York, 1967

Stevenson, Ian, *Twenty Cases Suggestive of Reincarnation*, University Press of Virginia, Charlottesville, 1974

Storr, Anthony, *Churchill's Black Dog, Kafka's Mice*, Ballantine Books, New York, 1990

Swedenborg, Emanuel, *Heaven and Hell*, Swedenborg Society, London, 1966

Tansley, David V., *Radionics and the Subtle Anatomy of Man*, C. W. Daniel, Essex, 1972

Torrey, E. Fuller, *Witchcraft and Psychiatrists*, Harper & Row, New York, 1986

Vaughan, Alan, *Incredible Coincidence*, Ballantine Books, New York, 1989

Von Franz, Marie-Louise, *On Divination and Synchronicity*, Inner City Books, Toronto, 1980

Van Dusen, Wilson, *The Presence of Other Worlds*, Harper & Row, New York, 1974

Van der Post, Laurens, *Jung and the Story of Our Time*, Vintage Books, New York, 1977

Watson, John, *Behaviorism*, Norton, New York, 1920

Watson, Lyall, *Supernature*, Sceptre Edition, London, 1986

Watson, Peter, *Twins*, Hutchinson, London, 1981

Watson, Sr., Robert I., *The Great Psychologists*, Lippincott, Philadelphia, 1978

Weil, Andrew, *Health and Healing*, Houghton Mifflin, Boston, 1983

White, John, ed., *Frontiers of Consciousness*, Julian Press, New York, 1974

Wilson, Colin, *The Occult*, Grafton Books, London, 1979

Winson, Jonathan, *Brain and Psyche*, Doubleday, New York, 1985

Woolger, Roger J., *Other Lives, Other Selves*, Bantam Books, New York, 1988

Zohar, Danah, *Through the Time Barrier*, Heinemann, London, 1982

Zukav, Gary, *The Dancing Wu Li Masters*, Bantam Books, New York, 1980

Index